Book of Confessions
Study Edition

Book of Confessions
Study Edition

[Part I of the Constitution of the Presbyterian Church (U.S.A.)]

Geneva Press
Louisville, Kentucky

THE CONSTITUTION
OF THE
PRESBYTERIAN CHURCH (U.S.A.)

PART I

BOOK OF CONFESSIONS
Geneva Press
Louisville, Kentucky

Copyright © 1996 by the Office of the General Assembly,
Presbyterian Church (U.S.A.)

Licensed to Geneva Press by the Office of the General Assembly,
Presbyterian Church (U.S.A.), 1999

Published by Geneva Press, Louisville, Kentucky

Library of Congress Cataloging-in-Publication Data

Book of confessions : Presbyterian Church (U.S.A.) : study edition.
    p.   cm.
   ISBN 0-664-50012-9
   1. Presbyterian Church (U.S.A.). Book of confessions.
  2. Presbyterian Church—Creeds—History and criticism.
  I. Presbyterian Church (U.S.A.)
  BX8969.5.B66   1999   98-48596
  238′.5137—dc21

CONTENTS

FOREWORD FROM THE PUBLISHER

Geneva Press is proud to publish this study edition of the *Book of Confessions* as a service to the Presbyterian Church (U.S.A.). The volume brings together the official texts of the eleven confessional documents that together form Part I of *The Constitution of the Presbyterian Church (U.S.A.)* and introductory essays that provide historical and theological background for each of these documents. The eleven documents are:

The Nicene Creed
The Apostles' Creed
The Scots Confession
The Heidelberg Catechism
The Second Helvetic Confession
The Westminster Standards
   The Westminster Confession of Faith
   The Shorter Catechism
   The Larger Catechism
The Theological Declaration of Barmen
The Confession of 1967
A Brief Statement of Faith—Presbyterian Church (U.S.A.)

In addition to these documents, two additional texts are included that are not constitutional documents but which the General Assembly has mandated to be published with the *Book of Confessions:* "The Confessional Nature of the Church" and "The Assessment of Proposed Amendments to the *Book of Confessions.*"

The introductory essays are designed to encourage study and understanding of the confessional documents and are not, of course, official constitutional texts themselves. These essays were written by outstanding Presbyterian scholars, but they are unsigned both because of the character of this book as a reference volume and study resource and because the spotlight in this volume falls on the creeds, confessions, and catechisms of the Presbyterian Church rather than on the persons writing about them.

We hope that this volume will provide new understanding of and appreciation for the rich confessional heritage of the Presbyterian Church (U.S.A.) and will support careful study of the church's confessional documents by seminary students, ministers, church officers, and laypersons. Moreover, we hope that this book will stimulate deeper curiosity about the history and theology of the confessions, prompting readers to seek out many other fine interpretations of the creeds, confessions, and catechisms readily available in theological libraries. Most of all, however, we hope that the *Book of Confessions: Study Edition* will help all who explore the creeds, confessions, and catechisms of the Presbyterian Church to understand the Christian faith more truly.

THE NICENE CREED

Introduction to the Nicene Creed

The Nicene Creed was the first and in fact is the only creed used ecumenically by the vast majority of Christians throughout the world. For more than fifteen hundred years, it has been the hallmark of orthodoxy. Before Nicaea, churches in various regions had baptismal confessions that agreed with each other on all major points. The wording differed, however, and few had any detail as to how the various points confessed were to be understood. But the Nicene Creed, the product of two councils—Nicaea in A.D. 325 and Constantinople in A.D. 381—was carefully worded, geared to explain the matters in dispute. With the exception of one phrase, a later addition in the West, the careful wording of Nicaea has remained constant. In that sense it is a creed.

What were the issues or problems that led to the calling of the Council of Nicaea? In order to understand what this creed is responding to we need to put ourselves back in that time and place. Once we do that, however, we will see that the issues dealt with then remain issues with which the church must deal in every time and place.

The time was 325. It was but a few years after the Emperor Constantine had eliminated all rivals and alone ruled the vast Roman Empire that surrounded the entirety of the Mediterranean Sea. He had shown great favor to the Christian church, ending all persecution. That persecution had been the most severe just before Constantine's climb to power. After his victory, he and his mother gave money for the construction of churches where Christians could worship openly and in peace. Although he was not yet baptized and still present at state functions Christians considered idolatrous, it was clear to everyone that Constantine supported the Christian church more than any other religious institution of the day, including the traditional forms of the Roman Empire. His mother was a baptized and practicing Christian.

Furthermore, the church was a young and vibrant movement with a network of bishops and congregations coextensive with the Empire itself and growing rapidly. Evidently the emperor hoped that if it became the dominant religion then perhaps it could unify the disparate areas and peoples. For this reason, when Constantine discovered that there was a threat to the unity of the church, he worked to eliminate the dissension. He himself called a council of all the bishops to discuss the issue in dispute and come to a decision as to the truth the whole church should believe. The imperial post carried the invitations and the emperor provided the hospitality for the gathering. During the time of persecution but a few years earlier, a meeting of this scale would have been impossible for the church to arrange.

More than three hundred bishops, mostly from the eastern area of the Empire, came to Nicaea, today a small town in Turkey, a few miles south of Instanbul across the Bosphorus. At that time it was the residence of Constantine while he awaited the completion of his new

1

capital city, Constantinople, the name it had until the Turks changed it to Istanbul after their conquest of the area in 1451.

EARLIER PROBLEMS

What was the issue that was dividing the church? To understand this, we will need to go back briefly to an even earlier time in the church. When Christians began to be a noticeable group in some of the major cities of the Roman Empire in the second and third centuries, they were asked questions they sometimes found difficult to answer. There were two questions in particular: First, How could Christians consider themselves monotheists and yet hold that both the God of Israel and Jesus are divine? Didn't that make two gods? Second, How can Christians use the Hebrew Scriptures as their holy book and yet disagree with the Jews on how it is to be interpreted? Christians found texts that pointed to Jesus, but Jews did not understand them in the same way. Whom should Greeks believe? The Jews had had much more time and history with these writings, so their opinion seemed more probable.

We should not think that these questions were simply posed to one Christian by a neighbor in private. Surely that happened. But debates also occurred in the city square, especially during times when there was little or no persecution. The debates were public, with representatives of different "philosophies"—not only Stoics, Epicureans, Platonists, and so forth, but also Jews and Christians. All these groups were mostly urban and accustomed to such debates (See Paul's invitation to participate in such a forum in Acts 17:16–21.) These latter two were considered philosophies because their teachings were for the purpose of showing how to live well, meaningfully, virtuously. What beliefs and practices led to such a life? Forms of worship were not the major concern, and therefore the traditional Greek and Roman cults were not part of the debates. Both Christians and Jews believed in one God, who had a certain character, who desired a certain style of life on the part of adherents.

Already in the second century, some who called themselves Christians had answered the questions posed to Christians very simply: The God of Israel has nothing to do with Jesus Christ. He represents a different God. Christians should not use the Old Testament. The church quickly said that that was contrary to the gospel. So the debates would be with those who held to the Old Testament as well as the gospel, and who believed that the God of Israel is indeed the God of Jesus Christ.

That left the more difficult question of monotheism. Christians were convinced that they were indeed monotheists. There was only one God: the God of Israel. At the same time, the center of the gospel was that this God had visited the people in an act of salvation in Jesus Christ. Jesus was God incarnate. The baptismal confessions held this, the writings of Paul and the Gospels held to it. How can this be understood?

2

An attempt had been made in the early third century that, for some, seemed to answer the question satisfactorily. It said that God had different modes of being God, even as water can be a liquid, or a vapor, or a solid. First God was "the Father," the creator of all things that the baptismal confessions held to. After paving the way in the nation of Israel, God ceased to be "the Father" and became "the Son." This was Jesus, who was born, lived among us, was crucified, died, and rose again. But the resurrection began a new mode of God, "the Holy Spirit." So Jesus is God, the Holy Spirit is God, as is the God of Israel. All are the same God, but only in one mode at a time, in sequence, with no return to earlier modes. This understanding is known as modalism or Sabellianism. It is monotheistic, since there is only one mode at a time, but the majority of the church found such a view seriously flawed. In fact, it created more problems than it solved. Above all, if Jesus really died, as the church clearly confessed, does that mean that God died? And to whom did Jesus pray? If Jesus was "conceived by the Holy Spirit," how could that have been when God was still in the first mode?

Though modalism had generally been rejected by the churches throughout the Empire, it still was a temptingly easy solution for many questions about monotheism, and it remained a threat in the life of the church. The significance of this background will become clearer after we deal with Nicaea itself.

ARIUS

Now we come to the time of Constantine. In Alexandria, a young, well-educated presbyter named Arius began to teach his own understanding of how the One who became incarnate as Jesus of Nazareth was related to the God of Israel. Arius was well trained in Greek philosophy, and much of this influenced his theology. His concern was not the issue of monotheism. Rather, for him, the true God, the God of Israel, could not be directly involved in the transient, changing world of creation. Greek philosophy considered the highest reality to be unchanging, eternally fixed. Any change would mean less than perfection. Therefore, for him the question was how this unchanging God could be involved in this constantly changing, clearly finite world. (It should be noted that the biblical perspective has no such question, but assumes that God created the world and continues to be involved with it, and was not less than true God in doing so. Arius's view shows the influence of Greek Platonism.) He solved the problem by holding that this high, true God had created an agent, divine to be sure, but a lesser being than God, through whom to create and interact with the finite, changing world. This agent is God's first creation, and is called the Word or Logos or Son. When the created world fell into sin, it was this Word or Logos who became incarnate in order to save it. Therefore, the one who became incarnate as Jesus of Nazareth is not the high God, but this divine agent, this created divinity, who is above all the rest of creation, but nonetheless, a creature.

For the philosophically inclined, this was an interesting view, and solved the problem that Platonic philosophy had with a God who constantly interacted with this changing world. But for those who were steeped in the church tradition more than in philosophy, Arius's view seriously compromised the monotheism to which the church was thoroughly committed. Arius's bishop, Alexander of Alexandria, therefore excommunicated this presbyter who was a teacher in Alexandria. The followers of Arius, most of whom were not in Alexandria but in the area around Antioch, still supported him. This is what caused the division that concerned the Emperor Constantine. Constantine was not particularly interested in the particularities of theology, but he did want a united church throughout the Empire. When it became obvious that this was a serious division, he therefore called a council of all the bishops to meet in Nicaea in 325. More than three hundred bishops attended—by no means all the bishops—but few from the western, Latin-speaking area of the church attended. Neither Platonic philosophy nor Arius's teachings had made many followers in the West, so the bishops were not concerned with the debate. They were also much farther from Nicaea and the influence of the emperor.

When the discussion at Nicaea began, the emperor himself presided. He did not presume to determine the decision of the council, but he did intend to enforce whatever decision the council made. The bishops in attendance included very few who actually supported Arius. (He was not a bishop and therefore could not address the assembly.) There were a few who really understood the issues and opposed Arius. Most were not really clear what Arius taught. Arius's opinion was clearly given by a bishop who agreed with him. At that point, many of the bishops who had not understood the issue before realized how distant Arius's teaching was from the faith the church professed. They therefore condemned his teachings. However, the opposition to Arius had to be couched in the philosophical language that Arius used, and not simply in the biblical language with which the majority of bishops were far more familiar.

The creedal statement made very clear that the One who became incarnate as Jesus of Nazareth—the Word or Logos or Son—was no creature, no lesser divinity. Rather he is "God of God," "Light of Light," "of the same substance as the Father."

The term "being of one substance with the Father"—in the Greek, *homoousios to patri*—is the critical point. For us, the terms "father" and "son" appear to imply a generation gap. Of course the father is before the son, earlier than the son in time. This is not what the creed means. In fact, it assumes that there never is a time when the Father exists without the Son. Rather, the creed is dealing with a very different issue. Our knowledge of human reproduction is very different from theirs, but if we were to put into contemporary language what Nicaea is saying, we could state that the Son, the Word, is of the same genetic material as the Father. Just as a human father produces a human child and not some other species, so the Son of God is of the same divinity as the Father, not a lesser form, not a creature. Human beings can create or make a painting or some other object totally different from themselves. But a child is not a creation in the same sense. It is of the same species, the same form, the same thing as the parent. For this reason the creed states that the Son is "begotten not made." He is not a creature as are all others. It is this Son, the only-begotten, who then, for our sake, became incarnate as Jesus of Nazareth.

Furthermore, it was not until the mid-nineteenth century that there was any awareness that the mother provided anything other than "matter." The ancients believed that just as the farmer plants all sorts of different seeds in the same ground, and it is the seed not the ground that determines what grows, the mother was like the ground, and the seed of the father determined what was produced. The gender-specific language was therefore part of the argument for them in a way that it would not be for us. The Son or Word of God is God, just as much as the Father is God. The analogy from human relationships was important. This was the statement against Arius, and was effective in opposing his teaching.

The council closed, declaring the sections on the Father and the Son of the creed we know in the form we know it. However, they added only the beginning of the section on the Holy Spirit, declaring only that they believed in the Holy Spirit. They included a list of "anathemas," statements of what was not to be believed.

The council may have solved the problem of Arius, but it soon became clear that many of the faithful in the church did not like the creed at all, not because they favored Arius, but because the way the creed was stated, it appeared to legitimate Sabellianism. If the Son was of the same substance as the Father, with no distinction, then the Father could become the Son and then the Spirit with no difficulty at all. The creed was therefore not well accepted. In addition, although Constantine had exiled those bishops and Arius who did not agree with the decision of Nicaea, eventually he changed his mind, and exiled those bishops who did not agree with an Arian confession. This confusion lasted for several years. Several suggestions were made, including using the Greek term *homoiousios* instead of *homoousios*, indicating that the Son was of a substance similar to the Father but not the same. That would have eliminated a Sabellian reading of the creed but would have left the door open again for Arianism.

It took another generation, with serious work on the part of several bishop-theologians, to find agreement to the language of Nicaea so that Arianism (the teachings of Arius) was condemned while still condemning Sabellian modalism. The language of the creed did not change, but the understanding did. Another council was called—by a later emperor—in 381

5

in the city of Constantinople. There the creed of Nicaea was reaffirmed, and a third paragraph was added, filling out what is believed concerning the Holy Spirit. The anathemas were also dropped.

Only one change has occurred since 381, and that only in the West. A century or so after the Council of Constantinople, Christians in Spain added the phrase that the Holy Spirit "proceeds from the Father *and the Son*." Before that, the creed said only that the Spirit proceeds from the Father. They added this in order to deal with a particular heresy that was local to Spain. Around the year 800, western missionaries in Eastern Europe discovered that the Greek-speaking church did not use this phrase. They therefore labeled the Greeks heretics, unaware that the Greeks were using the original form of the creed. It is not clear whether theological or political struggles raised this issue to great heights, eventually leading to the split between the Greek and Latin churches—the Roman Catholic and Eastern Orthodox. The Eastern church was furious that a creed, carefully worked out by a council of the whole church, could be altered by a part of that church, with no council at all. The West assumed they had such a right, especially in the office of the Bishop of Rome, the Pope. The discussion, and the division, continues to the present day on this phrase in the creed.

Though Constantine called the council for his own purposes, the church clearly stated its view that Jesus is indeed God—not a second, lesser god—making clear that there is only one God. Though they used language and analogies that need to be clarified for a contemporary audience, the decisions they made remain the bedrock of our faith. The fact that the decision was eventually confirmed by the whole church in spite of all the difficulties on the way to the Council of Constantinople shows that though emperors called councils, it was bishops who knew and loved the gospel who finally made the decisions.

QUESTIONS FOR STUDY

1. What do you think of the debate between East and West on the phrase about the Spirit proceeding from the Father *and the Son*? This is an ecumenical issue of significant proportions. Is our faith something limited to our congregation or even our denomination? To what degree do we confess the faith of the whole church, far wider than our own denominational family? We use the Nicene Creed in our denomination. How free should we be to alter decisions made by far wider expressions of the church?

2. How likely are contemporary Christians to hold beliefs similar to those of Arius? When we say Jesus is the Son of God, what do we mean? How do we explain this in modern language without denying the monotheism that is basic to the church's faith?

3. In addition to the English translation of the Nicene Creed accepted

as authoritative by the Presbyterian Church (U.S.A.) and included in the *Book of Confessions,* some congregations use in their worship a more recent English translation, which has been included in *The Presbyterian Hymnal* since its publication in 1990. In 1998, the 210th General Assembly sent this translation of the Nicene Creed to be voted upon affirmatively or negatively by the presbyteries. If approved by two-thirds of the presbyteries and approved and enacted by the 211th General Assembly, this newer translation will replace the current one in the *Book of Confessions.*

The current translation is included on page 9 (Version 1) and the newer translation is included on page 11 (Version 2). How are the earlier and later translations similar? different?

THE NICENE CREED, VERSION 1

WE BELIEVE in one God the Father Almighty, Maker of heaven and earth, and of all things visible and invisible; **1.1**

And in one Lord Jesus Christ, the only-begotten Son of God, begotten of the Father before all worlds, God of God, Light of Light, Very God of Very God, begotten, not made, being of one substance with the Father, by whom all things were made; who for us men, and for our salvation, came down from heaven, and was incarnate by the Holy Spirit of the Virgin Mary, and was made man, and was crucified also for us under Pontius Pilate. He suffered and was buried, and the third day he rose again according to the Scriptures, and ascended into heaven, and sitteth on the right hand of the Father. And he shall come again with glory to judge both the quick and the dead, whose kingdom shall have no end. **1.2**

And we believe in the Holy Spirit, the Lord and Giver of Life, who proceedeth from the Father and the Son, who with the Father and the Son together is worshipped and glorified, who spoke by the prophets. And we believe one holy catholic and apostolic Church. We acknowledge one baptism for the remission of sins. And we look for the resurrection of the dead, and the life of the world to come. Amen. **1.3**

---

*This translation of the Nicene Creed is the currently accepted version, pending action of the 211th General Assembly (see "Introduction to the Nicene Creed," Questions for Study, #3).

THE NICENE CREED, VERSION 2

We believe in one God,
the Father, the Almighty,
maker of heaven and earth,
of all that is, seen and unseen.

We believe in one Lord, Jesus Christ,
the only Son of God,
eternally begotten of the Father,
God from God, Light from Light,
true God from true God,
begotten, not made,
of one Being with the Father;
through him all things were made.
For us and for our salvation
he came down from heaven,
was incarnate of the Holy Spirit and the Virgin Mary
and became truly human.
For our sake he was crucified under Pontius Pilate;
he suffered death and was buried.
On the third day he rose again
in accordance with the Scriptures;
he ascended into heaven
and is seated at the right hand of the Father.
He will come again in glory to judge the living and the dead,
and his kingdom will have no end.

We believe in the Holy Spirit, the Lord, the giver of life,
who proceeds from the Father and the Son,
who with the Father and the Son is worshiped and glorified,
who has spoken through the prophets.
We believe in one holy catholic and apostolic church.
We acknowledge one baptism for the forgiveness of sins.
We look for the resurrection of the dead,
and the life of the world to come. Amen.

---

*This translation of the Nicene Creed may become the accepted text in the *Book of Confessions,* pending action of the 211th General Assembly.

THE APOSTLES' CREED

Introduction to the Apostles' Creed

According to an attractive legend, at Pentecost the apostles developed a creed that was their common statement of the essentials of the Christian faith. Each apostle, inspired by the gift of the Spirit, is claimed to have contributed a specific element. "Peter said, 'I believe in God the Father almighty . . . maker of heaven and earth' . . . Andrew said, 'and in Jesus Christ His Son . . . our only Lord' . . . James said 'Who was conceived by the Holy Spirit . . . born from the Virgin Mary' . . . Simon said 'the remission of sins' . . . Thaddaeus said 'the resurrection of the flesh' . . . Matthias said 'eternal life.'"

Although the origins of the account lie in pious imagination rather than actual events, the legend does disclose a crucial feature of Christian witness from the earliest age: the importance given to maintaining continuity with the witness of the apostles.

Christianity is a historical religion. It is founded on specific historical events reported by witnesses: the life, death, resurrection of Jesus, and the formation of the church. From the first century the church has sought to ensure that its ongoing proclamation of the gospel is consistent with the witness of the first followers of Jesus. Faithful transmission of the historical events has been viewed as essential to the integrity of the church's proclamation.

A purely historical recitation of these events has never been considered sufficient, however. From the first preaching of the apostles at Pentecost, the followers of Jesus have recognized the necessity of a theological interpretation of the historical data. Moreover, the conviction that these events are the definitive revelation of the will and activity of God has led Christians to seek to understand all things (God, the human condition, creation, history, the eschaton) in terms of these data.

Because acceptance of the Christian faith requires knowledge of specific historical events and understanding of their theological import, the task of instruction, both of interested outsiders and of believers, has always been central to the work of the church. The need to ensure the historical and theological integrity of that instruction led, even in the days of the apostles, to the formulation of summaries of the faith.

These early summaries were not official, fixed creeds of the kind that we know today; however, they were formulas that so effectively captured core elements of the gospel that they became standard elements of early Christian proclamation. Evidence for them can be found in the New Testament. Some of these formulas affirm Jesus as Lord (e.g., Acts 11:17, 16:31; 1 Cor. 15:3–5; Phil. 2:11; Col. 2:6); others refer to God and Jesus Christ (e.g., 1 Cor. 8:6; Gal 1:1; 1 Tim. 2:5–6; 6:13–15); another group is explicitly trinitarian (e.g., Matt. 28:19; Rom. 1:1–4; 2 Cor. 13:14; 1 Peter 1:2. The presence of these three basic patterns, each allowing variations of language, suggests that early Christians sought a general

15

correspondence of content, not uniformity of wording. Fixed language was a considerably later development.

ANTECEDENTS OF THE APOSTLES' CREED

The first appearance of the Apostles' Creed, as we know it today, was in the eighth century. That late date should not mislead, however. The roots of this creed are ancient. Its antecedents can be securely traced to the baptismal liturgy of the mid-second century which was itself based on the New Testament formulas.

As baptism in the second century was almost entirely restricted to adults, a profession of faith was expected as part of the ritual. The candidate, while standing in the water, was asked whether he or she believed in God the Father. The affirmation "I believe" was followed by immersion. A second question regarding Jesus Christ and a third regarding the Holy Spirit were each followed by the candidate's affirmation and then an immersion.

The explicitly trinitarian pattern of these *baptismal interrogations* derived from Jesus' injunction at the conclusion of Matthew (28:18–20) to baptize "in the name of the Father and of the Son and of the Holy Spirit." That injunction dominated baptismal practice from the first century on. Within this basic trinitarian framework, however, precise wording could vary. Clauses that described each of the three persons were often added. In particular, statements about the person and work of Christ were regularly incorporated.

As the use of questions at baptism indicates, assent to basic doctrinal formulations was a precondition for entrance into the church. Instruction or catechesis of the baptismal candidate was thus a necessity. In the second century summaries of Christian teaching, called *rules of faith,* developed. Employing such a rule, a catechist could instruct a group of catechumens by methodically explaining to them each of its elements.

Although the wording was not fixed, a rule of faith was usually trinitarian or binitarian (Father and Son) in outline. Typically, it emphasized the oneness of God, who is creator and Father of Jesus Christ; it listed the basic data of Christ's birth, life, death, resurrection, ascension, and future judgment; it often referred to the Holy Spirit as inspiring the prophets and guiding believers. Significantly, there was sufficient similarity of content among these rules that ancient writers, such as Irenaeus, Tertullian, and Origen, could confidently speak of the one apostolic faith held by the church.

In the third and fourth centuries, in response to increasing numbers of converts, the catechetical system became more formalized, and what are known as *declaratory creeds* developed. These had the form of brief, first-person declarations of trinitarian faith. The wording was fairly fixed. As part of the preparation for baptism, the local bishop would entrust the creed to those catechumens considered ready for its reception. They, in turn, would be expected to memorize it and recite it prior to their baptism as evidence of their acceptance of the essentials of the church's teaching.

Among these declaratory creeds was one that was to be the parent of all Western baptismal creeds of the next centuries: the *Old Roman Creed*. The Apostles' Creed, in the form that we use today, is an expanded version of the Old Roman Creed, which was itself a descendant of the early trinitarian baptismal interrogations. Unlike the baptismal interrogations, rules of faith, and declaratory creeds that predated it, the Apostles' Creed was to receive a fixed form and peculiarly authoritative status throughout the church in the West as a result of efforts by the Emperor Charlemagne (d. 814) to impose uniformity in liturgy and doctrine. The long era of fluidity in creedal wording had ended.

THEOLOGY OF THE APOSTLES' CREED

As the language that was to become the Apostles' Creed evolved out of a centuries-long process, the meanings attached to the words also evolved. As a result, it is not possible to speak of one definitive interpretation for this creed and its antecedents. Instead, what is to be found in the history of its interpretation, even of the first several centuries, is a range of allowable meaning associated with particular terms.

The three-article structure of the creed, one article for each person of the Trinity, undeniably reflects the most ancient trinitarian formulas, especially that of Matthew 28:18–20. Yet the significance attached to these titles has not remained static, as a brief consideration of the *first article* ("I believe in God the Father almighty, creator of heaven and earth") will illustrate.

In early Christian teaching the primary meaning associated with the term "Father" was that of God as the maker of all creation. The addition of the word "almighty" called attention to the dynamic character of God's work as creator and ruler of all that is. A secondary meaning that gained prominence, at least from the beginning of the third century, was that of God as Father of the believer. Christians were to understand themselves as holding a distinctively familiar relationship with God.

Although neither of these interpretations was lost, after the trinitarian controversy of the fourth century attention shifted to the relationship of the members of the Trinity to each other. The Father is the Father of the Son, as the Son is the Son of the Father, and the Holy Spirit is the Spirit of both Father and Son. In other words, the relational character of the terms was understood to refer to the relationship of the members of the Trinity to each other. It was a means to underscore that they all shared the same divine nature.

This shift in interpretation had the effect of detracting from the original interpretation of "Father" as creator. It would seem to have been the case that the phrase "creator of heaven and earth" was thus added to the creed as a means of safeguarding the fundamentally important conviction that God is the creator of all that is.

As in the case of the first article, the interpretation of the *second article* also evolved over time. The designations of Jesus as Son and as Lord were among the earliest Christian claims, as were the references to his birth, suffering, death, burial, resurrection, ascension, and anticipated coming again in judgment.

Nevertheless, this language could be and was used to counter various heresies as they emerged over the centuries. For example, the statements describing Jesus' distinctively human activity (birth, suffering, death, burial) were used to counter those who sought to deny the genuine humanity of the Savior (Docetists, Gnostics). In this regard it might be noted that the doctrine that he was "born from the Virgin Mary," which is sometimes used today as evidence of the deity of Jesus, was in the early centuries used to prove his humanity: He was born of a woman as are all of us. In contrast, the assertion that he was "conceived by the Holy Spirit" was employed centuries later to argue (against Adoptianism) that the Savior, although human, was also divine from the moment of conception.

Perhaps the most curious element of the second article is the claim that Jesus "descended into hell." Although several passages in the New Testament were early considered to be references to such a descent (e.g., Acts 2:27–31; Rom. 10:7; Col. 1:18; 1 Peter 3:19; 4:6), it was not mentioned in a creed until the mid-fourth century. Interpretations have varied. According to a prominent early view, the descent refers to Christ's liberation of the faithful of the Old Testament. A somewhat later view interpreted the descent in terms of Christ's victory over the kingdom of Satan. This latter understanding is consistent with the very ancient view that what is meant by Christ's ascension, seat at the right hand of God, and coming judgment is, in fact, his victory over death and evil. John Calvin, it might be noted, interpreted the descent as a reference to the interior torment that Christ suffered for us.

The *third article* begins with a profession of belief in the Holy Spirit. This profession formed a part of baptismal interrogations and declaratory creeds long before a doctrine of the Holy Spirit developed. In fact, it was not until the late fourth century that the church officially acknowledged the Holy Spirit to be God, equal in all ways to the Father and the Son.

That the church taught and required belief in the Holy Spirit even while the question of the Spirit's deity remained open suggests that the church's experience of the Holy Spirit required affirmation, even though precise language to describe the source of that experience remained elusive. At the very least, the remaining elements in this article identify the commonly acknowledged arenas of the Spirit's operation: the church ("holy catholic Church, the communion of saints"), baptism ("the forgiveness of sins"), and the achievement of eternal blessedness ("the resurrection of the body, and the life everlasting").

As with other elements of the creed, the range of meanings associated with these phrases requires explanation. For example, the phrase "holy catholic Church" came to prominence in the second century as a counter to the threat posed by heretical sects. It was an affirmation of the universal church, understood to be that worldwide assemblage of local congregations unified with each other by their adherence to the teaching of the apostles and sanctified through the indwelling of the Holy Spirit.

The following phrase, "communion of saints," although probably not added until the fourth century, is closely related to the notions both of unity and of holiness. Although over the centuries a variety of meanings has been attached to these words, two strands of thinking have dominated. Most frequently, it has been understood to refer to the fellowship enjoyed by believers not only with those still living but also with those who have died in the faith. A secondary but persistent interpretation has been that the phrase refers to believers' participation in the elements of the Eucharist. Regardless, both "communion of saints" and "holy catholic Church" testify to the operation of the Spirit among the people of God.

Also included within the work of the Spirit is the "forgiveness of sins." The phrase expresses the joyous ancient conviction that the believer emerges from the water of baptism as a radically new person, with all prior sins washed away. It was not until the second and third centuries that the church considered the possibility of forgiveness of any but minor sins after baptism. In the centuries that followed, as the church not only encouraged the baptism of infants but also accepted into its ranks persons of only minimal commitment, the assurance of forgiveness of sins came to apply not merely to baptism but to the efficacy of prayer and penitence for sins committed thereafter.

As it is through the operation of the Spirit that the church is made holy and the believer is forgiven, it is also through the Spirit that one may confidently hope for resurrection and eternal life. The phrase "resurrection of the body" is the claim of ancient Christianity that God's triumph over death applies not only to the soul but also to the body. The final phrase, "life everlasting," provides the further assurance that the life thereby granted is eternal. It is the blessed, eternal union with God, who is Life itself.

The summary of the church's belief, as we find it in the Apostles' Creed, is the result of centuries of disciplined reflection on Scripture, developing tradition, and the experience of grace. The creed states the central mysteries without precisely explaining them, and thus invites the church and the individual believer to join the centuries-long exploration and appropriation of the riches of the ancient apostolic faith.

QUESTIONS FOR STUDY

1. What values do you find in the creed which you understand to be fundamental to a lively Christian faith?

2. Of what importance is it for the church and the individual believer to maintain continuity with the faith of early Christians? To what extent do you find that the convictions of early Christians enrich or challenge your own convictions?

3. What advantages and problems do you see in the fluidity of language in early Christian teaching?

4. In addition to the English translation of the Apostles' Creed accepted as authoritative by the Presbyterian Church (U.S.A.), some congregations use a more recent translation that is included in *The Presbyterian Hymnal* and reads as follows:

I believe in God, the Father almighty, creator of heaven and earth.

I believe in Jesus Christ, God's only Son, our Lord, who was conceived by the Holy Spirit, born of the Virgin Mary, suffered under Pontius Pilate, was crucified, died, and was buried; he descended to the dead. On the third day he rose again; he ascended into heaven, he is seated at the right hand of the Father, and he will come to judge the living and the dead.

I believe in the Holy Spirit, the holy catholic Church, the communion of saints, the forgiveness of sins, the resurrection of the body, and the life everlasting. Amen.

How are the earlier and later English translations similar? How do they differ?

THE APOSTLES' CREED

I BELIEVE in God the Father Almighty, Maker of heaven and earth,   **2.1**

And in Jesus Christ his only Son our Lord; who was conceived by   **2.2**
the Holy Ghost, born of the Virgin Mary, suffered under Pontius
Pilate, was crucified, dead, and buried; he descended into hell; the
third day he rose again from the dead; he ascended into heaven, and
sitteth on the right hand of God the Father Almighty; from thence he
shall come to judge the quick and the dead.

I believe in the Holy Ghost; the holy catholic Church; the commu-   **2.3**
nion of saints; the forgiveness of sins; the resurrection of the body; and
the life everlasting. Amen.

THE SCOTS CONFESSION

Introduction to the Scots Confession

The Scots Confession, charter document of the Church of Scotland, emerged from a protracted period of political and ecclesiastical turmoil during which religious leadership often proved a risky business. Thus, for example, the Protestant preacher George Wishart was seized by authorities early in 1546 and burned as a heretic at St. Andrews on March 1. (His initials in stone still mark the spot.) The following decade Walter Myln, a Catholic priest, was burned in the same city, and there were iconoclastic riots at locations across Scotland.

Fortunes of the Reformation in Scotland varied according to alliances between Scottish nobles and the French crown, which was aligned with Roman Catholicism. These were designed to counter the interests of the English crown, which had opposed papal power since Henry VIII's establishment of the Church of England during the mid-1530s. However, on December 3, 1557, a group of Scottish Protestants entered into a covenant to nourish and defend "the whole congregation of Christ." They gained support from the English, and the ensuing conflict ended at Edinburgh on July 8, 1560, in a peace between the "covenanters" and Mary, Queen of France and Scotland, and her French allies.

The Treaty provided that a Scottish Parliament should meet at Edinburgh on August 1. The Parliament commissioned six prominent ministers (John Douglas, John Knox, John Row, John Spottiswood, John Willock and John Winram) to write a statement of Protestant Christian faith. Knox, who during periods of exile had studied in Geneva with John Calvin and also ministered to the English-speaking congregation there, is generally thought to have exerted a strong influence over the document. (He also claimed that it was written in four days.) Following its adoption, acts of Parliament abolished the Mass as well as the jurisdiction of the Pope, although the effects of these acts varied from place to place. Queen Mary remained at Paris and withheld her approval of the Parliament's actions. Full constitutional ratification of the Scots Confession therefore waited until the reign of James VI in 1567. Nevertheless, the Confession was translated immediately into Latin so that it could be shared internationally, and first printings in the original Scottish dialect were made in 1561 at Edinburgh and at London.

Especially as we now consider it within our *Book of Confessions*, we should also observe that the first official standard of Scottish Presbyterianism never functioned alone. Other Protestant documents were also used and approved, including Calvin's Geneva Catechism of 1545, the Heidelberg Catechism of 1563, and the Second Helvetic Confession of 1566. Indeed, Knox's *Book of Common Order* did not include the Scots Confession but the confession adopted by the English-speaking congregation at Geneva in 1556, and the *First Book of Discipline* required communicants to be familiar with not only the Scots Confession but also the Apostles' Creed. The Scots Confession was superseded (but not abrogated) in the

Church of Scotland when the Westminster Confession of Faith was approved in 1647 in the interest of sharing a common standard with English Presbyterians.

A further note before we turn to substantive themes. Although the Scots Confession contains more than its share of polemics, its literary style is simple and direct, and this is one reason why it remains a good choice for instruction in the faith more than four hundred years after it was written.

GOD'S PROMISE AND THE CHURCH

Chapter 1 of the Scots Confession acknowledges the one God who creates, upholds, rules, and guides all things, and the next two chapters treat the creation of human beings and their fall into sin. Then comes a rather remarkable fourth chapter on "The Revelation of the Promise." Here, we learn that, following Adam's disobedience, God "did seek Adam again . . . and in the end made unto him a most joyful promise," and that this promise has been received by all of the faithful "from Adam . . . onwards to the incarnation of Christ Jesus" (3.04).

It is at this point that the Confession turns to the Church, or as it is called in Scottish dialect, the Kirk. Consequently, the entire discussion of the Kirk falls within the frame of God's sweeping promise of grace and restoration. "God preserved, instructed, multiplied, honored, adorned, and called from death to life his Kirk in all ages since Adam until the coming of Christ Jesus in the flesh" (3.05). Adam, Noah, Abraham, Moses, David, the prophets—all share in the largesse of God's promise definitively revealed in Jesus Christ, and all therefore are counted within the true Kirk.

To say that same thing another way, the community of God's promise is the community of the elect. "By grace alone," God the Father "chose us in his Son Christ Jesus before the foundation of the world was laid, [and also] appointed him to be our head, our brother, our pastor, the great bishop of our souls" (3.08). This is why, "from the beginning there has been, now is, and . . . shall be, one Kirk," a catholic or universal company of persons "chosen of all ages, of all realms, nations, and tongues, be they of the Jews or be they of the Gentiles, who have communion and society with God the Father, and with his Son, Christ Jesus, through the sanctification of his Holy Spirit" (3.16). In short, the community of those who receive God's promise is the *invisible* Kirk, and it is made up of all those whom God has chosen. Known only to God, the invisible Kirk includes both the living and the departed.

THE NOTES OF THE TRUE KIRK

The true, *visible* Kirk, or "such Kirks [as] we the inhabitants of the realm of Scotland confessing Christ Jesus, do claim to have in our cities, towns, and reformed districts," is distinguished from false churches by three visible notes, signs, or marks (3.18). Much like Calvin in his *Institutes of the Christian Religion,* the Scots Confession claims that the first note is "the true preaching of the Word of God," and that the second is "the right administration of the sacraments" always in association "with the Word and promise of God" (3.18). However, unlike Calvin, who surely accorded the law and discipline a prominent place in the Christian life, the Scots Confession also raises to the level of a third mark of the church "ecclesiastical discipline . . . whereby vice is repressed and virtue nourished" (3.18). In this, it follows the Confession of Faith of the English-speaking Congregation at Geneva (1556).

The positive significance of the notes is to emphasize practices that are essential to the life of the church in history and society, and without which the church ceases to be the church. However, we cannot help but observe the harshly polemical and even anti-Semitic language with which the notes of the true Kirk are introduced. The writers of the Scots Confession tell us that "Satan has labored from the beginning to adorn his pestilent synagogue with the title of the Kirk." And so, lest we be deceived, "it is essential that the true Kirk be distinguished from the filthy synagogues by clear and perfect notes." Again, the true Kirk cannot be distinguished from the false and "horrible harlot" by "antiquity, usurped title, lineal succession, appointed place, nor the [substantial] numbers of men approving of an error"—all of these being either real or alleged characteristics of Roman Catholicism (3.18).

CHURCH COUNCILS AND THEIR DECLARATIONS

The Scots prove sharply Protestant and Reformed in their view of the status of church assemblies and pronouncements. Chapter XX states that the primary function of church councils is "to refute heresies, and to give public confession of their faith to generations following." Councils and pronouncements help the Kirk to articulate what it believes. They help it to protect sound doctrine, and to teach and hand on the authentic faith from generation to generation. Secondarily, councils also serve to articulate and ensure "good policy and order" in the church, its ceremonies and services of worship. For these reasons, "we do not rashly condemn what good men, assembled together in general councils lawfully gathered, have set before us." Indeed, we should respect past tradition and remain willing to be instructed by it.

Nevertheless, we should not accept it uncritically. For, "it is plain that, being human, [some general councils] have manifestly erred, and that in matters of great weight and importance." (Otherwise, why have a reformation?) Councils and their decrees are not "to forge for us new articles of faith," and they should be denied when they "make decisions contrary to the Word of God." In sum, councils, creeds, confessions, catechisms, declarations, statements of faith, and the like are human and their authority is therefore limited. They are subordinate to "the plain Word of God," and they should be tested for their conformity to it. Moreover, the policies and orders of worship that councils recommend should not be "appointed for all ages, times, and places . . . they may, and ought to be, changed, when they foster superstition rather than edify the Kirk"—a central Reformation criticism of the Roman Mass (3.20).

The Preface to the Scots Confession (which is appended to this introduction) dispels any doubts as to whether its authors intended their own work to be subjected to the same standard of criticism. It begins by recounting the trials and unexpected good fortune of the Protestant cause in Scotland. Next, it asks anyone who notes a chapter or sentence "in our Confession" that is "contrary to God's Holy Word" to "inform us of it in writing." Then, it declares, "and we, upon our honour, do promise him that by God's grace we shall give him satisfaction from the mouth of God, that is, from Holy Scripture, or else we shall alter whatever he can prove to be wrong."

THE SACRAMENTS

Chapters XXI–XXIII discuss the sacraments, and here the overarching theme of God's promise of grace comes to expression in an emphasis on our spiritual union with the Redeemer. The Scots note that we are engrafted into Jesus Christ and made partakers of his cleansing righteousness by baptism. They affirm that, in the Supper, "Christ Jesus is so joined with us that he becomes the very nourishment and food of our souls" (3.21). They reject transubstantiation, or the doctrine that the substances of the bread and wine are changed into Christ's body and blood, in favor of the idea that, by means of the Holy Spirit, the faithful "have such union with Christ Jesus as the natural man cannot apprehend." Indeed, Christ "remains in them and they in him" in such a manner that they gain life and immortality (3.21).

Reflecting the Reformed insistence that Word and sacrament belong together, the Scots maintain that the sacraments are rightly administered only by those who are lawfully appointed to preach in particular congregations and only in the manner appointed by God in the Scriptures. They reject Roman additions to baptism, such as "oil, salt, spittle," as well as the practice of withdrawing the cup from the people during celebrations of the Supper (3.22). Like John Calvin in his *Institutes* and also Heinrich Bullinger in the Second Helvetic Confession (5.207), they uphold the appropriateness of infant baptism, but claim that the Supper is only for those who can examine their own faith and morals (3.23).

Like Calvin and Bullinger also, the Scots reject the practice of allowing women (in their capacity as midwives) to baptize newborn infants who are in danger of dying unbaptized. For Calvin, a part of the reason was that there is no emergency. Baptism is a sign and seal of God's promise of grace, but God adopts the children of believers before they are born, and it is mere superstition to join God's grace to baptism in such a manner as to suggest that the unbaptized are condemned to eternal death. Indeed, says Calvin, "Few realize how much injury the dogma that baptism is necessary for salvation, badly expounded, has entailed" (*Institutes of the Christian Religion* 4.15.20). However, the Scots simply claim that the Roman Church is wrong to let women baptize, since "the Holy Ghost will not permit [women] to preach in the congregation" (3.22), a point that stands in flat opposition to A Brief Statement of Faith when it says that the Spirit "calls women and men to all ministries of the Church" (10.4).

CIVIL AUTHORITY

Chapter XXIV of the Scots Confession, "The Civil Magistrate," articulates a central affirmation of social ethics in the Reformed tradition: namely, the sovereignty of God over civil authority. The Scots affirm that civil dominions and their ruling authorities are appointed and ordained by God "for the manifestation of his own glory and for the good and well-being of all men" (3.24). The civil authorities are to pursue these ends by wielding the sword for the defense of good persons, the punishment of "all open evildoers," the maintenance of "true religion," and the suppression of "all idolatry and superstition." Clearly, there is no separation of church and state here, and it may be instructive to compare the Scots' position with both the original and revised texts of the chapter entitled "Of the Civil Magistrate" in the Westminster Confession of Faith (6.127–.130), as well as with what the Theological Declaration of Barmen says in response to a totalitarian regime (8.22–.24).

The idea that civil government has a divinely appointed function within God's sovereign reign supports an ethic of worldly engagement that regards both public office and citizenship as worthy callings of genuine importance. It also encourages obedience to civil authority at the same time that it does not entirely rule out legitimate resistance (a possibility with which Scottish Presbyterians believed they had firsthand experience). We are not to resist governmental powers "so long as they are acting in their own spheres," and we are to aid and serve "princes and rulers," so long as they "vigilantly fulfill their office" (3.24). In setting these limits to our obedience to and cooperation with civil authorities under God, Chapter XXIV connects with the account of good works in Chapter XIV. There, the Scots affirm that we are "to honor father, mother, princes, rulers, and superior powers; to love them, to support them, to obey their orders if they are not contrary to the commands of God, to save the lives of the innocent, to repress tyranny, to defend the oppressed" (3.14). And this accords with Calvin's exposition of the Fifth Commandment, which he also takes to refer not only to parents but also to authorities of all kinds. Calvin writes, "Hence, if they spur us to transgress [God's] law, we have a perfect right to regard them not as parents, but as strangers who are trying to lead us away from obedience to our true Father. So should we act toward princes, lords, and every kind of superiors" (*Institutes* 2.8.38).

LAST THINGS

The Scots Confession closes with a treatment of the consummation of God's promise under the title "The Gifts Freely Given to the Kirk." The gifts in question are those given to the true, invisible Kirk, as the Kirk's visible company includes both reprobate and those who truly believe. At the last judgment, the reprobate "shall be condemned to the fire unquenchable" (3.25). The elect, who receive from Christ the gift of forgiveness and remission of sins in this life, shall also receive the gift of incorruptible resurrection to glory. Then the one "eternal, infinite, immeasurable, incomprehensible, omnipotent, invisible" God, whom the Scots acknowledged in Chapter I, shall be "all in all things" (3.01, 3.25).

A MOVEMENT WITH A MISSION

"Long we have thirsted, dear brethren, to have made known to the world the doctrine which we profess and for which we have suffered abuse and danger." These words from the Preface to the Scots Confession express the sense of struggle and evangelical urgency that accompanied the Reformation in Scotland. This same sense comes through in the Confession's final prayer, which calls upon God to confound God's enemies, empower true servants to proclaim God's Word, and turn every nation toward the truth. It reminds us that this first confessional standard of Presbyterianism was written in turbulent times.

QUESTIONS FOR STUDY

1. How does the theme of God's promise of grace tie together much that the Scots Confession says about church and sacraments? Do you find this theme helpful for understanding your own faith?

2. What is the status of church councils and their confessions according to the Scots Confession? What is their value? How does the Scots Confession on this point compare with the Westminster Confession of Faith (6.175) and the Confession of 1967 (9.01–.06)?

3. How shall we understand disagreements among documents in our *Book of Confessions,* such as the one over whether the Spirit calls women to all ministries of the church? What shall we make of the statements concerning Satan's "pestilent synagogues" and "filthy synagogues" that appear in the Scots Confession (3.18)?

4. How does the Scots Confession understand civil authority under God?

ADDENDUM: THE PREFACE TO THE SCOTS CONFESSION OF 1560 *

And this glad tidings of the Kingdom shall be preached through the whole world for a witness to all nations; and then shall the end come (Matt. 24:14).

The Estates of Scotland, with the inhabitants of Scotland who profess the holy Evangel of Jesus Christ, to their fellow country-men and to all other nations who confess the Lord Jesus with them, wish grace, mercy, and peace from God the Father of our Lord Jesus Christ, with the Spirit of righteous judgment, for salvation.

Long have we thirsted, dear brethren, to have made known to the world the doctrine which we profess and for which we have suffered abuse and danger; but such has been the rage of Satan against us, and against the eternal truth of Christ now recently reborn among us, that until this day we have had neither time nor opportunity to set forth our faith, as gladly we would have done. For how we have been afflicted until now the greater part of Europe, we suppose, knows well.

But since by the infinite goodness of our God (who never suffers His afflicted to be utterly confounded) we have received unexpected rest and liberty, we could not do other than set forth this brief and plain Confession of that doctrine which is set before us, and which we believe and confess; partly to satisfy our brethren whose hearts, we suspect, have been and are grieved by the slanders against us; and partly to silence impudent blasphemers who boldly condemn that which they have not heard and do not understand.

We do not suppose that such malice can be cured merely by our Confession, for we know that the sweet savour of the Gospel is, and shall be, death to the sons of perdition; but we are considering chiefly our own weaker brethren, to whom we would communicate our deepest thoughts, lest they be troubled or carried away by the different rumours which Satan spreads against us to defeat our godly enterprise, protesting that if any man will note in our Confession any chapter or sentence contrary to God's Holy Word, that it would please him of his gentleness and for Christian charity's sake to inform us of it in writing; and we, upon our honour, do promise him that by God's grace we shall give him satisfaction from the mouth of God, that is, from Holy Scripture, or else we shall alter whatever he can prove to be wrong. For we call on God to record that from our hearts we abhor all heretical sects and all teachers of false doctrine, and that with all humility we embrace the purity of Christ's Gospel, which is the one food of our souls and therefore so precious to us that we are determined to suffer the greatest of worldly dangers, rather than let our souls be defrauded of it. For we are completely convinced that whoever denies Christ Jesus, or is ashamed of Him in the presence of men, shall be denied before the Father and before His holy angels. Therefore by the aid of the mighty Spirit of our Lord Jesus Christ we firmly intend to endure to the end in the confession of our faith, as in the following chapters.

---

*Arthur C. Cochrane, ed., *Reformed Confessions of the 16th Century* (Philadelphia: Westminster Press, 1966), 163–65.

THE SCOTS CONFESSION[1]

CHAPTER I

God

We confess and acknowledge one God alone, to whom alone we must cleave, whom alone we must serve, whom only we must worship, and in whom alone we put our trust. Who is eternal, infinite, immeasurable, incomprehensible, omnipotent, invisible; one in substance and yet distinct in three persons, the Father, the Son, and the Holy Ghost. By whom we confess and believe all things in heaven and earth, visible and invisible, to have been created, to be retained in their being, and to be ruled and guided by his inscrutable providence for such end as his eternal wisdom, goodness, and justice have appointed, and to the manifestation of his own glory.

3.01

CHAPTER II

The Creation of Man

We confess and acknowledge that our God has created man, i.e., our first father, Adam, after his own image and likeness, to whom he gave wisdom, lordship, justice, free will, and self-consciousness, so that in the whole nature of man no imperfection could be found. From this dignity and perfection man and woman both fell; the woman being deceived by the serpent and man obeying the voice of the woman, both conspiring against the sovereign majesty of God, who in clear words had previously threatened death if they presumed to eat of the forbidden tree.

3.02

CHAPTER III

Original Sin

By this transgression, generally known as original sin, the image of God was utterly defaced in man, and he and his children became by

3.03

---

[1] Reprinted from *The Scots Confession: 1560*. Edited with an Introduction by G. D. Henderson. Rendered into modern English by James Bulloch. The Saint Andrew Press, Edinburgh, 1960, pp. 58-80. Used by permission.

33

nature hostile to God, slaves to Satan, and servants to sin. And thus everlasting death has had, and shall have, power and dominion over all who have not been, are not, or shall not be reborn from above. This rebirth is wrought by the power of the Holy Ghost creating in the hearts of God's chosen ones an assured faith in the promise of God revealed to us in his Word; by this faith we grasp Christ Jesus with the graces and blessings promised in him.

CHAPTER IV

The Revelation of the Promise

3.04   We constantly believe that God, after the fearful and horrible departure of man from his obedience, did seek Adam again, call upon him, rebuke and convict him of his sin, and in the end made unto him a most joyful promise, that "the seed of the woman should bruise the head of the serpent," that is, that he should destroy the works of the devil. This promise was repeated and made clearer from time to time; it was embraced with joy, and most constantly received by all the faithful from Adam to Noah, from Noah to Abraham, from Abraham to David, and so onwards to the incarnation of Christ Jesus; all (we mean the believing fathers under the law) did see the joyful day of Christ Jesus, and did rejoice.

CHAPTER V

The Continuance, Increase, and Preservation of the Kirk

3.05   We most surely believe that God preserved, instructed, multiplied, honored, adorned, and called from death to life his Kirk in all ages since Adam until the coming of Christ Jesus in the flesh. For he called Abraham from his father's country, instructed him, and multiplied his seed; he marvelously preserved him, and more marvelously delivered his seed from the bondage and tyranny of Pharaoh; to them he gave his laws, constitutions, and ceremonies; to them he gave the land of Canaan; after he had given them judges, and afterwards Saul, he gave David to be king, to whom he gave promise that of the fruit of his loins should one sit forever upon his royal throne. To this same people from time to time he sent prophets, to recall them to the right way of their God, from which sometimes they strayed by idolatry. And although, because of their stubborn contempt for righteousness he was compelled to give them into the hands of their enemies, as had previously been threatened by the mouth of Moses, so that the holy city was destroyed, the temple burned with fire, and the whole land desolate for seventy years, yet in mercy he restored them again to Jerusalem, where the city and temple were rebuilt, and they endured against all temptations and assaults of Satan till the Messiah came according to the promise.

CHAPTER VI

The Incarnation of Christ Jesus

When the fullness of time came God sent his Son, his eternal   **3.06**
wisdom, the substance of his own glory, into this world, who took the nature of humanity from the substance of a woman, a virgin, by means of the Holy Ghost. And so was born the "just seed of David," the "Angel of the great counsel of God," the very Messiah promised, whom we confess and acknowledge to be Emmanuel, true God and true man, two perfect natures united and joined in one person. So by our Confession we condemn the damnable and pestilent heresies of Arius, Marcion, Eutyches, Nestorius, and such others as did either deny the eternity of his Godhead, or the truth of his humanity, or confounded them, or else divided them.

CHAPTER VII

Why the Mediator Had to Be
True God and True Man

We acknowledge and confess that this wonderful union between the   **3.07**
Godhead and the humanity in Christ Jesus did arise from the eternal and immutable decree of God from which all our salvation springs and depends.

CHAPTER VIII

Election

That same eternal God and Father, who by grace alone chose us in   **3.08**
his Son Christ Jesus before the foundation of the world was laid, appointed him to be our head, our brother, our pastor, and the great bishop of our souls. But since the opposition between the justice of God and our sins was such that no flesh by itself could or might have attained unto God, it behooved the Son of God to descend unto us and take himself a body of our body, flesh of our flesh, and bone of our bone, and so become the Mediator between God and man, giving power to as many as believe in him to be the sons of God; as he himself says, "I ascend to my Father and to your Father, to my God and to your God." By this most holy brotherhood whatever we have lost in Adam is restored to us again. Therefore we are not afraid to call God our Father, not so much because he has created us, which we have in

common with the reprobate, as because he has given unto us his only Son to be our brother, and given us grace to acknowledge and embrace him as our only Mediator. Further, it behooved the Messiah and Redeemer to be true God and true man, because he was able to undergo the punishment of our transgressions and to present himself in the presence of his Father's judgment, as in our stead, to suffer for our transgression and disobedience, and by death to overcome him that was the author of death. But because the Godhead alone could not suffer death, and neither could manhood overcome death, he joined both together in one person, that the weakness of one should suffer and be subject to death—which we had deserved—and the infinite and invincible power of the other, that is, of the Godhead, should triumph, and purchase for us life, liberty, and perpetual victory. So we confess, and most undoubtedly believe.

CHAPTER IX

Christ's Death, Passion, and Burial

3.09   That our Lord Jesus offered himself a voluntary sacrifice unto his Father for us, that he suffered contradiction of sinners, that he was wounded and plagued for our transgressions, that he, the clean innocent Lamb of God, was condemned in the presence of an earthly judge, that we should be absolved before the judgment seat of our God; that he suffered not only the cruel death of the cross, which was accursed by the sentence of God; but also that he suffered for a season the wrath of his Father which sinners had deserved. But yet we avow that he remained the only, well beloved, and blessed Son of his Father even in the midst of his anguish and torment which he suffered in body and soul to make full atonement for the sins of his people. From this we confess and avow that there remains no other sacrifice for sin; if any affirm so, we do not hesitate to say that they are blasphemers against Christ's death and the everlasting atonement thereby purchased for us.

CHAPTER X

The Resurrection

3.10   We undoubtedly believe, since it was impossible that the sorrows of death should retain in bondage the Author of life, that our Lord Jesus crucified, dead, and buried, who descended into hell, did rise again for our justification, and the destruction of him who was the author of death, and brought life again to us who were subject to death and its bondage. We know that his resurrection was confirmed by the testimony of his enemies, and by the resurrection of the dead, whose sepulchres did open, and they did rise and appear to many within the city of Jerusalem. It was also confirmed by the testimony of his angels, and by the senses and judgment of his apostles and of others, who had conversation, and did eat and drink with him after his resurrection.

CHAPTER XI

The Ascension

We do not doubt but that the selfsame body which was born of the   3.11
virgin, was crucified, dead, and buried, and which did rise again, did ascend into the heavens, for the accomplishment of all things, where in our name and for our comfort he has received all power in heaven and earth, where he sits at the right hand of the Father, having received his kingdom, the only advocate and mediator for us. Which glory, honor, and prerogative, he alone amongst the brethren shall possess till all his enemies are made his footstool, as we undoubtedly believe they shall be in the Last Judgment. We believe that the same Lord Jesus shall visibly return for this Last Judgment as he was seen to ascend. And then, we firmly believe, the time of refreshing and restitution of all things shall come, so that those who from the beginning have suffered violence, injury, and wrong, for righteousness' sake, shall inherit that blessed immortality promised them from the beginning. But, on the other hand, the stubborn, disobedient, cruel persecutors, filthy persons, idolators, and all sorts of the unbelieving, shall be cast into the dungeon of utter darkness, where their worm shall not die, nor their fire be quenched. The remembrance of that day, and of the Judgment to be executed in it, is not only a bridle by which our carnal lusts are restrained but also such inestimable comfort that neither the threatening of worldly princes, nor the fear of present danger or of temporal death, may move us to renounce and forsake that blessed society which we, the members, have with our Head and only Mediator, Christ Jesus: whom we confess and avow to be the promised Messiah, the only Head of his Kirk, our just Lawgiver, our only High Priest, Advocate, and Mediator. To which honors and offices, if man or angel presume to intrude themselves, we utterly detest and abhor them, as blasphemous to our sovereign and supreme Governor, Christ Jesus.

CHAPTER XII

Faith in the Holy Ghost

Our faith and its assurance do not proceed from flesh and blood,   3.12
that is to say, from natural powers within us, but are the inspiration of the Holy Ghost; whom we confess to be God, equal with the Father

and with his Son, who sanctifies us, and brings us into all truth by his own working, without whom we should remain forever enemies to God and ignorant of his Son, Christ Jesus. For by nature we are so dead, blind, and perverse, that neither can we feel when we are pricked, see the light when it shines, nor assent to the will of God when it is revealed, unless the Spirit of the Lord Jesus quicken that which is dead, remove the darkness from our minds, and bow our stubborn hearts to the obedience of his blessed will. And so, as we confess that God the Father created us when we were not, as his Son our Lord Jesus redeemed us when we were enemies to him, so also do we confess that the Holy Ghost does sanctify and regenerate us, without respect to any merit proceeding from us, be it before or be it after our regeneration. To put this even more plainly; as we willingly disclaim any honor and glory for our own creation and redemption, so do we willingly also for our regeneration and sanctification; for by ourselves we are not capable of thinking one good thought, but he who has begun the work in us alone continues us in it, to the praise and glory of his undeserved grace.

CHAPTER XIII

The Cause of Good Works

3.13   The cause of good works, we confess, is not our free will, but the Spirit of the Lord Jesus, who dwells in our hearts by true faith, brings forth such works as God has prepared for us to walk in. For we most boldly affirm that it is blasphemy to say that Christ abides in the hearts of those in whom is no spirit of sanctification. Therefore we do not hesitate to affirm that murderers, oppressors, cruel persecuters, adulterers, filthy persons, idolators, drunkards, thieves, and all workers of iniquity, have neither true faith nor anything of the Spirit of the Lord Jesus, so long as they obstinately continue in wickedness. For as soon as the Spirit of the Lord Jesus, whom God's chosen children receive by true faith, takes possession of the heart of any man, so soon does he regenerate and renew him, so that he begins to hate what before he loved, and to love what he hated before. Thence comes that continual battle which is between the flesh and the Spirit in God's children, while the flesh and the natural man, being corrupt, lust for things pleasant and delightful to themselves, are envious in adversity and proud in prosperity, and every moment prone and ready to offend the majesty of God. But the Spirit of God, who bears witness to our spirit that we are the sons of God, makes us resist filthy pleasures and groan in God's presence for deliverance from this bondage of corruption, and finally to triumph over sin so that it does not reign in our mortal bodies. Other men do not share this conflict since they do not have God's Spirit, but they readily follow and obey sin and feel no regrets, since they act as the devil and their corrupt nature urge. But the sons of God fight against sin; sob and mourn when they find themselves tempted to do evil; and, if they fall, rise again with earnest and unfeigned repentance. They do these things, not by their own power, but by the power of the Lord Jesus, apart from whom they can do nothing.

CHAPTER XIV

The Works Which Are Counted Good Before God

We confess and acknowledge that God has given to man his holy law, in which not only all such works as displease and offend his godly majesty are forbidden, but also those which please him and which he has promised to reward are commanded. These works are of two kinds. The one is done to the honor of God, the other to the profit of our neighbor, and both have the revealed will of God as their assurance. To have one God, to worship and honor him, to call upon him in all our troubles, to reverence his holy Name, to hear his Word and to believe it, and to share in his holy sacraments, belong to the first kind. To honor father, mother, princes, rulers, and superior powers; to love them, to support them, to obey their orders if they are not contrary to the commands of God, to save the lives of the innocent, to repress tyranny, to defend the oppressed, to keep our bodies clean and holy, to live in soberness and temperance, to deal justly with all men in word and deed, and, finally, to repress any desire to harm our neighbor, are the good works of the second kind, and these are most pleasing and acceptable to God as he has commanded them himself. Acts to the contrary are sins, which always displease him and provoke him to anger, such as, not to call upon him alone when we have need, not to hear his Word with reverence, but to condemn and despise it, to have or worship idols, to maintain and defend idolatry, lightly to esteem the reverend name of God, to profane, abuse, or condemn the sacraments of Christ Jesus, to disobey or resist any whom God has placed in authority, so long as they do not exceed the bounds of their office, to murder, or to consent thereto, to bear hatred, or to let innocent blood be shed if we can prevent it. In conclusion, we confess and affirm that the breach of any other commandment of the first or second kind is sin, by which God's anger and displeasure are kindled against the proud, unthankful world. So that we affirm good works to be those alone which are done in faith and at the command of God who, in his law, has set forth the things that please him. We affirm that evil works are not only those expressly done against God's command, but also, in religious matters and the worship of God, those things which have no other warrant than the invention and opinion of man. From the beginning God has rejected such, as we learn from the words of the prophet Isaiah and of our master, Christ Jesus, "In vain do they worship Me, teaching the doctrines and commandments of men."

CHAPTER XV

The Perfection of the Law and the Imperfection of Man

3.15   We confess and acknowledge that the law of God is most just, equal, holy, and perfect, commanding those things which, when perfectly done, can give life and bring man to eternal felicity; but our nature is so corrupt, weak, and imperfect, that we are never able perfectly to fulfill the works of the law. Even after we are reborn, if we say that we have no sin, we deceive ourselves and the truth of God is not in us. It is therefore essential for us to lay hold on Christ Jesus, in his righteousness and his atonement, since he is the end and consummation of the Law and since it is by him that we are set at liberty so that the curse of God may not fall upon us, even though we do not fulfill the Law in all points. For as God the Father beholds us in the body of his Son Christ Jesus, he accepts our imperfect obedience as if it were perfect, and covers our works, which are defiled with many stains, with the righteousness of his Son. We do not mean that we are so set at liberty that we owe no obedience to the Law—for we have already acknowledged its place—but we affirm that no man on earth, with the sole exception of Christ Jesus, has given, gives, or shall give in action that obedience to the Law which the Law requires. When we have done all things we must fall down and unfeignedly confess that we are unprofitable servants. Therefore, whoever boasts of the merits of his own works or puts his trust in works of supererogation, boasts of what does not exist, and puts his trust in damnable idolatry.

CHAPTER XVI

The Kirk

3.16   As we believe in one God, Father, Son, and Holy Ghost, so we firmly believe that from the beginning there has been, now is, and to the end of the world shall be, one Kirk, that is to say, one company and multitude of men chosen by God, who rightly worship and embrace him by true faith in Christ Jesus, who is the only Head of the Kirk, even as it is the body and spouse of Christ Jesus. This Kirk is catholic, that is, universal, because it contains the chosen of all ages, of all realms, nations, and tongues, be they of the Jews or be they of the Gentiles, who have communion and society with God the Father, and with his Son, Christ Jesus, through the sanctification of his Holy Spirit. It is therefore called the communion, not of profane persons, but of saints, who, as citizens of the heavenly Jerusalem, have the fruit of inestimable benefits, one God, one Lord Jesus, one faith, and one baptism. Out of this Kirk there is neither life nor eternal felicity. Therefore we utterly abhor the blasphemy of those who hold that men who live according to equity and justice shall be saved, no matter what religion they profess. For since there is neither life nor salvation without Christ Jesus; so shall none have part therein but those whom the Father has given unto his Son Christ Jesus, and those who in time come to him, avow his doctrine, and believe in him. (We include the children with the believing parents.) This Kirk is invisible, known only to God, who alone knows whom he has chosen, and includes both the chosen who are departed, the Kirk triumphant, those who yet live and fight against sin and Satan, and those who shall live hereafter.

CHAPTER XVII

The Immortality of Souls

The chosen departed are in peace, and rest from their labors; not that they sleep and are lost in oblivion as some fanatics hold, for they are delivered from all fear and torment, and all the temptations to which we and all God's chosen are subject in this life, and because of which we are called the Kirk Militant. On the other hand, the reprobate and unfaithful departed have anguish, torment, and pain which cannot be expressed. Neither the one nor the other is in such sleep that they feel no joy or torment, as is testified by Christ's parable in St. Luke XVI, his words to the thief, and the words of the souls crying under the altar, "O Lord, thou that art righteous and just, how long shalt thou not revenge our blood upon those that dwell in the earth?" 3.17

CHAPTER XVIII

The Notes by Which the True Kirk Shall Be Determined from the False, and Who Shall Be Judge of Doctrine

Since Satan has labored from the beginning to adorn his pestilent synagogue with the title of the Kirk of God, and has incited cruel murderers to persecute, trouble, and molest the true Kirk and its members, as Cain did to Abel, Ishmael to Isaac, Esau to Jacob, and the whole priesthood of the Jews to Christ Jesus himself and his apostles after him. So it is essential that the true Kirk be distinguished from the filthy synagogues by clear and perfect notes lest we, being deceived, receive and embrace, to our own condemnation, the one for the other. The notes, signs, and assured tokens whereby the spotless bride of Christ is known from the horrible harlot, the false Kirk, we state, are neither antiquity, usurped title, lineal succession, appointed place, nor the numbers of men approving an error. For Cain was before Abel and Seth in age and title; Jerusalem had precedence above all other parts of the earth, for in it were priests lineally descended from Aaron, and greater numbers followed the scribes, pharisees, and priests, than unfeignedly believed and followed Christ Jesus and his 3.18

doctrine . . . and yet no man of judgment, we suppose, will hold that any of the forenamed were the Kirk of God. The notes of the true Kirk, therefore, we believe, confess, and avow to be: first, the true preaching of the Word of God, in which God has revealed himself to us, as the writings of the prophets and apostles declare; secondly, the right administration of the sacraments of Christ Jesus, with which must be associated the Word and promise of God to seal and confirm them in our hearts; and lastly, ecclesiastical discipline uprightly ministered, as God's Word prescribes, whereby vice is repressed and virtue nourished. Then wherever these notes are seen and continue for any time, be the number complete or not, there, beyond any doubt, is the true Kirk of Christ, who, according to his promise, is in its midst. This is not that universal Kirk of which we have spoken before, but particular Kirks, such as were in Corinth, Galatia, Ephesus, and other places where the ministry was planted by Paul and which he himself called Kirks of God. Such Kirks, we the inhabitants of the realm of Scotland confessing Christ Jesus, do claim to have in our cities, towns, and reformed districts because of the doctrine taught in our Kirks, contained in the written Word of God, that is, the Old and New Testaments, in those books which were originally reckoned canonical. We affirm that in these all things necessary to be believed for the salvation of man are sufficiently expressed. The interpretation of Scripture, we confess, does not belong to any private or public person, nor yet to any Kirk for pre-eminence or precedence, personal or local, which it has above others, but pertains to the Spirit of God by whom the Scriptures were written. When controversy arises about the right understanding of any passage or sentence of Scripture, or for the reformation of any abuse within the Kirk of God, we ought not so much to ask what men have said or done before us, as what the Holy Ghost uniformly speaks within the body of the Scriptures and what Christ Jesus himself did and commanded. For it is agreed by all that the Spirit of God, who is the Spirit of unity, cannot contradict himself. So if the interpretation or opinion of any theologian, Kirk, or council, is contrary to the plain Word of God written in any other passage of the Scripture, it is most certain that this is not the true understanding and meaning of the Holy Ghost, although councils, realms, and nations have approved and received it. We dare not receive or admit any interpretation which is contrary to any principal point of our faith, or to any other plain text of Scripture, or to the rule of love.

CHAPTER XIX

The Authority of the Scriptures

3.19   As we believe and confess the Scriptures of God sufficient to instruct and make perfect the man of God, so do we affirm and avow their authority to be from God, and not to depend on men or angels.

We affirm, therefore, that those who say the Scriptures have no other authority save that which they have received from the Kirk are blasphemous against God and injurious to the true Kirk, which always hears and obeys the voice of her own Spouse and Pastor, but takes not upon her to be mistress over the same.

CHAPTER XX

General Councils, Their Power, Authority, and the Cause of Their Summoning

As we do not rashly condemn what good men, assembled together in general councils lawfully gathered, have set before us; so we do not receive uncritically whatever has been declared to men under the name of the general councils, for it is plain that, being human, some of them have manifestly erred, and that in matters of great weight and importance. So far then as the council confirms its decrees by the plain Word of God, so far do we reverence and embrace them. But if men, under the name of a council, pretend to forge for us new articles of faith, or to make decisions contrary to the Word of God, then we must utterly deny them as the doctrine of devils, drawing our souls from the voice of the one God to follow the doctrines and teachings of men. The reason why the general councils met was not to make any permanent law which God had not made before, nor yet to form new articles for our belief, nor to give the Word of God authority; much less to make that to be his Word, or even the true interpretation of it, which was not expressed previously by his holy will in his Word; but the reason for councils, at least of those that deserve that name, was partly to refute heresies, and to give public confession of their faith to the generations following, which they did by the authority of God's written Word, and not by any opinion or prerogative that they could not err by reason of their numbers. This, we judge, was the primary reason for general councils. The second was that good policy and order should be constituted and observed in the Kirk where, as in the house of God, it becomes all things to be done decently and in order. Not that we think any policy or order of ceremonies can be appointed for all ages, times, and places; for as ceremonies which men have devised are but temporal, so they may, and ought to be, changed, when they foster superstition rather than edify the Kirk.

3.20

CHAPTER XXI

The Sacraments

As the fathers under the Law, besides the reality of the sacrifices, had two chief sacraments, that is, circumcision and the passover, and those who rejected these were not reckoned among God's people; so

3.21

43

do we acknowledge and confess that now in the time of the gospel we have two chief sacraments, which alone were instituted by the Lord Jesus and commanded to be used by all who will be counted members of his body, that is, Baptism and the Supper or Table of the Lord Jesus, also called the Communion of His Body and Blood. These sacraments, both of the Old Testament and of the New, were instituted by God not only to make a visible distinction between his people and those who were without the Covenant, but also to exercise the faith of his children and, by participation of these sacraments, to seal in their hearts the assurance of his promise, and of that most blessed conjunction, union, and society, which the chosen have with their Head, Christ Jesus. And so we utterly condemn the vanity of those who affirm the sacraments to be nothing else than naked and bare signs. No, we assuredly believe that by Baptism we are engrafted into Christ Jesus, to be made partakers of his righteousness, by which our sins are covered and remitted, and also that in the Supper rightly used, Christ Jesus is so joined with us that he becomes the very nourishment and food of our souls. Not that we imagine any transubstantiation of bread into Christ's body, and of wine into his natural blood, as the Romanists have perniciously taught and wrongly believed; but this union and conjunction which we have with the body and blood of Christ Jesus in the right use of the sacraments is wrought by means of the Holy Ghost, who by true faith carries us above all things that are visible, carnal, and earthly, and makes us feed upon the body and blood of Christ Jesus, once broken and shed for us but now in heaven, and appearing for us in the presence of his Father. Notwithstanding the distance between his glorified body in heaven and mortal men on earth, yet we must assuredly believe that the bread which we break is the communion of Christ's body and the cup which we bless the communion of his blood. Thus we confess and believe without doubt that the faithful, in the right use of the Lord's Table, do so eat the body and drink the blood of the Lord Jesus that he remains in them and they in him; they are so made flesh of his flesh and bone of his bone that as the eternal Godhood has given to the flesh of Christ Jesus, which by nature was corruptible and mortal, life and immortality, so the eating and drinking of the flesh and blood of Christ Jesus does the like for us. We grant that this is neither given to us merely at the time nor by the power and virtue of the sacrament alone, but we affirm that the faithful, in the right use of the Lord's Table, have such union with Christ Jesus as the natural man cannot apprehend. Further we affirm that although the faithful, hindered by negligence and human weakness, do not profit as much as they ought in the actual moment of the Supper, yet afterwards it shall bring forth fruit, being living seed sown in good ground; for the Holy Spirit, who can never be separated from the right institution of the Lord Jesus, will not deprive the faithful of the fruit of that mystical action. Yet all this, we say again, comes of that true faith which apprehends Christ Jesus, who alone makes the sacrament effective in us. Therefore, if anyone slanders us by saying that we affirm or believe the sacraments to be symbols and nothing more, they are libelous and speak against the plain facts. On the other hand we readily admit that we make a distinction between Christ Jesus in his eternal substance and the elements of the sacramental signs. So we neither worship the elements, in place of that which they signify, nor yet do we despise them or undervalue them, but we use them with great reverence, examining ourselves diligently before we participate, since we are assured by the mouth of the apostle that "whosoever shall eat this bread, and drink this cup of the Lord, unworthily, shall be guilty of the body and blood of the Lord."

CHAPTER XXII

The Right Administration of the Sacraments

Two things are necessary for the right administration of the sacra-   **3.22** ments. The first is that they should be ministered by lawful ministers, and we declare that these are men appointed to preach the Word, unto whom God has given the power to preach the gospel, and who are lawfully called by some Kirk. The second is that they should be ministered in the elements and manner which God has appointed. Otherwise they cease to be the sacraments of Christ Jesus. This is why we abandon the teaching of the Roman Church and withdraw from its sacraments; firstly, because their ministers are not true ministers of Christ Jesus (indeed they even allow women, whom the Holy Ghost will not permit to preach in the congregation to baptize) and, secondly, because they have so adulterated both the sacraments with their own additions that no part of Christ's original act remains in its original simplicity. The addition of oil, salt, spittle, and such like in baptism, are merely human additions. To adore or venerate the sacrament, to carry it through streets and towns in procession, or to reserve it in a special case, is not the proper use of Christ's sacrament but an abuse of it. Christ Jesus said, "Take ye, eat ye," and "Do this in remembrance of Me." By these words and commands he sanctified bread and wine to be the sacrament of his holy body and blood, so that the one should be eaten and that all should drink of the other, and not that they should be reserved for worship or honored as God, as the Romanists do. Further, in withdrawing one part of the sacrament—the blessed cup—from the people, they have committed sacrilege. Moreover, if the sacraments are to be rightly used it is essential that the end and purpose of their institution should be understood, not only by the minister but by the recipients. For if the recipient does not understand what is being done, the sacrament is not being rightly used, as is seen in the case of the Old Testament sacrifices. Similarly, if the teacher teaches false doctrine which is hateful to God, even though the sacraments are his own ordinance, they are not rightly used, since wicked men have used them for another end than what God commanded. We affirm that this has been done to the sacraments in the Roman

Church, for there the whole action of the Lord Jesus is adulterated in form, purpose, and meaning. What Christ Jesus did, and commanded to be done, is evident from the Gospels and from St. Paul; what the priest does at the altar we do not need to tell. The end and purpose of Christ's institution, for which it should be used, is set forth in the words, "Do this in remembrance of Me," and "For as often as ye eat this bread and drink this cup ye do show"—that is, extol, preach, magnify, and praise—"the Lord's death, till He come." But let the words of the mass, and their own doctors and teachings witness, what is the purpose and meaning of the mass; it is that, as mediators between Christ and his Kirk, they should offer to God the Father, a sacrifice in propitiation for the sins of the living and of the dead. This doctrine is blasphemous to Christ Jesus and would deprive his unique sacrifice, once offered on the cross for the cleansing of all who are to be sanctified, of its sufficiency; so we detest and renounce it.

CHAPTER XXIII

To Whom Sacraments Appertain

3.23   We hold that baptism applies as much to the children of the faithful as to those who are of age and discretion, and so we condemn the error of the Anabaptists, who deny that children should be baptized before they have faith and understanding. But we hold that the Supper of the Lord is only for those who are of the household of faith and can try and examine themselves both in their faith and their duty to their neighbors. Those who eat and drink at that holy table without faith, or without peace and goodwill to their brethren, eat unworthily. This is the reason why ministers in our Kirk make public and individual examination of those who are to be admitted to the table of the Lord Jesus.

CHAPTER XXIV

The Civil Magistrate

3.24   We confess and acknowledge that empires, kingdoms, dominions, and cities are appointed and ordained by God; the powers and authorities in them, emperors in empires, kings in their realms, dukes and princes in their dominions, and magistrates in cities, are ordained by God's holy ordinance for the manifestation of his own glory and for the good and well being of all men. We hold that any men who conspire to rebel or to overturn the civil powers, as duly established, are not merely enemies to humanity but rebels against God's will. Further, we confess and acknowledge that such persons as are set in authority are to be loved, honored, feared, and held in the highest respect, because they are the lieutenants of God, and in their councils God himself doth sit and judge. They are the judges and princes to whom God has given the sword for the praise and defense of good men and the punishment of all open evil doers. Moreover, we state that the preservation and purification of religion is particularly the duty of kings, princes, rulers, and magistrates. They are not only appointed for civil government but also to maintain true religion and to suppress all idolatry and superstition. This may be seen in David, Jehosaphat, Hezekiah, Josiah, and others highly commended for their zeal in that cause.

Therefore we confess and avow that those who resist the supreme powers, so long as they are acting in their own spheres, are resisting God's ordinance and cannot be held guiltless. We further state that so long as princes and rulers vigilantly fulfill their office, anyone who denies them aid, counsel, or service, denies it to God, who by his lieutenant craves it of them.

CHAPTER XXV

The Gifts Freely Given to the Kirk

Although the Word of God truly preached, the sacraments rightly ministered, and discipline executed according to the Word of God, are certain and infallible signs of the true Kirk, we do not mean that every individual person in that company is a chosen member of Christ Jesus. We acknowledge and confess that many weeds and tares are sown among the corn and grow in great abundance in its midst, and that the reprobate may be found in the fellowship of the chosen and may take an outward part with them in the benefits of the Word and sacraments. But since they only confess God for a time with their mouths and not with their hearts, they lapse, and do not continue to the end. Therefore they do not share the fruits of Christ's death, resurrection, and ascension. But such as unfeignedly believe with the heart and boldly confess the Lord Jesus with their mouths shall certainly receive his gifts. Firstly, in this life, they shall receive remission of sins and that by faith in Christ's blood alone; for though sin shall remain and continually abide in our mortal bodies, yet it shall not be counted against us, but be pardoned, and covered with Christ's righteousness. Secondly, in the general judgment, there shall be given to every man and woman resurrection of the flesh. The seas shall give up her dead, and the earth those who are buried within her. Yea, the Eternal, our God, shall stretch out his hand on the dust, and the dead shall arise incorruptible, and in the very substance of the selfsame flesh which every man now bears, to receive according to their works, glory or punishment. Such as now delight in vanity, cruelty, filthiness, superstition, or idolatry, shall be condemned to the fire unquenchable, in which those who now serve the devil in all abominations shall be tormented forever, both in body and in spirit. But such as continue in well doing to the end, boldly confessing the Lord Jesus, shall receive glory, honor, and immortality, we constantly believe, to reign forever in life everlasting with Christ Jesus, to whose glorified body all his chosen shall be made like, when he shall appear again in judgment and shall render up the Kingdom to God his Father, who then shall be and ever shall remain, all in all things, God blessed forever. To whom, with the Son and the Holy Ghost, be all honor and glory, now and ever. Amen.

Arise, O Lord, and let thine enemies be confounded; let them flee from thy presence that hate thy godly Name. Give thy servants strength to speak thy Word with boldness, and let all nations cleave to the true knowledge of thee. Amen.

THE HEIDELBERG CATECHISM

Introduction to the Heidelberg Catechism

The Heidelberg Catechism is both ecumenical and deeply personal. It became the doctrinal standard for Reformed churches in Holland, Germany, and Hungary. Dutch explorers brought it with them to Manhattan Island in 1609, thus making it the first Reformed confession in the North American colonies. Its continuing influence can be seen in the opening line of A Brief Statement of Faith, adopted by the Presbyterian Church (U.S.A.) in 1991 after the reunion of 1983: "In life and in death we belong to God." This affirmation echoes the first question and answer of the Heidelberg Catechism:

Q. 1. What is your only comfort, in life and in death?

A. That I belong—body and soul, in life and in death—not to myself but to my faithful Savior, Jesus Christ.

Note the use of the first person—"I belong." The Heidelberg Catechism is the confession of personal piety and individual faith. However, it was published as part of a new liturgy, so its doctrinal instruction is intimately linked to the corporate worship of God. Furthermore, because it focused on enduring questions of human existence rather than complicated theological arguments, it became a confessional standard for Reformed churches in many lands.

HISTORICAL BACKGROUND

The Heidelberg Catechism was composed in the midst of controversy. In the Palatinate, where Heidelberg was located, theologians vehemently debated the doctrine of the Lord's Supper and specifically how Christ was present in the sacrament. The Palatinate was basically Lutheran, and following Luther some argued that Christ's body and blood are really present "in, with, and under" the substance of the bread and the wine. Those who sided with Ulrich Zwingli insisted that Christ's body was resurrected and that the Lord's Supper celebrated the memory of Christ's presence. Calvinist interpreters maintained that in the Supper we have a real and spiritually nourishing communion with Christ by the power of the Holy Spirit.

Such debates may seem arcane more than four hundred years later, but they shaped the politics and Protestantism of the sixteenth century. Otto Henry, the Protestant Elector of the Palatinate, died in 1559. The Palatinate was a German province, and Heidelberg was the capital. Since Otto Henry did not have any children, the crown passed to his nephew, Frederick III.

Although Frederick was raised as a Catholic, he willingly converted to Protestantism when he married Princess Maira of Brandenburg-Kulmback in 1537. She was an ardent Lutheran, and through her influence of Frederick the elector absorbed a great deal of Protestant and especially Lutheran doctrine. He promised her that he would read the Bible daily and study theology. By the time he ascended the throne in 1559, he had developed a reputation for his piety and learning.

Both were required to deal with the conflict over the interpretation of the Lord's Supper in the Palatinate and especially in Heidelberg itself. Frederick III consulted with Luther's friend and successor, Philip Melanchthon, who advised him: "In all things seek peace and moderation. This is done best by holding carefully to a fixed doctrinal position as regards the Lord's Supper and all other matters of faith."

Good advice; but it begged the question of which "fixed doctrinal position" should be used. According to tradition, in 1562, Frederick III turned to two young Reformed theologians for advice—Kaspar Olevianus and Zacharias Ursinus. Scholars debate the influence of Olevianus in shaping the Heidelberg Catechism, but most agree that Ursinus was the principal author and genius behind the document. Frederick's choice of Reformed theologians to resolve theological disputes within the Lutheran churches of the Palatinate was curious and courageous. Frederick's Lutheran wife had suspected, with justification, that he was becoming more Reformed in his own convictions. There is evidence that Frederick himself sought to move beyond the theological disputes by appealing to Scripture, and he undoubtedly hoped that a perspective based on Scripture would provide a mediating position that would create consensus in his realm.

Frederick III commissioned the catechism to order the life of the church and to educate people "according to the pure and consistent doctrine of the holy gospel." Ursinus had earlier composed a long document of 323 questions and answers, *Summa Theologiae*. He then condensed that document into a shorter version of 108 questions. *Catechesis Minor*, which became the basis for the Heidelberg Catechism. According to Frederick's preface to the Catechism, the draft was given to "our entire theological faculty in this place, and all the superintendents, and distinguished servants of the church." Frederick III supervised the proceedings closely, even ordering that one question be rewritten because it had too much Zwinglian language.

A synod adopted the Heidelberg Catechism in January 1563, yet the text was revised in three editions that year. Frederick III insisted on adding question 80 to condemn the Latin Mass in answer to the Council of Trent in 1562; this sharply polemical statement is the exception to the otherwise peaceful and conciliatory tone of the catechism. The fourth and final edition included a book of church order and liturgy for the Palatinate churches, thus becoming a statement of church doctrine, discipline, and worship.

What was intended as a document to bring peace to the church produced further conflict and debate. Frederick III was accused of having deposed the authority of the Augsburg Confession, and the Holy Roman

Emperor Maximilian summoned him to appear before the German Diet in 1566. As he entered the hall, he was accompanied by his son, who carried symbolically copies of the Augsburg Confession and the Bible. He testified as follows: "What men understand by Calvinism, I do not know. I can say with a pure conscience that I have never read Calvin's writings. As to the. . . . Augsburg Confession. . . . that I signed with the other princes . . . in that faith I continue firmly, on no other ground than that I find it established in the Holy Scriptures."

Frederick III insisted that the authority for the Heidelberg Catechism was the Bible. "My own catechism," he declared, "is drawn word for word from divine, not human sources, as the references in the margins will prove." Then he issued a challenge: "If any person, regardless of age, station, or class, even the humblest, can teach me something better from the Holy Scriptures, I will give him hearty thanks and be readily obedient to divine truth. . . . Here are the Scriptures. . . . Would it please your Imperial Majesty to do this I would take it as a great favor."

It was a dramatic moment; no one answered his challenge. One of Frederick's friends told him, "Fritz, you are more pious than the lot of us." The debate was left unresolved, but Frederick was acquitted of all charges. He continued to hold the Augsburg Confession as the authority for doctrine, second only to Scripture, and even included an affirmation of Augsburg in his will. His defense of the Heidelberg Catechism on the basis of Scripture made it an increasingly popular document for the Reformed churches, and he became known to subsequent generations by the nickname the emperor had given him—"Frederick the Pious."

THE STRUCTURE OF THE HEIDELBERG CATECHISM

Structure often shapes content. Like most catechisms, the Heidelberg Catechism covers the Ten Commandments, the Apostles' Creed, and the Lord's Prayer. It also discusses the two Protestant sacraments: Baptism and the Lord's Supper. But the Heidelberg Catechism is distinctive, if not unique, in placing all these discussions within a three-part structure based on what one theologian calls "a spiritual autobiography." Part I treats the misery of humanity; Part II, human redemption; and Part III, thankfulness. In other words, the three themes have often been described as guilt, grace, and gratitude. They encompass the journey of the Christian: first, the awareness of our sinful condition and our inability to save ourselves; then the conviction that we are saved by the love of God in Jesus Christ; and then our grateful response to God in lives of obedience and service.

Many interpreters have noted that this three-part structure is also the pattern of Paul's letter to the Romans, and the threefold character of the confession is matched by a similar structure in the Palatinate Church Liturgy. In addition, the 129 questions are arranged in 52 groups—one for each Sunday. Clearly this is a catechism designed not only for individual study but also for corporate worship and preaching. Indeed, in the Dutch Reformed churches in the United States, it has been a long-standing tradition that on Sunday morning, the sermon is based on Scripture; on Sunday evening, the sermon focuses on the sections of the Heidelberg Catechism for that Sunday. Even today, the Reformed Church in America requires that the points of doctrine in the Heidelberg Catechism shall be preached within a span of four years, and in the Christian Reformed Church the doctrines shall be covered in sermons every year.

THEMES OF THE HEIDELBERG CATECHISM

Many commentators have identified themes that run through the entire catechism and unite its three parts and 129 questions and answers.

Its Biblical Foundation

Frederick III wanted a catechism rooted in Scripture, and the Heidelberg Catechism breathes the language of the Bible, especially Romans. Although the text in the *Book of Confessions* does not include scriptural citations, the original text and many subsequent translations include numerous biblical texts as the basis for each answer. This is more than simply proof-texting; the answers are attempts to capture the character of what the Bible actually says about many aspects of the Christian life. The answers are designed to make the words of Scripture come alive and to encourage the believer and the community of faith to study and rely on Scripture for instruction and guidance in living faithful lives.

Its Ecumenical Character

As noted earlier, the Heidelberg Catechism was an attempt to create peace at a time of dissension and debate. It did not succeed, but of all the Protestant creeds and confessions, it is the most widely recognized as a basis for common affirmation of faith. It almost completely avoids the issue of predestination and election, which has been the source of countless theological debates since the sixteenth century. Aside from the condemnation of the Latin Mass and the usual Protestant assertion of only two sacraments in contrast to seven sacraments in the Roman Catholic and Orthodox traditions, there is a great deal in the Heidelberg Catechism that all Christians can affirm. In spirit and in substance, the Heidelberg Catechism defines what Christians are for, rather than what they are against.

Its Focus on Jesus Christ

The Heidelberg Catechism is about salvation in Jesus Christ. Beginning with human sin, it poses the crucial question: How can humanity be saved from itself? That question is all the more poignant in this century marked by incredible violence and cruelty. The catechism does not dwell on the problem. In fact, the first section on humanity's misery is the shortest one in the entire catechism. Instead, the vast bulk of the catechism is an attempt to describe God's saving work in Jesus Christ and our response to Christ's redemption in lives of gratitude. The key to the catechism is Jesus Christ. Everything hinges on Christ and God's love that seeks us while we are sinners and offers us new and abundant life.

Its Personal Nature

Virtually every question and answer follow the same format. The question is addressed to "you." The answer is a response by the individual ("I") or a community ("we"). This format is remarkable, given the circumstances in which the Heidelberg Catechism was written. The great issue of the day was "the presence" of Christ in the Lord's Supper, which involved very complex philosophical and theological concepts. The Heidelberg Catechism seems to put all that aside. Instead, it addresses the enduring questions of human existence: Am I worth anything? Does God love me? How can I find peace and wholeness? How shall I live in this world? The Heidelberg Catechism speaks to each person about what it means to be a Christian and how to live as Christians. It is a pastoral document, consoling and inspiring, even as it teaches the faith. Even though it was written centuries later, the hymn "Blessed Assurance" captures some of the spirit of Heidelberg:

> "Blessed assurance, Jesus is mine!
> O what a foretaste of glory divine!"

Its Practical Character

Frederick III wanted a catechism that could be used with all the people, young and old, in all stations of life. The entire Heidelberg Catechism keeps its audience in view. Throughout the catechism the question is asked, How does this profit you? Or, how does this comfort you? There is a constant concern for the personal and practical significance of Christian doctrine.

Note that the Ten Commandments are treated in Part III. The law does not merely convict us of our sins; it provides a way for us to order our lives and the life of the world because we give thanks to God for salvation in Jesus Christ. Christians obey the commandments not merely because they were given by God but because we are grateful for the gift of forgiveness and life in Jesus Christ. This puts what is often called stewardship in the context of God's redemption, rather than God's creation of the world. It also accents the importance of sanctification in the Christian life (see the phrase "more and more," which appears at several key points. The catechism also puts a positive emphasis on the nature of law itself—a characteristic of the Reformed tradition that has encouraged people to be involved in the reform of society. Politics and economics are not the arenas of what are inherently sinful but what are potentially gracious.

Its Devotional Value

The Heidelberg Catechism reflects the spirit of its sponsor—Frederick the Pious. Its tone is reverential; its language evokes a sense of awe about the mystery of God's love. One commentator observed that much of the catechism "seems to have been written from bended knees." James Moffatt, the New Testament scholar, maintained that the Heidelberg Catechism is the pinnacle of devotional literature of the Reformation and that by slightly revising the language, each of the questions can be turned into a prayer. The catechism that begins with humanity's misery concludes with a section on prayer—the opening of ourselves to God and God's love.

THE HEIDELBERG CATECHISM FOR TODAY

No confession is perfect. Each is a reflection of its time and place, and Heidelberg is no exception. Some contemporary readers will be put off by the heavily masculine language in the text of the *Book of Confessions*. Presbyterians today will be shocked by the prohibition against pictures and images in churches contained in Question 98. Still others will be offended by the condemnation of "homosexual perversion" in Question 87. But there are also hidden gems. Theological educators may be surprised to discover that the Heidelberg Catechism explains the meaning of the commandment to remember the Sabbath as the basis for maintaining "the ministry of the gospel and Christian education." Few today would imagine a connection between Sabbath observance and theological seminaries and Christian education!

Most important, the Heidelberg Catechism reminds us that our only comfort is that we belong, in life and in death, to our faithful Savior, Jesus Christ. The message is as old as Paul's affirmation in Romans 8:38–39 (NRSV): "For I am convinced that neither death, nor life, nor angels, nor rulers, nor things present, nor things to come, nor powers, nor height, nor depth, nor anything else in all creation, will be able to separate us from the love of God in Christ Jesus our Lord."

Across the centuries, that message still needs to be heard. We are not alone. We belong to God in Jesus Christ.

QUESTIONS FOR STUDY

1. What does it mean to "belong" to God?
2. What are the signs of humanity's "misery" today?

3. How has the love of God in Jesus Christ changed your life?

4. What does it mean to live gratefully?

ADDENDUM

The following is Frederick III's preface to the Heidelberg Catechism. It is not part of the current Heidelberg Catechism of the Presbyterian Church (U.S.A.).

Frederick, by the grace of God, First Lord High Steward and Elector of the Holy Roman Empire, Duke in Bavaria, Elector Palatine on the Rhine, etc. Grace and greeting to each and every superintendent, pastor, and schoolmaster throughout our Electorate.

We acknowledge that we are bound by the admonition of the Divine Word, as well as by natural duty and relation. We therefore have finally determined to order and administer our office, calling, and government not only to promote peace, quiet, and virtuous living among our subjects, but also (and above all) to admonish and lead them to devout knowledge and fear of the Almighty and his holy word of salvation, as the only foundation of all virtue and obedience. Indeed, we shall make every effort with all sincerity to promote, defend, and maintain their eternal and temporal welfare.

At the outset of our administration, we were informed of how our dear cousins and predecessors, Counts Palatine, Electors, etc., of noble and blessed memory instituted and proposed diverse Christian and helpful preparations and arrangements in order to further the glory of God and to uphold civil propriety and order. However, this was not always earnestly pursued, and the desired fruit failed to materialize. Now, we are determined not only to renew these measures but also to improve, reform, and extend them as present times demand. We have discovered that an important defect in our system is exposed by the fact that young people in both our schools and our churches tend to be lax in their Christian doctrine. Without any established catechism, some receive no instruction, while others are inconsistently taught according to individual plans and judgments. Consequently, too many have grown up without fear of God and knowledge of God's word, or else they have been perplexed with irrelevant and needless questions. Occasionally, they have been burdened with unsound doctrines.

And now, since both Christian and worldly offices, authority, and households cannot otherwise be maintained—and in order that discipline and obedience to authority as well as other virtues may increase—it is essential that our young people be trained early in life (and above all) in the pure and consistent doctrine of the holy Gospel, and that they be well trained in the proper knowledge of God.

Therefore, we have recognized it as a high obligation and most important duty of our government to eliminate the defect in our system and to introduce the needed improvements. With the advice and cooperation of our entire theological faculty in this place, and of all superintendents and distinguished servants of the church, we have secured the composition of a summary course of instruction or catechism of our Christian religion according to the word of God, in both German and Latin. We have done this not only so that young people may be piously and consistently instructed in this Christian doctrine, but also so that pastors and schoolmasters themselves may have a clear and fixed form and standard to follow, rather than introduce daily changes or unsound doctrine on their own.

We affectionately admonish and enjoin every one of you thankfully to accept this catechism or course of instruction for the honor of God as well as for the good of our subjects and your own souls. We ask you to teach, act, and live according to it. We also ask you to present it and explain its true meaning to young people in our schools and churches, as well as to the general population from the pulpit. We have made this provision in the sure hope that, if our youth are earnestly instructed and educated in the word of God, it will please the Almighty to grant the amendment of our lives as well as our temporal and eternal welfare.

Given at Heidelberg, Tuesday, the nineteenth of January, in the year 1563 after the birth of Christ, our dear Lord and Savior.

THE HEIDELBERG CATECHISM[1]

Q. 1. What is your only comfort, in life and in death?   4.001
A. That I belong—body and soul, in life and in death—not to myself but to my faithful Savior, Jesus Christ, who at the cost of his own blood has fully paid for all my sins and has completely freed me from the dominion of the devil; that he protects me so well that without the will of my Father in heaven not a hair can fall from my head; indeed, that everything must fit his purpose for my salvation. Therefore, by his Holy Spirit, he also assures me of eternal life, and makes me wholeheartedly willing and ready from now on to live for him.

Q. 2. How many things must you know that you may live and die in the blessedness of this comfort?   4.002
A. Three. First, the greatness of my sin and wretchedness. Second, how I am freed from all my sins and their wretched consequences. Third, what gratitude I owe to God for such redemption.

PART I

Of Man's Misery

Q. 3. Where do you learn of your sin and its wretched consequences?   4.003
A. From the Law of God.

Q. 4. What does the Law of God require of us?   4.004
A. Jesus Christ teaches this in a summary in Matthew 22:37-40: "You shall love the Lord your God with all your heart, and with all your soul, and with all your mind. This is the great and first commandment. And a second is like it, you shall love your neighbor as yourself. On these two commandments depend all the law and the prophets." (Cf. Luke 10:27.)

Q. 5. Can you keep all this perfectly?   4.005
A. No, for by nature I am prone to hate God and my neighbor.

---

[1]Reprinted from *The Heidelberg Catechism, 1563-1963. 400th Anniversary Edition.* Copyright 1962. United Church Press. Used by permission.

4.006   **Q. 6. Did God create man evil and perverse like this?**
A. No. On the contrary, God created man good and in his image, that is, in true righteousness and holiness, so that he might rightly know God his Creator, love him with his whole heart, and live with him in eternal blessedness, praising and glorifying him.

4.007   **Q. 7. Where, then, does this corruption of human nature come from?**
A. From the fall and disobedience of our first parents, Adam and Eve, in the Garden of Eden; whereby our human life is so poisoned that we are all conceived and born in the state of sin.

4.008   **Q. 8. But are we so perverted that we are altogether unable to do good and prone to do evil?**
A. Yes, unless we are born again through the Spirit of God.

4.009   **Q. 9. Is not God unjust in requiring of man in his Law what he cannot do?**
A. No, for God so created man that he could do it. But man, upon the instigation of the devil, by deliberate disobedience, has cheated himself and all his descendants out of these gifts.

4.010   **Q. 10. Will God let man get by with such disobedience and defection?**
A. Certainly not, for the wrath of God is revealed from heaven, both against our inborn sinfulness and our actual sins, and he will punish them according to his righteous judgment in time and in eternity, as he has declared: "Cursed be everyone who does not abide by all things written in the book of the Law, and do them."

4.011   **Q. 11. But is not God also merciful?**
A. God is indeed merciful and gracious, but he is also righteous. It is his righteousness which requires that sin committed against the supreme majesty of God be punished with extreme, that is, with eternal punishment of body and soul.

PART II

Of Man's Redemption

4.012   **Q. 12. Since, then, by the righteous judgment of God we have deserved temporal and eternal punishment, how may we escape this punishment, come again to grace, and be reconciled to God?**

A. God wills that his righteousness be satisfied; therefore, payment in full must be made to his righteousness, either by ourselves or by another.

Q. 13. Can we make this payment ourselves? 4.013
A. By no means. On the contrary, we increase our debt each day.

Q. 14. Can any mere creature make the payment for us? 4.014
A. No one. First of all, God does not want to punish any other creature for man's debt. Moreover, no mere creature can bear the burden of God's eternal wrath against sin and redeem others from it.

Q. 15. Then what kind of mediator and redeemer must we seek? 4.015
A. One who is a true and righteous man and yet more powerful than all creatures, that is, one who is at the same time true God.

LORD'S DAY 6

Q. 16. Why must he be a true and righteous man? 4.016
A. Because God's righteousness requires that man who has sinned should make reparation for sin, but the man who is himself a sinner cannot pay for others.

Q. 17. Why must he at the same time be true God? 4.017
A. So that by the power of his divinity he might bear as a man the burden of God's wrath, and recover for us and restore to us righteousness and life.

Q. 18. Who is this mediator who is at the same time true God and a true and perfectly righteous man? 4.018
A. Our Lord Jesus Christ, who is freely given to us for complete redemption and righteousness.

Q. 19. Whence do you know this? 4.019
A. From the holy gospel, which God himself revealed in the beginning in the Garden of Eden, afterward proclaimed through the holy patriarchs and prophets and foreshadowed through the sacrifices and other rites of the Old Covenant, and finally fulfilled through his own well-beloved Son.

LORD'S DAY 7

Q. 20. Will all men, then, be saved through Christ as they became lost through Adam? 4.020
A. No. Only those who, by true faith, are incorporated into him and accept all his benefits.

Q. 21. What is true faith? 4.021
A. It is not only a certain knowledge by which I accept as true all

that God has revealed to us in his Word, but also a wholehearted trust which the Holy Spirit creates in me through the gospel, that, not only to others, but to me also God has given the forgiveness of sins, everlasting righteousness and salvation, out of sheer grace solely for the sake of Christ's saving work.

4.022   **Q. 22. What, then, must a Christian believe?**
A. All that is promised us in the gospel, a summary of which is taught us in the articles of the Apostles' Creed, our universally acknowledged confession of faith.

4.023   **Q. 23. What are these articles?**
A. I believe in God the Father Almighty, Maker of Heaven and earth; And in Jesus Christ, his only-begotten Son, our Lord; who was conceived by the Holy Spirit, born of the Virgin Mary; suffered under Pontius Pilate, was crucified, dead, and buried; he descended into hell; the third day he rose again from the dead; he ascended into heaven, and sits at the right hand of God the Father Almighty; from thence he shall come to judge the living and the dead.
I believe in the Holy Spirit; the holy catholic Church; the communion of saints; the forgiveness of sins; the resurrection of the body; and the life everlasting.

LORD'S DAY 8

4.024   **Q. 24. How are these articles divided?**
A. Into three parts: The first concerns God *the Father* and our *creation;* the second, God *the Son* and our *redemption;* and the third, God *the Holy Spirit* and our *sanctification.*

4.025   **Q. 25. Since there is only one Divine Being, why do you speak of three, Father, Son, and Holy Spirit?**
A. Because God has thus revealed himself in his Word, that these three distinct persons are the one, true, eternal God.

Of God the Father

LORD'S DAY 9

4.026   **Q. 26. What do you believe when you say: "I believe in God the Father Almighty, Maker of heaven and earth"?**
A. That the eternal Father of our Lord Jesus Christ, who out of nothing created heaven and earth with all that is in them, who also upholds and governs them by his eternal counsel and providence, is for the sake of Christ his Son my God and my Father. I trust in him so completely that I have no doubt that he will provide me with all things necessary for body and soul. Moreover, whatever evil he sends upon me in this troubled life he will turn to my good, for he is able to do it, being almighty God, and is determined to do it, being a faithful Father.

Q. 27. What do you understand by the providence of God?   4.027
A. The almighty and ever-present power of God whereby he still
upholds, as it were by his own hand, heaven and earth together with
all creatures, and rules in such a way that leaves and grass, rain and
drought, fruitful and unfruitful years, food and drink, health and
sickness, riches and poverty, and everything else, come to us not by
chance but by his fatherly hand.

Q. 28. What advantage comes from acknowledging God's crea-   4.028
tion and providence?
A. We learn that we are to be patient in adversity, grateful in the
midst of blessing, and to trust our faithful God and Father for the
future, assured that no creature shall separate us from his love, since
all creatures are so completely in his hand that without his will they
cannot even move.

Of God the Son

Q. 29. Why is the Son of God called JESUS, which means   4.029
SAVIOR?
A. Because he saves us from our sins, and because salvation is to
be sought or found in no other.

Q. 30. Do those who seek their salvation and well-being from   4.030
saints, by their own efforts, or by other means really believe in the
only Savior Jesus?
A. No. Rather, by such actions they deny Jesus, the only Savior and
Redeemer, even though they boast of belonging to him. It therefore
follows that either Jesus is not a perfect Savior, or those who receive
this Savior with true faith must possess in him all that is necessary for
their salvation.

Q. 31. Why is he called CHRIST, that is, the ANOINTED ONE?   4.031
A. Because he is ordained by God the Father and anointed with the
Holy Spirit to be *our chief Prophet* and *Teacher*, fully revealing to us
the secret purpose and will of God concerning our redemption; to be
our only High Priest, having redeemed us by the one sacrifice of his
body and ever interceding for us with the Father; and to be *our eternal
King*, governing us by his Word and Spirit, and defending and sustain-
ing us in the redemption he has won for us.

Q. 32. But why are you called a Christian?   4.032

A. Because through faith I share in Christ and thus in his anointing, so that I may confess his name, offer myself a living sacrifice of gratitude to him, and fight against sin and the devil with a free and good conscience throughout this life and hereafter rule with him in eternity over all creatures.

LORD'S DAY 13

4.033   Q. 33. Why is he called GOD'S ONLY-BEGOTTEN SON, since we also are God's children?
A. Because Christ alone is God's own eternal Son, whereas we are accepted for his sake as children of God by grace.

4.034   Q. 34. Why do you call him OUR LORD?
A. Because, not with gold or silver but at the cost of his blood, he has redeemed us body and soul from sin and all the dominion of the devil, and has bought us for his very own.

LORD'S DAY 14

4.035   Q. 35. What is the meaning of: "Conceived by the Holy Spirit, born of the Virgin Mary"?
A. That the eternal Son of God, who is and remains true and eternal God, took upon himself our true manhood from the flesh and blood of the Virgin Mary through the action of the Holy Spirit, so that he might also be the true seed of David, like his fellow men in all things, except for sin.

4.036   Q. 36. What benefit do you receive from the holy conception and birth of Christ?
A. That he is our Mediator, and that, in God's sight, he covers over with his innocence and perfect holiness the sinfulness in which I have been conceived.

LORD'S DAY 15

4.037   Q. 37. What do you understand by the word "suffered"?
A. That throughout his life on earth, but especially at the end of it, he bore in body and soul the wrath of God against the sin of the whole human race, so that by his suffering, as the only expiatory sacrifice, he might redeem our body and soul from everlasting damnation, and might obtain for us God's grace, righteousness, and eternal life.

4.038   Q. 38. Why did he suffer "under Pontius Pilate" as his judge?
A. That he, being innocent, might be condemned by an earthly judge, and thereby set us free from the judgment of God which, in all its severity, ought to fall upon us.

4.039   Q. 39. Is there something more in his having been crucified than if he had died some other death?

A. Yes, for by this I am assured that he took upon himself the curse which lay upon me, because the death of the cross was cursed by God.

LORD'S DAY 16

Q. 40. Why did Christ have to suffer "death"?   4.040
A. Because the righteousness and truth of God are such that nothing else could make reparation for our sins except the death of the Son of God.

Q. 41. Why was he "buried"?   4.041
A. To confirm the fact that he was really dead.

Q. 42. Since, then, Christ died for us, why must we also die?   4.042
A. Our death is not a reparation for our sins, but only a dying to sin and an entering into eternal life.

Q. 43. What further benefit do we receive from the sacrifice and death of Christ on the cross?   4.043
A. That by his power our old self is crucified, put to death, and buried with him, so that the evil passions of our mortal bodies may reign in us no more, but that we may offer ourselves to him as a sacrifice of thanksgiving.

Q. 44. Why is there added: "He descended into hell"?   4.044
A. That in my severest tribulations I may be assured that Christ my Lord has redeemed me from hellish anxieties and torment by the unspeakable anguish, pains, and terrors which he suffered in his soul both on the cross and before.

LORD'S DAY 17

Q. 45. What benefit do we receive from "the resurrection" of Christ?   4.045
A. First, by his resurrection he has overcome death that he might make us share in the righteousness which he has obtained for us through his death. Second, we too are now raised by his power to a new life. Third, the resurrection of Christ is a sure pledge to us of our blessed resurrection.

LORD'S DAY 18

Q. 46. How do you understand the words: "He ascended into heaven"?   4.046
A. That Christ was taken up from the earth into heaven before the eyes of his disciples and remains there on our behalf until he comes again to judge the living and the dead.

Q. 47. Then, is not Christ with us unto the end of the world, as he has promised us?   4.047

A. Christ is true man and true God. As a man he is no longer on earth, but in his divinity, majesty, grace, and Spirit, he is never absent from us.

4.048   **Q. 48. But are not the two natures in Christ separated from each other in this way, if the humanity is not wherever the divinity is?**

A. Not at all; for since divinity is incomprehensible and everywhere present, it must follow that the divinity is indeed beyond the bounds of the humanity which it has assumed, and is nonetheless ever in that humanity as well, and remains personally united to it.

4.049   **Q. 49. What benefit do we receive from Christ's ascension into heaven?**

A. First, that he is our Advocate in the presence of his Father in heaven. Second, that we have our flesh in heaven as a sure pledge that he, as the Head, will also take us, his members, up to himself. Third, that he sends us his Spirit as a counterpledge by whose power we seek what is above, where Christ is, sitting at the right hand of God, and not things that are on earth.

LORD'S DAY 19

4.050   **Q. 50. Why is there added: "And sits at the right hand of God"?**

A. Because Christ ascended into heaven so that he might manifest himself there as the Head of his Church, through whom the Father governs all things.

4.051   **Q. 51. What benefit do we receive from this glory of Christ, our Head?**

A. First, that through his Holy Spirit he pours out heavenly gifts upon us, his members. Second, that by his power he defends and supports us against all our enemies.

4.052   **Q. 52. What comfort does the return of Christ "to judge the living and the dead" give you?**

A. That in all affliction and persecution I may await with head held high the very Judge from heaven who has already submitted himself to the judgment of God for me and has removed all the curse from me; that he will cast all his enemies and mine into everlasting condemnation, but he shall take me, together with all his elect, to himself into heavenly joy and glory.

The Holy Spirit

LORD'S DAY 20

4.053   **Q. 53. What do you believe concerning "the Holy Spirit"?**

A. First, that, with the Father and the Son, he is equally eternal God; second, that God's Spirit is also given to me, preparing me through a true faith to share in Christ and all his benefits, that he comforts me and will abide with me forever.

LORD'S DAY 21

Q. 54. What do you believe concerning "the Holy Catholic Church"? 4.054
A. I believe that, from the beginning to the end of the world, and from among the whole human race, the Son of God, by his Spirit and his Word, gathers, protects, and preserves for himself, in the unity of the true faith, a congregation chosen for eternal life. Moreover, I believe that I am and forever will remain a living member of it.

Q. 55. What do you understand by "the communion of saints"? 4.055
A. First, that believers one and all, as partakers of the Lord Christ, and all his treasures and gifts, shall share in one fellowship. Second, that each one ought to know that he is obliged to use his gifts freely and with joy for the benefit and welfare of other members.

Q. 56. What do you believe concerning "the forgiveness of sins"? 4.056
A. That, for the sake of Christ's reconciling work, God will no more remember my sins or the sinfulness with which I have to struggle all my life long; but that he graciously imparts to me the righteousness of Christ so that I may never come into condemnation.

LORD'S DAY 22

Q. 57. What comfort does "the resurrection of the body" give you? 4.057
A. That after this life my soul shall be immediately taken up to Christ, its Head, and that this flesh of mine, raised by the power of Christ, shall be reunited with my soul, and be conformed to the glorious body of Christ.

Q. 58. What comfort does the article concerning "the life everlasting" give you? 4.058
A. That, since I now feel in my heart the beginning of eternal joy, I shall possess, after this life, perfect blessedness, which no eye has seen, nor ear heard, nor the heart of man conceived, and thereby praise God forever.

LORD'S DAY 23

Q. 59. But how does it help you now that you believe all this? 4.059
A. That I am righteous in Christ before God, and an heir of eternal life.

Q. 60. How are you righteous before God? 4.060

A. Only by true faith in Jesus Christ. In spite of the fact that my conscience accuses me that I have grievously sinned against all the commandments of God, and have not kept any one of them, and that I am still ever prone to all that is evil, nevertheless, God, without any merit of my own, out of pure grace, grants me the benefits of the perfect expiation of Christ, imputing to me his righteousness and holiness as if I had never committed a single sin or had ever been sinful, having fulfilled myself all the obedience which Christ has carried out for me, if only I accept such favor with a trusting heart.

4.061   **Q. 61. Why do you say that you are righteous by faith alone?**
A. Not because I please God by virtue of the worthiness of my faith, but because the satisfaction, righteousness, and holiness of Christ alone are my righteousness before God, and because I can accept it and make it mine in no other way than by faith alone.

LORD'S DAY 24

4.062   **Q. 62. But why cannot our good works be our righteousness before God, or at least a part of it?**
A. Because the righteousness which can stand before the judgment of God must be absolutely perfect and wholly in conformity with the divine Law. But even our best works in this life are all imperfect and defiled with sin.

4.063   **Q. 63. Will our good works merit nothing, even when it is God's purpose to reward them in this life, and in the future life as well?**
A. This reward is not given because of merit, but out of grace.

4.064   **Q. 64. But does not this teaching make people careless and sinful?**
A. No, for it is impossible for those who are ingrafted into Christ by true faith not to bring forth the fruit of gratitude.

The Holy Sacraments

LORD'S DAY 25

4.065   **Q. 65. Since, then, faith alone makes us share in Christ and all his benefits, where does such faith originate?**
A. The Holy Spirit creates it in our hearts by the preaching of the holy gospel, and confirms it by the use of the holy Sacraments.

4.066   **Q. 66. What are the Sacraments?**
A. They are visible, holy signs and seals instituted by God in order that by their use he may the more fully disclose and seal to us the promise of the gospel, namely, that because of the one sacrifice of Christ accomplished on the cross he graciously grants us the forgiveness of sins and eternal life.

Q. 67. Are both the Word and the Sacraments designed to direct our faith to the one sacrifice of Jesus Christ on the cross as the only ground of our salvation?   4.067

A. Yes, indeed, for the Holy Spirit teaches in the gospel and confirms by the holy Sacraments that our whole salvation is rooted in the one sacrifice of Christ offered for us on the cross.

Q. 68. How many Sacraments has Christ instituted in the New Testament?   4.068

A. Two, holy Baptism and the holy Supper.

Holy Baptism

LORD'S DAY 26

Q. 69. How does holy Baptism remind and assure you that the one sacrifice of Christ on the cross avails for you?   4.069

A. In this way: Christ has instituted this external washing with water and by it has promised that I am as certainly washed with his blood and Spirit from the uncleanness of my soul and from all my sins, as I am washed externally with water which is used to remove the dirt from my body.

Q. 70. What does it mean to be washed with the blood and Spirit of Christ?   4.070

A. It means to have the forgiveness of sins from God, through grace, for the sake of Christ's blood which he shed for us in his sacrifice on the cross, and also to be renewed by the Holy Spirit and sanctified as members of Christ, so that we may more and more die unto sin and live in a consecrated and blameless way.

Q. 71. Where has Christ promised that we are as certainly washed with his blood and Spirit as with the water of baptism?   4.071

A. In the institution of Baptism which runs thus: "Go therefore and make disciples of all nations, baptizing them in the name of the Father and of the Son and of the Holy Spirit." "He who believes and is baptized will be saved: but he who does not believe will be condemned." This promise is also repeated where the Scriptures call baptism "the water of rebirth" and the washing away of sins.

LORD'S DAY 27

Q. 72. Does merely the outward washing with water itself wash away sins?   4.072

A. No; for only the blood of Jesus Christ and the Holy Spirit cleanse us from all sins.

Q. 73. Then why does the Holy Spirit call baptism the water of rebirth and the washing away of sins?   4.073

A. God does not speak in this way except for a strong reason. Not only does he teach us by Baptism that just as the dirt of the body is taken away by water, so our sins are removed by the blood and Spirit of Christ; but more important still, by the divine pledge and sign he wishes to assure us that we are just as truly washed from our sins spiritually as our bodies are washed with water.

4.074   **Q. 74. Are infants also to be baptized?**

A. Yes, because they, as well as their parents, are included in the covenant and belong to the people of God. Since both redemption from sin through the blood of Christ and the gift of faith from the Holy Spirit are promised to these children no less than to their parents, infants are also by baptism, as a sign of the covenant, to be incorporated into the Christian church and distinguished from the children of unbelievers. This was done in the Old Covenant by circumcision. In the New Covenant baptism has been instituted to take its place.

The Holy Supper

LORD'S DAY 28

4.075   **Q. 75. How are you reminded and assured in the Holy Supper that you participate in the one sacrifice of Christ on the cross and in all his benefits?**

A. In this way: Christ has commanded me and all believers to eat of this broken bread, and to drink of this cup in remembrance of him. He has thereby promised that his body was offered and broken on the cross for me, and his blood was shed for me, as surely as I see with my eyes that the bread of the Lord is broken for me, and that the cup is shared with me. Also, he has promised that he himself as certainly feeds and nourishes my soul to everlasting life with his crucified body and shed blood as I receive from the hand of the minister and actually taste the bread and the cup of the Lord which are given to me as sure signs of the body and blood of Christ.

4.076   **Q. 76. What does it mean to eat the crucified body of Christ and to drink his shed blood?**

A. It is not only to embrace with a trusting heart the whole passion and death of Christ, and by it to receive the forgiveness of sins and eternal life. In addition, it is to be so united more and more to his blessed body by the Holy Spirit dwelling both in Christ and in us that, although he is in heaven and we are on earth, we are nevertheless flesh of his flesh and bone of his bone, always living and being governed by one Spirit, as the members of our bodies are governed by one soul.

4.077   **Q. 77. Where has Christ promised that he will feed and nourish believers with his body and blood just as surely as they eat of this broken bread and drink of this cup?**

A. In the institution of the holy Supper which reads: The Lord Jesus on the night when he was betrayed took bread, and when he had given thanks, he broke it, and said, "this is my body which is for you. Do this in remembrance of me." In the same way also the cup, after supper, saying, "this cup is the new covenant in my blood. Do this, as often as you drink it, in remembrance of me." For as often as you eat this bread and drink the cup, you proclaim the Lord's death until he comes.

This promise is also repeated by the apostle Paul: When we bless "the cup of blessing," is it not a means of sharing in the blood of Christ? When we break the bread, is it not a means of sharing the body of Christ? Because there is one loaf, we, many as we are, are one body; for it is one loaf of which we all partake.

LORD'S DAY 29

Q. 78. Do the bread and wine become the very body and blood of Christ?   4.078

A. No, for as the water in baptism is not changed into the blood of Christ, nor becomes the washing away of sins by itself, but is only a divine sign and confirmation of it, so also in the Lord's Supper the sacred bread does not become the body of Christ itself, although, in accordance with the nature and usage of sacraments, it is called the body of Christ.

Q. 79. Then why does Christ call the bread his body, and the cup his blood, or the New Covenant in his blood, and why does the apostle Paul call the Supper "a means of sharing" in the body and blood of Christ?   4.079

A. Christ does not speak in this way except for a strong reason. He wishes to teach us by it that as bread and wine sustain this temporal life so his crucified body and shed blood are the true food and drink of our souls for eternal life. Even more, he wishes to assure us by this visible sign and pledge that we come to share in his true body and blood through the working of the Holy Spirit as surely as we receive with our mouth these holy tokens in remembrance of him, and that all his sufferings and his death are our own as certainly as if we had ourselves suffered and rendered satisfaction in our own persons.

LORD'S DAY 30

Q. 80. What difference is there between the Lord's Supper and the papal Mass?[2]   4.080

A. The Lord's Supper testifies to us that we have complete forgiveness of all our sins through the one sacrifice of Jesus Christ which he himself has accomplished on the cross once for all; (and that through

---

[2]This question first appeared in part in the second edition. The sections in parentheses were added in the third.

the Holy Spirit we are incorporated into Christ, who is now in heaven with his true body at the right hand of the Father and is there to be worshiped). But the Mass teaches that the living and the dead do not have forgiveness of sins through the sufferings of Christ unless Christ is again offered for them daily by the priest (and that Christ is bodily under the form of bread and wine and is therefore to be worshiped in them). Therefore the Mass is fundamentally a complete denial of the once for all sacrifice and passion of Jesus Christ (and as such an idolatry to be condemned).

4.081   **Q. 81. Who ought to come to the table of the Lord?**
A. Those who are displeased with themselves for their sins, and who nevertheless trust that these sins have been forgiven them and that their remaining weakness is covered by the passion and death of Christ, and who also desire more and more to strengthen their faith and improve their life. The impenitent and hypocrites, however, eat and drink judgment to themselves.

4.082   **Q. 82. Should those who show themselves to be unbelievers and enemies of God by their confession and life be admitted to this Supper?**
A. No, for then the covenant of God would be profaned and his wrath provoked against the whole congregation. According to the ordinance of Christ and his apostles, therefore, the Christian church is under obligation, by the office of the keys, to exclude such persons until they amend their lives.

LORD'S DAY 31

4.083   **Q. 83. What is the office of the keys?**
A. The preaching of the holy gospel and Christian discipline. By these two means the kingdom of heaven is opened to believers and shut against unbelievers.

4.084   **Q. 84. How is the kingdom of heaven opened and shut by the preaching of the holy gospel?**
A. In this way: The kingdom of heaven is opened when it is proclaimed and openly testified to believers, one and all, according to the command of Christ, that as often as they accept the promise of the gospel with true faith all their sins are truly forgiven them by God for the sake of Christ's gracious work. On the contrary, the wrath of God and eternal condemnation fall upon all unbelievers and hypocrites as long as they do not repent. It is according to this witness of the gospel that God will judge the one and the other in this life and in the life to come.

4.085   **Q. 85. How is the kingdom of heaven shut and opened by Christian discipline?**
A. In this way: Christ commanded that those who bear the Christian name in an unchristian way either in doctrine or in life should be

given brotherly admonition. If they do not give up their errors or evil ways, notification is given to the church or to those ordained for this by the church. Then, if they do not change after this warning, they are forbidden to partake of the holy Sacraments and are thus excluded from the communion of the church and by God himself from the kingdom of Christ. However, if they promise and show real amendment, they are received again as members of Christ and of the church.

PART III

Thankfulness

Q. 86. Since we are redeemed from our sin and its wretched consequences by grace through Christ without any merit of our own, why must we do good works?   4.086

A. Because just as Christ has redeemed us with his blood he also renews us through his Holy Spirit according to his own image, so that with our whole life we may show ourselves grateful to God for his goodness and that he may be glorified through us; and further, so that we ourselves may be assured of our faith by its fruits and by our reverent behavior may win our neighbors to Christ.

Q. 87. Can those who do not turn to God from their ungrateful, impenitent life be saved?   4.087

A. Certainly not! Scripture says, "Surely you know that the unjust will never come into possession of the kingdom of God. Make no mistake: no fornicator or idolater, none who are guilty either of adultery or of homosexual perversion, no thieves or grabbers or drunkards or slanderers or swindlers, will possess the kingdom of God."

Q. 88. How many parts are there to the true repentance or conversion of man?   4.088

A. Two: the dying of the old self and the birth of the new.

Q. 89. What is the dying of the old self?   4.089

A. Sincere sorrow over our sins and more and more to hate them and to flee from them.

Q. 90. What is the birth of the new self?   4.090

A. Complete joy in God through Christ and a strong desire to live according to the will of God in all good works.

Q. 91. But what are good works?   4.091

A. Only those which are done out of true faith, in accordance with the Law of God, and for his glory, and not those based on our own opinion or on the traditions of men.

LORD'S DAY 34

4.092   **Q. 92. What is the Law of God?**
A. God spoke all these words saying:

FIRST COMMANDMENT

"I am the Lord your God, who brought you out of the land of Egypt, out of the house of bondage. You shall have no other gods before Me."

SECOND COMMANDMENT

"You shall not make for yourself a graven image, or any likeness of anything that is in heaven above, or that is in the earth beneath, or that is in the water under the earth; you shall not bow down to them or serve them; for I the Lord your God am a jealous God, visiting the iniquity of the fathers upon the children to the third and fourth generation of those who hate Me, but showing steadfast love to thousands of those who love Me and keep My commandments."

THIRD COMMANDMENT

"You shall not take the name of the Lord your God in vain; for the Lord will not hold him guiltless who takes His name in vain."

FOURTH COMMANDMENT

"Remember the sabbath day, to keep it holy. Six days you shall labor, and do all your work; but the seventh day is a sabbath to the Lord your God; in it you shall not do any work, you, or your son, or your daughter, your manservant, or your maidservant, or your cattle, or the sojourner who is within your gates; for in six days the Lord made heaven and earth, and the sea, and all that is in them, and rested the seventh day; therefore the Lord blessed the sabbath day and hallowed it."

FIFTH COMMANDMENT

"Honor your father and your mother, that your days may be long in the land which the Lord your God gives you."

SIXTH COMMANDMENT

"You shall not kill."

SEVENTH COMMANDMENT

"You shall not commit adultery."

EIGHTH COMMANDMENT
"You shall not steal."

NINTH COMMANDMENT
"You shall not bear false witness against your neighbor."

TENTH COMMANDMENT
"You shall not covet your neighbor's house; you shall not covet your neighbor's wife, or his manservant, or his maidservant, or his ox, or his ass, or anything that is your neighbor's."

Q. 93. How are these commandments divided? 4.093
A. Into two tables, the first of which teaches us in four commandments how we ought to live in relation to God; the other, in six commandments, what we owe to our neighbor.

Q. 94. What does the Lord require in the first commandment? 4.094
A. That I must avoid and flee all idolatry, sorcery, enchantments, invocation of saints or other creatures because of the risk of losing my salvation. Indeed, I ought properly to acknowledge the only true God, trust in him alone, in humility and patience expect all good from him only, and love, fear and honor him with my whole heart. In short, I should rather turn my back on all creatures than do the least thing against his will.

Q. 95. What is idolatry? 4.095
A. It is to imagine or possess something in which to put one's trust in place of or beside the one true God who has revealed himself in his Word.

LORD'S DAY 35

Q. 96. What does God require in the second commandment? 4.096
A. That we should not represent him or worship him in any other manner than he has commanded in his word.

Q. 97. Should we, then, not make any images at all? 4.097
A. God cannot and should not be pictured in any way. As for creatures, although they may indeed be portrayed, God forbids making or having any likeness of them in order to worship them, or to use them to serve him.

Q. 98. But may not pictures be tolerated in churches in place of books for unlearned people? 4.098
A. No, for we must not try to be wiser than God who does not want his people to be taught by means of lifeless idols, but through the living preaching of his Word.

4.099   **Q. 99. What is required in the third commandment?**
A. That we must not profane or abuse the name of God by cursing, by perjury, or by unnecessary oaths. Nor are we to participate in such horrible sins by keeping quiet and thus giving silent consent. In a word, we must not use the holy name of God except with fear and reverence so that he may be rightly confessed and addressed by us, and be glorified in all our words and works.

4.100   **Q. 100. Is it, therefore, so great a sin to blaspheme God's name by cursing and swearing that God is also angry with those who do not try to prevent and forbid it as much as they can?**
A. Yes, indeed; for no sin is greater or provokes his wrath more than the profaning of his name. That is why he commanded it to be punished with death.

4.101   **Q. 101. But may we not swear oaths by the name of God in a devout manner?**
A. Yes, when the civil authorities require it of their subjects, or when it is otherwise needed to maintain and promote fidelity and truth, to the glory of God and the welfare of our neighbor. Such oath-taking is grounded in God's Word and has therefore been rightly used by God's people under the Old and New Covenants.

4.102   **Q. 102. May we also swear by the saints or other creatures?**
A. No; for a lawful oath is a calling upon God, as the only searcher of hearts, to bear witness to the truth, and to punish me if I swear falsely. No creature deserves such honor.

4.103   **Q. 103. What does God require in the fourth commandment?**
A. First, that the ministry of the gospel and Christian education be maintained, and that I diligently attend church, especially on the Lord's day, to hear the Word of God, to participate in the holy Sacraments, to call publicly upon the Lord, and to give Christian service to those in need. Second, that I cease from my evil works all the days of my life, allow the Lord to work in me through his Spirit, and thus begin in this life the eternal Sabbath.

4.104   **Q. 104. What does God require in the fifth commandment?**
A. That I show honor, love, and faithfulness to my father and mother and to all who are set in authority over me; that I submit

myself with respectful obedience to all their careful instruction and discipline; and that I also bear patiently their failures, since it is God's will to govern us by their hand.

LORD'S DAY 40

Q. 105. What does God require in the sixth commandment?   4.105
A. That I am not to abuse, hate, injure, or kill my neighbor, either with thought, or by word or gesture, much less by deed, whether by myself or through another, but to lay aside all desire for revenge; and that I do not harm myself or willfully expose myself to danger. This is why the authorities are armed with the means to prevent murder.

Q. 106. But does this commandment speak only of killing?   4.106
A. In forbidding murder God means to teach us that he abhors the root of murder, which is envy, hatred, anger, and desire for revenge, and that he regards all these as hidden murder.

Q. 107. Is it enough, then, if we do not kill our neighbor in any of these ways?   4.107
A. No; for when God condemns envy, hatred, and anger, he requires us to love our neighbor as ourselves, to show patience, peace, gentleness, mercy, and friendliness toward him, to prevent injury to him as much as we can, also to do good to our enemies.

LORD'S DAY 41

Q. 108. What does the seventh commandment teach us?   4.108
A. That all unchastity is condemned by God, and that we should therefore detest it from the heart, and live chaste and disciplined lives, whether in holy wedlock or in single life.

Q. 109. Does God forbid nothing more than adultery and such gross sins in this commandment?   4.109
A. Since both our body and soul are a temple of the Holy Spirit, it is his will that we keep both pure and holy. Therefore he forbids all unchaste actions, gestures, words, thoughts, desires and whatever may excite another person to them.

LORD'S DAY 42

Q. 110. What does God forbid in the eighth commandment?   4.110
A. He forbids not only the theft and robbery which civil authorities punish, but God also labels as theft all wicked tricks and schemes by which we seek to get for ourselves our neighbor's goods, whether by force or under the pretext of right, such as false weights and measures, deceptive advertising or merchandising, counterfeit money, exorbitant interest, or any other means forbidden by God. He also forbids all greed and misuse and waste of his gifts.

4.111   **Q. 111. But what does God require of you in this commandment?**
A. That I work for the good of my neighbor wherever I can and may, deal with him as I would have others deal with me, and do my work well so that I may be able to help the poor in their need.

4.112   **Q. 112. What is required in the ninth commandment?**
A. That I do not bear false witness against anyone, twist anyone's words, be a gossip or a slanderer, or condemn anyone lightly without a hearing. Rather I am required to avoid, under penalty of God's wrath, all lying and deceit as the works of the devil himself. In judicial and all other matters I am to love the truth, and to speak and confess it honestly. Indeed, insofar as I am able, I am to defend and promote my neighbor's good name.

4.113   **Q. 113. What is required in the tenth commandment?**
A. That there should never enter our heart even the least inclination or thought contrary to any commandment of God, but that we should always hate sin with our whole heart and find satisfaction and joy in all righteousness.

4.114   **Q. 114. But can those who are converted to God keep these commandments perfectly?**
A. No, for even the holiest of them make only a small beginning in obedience in this life. Nevertheless, they begin with serious purpose to conform not only to some, but to all the commandments of God.

4.115   **Q. 115. Why, then, does God have the ten commandments preached so strictly since no one can keep them in this life?**
A. First, that all our life long we may become increasingly aware of our sinfulness, and therefore more eagerly seek forgiveness of sins and righteousness in Christ. Second, that we may constantly and diligently pray to God for the grace of the Holy Spirit, so that more and more we may be renewed in the image of God, until we attain the goal of full perfection after this life.

Prayer

4.116   **Q. 116. Why is prayer necessary for Christians?**
A. Because it is the chief part of the gratitude which God requires of us, and because God will give his grace and Holy Spirit only to those who sincerely beseech him in prayer without ceasing, and who thank him for these gifts.

Q. 117. What is contained in a prayer which pleases God and is heard by him?   4.117

A. First, that we sincerely call upon the one true God, who has revealed himself to us in his Word, for all that he has commanded us to ask of him. Then, that we thoroughly acknowledge our need and evil condition so that we may humble ourselves in the presence of his majesty. Third, that we rest assured that, in spite of our unworthiness, he will certainly hear our prayer for the sake of Christ our Lord, as he has promised us in his Word.

Q. 118. What has God commanded us to ask of him?   4.118

A. All things necessary for soul and body which Christ the Lord has included in the prayer which he himself taught us.

Q. 119. What is the Lord's Prayer?   4.119

A. "Our Father who art in heaven, hallowed be thy name. Thy kingdom come, thy will be done, on earth as it is in heaven. Give us this day our daily bread; and forgive us our debts, as we also have forgiven our debtors; and lead us not into temptation, but deliver us from evil, for thine is the kingdom and the power and the glory, forever. Amen."

Our Lord's Prayer

LORD'S DAY 46

Q. 120. Why has Christ commanded us to address God: "Our Father"?   4.120

A. That at the very beginning of our prayer he may awaken in us the childlike reverence and trust toward God which should be the motivation of our prayer, which is that God has become our Father through Christ and will much less deny us what we ask him in faith than our human fathers will refuse us earthly things.

Q. 121. Why is there added: "who art in heaven"?   4.121

A. That we may have no earthly conception of the heavenly majesty of God, but that we may expect from his almighty power all things that are needed for body and soul.

LORD'S DAY 47

Q. 122. What is the first petition?   4.122

A. "Hallowed be thy name." That is: help us first of all to know thee rightly, and to hallow, glorify, and praise thee in all thy works through which there shine thine almighty power, wisdom, goodness, righteousness, mercy, and truth. And so order our whole life in thought, word, and deed that thy name may never be blasphemed on our account, but may always be honored and praised.

4.123   **Q. 123. What is the second petition?**
A. "Thy kingdom come." That is: so govern us by the Word and Spirit that we may more and more submit ourselves unto thee. Uphold and increase thy church. Destroy the works of the devil, every power that raises itself against thee, and all wicked schemes thought up against thy holy Word, until the full coming of thy kingdom in which thou shalt be all in all.

4.124   **Q. 124. What is the third petition?**
A. "Thy will be done, on earth as it is in heaven." That is: grant that we and all men may renounce our own will and obey thy will, which alone is good, without grumbling, so that everyone may carry out his office and calling as willingly and faithfully as the angels in heaven.

4.125   **Q. 125. What is the fourth petition?**
A. "Give us this day our daily bread." That is: be pleased to provide for all our bodily needs so that thereby we may acknowledge that thou art the only source of all that is good, and that without thy blessing neither our care and labor nor thy gifts can do us any good. Therefore, may we withdraw our trust from all creatures and place it in thee alone.

4.126   **Q. 126. What is the fifth petition?**
A. "And forgive us our debts, as we also have forgiven our debtors." That is: be pleased, for the sake of Christ's blood, not to charge to us, miserable sinners, our many transgressions, nor the evil which still clings to us. We also find this witness of thy grace in us, that it is our sincere intention heartily to forgive our neighbor.

4.127   **Q. 127. What is the sixth petition?**
A. "And lead us not into temptation, but deliver us from evil." That is: since we are so weak that we cannot stand by ourselves for one moment, and besides, since our sworn enemies, the devil, the world, and our own sin, ceaselessly assail us, be pleased to preserve and strengthen us through the power of the Holy Spirit so that we may stand firm against them, and not be defeated in this spiritual warfare, until at last we obtain complete victory.

Q. 128. How do you close this prayer?

A. "For thine is the kingdom and the power and the glory, forever."
That is: we ask all this of thee because, as our King, thou art willing
and able to give us all that is good since thou hast power over all
things, and that by this not we ourselves but thy holy name may be
glorified forever.

Q. 129. What is the meaning of the little word "Amen"?

A. Amen means: this shall truly and certainly be. For my prayer is
much more certainly heard by God than I am persuaded in my heart
that I desire such things from him.

THE SECOND HELVETIC
CONFESSION

Introduction to the Second Helvetic Confession

"Helvetic" (from the Latin word for Switzerland, *Helvetia*) means "Swiss." Unlike most other Reformed confessions, the Second Helvetic Confession was written by one man, Heinrich Bullinger (1504–1575), who was principal author of an earlier Swiss confession, the First Helvetic Confession.

Bullinger was a pupil and friend of Ulrich Zwingli, who was the "father" of the Reformation in Switzerland as Luther was in Germany. After Zwingli died in 1531, he took Zwingli's place as preacher and pastor of the cathedral church in Zurich. During his forty-four-year pastorate (which began before and lasted longer than his friend Calvin's activity in Geneva), he became adviser and "senior pastor and theologian" to three generations of reformers. He exchanged correspondence with Luther, Calvin, and other reformers on the continent and in the British Isles. His sermons were circulated and widely read.

Bullinger intended to leave the Second Helvetic Confession as his personal legacy to the church in Zurich, but had it published in 1566 in an attempt to help reconcile Lutheran and Reformed Christians in Germany. It was enthusiastically received and subsequently adopted or recognized as an authoritative statement of faith by Reformed churches in Switzerland, Scotland, France, Holland, Germany, Hungary, Poland, and Czechoslovakia. Later it was a major influence on the English Puritans and (through Professor Charles Hodge of Princeton Theological Seminary) on Presbyterians in the United States. With the Heidelberg Catechism it is the most widely recognized confessional statement in the worldwide family of Reformed churches.

The confession reflects the person and work of its author. It is the most pastoral and practical of all Reformed confessions of the sixteenth century, always concerned to relate the interpretation of Scripture and Christian faith to the everyday life of Christians and the church. Although it condemns ancient heresies and distinguishes the faith of Reformed Christians from that of Roman Catholics, Lutherans, and Anabaptists in its time, it is ecumenical in spirit, seeking the unity of the one catholic Church. While readers untrained in the history of theology may have trouble understanding some of the issues involved in what it is against, the positive things it has to say are so clearly and simply expressed (with more biblical references than are found in most confessions) that it is still accessible to "ordinary Christians" like those Bullinger had in mind when he composed it.

Of course the Second Helvetic Confession also reflects some social customs, political assumptions, and theological convictions of Reformed churches in the sixteenth century that are different from those of the Presbyterian Church (U.S.A.) today. For example, it excludes women from "ecclesiastical duties" (5.191). It takes for granted a monarchical form of government, and says that "the magistrate" should "suppress" and even "execute" heretics and "blasphemers" (5.255). It is so preoccupied with the reformation of the inner life of the church that it has little to say about evangelism and the mission of the church in and for the world. But despite such limitations, this confession as a whole lays out the fundamental understanding of Christian faith and life that sixteenth- and twentieth-century Reformed confessions have in common. It does so with a clarity, commonsense wisdom, pastoral sensitivity, ecumenical goodwill—and with some theological insights ahead of its time—that make it a unique contribution to the *Book of Confessions*.

Despite the length of the confession (the longest in the *Book*), its outline is easy to follow:

Chapter	Outline
I–II	Scripture and Preaching
III–V	God and the True Worship of God
VI–VII	Providence and Creation
VIII–IX	Sin and Free Will
X–XI	Predestination/Election and Salvation
XII–XVI	Reception of Salvation and New Life in Christ
XVII–XXI	Church, Ministry, and Sacraments
XXII–XXVIII	Life and Work of the Church
XXIX–XXX	Family and State

Without attempting to summarize everything in these chapters, we will identify here some of the most distinctive contributions of the Second Helvetic Confession to Reformed confessional tradition.

EMPHASIS ON PREACHING

Unique among classical Reformed confessions, the Second Helvetic Confession emphasizes in Chapter I that the God who once spoke through the prophets and apostles continues to speak through preaching. "The preaching of the Word of God is the Word of God. Wherefore when this Word of God is now preached in the church by preachers lawfully called, we believe that the very Word of God is proclaimed, and received by the faithful" (5.004). It is an indication of Bullinger's practical concern that this confession is less interested in arguing at length about the origin and authority of Scripture than in talking about how it actually functions in the faith and life of Christians when it is faithfully interpreted, proclaimed, and heard.

THE SOVEREIGNTY OF GOD AND HUMAN FREEDOM AND RESPONSIBILITY

The Second Helvetic Confession agrees with the whole of Reformed tradition in seeking to affirm God's sovereign rule without destroying human freedom and responsibility. Chapter VI discusses the doctrine of providence in such a way that it emphasizes God's care for us (not just God's power over us), and our responsibility to use the "means" God has provided for us to care for others and ourselves. Chapter IX is one of the clearest brief discussions of "free will" in all of Reformed confessional literature.

PREDESTINATION/ELECTION

A major contribution of this confession to Reformed faith in the twentieth century is that its doctrine of predestination (Chapter X) is based on the good news of God in Jesus Christ—not on speculation about God's "eternal decree" (as in Chapter III of the Westminster Confession). "We are elected or predestined in Christ" (5.053). "Let Christ, therefore be the looking glass, in whom we may contemplate our predestination" (5.060). "[I]t is to be held as beyond doubt that if you believe and are in Christ, you are elected" (5.059). Looking at predestination in light of the revelation of the will and plan of God in Christ leads the confession to say, "We are to have a good hope for all. And although God knows who are his, and here and there mention is made of the small number of the elect, yet we must hope well of all, and not rashly judge any man to be a reprobate" (5.055).

Another consequence of the confession's christological approach is the insight that the purpose of predestination/election is not just that we may be saved but that God chose us in Christ "that we should be holy and blameless before him in love" (5.054).

CHRISTIAN FAITH AND LIFE

Chapters XII–XVI give a simple, straightforward summary of the Reformed understanding of repentance and conversion, justification and sanctification. In agreement with Calvin and the Heidelberg Catechism, it says that the motive for "good works" is not to earn God's approval and blessing, or for our own personal gain, but "to show gratitude to God, and for the profit of the neighbor" (5.117).

THE CHURCH

In Chapter XVII the Second Helvetic Confession defines the church in language similar to other Reformed confessions. But it demonstrates again the author's concentration on practical issues. It has some good advice about how we are to maintain order and have serious debate without dissension and strife in the church (5.132–.133). Echoing what it has said about predestination, it also offers advice about how we are to deal with the ancient claim that there is no salvation outside the church: ". . .

we know that God had some friends in the world outside the commonwealth of Israel" (5.137). "We must not judge rashly or prematurely. Hence we must be very careful not to judge before the time, nor undertake to exclude, reject or cut off those whom the Lord does not want to have excluded or rejected, and those we cannot eliminate without loss to the Church" (5.140). "On the other hand," Bullinger adds with wit unusual in confessional statements, "we must be vigilant lest while the pious snore the wicked gain ground and do harm to the Church."

MINISTERS

Chapter XVIII, although it recognizes the priesthood of all believers, discusses in detail the calling, ordination, duties, and personal character of ministers. Here again the author's practical interest is evident. Ministers are to be "capable men [sic] distinguished by sufficient consecrated learning, pious eloquence, simple wisdom . . . moderation and an honorable reputation." They are to be carefully chosen and duly elected "in a proper order without any uproar, dissension and rivalry" (5.150). No more comprehensive and realistic description of "the duties of ministers" can be found in Reformed confessional literature than the list in 5.163.

This chapter also includes a section on the exercise of discipline in the church (sometimes considered a third "mark" of the church along with true preaching of the gospel and right administration of the sacraments). The rule is that "everything is to be done for edification, decently and honorably, without oppression or strife . . . for building up and not for destroying" (5.165).

Practical Bullinger concludes the chapter by saying that ministers are to "receive a stipend, and all things that be necessary for themselves and their family" (5.168).

SACRAMENTS

Chapters XIX–XXI lay out in a clear way the Reformed understanding of the sacraments, a topic on which in the sixteenth century (as ever since) there was bitter, church-splitting controversy. It is a sign of Bullinger's ecumenical concern for the unity of the whole church that the discussion here is not defensive or polemical. Although it criticizes alternative views, it describes the Reformed understanding of Baptism and the Lord's Supper in mostly positive language.

THE EVERYDAY LIFE OF THE CHURCH

Chapters XXII–XXVIII give us a picture of the life of a Reformed congregation in the sixteenth century. Some of the topics discussed are no longer pressing issues for us. But what Bullinger writes here is still instructive for Presbyterians in the twentieth century—especially concerning public worship (Chapters XXII–XXIII), Christian education of youth and visitation of the sick (Chapter XXV), funerals and our attitude toward those who have died (Chapter XXVI), and the proper use of the church's money (Chapter XXVIII). Some examples of the author's Reformed perspective, common sense, and wit:

In a paragraph on "the true ornamentation of sanctuaries," the Second Helvetic Confession underlines the protest of all the Swiss reformers against ostentation and pomp in the church. "Therefore, all luxurious attire, all pride, and everything unbecoming to Christian humility, discipline and modesty, are to be banished from the sanctuaries and places of prayer of Christians. For the true ornamentation of churches does not consist in ivory, gold, and precious stones, but in the frugality, piety, and virtues of those who are in the Church" (5.216).

Public prayers should not be "excessively long and irksome. The greater part of meetings for worship is therefore to be given to evangelical teaching, and care is to be taken lest the congregation is wearied by too lengthy prayers and when they are to hear the preaching of the Gospel they either leave the meeting or, having been exhausted, want to do away with it altogether" (5.220).

The greatest care is to be taken that young people ("even from infancy") be properly instructed, "laying the first grounds of faith and faithfully teaching the rudiments of our religion by expounding the Ten Commandments, the Apostles' Creed, the Lord's Prayer, and the doctrine of the Sacraments" (5.233).

Pastors should visit the sick—and when possible the sick ought to let them know that they are sick (5.234)!

Still relevant in our time and in agreement with Reformed tradition past and present: We may give thanksgiving for the lives of the dead, but we do not need to pray for them, "for we believe that the faithful, after bodily death, go directly to Christ" (5.237). And concerning the appearance of the dead to the living: "We count those apparitions among the laughingstocks, crafts, and deceptions of the devil," and there is to be no "commerce" with them (5.239).

FAMILY LIFE AND POLITICS

Unlike many Reformed confessions, the Second Helvetic Confession does not end with anticipation of the future life (which it has discussed earlier) or the coming of the kingdom of God at the end of time. It ends very much in the middle of this life.

Chapter XXIX is the fullest treatment of marriage and family life to be found in any of the confessions in the Book of Confessions. It recognizes that single life and celibacy are the gift of God to some, but it emphasizes marriage and the family—with the same theological seriousness and down-to-earth realism that is characteristic of the confession as a whole.

God wills that married couples "live together in complete love and concord" (5.246), "with utmost faithfulness, piety, love and purity" (5.247). Then comes the warning: "Therefore let them guard against quarrels, dissensions, lust and adultery" (5.247).

Children are to be brought up "in the fear of the Lord." Parents "should teach their children honest trades or professions by which they may support themselves. They should keep them from idleness and in all these things instill in them true faith in God, lest through a lack of confidence or too much security or filthy greed they become dissolute and achieve no success" (5.249).

The confession ends with Chapter XXX on "the magistracy" (government). For us who live in a democratic society that is committed to freedom of religion and the separation of church and state, it is out of date in taking for granted (as did all Reformed confessions in the sixteenth and seventeenth centuries) that all governments are ruled by kings and princes who do what God has ordained them to do when they support—and enforce—true preaching of the gospel and Christian "piety." But what is of enduring importance for the Reformed tradition is the great respect the Second Helvetic Confession (with all other Reformed confessions) has for government itself and the public responsibility of Christians. Political authority is "instituted by God himself," and political leaders (not preachers!) "should have the chief place in the world" (5.252) because they have a God-ordained responsibility to "secure and preserve peace and public tranquility," "exercise judgment by judging uprightly," "protect widows, orphans and the afflicted," punish "criminals" and "oppressors," and, when all attempts to preserve peace have been exhausted, wage war (5.254–.256).

Christian citizens, then, are to honor their political leaders as "ministers of God," love and pray for them, "obey all just and fair commands," "pay taxes faithfully and willingly," and "if public safety and justice require it . . . lay down their lives and pour out their blood" (5.258).

From the beginning, commitment to the common good, social justice, reconciliation, and peace have always been an essential part of Reformed faith.

The Second Helvetic Confession concludes with a prayer (one quite different from the prayer at the end of the Scots Confession): "We beseech God, our most merciful Father in heaven, that he will bless the rulers of the people, and us, and his whole people, through Jesus Christ, our only Lord and Savior; to whom be praise and glory and thanksgiving, for all ages. Amen."

QUESTIONS FOR STUDY

1. To what extent, according to Chapter IX, do human beings have free will?

2. According to Chapter X, who is elected or predestined to salvation? How does the doctrine of election/predestination in the Second Helvetic Confession compare with that in the Westminster Confession of Faith, Chapter III?

3. To what extent is Chapter XXIX on marriage and family life still relevant/helpful today?

4. What guidelines for the worship and life of the church today can be found in Chapters XXII–XXVIII?

THE SECOND HELVETIC CONFESSION[1]

CHAPTER I

Of the Holy Scripture Being the True
Word of God

CANONICAL SCRIPTURE. We believe and confess the canonical Scriptures of the holy prophets and apostles of both Testaments to be the true Word of God, and to have sufficient authority of themselves, not of men. For God himself spoke to the fathers, prophets, apostles, and still speaks to us through the Holy Scriptures. **5.001**

And in this Holy Scripture, the universal Church of Christ has the most complete exposition of all that pertains to a saving faith, and also to the framing of a life acceptable to God; and in this respect it is expressly commanded by God that nothing be either added to or taken from the same. **5.002**

SCRIPTURE TEACHES FULLY ALL GODLINESS. We judge, therefore, that from these Scriptures are to be derived true wisdom and godliness, the reformation and government of churches; as also instruction in all duties of piety; and, to be short, the confirmation of doctrines, and the rejection of all errors, moreover, all exhortations according to that word of the apostle, "All Scripture is inspired by God and profitable for teaching, for reproof," etc. (II Tim. 3:16-17). Again, "I am writing these instructions to you," says the apostle to Timothy, "so that you may know how one ought to behave in the household of God," etc. (I Tim. 3:14-15). SCRIPTURE IS THE WORD OF GOD. Again, the selfsame apostle to the Thessalonians: "When," says he, "you received the Word of God which you heard from us, you accepted it, not as the word of men but as what it really is, the Word of God," etc. (I Thess. 2:13). For the Lord himself has said in the Gospel, "It is not you who speak, but the Spirit of my Father speaking through you"; therefore "he who hears you hears me, and he who rejects me rejects him who sent me" (Matt. 10:20; Luke 10:16; John 13:20). **5.003**

THE PREACHING OF THE WORD OF GOD IS THE WORD OF GOD. Wherefore when this Word of God is now preached in the church by **5.004**

---

preachers lawfully called, we believe that the very Word of God is proclaimed, and received by the faithful; and that neither any other Word of God is to be invented nor is to be expected from heaven: and that now the Word itself which is preached is to be regarded, not the minister that preaches; for even if he be evil and a sinner, nevertheless the Word of God remains still true and good.

5.005   Neither do we think that therefore the outward preaching is to be thought as fruitless because the instruction in true religion depends on the inward illumination of the Spirit, or because it is written "And no longer shall each man teach his neighbor . . ., for they shall all know me" (Jer. 31:34), and "Neither he who plants nor he who waters is anything, but only God who gives the growth" (I Cor. 3:7). For although "no one can come to Christ unless he be drawn by the Father" (John 6:44), and unless the Holy Spirit inwardly illumines him, yet we know that it is surely the will of God that his Word should be preached outwardly also. God could indeed, by his Holy Spirit, or by the ministry of an angel, without the ministry of St. Peter, have taught Cornelius in the Acts; but, nevertheless, he refers him to Peter, of whom the angel speaking says, "He shall tell you what you ought to do."

5.006   INWARD ILLUMINATION DOES NOT ELIMINATE EXTERNAL PREACH- ING. For he that illuminates inwardly by giving men the Holy Spirit, the same one, by way of commandment, said unto his disciples, "Go into all the world, and preach the Gospel to the whole creation" (Mark 16:15). And so in Philippi, Paul preached the Word outwardly to Lydia, a seller of purple goods; but the Lord inwardly opened the woman's heart (Acts 16:14). And the same Paul, after a beautiful development of his thought, in Rom. 10:17 at length comes to the conclusion, "So faith comes from hearing, and hearing from the Word of God by the preaching of Christ."

5.007   At the same time we recognize that God can illuminate whom and when he will, even without the external ministry, for that is in his power; but we speak of the usual way of instructing men, delivered unto us from God, both by commandment and examples.

5.008   HERESIES. We therefore detest all the heresies of Artemon, the Manichaeans, the Valentinians, of Cerdon, and the Marcionites, who denied that the Scriptures proceeded from the Holy Spirit; or did not accept some parts of them, or interpolated and corrupted them.

5.009   APOCRYPHA. And yet we do not conceal the fact that certain books of the Old Testament were by the ancient authors called *Apocryphal*, and by others *Ecclesiastical;* inasmuch as some would have them read in the churches, but not advanced as an authority from which the faith is to be established. As Augustine also, in his *De Civitate Dei,* book 18, ch. 38, remarks that "in the books of the Kings, the names and books of certain prophets are cited"; but he adds that "they are not in the canon"; and that "those books which we have suffice unto godliness."

CHAPTER II

Of Interpreting the Holy Scriptures; and of Fathers, Councils, and Traditions

THE TRUE INTERPRETATION OF SCRIPTURE. The apostle Peter has **5.010** said that the Holy Scriptures are not of private interpretation (II Peter 1:20), and thus we do not allow all possible interpretations. Nor consequently do we acknowledge as the true or genuine interpretation of the Scriptures what is called the conception of the Roman Church, that is, what the defenders of the Roman Church plainly maintain should be thrust upon all for acceptance. But we hold that interpretation of the Scripture to be orthodox and genuine which is gleaned from the Scriptures themselves (from the nature of the language in which they were written, likewise according to the circumstances in which they were set down, and expounded in the light of like and unlike passages and of many and clearer passages) and which agree with the rule of faith and love, and contributes much to the glory of God and man's salvation.

INTERPRETATIONS OF THE HOLY FATHERS. Wherefore we do not **5.011** despise the interpretations of the holy Greek and Latin fathers, nor reject their disputations and treatises concerning sacred matters as far as they agree with the Scriptures; but we modestly dissent from them when they are found to set down things differing from, or altogether contrary to, the Scriptures. Neither do we think that we do them any wrong in this matter; seeing that they all, with one consent, will not have their writings equated with the canonical Scriptures, but command us to prove how far they agree or disagree with them, and to accept what is in agreement and to reject what is in disagreement.

COUNCILS. And in the same order also we place the decrees and **5.012** canons of councils.

Wherefore we do not permit ourselves, in controversies about **5.013** religion or matters of faith, to urge our case with only the opinions of the fathers or decrees of councils; much less by received customs, or by the large number of those who share the same opinion, or by the prescription of a long time. WHO IS THE JUDGE? Therefore, we do not admit any other judge than God himself, who proclaims by the Holy Scriptures what is true, what is false, what is to be followed, or what to be avoided. So we do assent to the judgments of spiritual men which are drawn from the Word of God. Certainly Jeremiah and other prophets vehemently condemned the assemblies of priests which were set up against the law of God; and diligently admonished us that we should not listen to the fathers, or tread in their path who, walking in their own inventions, swerved from the law of God.

TRADITIONS OF MEN. Likewise we reject human traditions, even if **5.014** they be adorned with high-sounding titles, as though they were divine and apostolical, delivered to the Church by the living voice of the apostles, and, as it were, through the hands of apostolical men to succeeding bishops which, when compared with the Scriptures, disagree with them; and by their disagreement show that they are not apostolic at all. For as the apostles did not contradict themselves in doctrine, so the apostolic men did not set forth things contrary to the apostles. On the contrary, it would be wicked to assert that the apostles by a living voice delivered anything contrary to their writings. Paul affirms expressly that he taught the same things in all churches (I Cor. 4:17). And, again, "For we write you nothing but what you can read and understand" (II Cor. 1:13). Also, in another place, he testifies that he and his disciples—that is, apostolic men—walked in the same way, and jointly by the same Spirit did all things (II Cor. 12:18). Moreover, the Jews in former times had the traditions of their elders; but these traditions were severely rejected by the Lord, indicating that the keeping of them hinders God's law, and that God is worshipped in vain by such traditions (Matt. 15:1 ff.; Mark 7:1 ff.).

CHAPTER III

Of God, His Unity and Trinity

5.015   GOD IS ONE. We believe and teach that God is one in essence or nature, subsisting in himself, all sufficient in himself, invisible, incorporeal, immense, eternal, Creator of all things both visible and invisible, the greatest good, living, quickening and preserving all things, omnipotent and supremely wise, kind and merciful, just and true. Truly we detest many gods because it is expressly written: "The Lord your God is one Lord" (Deut. 6:4). "I am the Lord your God. You shall have no other gods before me" (Ex. 20:2-3). "I am the Lord, and there is no other god besides me. Am I not the Lord, and there is no other God beside me? A righteous God and a Savior; there is none besides me" (Isa. 45:5, 21). "The Lord, the Lord, a God merciful and gracious, slow to anger, and abounding in steadfast love and faithfulness" (Ex. 34:6).

5.016   GOD IS THREE. Notwithstanding we believe and teach that the same immense, one and indivisible God is in person inseparably and without confusion distinguished as Father, Son and Holy Spirit so, as the Father has begotten the Son from eternity, the Son is begotten by an ineffable generation, and the Holy Spirit truly proceeds from them both, and the same from eternity and is to be worshipped with both.

5.017   Thus there are not three gods, but three persons, consubstantial, coeternal, and coequal; distinct with respect to hypostases, and with respect to order, the one preceding the other yet without any inequality. For according to the nature or essence they are so joined together that they are one God, and the divine nature is common to the Father, Son and Holy Spirit.

5.018   For Scripture has delivered to us a manifest distinction of persons, the angel saying, among other things, to the Blessed Virgin, "The Holy

Spirit will come upon you, and the power of the Most High will overshadow you; therefore the child to be born will be called holy, the Son of God" (Luke 1:35). And also in the baptism of Christ a voice is heard from heaven concerning Christ, saying, "This is my beloved Son" (Matt. 3:17). The Holy Spirit also appeared in the form of a dove (John 1:32). And when the Lord himself commanded the apostles to baptize, he commanded them to baptize "in the name of the Father, and the Son, and the Holy Spirit" (Matt. 28:19). Elsewhere in the Gospel he said: "The Father will send the Holy Spirit in my name" (John 14:26), and again he said: "When the Counselor comes, whom I shall send to you from the Father, even the Spirit of truth, who proceeds from the Father, he will bear witness to me," etc. (John 15:26). In short, we receive the Apostles' Creed because it delivers to us the true faith.

HERESIES. Therefore we condemn the Jews and Mohammedans, and   5.019
all those who blaspheme that sacred and adorable Trinity. We also condemn all heresies and heretics who teach that the Son and Holy Spirit are God in name only, and also that there is something created and subservient, or subordinate to another in the Trinity, and that there is something unequal in it, a greater or a less, something corporeal or corporeally conceived, something different with respect to character or will, something mixed or solitary, as if the Son and Holy Spirit were the affections and properties of one God the Father, as the Monarchians, Novatians, Praxeas, Patripassians, Sabellius, Paul of Samosata, Aëtius, Macedonius, Anthropomorphites, Arius, and such like, have thought.

CHAPTER IV

Of Idols or Images of God, Christ and the Saints

IMAGES OF GOD. Since God as Spirit is in essence invisible and   5.020
immense, he cannot really be expressed by any art or image. For this reason we have no fear pronouncing with Scripture that images of God are mere lies. Therefore we reject not only the idols of the Gentiles, but also the images of Christians. IMAGES OF CHRIST. Although Christ assumed human nature, yet he did not on that account assume it in order to provide a model for carvers and painters. He denied that he had come "to abolish the law and the prophets" (Matt. 5:17). But images are forbidden by the law and the prophets (Deut. 4:15; Isa. 44:9). He denied that his bodily presence would be profitable for the Church, and promised that he would be near us by his Spirit forever (John 16:7). Who, therefore, would believe that a shadow or likeness of his body would contribute any benefit to the pious? (II Cor. 5:5). Since he abides in us by his Spirit, we are therefore the temple of God (I Cor. 3:16). But "what agreement has the temple of God with

idols?" (II Cor. 6:16). IMAGES OF SAINTS. And since the blessed spirits and saints in heaven, while they lived here on earth, rejected all worship of themselves (Acts 3:12 f.; 14:11 ff.; Rev. 14:7; 22:9) and condemned images, shall anyone find it likely that the heavenly saints and angels are pleased with their own images before which men kneel, uncover their heads, and bestow other honors?

5.021   But in fact in order to instruct men in religion and to remind them of divine things and of their salvation, the Lord commanded the preaching of the Gospel (Mark 16:15)—not to paint and to teach the laity by means of pictures. Moreover, he instituted Sacraments, but nowhere did he set up images. THE SCRIPTURES OF THE LAITY. Furthermore, wherever we turn our eyes, we see the living and true creatures of God which, if they be observed, as is proper, make a much more vivid impression on the beholders than all the images or vain, motionless, feeble and dead pictures made by men, of which the prophet truly said: "They have eyes, but do not see" (Ps. 115:5).

5.022   LACTANTIUS. Therefore we approved the judgment of Lactantius, an ancient writer, who says: "Undoubtedly no religion exists where there is an image." EPIPHANIUS AND JEROME. We also assert that the blessed bishop Epiphanius did right when, finding on the doors of a church a veil on which was painted a picture supposedly of Christ or some saint, he ripped it down and took it away, because to see a picture of a man hanging in the Church of Christ was contrary to the authority of Scripture. Wherefore he charged that from henceforth no such veils, which were contrary to our religion, should be hung in the Church of Christ, and that rather such questionable things, unworthy of the Church of Christ and the faithful people, should be removed. Moreover, we approve of this opinion of St. Augustine concerning true religion: "Let not the worship of the works of men be a religion for us. For the artists themselves who make such things are better; yet we ought not to worship them" (*De Vera Religione*, cap. 55).

CHAPTER V

Of the Adoration, Worship and Invocation of God Through the Only Mediator Jesus Christ

5.023   GOD ALONE IS TO BE ADORED AND WORSHIPPED. We teach that the true God alone is to be adored and worshipped. This honor we impart to none other, according to the commandment of the Lord, "You shall worship the Lord your God and him only shall you serve" (Matt. 4:10). Indeed, all the prophets severely inveighed against the people of Israel whenever they adored and worshipped strange gods, and not the only true God. But we teach that God is to be adored and worshipped as he himself has taught us to worship, namely, "in spirit and in truth" (John 4:23 f.), not with any superstition, but with sincerity, according to his Word; lest at any time he should say to us: "Who has required these things from your hands?" (Isa. 1:12; Jer. 6:20). For Paul also says: "God is not served by human hands, as though he needed anything," etc. (Acts 17:25).

GOD ALONE IS TO BE INVOKED THROUGH THE MEDIATION OF CHRIST ALONE. In all crises and trials of our life we call upon him alone, and that by the mediation of our only mediator and intercessor, Jesus Christ. For we have been explicitly commanded: "Call upon me in the day of trouble; I will deliver you, and you shall glorify me" (Ps. 50:15). Moreover, we have a most generous promise from the Lord who said: "If you ask anything of the Father, he will give it to you" (John 16:23), and: "Come to me, all who labor and are heavy laden and I will give you rest" (Matt 11:28). And since it is written: "How are men to call upon him in whom they have not believed?" (Rom. 10:14), and since we do believe in God alone, we assuredly call upon him alone, and we do so through Christ. For as the apostle says, "There is one God and there is one mediator between God and men, the man Christ Jesus" (I Tim. 2:5), and, "If any one does sin, we have an advocate with the Father, Jesus Christ the righteous," etc. (I John 2:1). | **5.024**

THE SAINTS ARE NOT TO BE ADORED, WORSHIPPED OR INVOKED. For this reason we do not adore, worship, or pray to the saints in heaven, or to other gods, and we do not acknowledge them as our intercessors or mediators before the Father in heaven. For God and Christ the Mediator are sufficient for us; neither do we give to others the honor that is due to God alone and to his Son, because he has expressly said: "My glory I give to no other" (Isa. 42:8), and because Peter has said: "There is no other name under heaven given among men by which we must be saved," except the name of Christ (Acts 4:12). In him, those who give their assent by faith do not seek anything outside Christ. | **5.025**

THE DUE HONOR TO BE RENDERED TO THE SAINTS. At the same time we do not despise the saints or think basely of them. For we acknowledge them to be living members of Christ and friends of God who have gloriously overcome the flesh and the world. Hence we love them as brothers, and also honor them; yet not with any kind of worship but by an honorable opinion of them and just praises of them. We also imitate them. For with ardent longings and supplications we earnestly desire to be imitators of their faith and virtues, to share eternal salvation with them, to dwell eternally with them in the presence of God, and to rejoice with them in Christ. And in this respect we approve of the opinion of St. Augustine in *De Vera Religione:* "Let not our religion be the cult of men who have died. For if they have lived holy lives, they are not to be thought of as seeking such honors; on the contrary, they want us to worship him by whose illumination they rejoice that we are fellow-servants of his merits. They are therefore to be honored by way of imitation, but not to be adored in a religious manner," etc. | **5.026**

5.027 RELICS OF THE SAINTS. Much less do we believe that the relics of the saints are to be adored and reverenced. Those ancient saints seemed to have sufficiently honored their dead when they decently committed their remains to the earth after the spirit had ascended on high. And they thought that the most noble relics of their ancestors were their virtues, their doctrine, and their faith. Moreover, as they commend these "relics" when praising the dead, so they strive to copy them during their life on earth.

5.028 SWEARING BY GOD'S NAME ALONE. These ancient men did not swear except by the name of the only God, Yahweh, as prescribed by the divine law. Therefore, as it is forbidden to swear by the names of strange gods (Ex. 23:13; Deut. 10:20), so we do not perform oaths to the saints that are demanded of us. We therefore reject in all these matters a doctrine that ascribes much to the saints in heaven.

CHAPTER VI

Of the Providence of God

5.029 ALL THINGS ARE GOVERNED BY THE PROVIDENCE OF GOD. We believe that all things in heaven and on earth, and in all creatures, are preserved and governed by the providence of this wise, eternal and almighty God. For David testifies and says: "The Lord is high above all nations, and his glory above the heavens! Who is like the Lord our God, who is seated on high, who looks far down upon the heavens and the earth?" (Ps. 113:4 ff.). Again: "Thou searchest out . . . all my ways. Even before a word is on my tongue, lo, O Lord, Thou knowest it altogether" (Ps. 139:3 f.). Paul also testifies and declares: "In him we live and move and have our being" (Acts 17:28), and "from him and through him and to him are all things" (Rom. 11:36). Therefore Augustine most truly and according to Scripture declared in his book *De Agone Christi*, cap. 8, "The Lord said, 'Are not two sparrows sold for a penny? And not one of them will fall to the ground without your Father's will' " (Matt. 10:29). By speaking thus, he wanted to show that what men regard as of least value is governed by God's omnipotence. For he who is the truth says that the birds of the air are fed by him and the lilies of the field are clothed by him; he also says that the hairs of our head are numbered (Matt. 6:26 ff.).

5.030 THE EPICUREANS. We therefore condemn the Epicureans who deny the providence of God, and all those who blasphemously say that God is busy with the heavens and neither sees nor cares about us and our affairs. David, the royal prophet, also condemned this when he said: "O Lord, how long shall the wicked exult? They say, 'The Lord does not see; the God of Jacob does not perceive.' Understand, O dullest of the people! Fools, when will you be wise? He who planted the ear, does he not hear? He who formed the eye, does he not see?" (Ps. 94:3, 7-9).

MEANS NOT TO BE DESPISED. Nevertheless, we do not spurn as   **5.031**
useless the means by which divine providence works, but we teach that
we are to adapt ourselves to them in so far as they are recommended to
us in the Word of God. Wherefore we disapprove of the rash statements of those who say that if all things are managed by the providence
of God, then our efforts and endeavors are in vain. It will be sufficient
if we leave everything to the governance of divine providence, and we
will not have to worry about anything or do anything. For although
Paul understood that he sailed under the providence of God who had
said to him: "You must bear witness also at Rome" (Acts 23:11), and
in addition had given him the promise, "There will be no loss of life
among you . . . and not a hair is to perish from the head of any of you"
(Acts 27:22, 34), yet when the sailors were nevertheless thinking about
abandoning ship the same Paul said to the centurion and the soldiers:
"Unless these men stay in the ship, you cannot be saved" (Acts
27:31). For God, who has appointed to everything its end, has
ordained the beginning and the means by which it reaches its goal. The
heathen ascribe things to blind fortune and uncertain chance. But St.
James does not want us to say: "Today or tomorrow we will go into
such and such a town and trade," but adds: "Instead you ought to say,
'If the Lord wills, we shall live and we shall do this or that'" (James
4:13, 15). And Augustine says: "Everything which to vain men seems
to happen in nature by accident, occurs only by his Word, because it
happens only at his command" (*Enarrationes in Psalmos* 148). Thus it
seemed to happen by mere chance when Saul, while seeking his
father's asses, unexpectedly fell in with the prophet Samuel. But
previously the Lord had said to the prophet: "Tomorrow I will send to
you a man from the land of Benjamin" (I Sam. 9:16).

CHAPTER VII

Of the Creation of All Things: Of Angels,
the Devil, and Man

GOD CREATED ALL THINGS. This good and almighty God created all   **5.032**
things, both visible and invisible, by his co-eternal Word, and
preserves them by his co-eternal Spirit, as David testified when he
said: "By the word of the Lord the heavens were made, and all their
host by the breath of his mouth" (Ps. 33:6). And, as Scripture says,
everything that God had made was very good, and was made for the
profit and use of man. Now we assert that all those things proceed
from one beginning. MANICHAEANS AND MARCIONITES. Therefore,
we condemn the Manichaeans and Marcionites who impiously
imagined two substances and natures, one good, the other evil; also
two beginnings and two gods contrary to each other, a good and an evil
one.

5.033   OF ANGELS AND THE DEVIL. Among all creatures, angels and men are most excellent. Concerning angels, Holy Scripture declares: "Who makest the winds thy messengers, fire and flame thy ministers" (Ps. 104:4). Also it says: "Are they not all ministering spirits sent forth to serve, for the sake of those who are to obtain salvation?" (Heb. 1:14). Concerning the devil, the Lord Jesus himself testifies: "He was a murderer from the beginning, and has nothing to do with the truth, because there is no truth in him. When he lies, he speaks according to his own nature, for he is a liar and the father of lies" (John 8:44). Consequently we teach that some angels persisted in obedience and were appointed for faithful service to God and men, but others fell of their own free will and were cast into destruction, becoming enemies of all good and of the faithful, etc.

5.034   OF MAN. Now concerning man, Scripture says that in the beginning he was made good according to the image and likeness of God;[2] that God placed him in Paradise and made all things subject to him (Gen., ch. 2). This is what David magnificently sets forth in Psalm 8. Moreover, God gave him a wife and blessed them. We also affirm that man consists of two different substances in one person: an immortal soul which, when separated from the body, neither sleeps nor dies, and a mortal body which will nevertheless be raised up from the dead at the last judgment, in order that then the whole man, either in life or in death, abide forever.

5.035   THE SECTS. We condemn all who ridicule or by subtle arguments cast doubt upon the immortality of souls, or who say that the soul sleeps or is a part of God. In short, we condemn all opinions of all men, however many, that depart from what has been delivered unto us by the Holy Scriptures in the apostolic Church of Christ concerning creation, angels, and demons, and man.

CHAPTER VIII

Of Man's Fall, Sin and the Cause of Sin

5.036   THE FALL OF MAN. In the beginning, man was made according to the image of God, in righteousness and true holiness, good and upright. But when at the instigation of the serpent and by his own fault he abandoned goodness and righteousness, he became subject to sin, death and various calamities. And what he became by the fall, that is, subject to sin, death and various calamities, so are all those who have descended from him.

5.037   SIN. By sin we understand that innate corruption of man which has been derived or propagated in us all from our first parents, by which we, immersed in perverse desires and averse to all good, are inclined

---

[2] *Ad imaginem et simulitudinem Dei.*

to all evil. Full of all wickedness, distrust, contempt and hatred of God, we are unable to do or even to think anything good of ourselves. Moreover, even as we grow older, so by wicked thoughts, words and deeds committed against God's law, we bring forth corrupt fruit worthy of an evil tree (Matt. 12:33 ff.). For this reason by our own deserts, being subject to the wrath of God, we are liable to just punishment, so that all of us would have been cast away by God if Christ, the Deliverer, had not brought us back.

DEATH. By death we understand not only bodily death, which all of   **5.038**
us must once suffer on account of sins, but also eternal punishment due to our sins and corruption. For the apostle says: "We were dead through trespasses and sins . . . and were by nature children of wrath, like the rest of mankind. But God, who is rich in mercy . . . even when we were dead through our trespasses, made us alive together with Christ" (Eph. 2:1 ff.). Also: "As sin came into the world through one man and death through sin, and so death spread to all men because all men sinned" (Rom. 5:12).

ORIGINAL SIN. We therefore acknowledge that there is original sin   **5.039**
in all men. ACTUAL SINS. We acknowledge that all other sins which arise from it are called and truly are sins, no matter by what name they may be called, whether mortal, venial or that which is said to be the sin against the Holy Spirit which is never forgiven (Mark 3:29; I John 5:16). We also confess that sins are not equal; although they arise from the same fountain of corruption and unbelief, some are more serious than others. As the Lord said, it will be more tolerable for Sodom than for the city that rejects the word of the Gospel (Matt. 10:14 f.; 11:20 ff.).

THE SECTS. We therefore condemn all who have taught contrary to   **5.040**
this, especially Pelagius and all Pelagians, together with the Jovinians who, with the Stoics, regard all sins as equal. In this whole matter we agree with St. Augustine who derived and defended his view from Holy Scriptures. Moreover, we condemn Florinus and Blastus, against whom Irenaeus wrote, and all who make God the author of sin.

GOD IS NOT THE AUTHOR OF SIN, AND HOW FAR HE IS SAID TO   **5.041**
HARDEN. It is expressly written: "Thou art not a God who delights in wickedness. Thou hatest all evildoers. Thou destroyest those who speak lies" (Ps. 5:4 ff.). And again: "When the devil lies, he speaks according to his own nature, for he is a liar and the father of lies" (John 8:44). Moreover, there is enough sinfulness and corruption in us that it is not necessary for God to infuse into us a new or still greater perversity. When, therefore, it is said in Scripture that God hardens, blinds and delivers up to a reprobate mind, it is to be understood that God does it by a just judgment as a just Judge and Avenger. Finally, as often as God in Scripture is said or seems to do something evil, it is not thereby said that man does not do evil, but that God permits it and does not prevent it, according to his just judgment, who could prevent it if he wished, or because he turns man's evil into good, as he did in the case of the sin of Joseph's brethren, or because he governs sins lest

they break out and rage more than is appropriate. St. Augustine writes in his *Enchiridion:* "What happens contrary to his will occurs, in a wonderful and ineffable way, not apart from his will. For it would not happen if he did not allow it. And yet he does not allow it unwillingly but willingly. But he who is good would not permit evil to be done, unless, being omnipotent, he could bring good out of evil." Thus wrote Augustine.

5.042   CURIOUS QUESTIONS. Other questions, such as whether God willed Adam to fall, or incited him to fall, or why he did not prevent the fall, and similar questions, we reckon among curious questions (unless perchance the wickedness of heretics or of other churlish men compels us also to explain them out of the Word of God, as the godly teachers of the Church have frequently done), knowing that the Lord forbade man to eat of the forbidden fruit and punished his transgression. We also know that what things are done are not evil with respect to the providence, will, and power of God, but in respect of Satan and our will opposing the will of God.

CHAPTER IX

Of Free Will, and Thus of Human Powers

5.043   In this matter, which has always produced many conflicts in the Church, we teach that a threefold condition or state of man is to be considered. WHAT MAN WAS BEFORE THE FALL. There is the state in which man was in the beginning before the fall, namely, upright and free, so that he could both continue in goodness and decline to evil. However, he declined to evil, and has involved himself and the whole human race in sin and death, as has been said already. WHAT MAN WAS AFTER THE FALL. Then we are to consider what man was after the fall. To be sure, his reason was not taken from him, nor was he deprived of will, and he was not entirely changed into a stone or a tree. But they were so altered and weakened that they no longer can do what they could before the fall. For the understanding is darkened, and the will which was free has become an enslaved will. Now it serves sin, not unwillingly but willingly. And indeed, it is called a will, not an unwill (ing).[3]

5.044   MAN DOES EVIL BY HIS OWN FREE WILL. Therefore, in regard to evil or sin, man is not forced by God or by the devil but does evil by his own free will, and in this respect he has a most free will. But when we frequently see that the worst crimes and designs of men are prevented by God from reaching their purpose, this does not take away man's freedom in doing evil, but God by his own power prevents what

---

[3] *Etenim voluntas, non noluntas dicitur.*

man freely planned otherwise. Thus Joseph's brothers freely determined to get rid of him, but they were unable to do it because something else seemed good to the counsel of God.

MAN IS NOT CAPABLE OF GOOD *Per Se.* In regard to goodness and   **5.045**
virtue man's reason does not judge rightly of itself concerning divine things. For the evangelical and apostolic Scripture requires regeneration of whoever among us wishes to be saved. Hence our first birth from Adam contributes nothing to our salvation. Paul says: "The unspiritual man does not receive the gifts of the Spirit of God," etc. (I Cor. 2:14). And in another place he denies that we of ourselves are capable of thinking anything good (II Cor. 3:5). Now it is known that the mind or intellect is the guide of the will, and when the guide is blind, it is obvious how far the will reaches. Wherefore, man not yet regenerate has no free will for good, no strength to perform what is good. The Lord says in the Gospel: "Truly, truly, I say to you, everyone who commits sin is a slave to sin" (John 8:34). And the apostle Paul says: "The mind that is set on the flesh is hostile to God; it does not submit to God's law, indeed it cannot" (Rom. 8:7). Yet in regard to earthly things, fallen man is not entirely lacking in understanding.

UNDERSTANDING OF THE ARTS. For God in his mercy has permitted   **5.046**
the powers of the intellect to remain, though differing greatly from what was in man before the fall. God commands us to cultivate our natural talents, and meanwhile adds both gifts and success. And it is obvious that we make no progress in all the arts without God's blessing. In any case, Scripture refers all the arts to God; and, indeed, the heathen trace the origin of the arts to the gods who invented them.

OF WHAT KIND ARE THE POWERS OF THE REGENERATE, AND IN   **5.047**
WHAT WAY THEIR WILLS ARE FREE. Finally, we must see whether the regenerate have free wills, and to what extent. In regeneration the understanding is illumined by the Holy Spirit in order that it may understand both the mysteries and the will of God. And the will itself is not only changed by the Spirit, but it is also equipped with faculties so that it wills and is able to do the good of its own accord (Rom. 8:1 ff.) Unless we grant this, we will deny Christian liberty and introduce a legal bondage. But the prophet has God saying: "I will put my law within them, and I will write it upon their hearts" (Jer. 31:33; Ezek. 36:26 f.). The Lord also says in the Gospel: "If the Son makes you free, you will be free indeed" (John 8:36). Paul also writes to the Philippians: "It has been granted to you that for the sake of Christ you should not only believe in him but also suffer for his sake" (Phil. 1:29). Again: "I am sure that he who began a good work in you will bring it to completion at the day of Jesus Christ" (v. 6). Also: "God is at work in you, both to will and to work for his good pleasure" (ch. 2:13).

THE REGENERATE WORK NOT ONLY PASSIVELY BUT ACTIVELY.   **5.048**
However, in this connection we teach that there are two things to be observed: First, that the regenerate, in choosing and doing good, work

not only passively but actively. For they are moved by God that they may do themselves what they do. For Augustine rightly adduces the saying that "God is said to be our helper. But no one can be helped unless he does something." The Manichaeans robbed man of all activity and made him like a stone or a block of wood.

5.049   THE FREE WILL IS WEAK IN THE REGENERATE. Secondly, in the regenerate a weakness remains. For since sin dwells in us, and in the regenerate the flesh struggles against the Spirit till the end of our lives, they do not easily accomplish in all things what they had planned. These things are confirmed by the apostle in Rom., ch. 7, and Gal., ch. 5. Therefore that free will is weak in us on account of the remnants of the old Adam and of innate human corruption remaining in us until the end of our lives. Meanwhile, since the powers of the flesh and the remnants of the old man are not so efficacious that they wholly extinguish the work of the Spirit, for that reason the faithful are said to be free, yet so that they acknowledge their infirmity and do not glory at all in their free will. For believers ought always to keep in mind what St. Augustine so many times inculcated according to the apostle: "What have you that you did not receive? If then you received it, why do you boast as if it were not a gift?" To this he adds that what we have planned does not immediately come to pass. For the issue of things lies in the hand of God. This is the reason Paul prayed to the Lord to prosper his journey (Rom. 1:10). And this also is the reason the free will is weak.

5.050   IN EXTERNAL THINGS THERE IS LIBERTY. Moreover, no one denies that in external things both the regenerate and the unregenerate enjoy free will. For man has in common with other living creatures (to which he is not inferior) this nature to will some things and not to will others. Thus he is able to speak or to keep silent, to go out of his house or to remain at home, etc. However, even here God's power is always to be observed, for it was the cause that Balaam could not go as far as he wanted (Num., ch. 24), and Zacharias upon returning from the temple could not speak as he wanted (Luke, ch. 1).

5.051   HERESIES. In this matter we condemn the Manichaeans who deny that the beginning of evil was for man [created] good, from his free will. We also condemn the Pelagians who assert that an evil man has sufficient free will to do the good that is commanded. Both are refuted by Holy Scripture which says to the former, "God made man upright" and to the latter, "If the Son makes you free, you will be free indeed" (John 8:36).

CHAPTER X

Of the Predestination of God and the Election of the Saints

5.052   GOD HAS ELECTED US OUT OF GRACE. From eternity God has freely, and of his mere grace, without any respect to men, predestinated or elected the saints whom he wills to save in Christ, according to the saying of the apostle, "God chose us in him before the foundation of the world" (Eph. 1:4). And again: "Who saved us and called us with a holy calling, not in virtue of our works but in virtue of his own purpose and the grace which he gave us in Christ Jesus ages ago, and now has manifested through the appearing of our Savior Christ Jesus" (II Tim. 1:9 f.).

WE ARE ELECTED OR PREDESTINATED IN CHRIST. Therefore, although not on account of any merit of ours, God has elected us, not directly, but in Christ, and on account of Christ, in order that those who are now ingrafted into Christ by faith might also be elected. But those who were outside Christ were rejected, according to the word of the apostle, "Examine yourselves, to see whether you are holding to your faith. Test yourselves. Do you not realize that Jesus Christ is in you?—unless indeed you fail to meet the test!" (II Cor. 13:5).   **5.053**

WE ARE ELECTED FOR A DEFINITE PURPOSE. Finally, the saints are chosen in Christ by God for a definite purpose, which the apostle himself explains when he says, "He chose us in him for adoption that we should be holy and blameless before him in love. He destined us for adoption to be his sons through Jesus Christ that they should be to the praise of the glory of his grace" (Eph. 1:4 ff.).   **5.054**

WE ARE TO HAVE A GOOD HOPE FOR ALL. And although God knows who are his, and here and there mention is made of the small number of elect, yet we must hope well of all, and not rashly judge any man to be a reprobate. For Paul says to the Philippians, "I thank my God for you all" (now he speaks of the whole Church in Philippi), "because of your fellowship in the Gospel, being persuaded that he who began a good work in you will bring it to completion at the day of Jesus Christ. It is also right that I have this opinion of you all" (Phil. 1:3 ff.).   **5.055**

WHETHER FEW ARE ELECT. And when the Lord was asked whether there were few that should be saved, he does not answer and tell them that few or many should be saved or damned, but rather he exhorts every man to "strive to enter by the narrow door" (Luke 13:24): as if he should say, It is not for you curiously to inquire about these matters, but rather to endeavor that you may enter into heaven by the straight way.   **5.056**

WHAT IN THIS MATTER IS TO BE CONDEMNED. Therefore we do not approve of the impious speeches of some who say, "Few are chosen, and since I do not know whether I am among the number of the few, I will enjoy myself." Others say, "If I am predestinated and elected by God, nothing can hinder me from salvation, which is already certainly appointed for me, no matter what I do. But if I am in the number of the reprobate, no faith or repentance will help me, since the decree of God cannot be changed. Therefore all doctrines and admonitions are useless." Now the saying of the apostle contradicts these men: "The Lord's servant must be ready to teach, instructing those who oppose him, so that if God should grant that they repent to know the truth,   **5.057** they may recover from the snare of the devil, after being held captive by him to do his will" (II Tim. 2:23 ff.).

5.058 ADMONITIONS ARE NOT IN VAIN BECAUSE SALVATION PROCEEDS FROM ELECTION. Augustine also shows that both the grace of free election and predestination, and also salutary admonitions and doctrines, are to be preached (*Lib. de Dono Perseverantiae*, cap. 14 ff.).

5.059 WHETHER WE ARE ELECTED. We therefore find fault with those who outside of Christ ask whether they are elected.[4] And what has God decreed concerning them before all eternity? For the preaching of the Gospel is to be heard, and it is to be believed; and it is to be held as beyond doubt that if you believe and are in Christ, you are elected. For the Father has revealed unto us in Christ the eternal purpose of his predestination, as I have just now shown from the apostle in II Tim. 1:9-10. This is therefore above all to be taught and considered, what great love of the Father toward us is revealed to us in Christ. We must hear what the Lord himself daily preaches to us in the Gospel, how he calls and says: "Come to me all who labor and are heavy-laden, and I will give you rest" (Matt. 11:28). "God so loved the world, that he gave his only Son, that whoever believes in him should not perish, but have eternal life" (John 3:16). Also, "It is not the will of my Father that one of these little ones should perish" (Matt. 18:14).

5.060 Let Christ, therefore be the looking glass, in whom we may contemplate our predestination. We shall have a sufficiently clear and sure testimony that we are inscribed in the Book of Life if we have fellowship with Christ, and he is ours and we are his in true faith.

5.061 TEMPTATION IN REGARD TO PREDESTINATION. In the temptation in regard to predestination, than which there is scarcely any other more dangerous, we are confronted by the fact that God's promises apply to all the faithful, for he says: "Ask, and everyone who seeks, shall receive" (Luke 11:9 f.). This finally we pray, with the whole Church of God, "Our Father who art in heaven" (Matt. 6:9), both because by baptism we are ingrafted into the body of Christ, and we are often fed in his Church with his flesh and blood unto life eternal. Thereby, being strengthened, we are commanded to work out our salvation with fear and trembling, according to the precept of Paul.

CHAPTER XI

Of Jesus Christ, True God and Man,
the Only Savior of the World

5.062 CHRIST IS TRUE GOD. We further believe and teach that the Son of God, our Lord Jesus Christ, was predestinated or foreordained from eternity by the Father to be the Savior of the world. And we believe

---

[4]Ed. 1568 reads: "whether they are elected from eternity?"

that he was born, not only when he assumed flesh of the Virgin Mary, and not only before the foundation of the world was laid, but by the Father before all eternity in an inexpressible manner. For Isaiah said: "Who can tell his generation?" (Ch. 53:8). And Micah says: "His origin is from of old, from ancient days" (Micah 5:2). And John said in the Gospel: "In the beginning was the Word, and the Word was with God, and the Word was God," etc. (Ch. 1:1). Therefore, with respect to his divinity the Son is coequal and consubstantial with the Father; true God (Phil. 2:11), not only in name or by adoption or by any merit, but in substance and nature, as the apostle John has often said: "This is the true God and eternal life" (I John 5:20). Paul also says: "He appointed the Son the heir of all things, through whom also he created the world. He reflects the glory of God and bears the very stamp of his nature, upholding all things by his word of power" (Heb. 1:2 f.). For in the Gospel the Lord himself said: "Father, glorify Thou me in Thy own presence with the glory which I had with Thee before the world was made" (John 17:5). And in another place in the Gospel it is written: "The Jews sought all the more to kill him because he . . . called God his Father, making himself equal with God" (John 5:18).

THE SECTS. We therefore abhor the impious doctrine of Arius and the Arians against the Son of God, and especially the blasphemies of the Spaniard, Michael Servetus, and all his followers, which Satan through them has, as it were, dragged up out of hell and has most audaciously and impiously spread abroad in the world.   5.063

CHRIST IS TRUE MAN, HAVING REAL FLESH. We also believe and teach that the eternal Son of the eternal God was made the Son of man, from the seed of Abraham and David, not from the coitus of a man, as the Ebionites said, but was most chastely conceived by the Holy Spirit and born of the ever virgin Mary, as the evangelical history carefully explains to us (Matt., ch. 1). And Paul says: "He took not on him the nature of angels, but of the seed of Abraham." Also the apostle John says that whoever does not believe that Jesus Christ has come in the flesh, is not of God. Therefore, the flesh of Christ was neither imaginary nor brought from heaven, as Valentinus and Marcion wrongly imagined.   5.064

A RATIONAL SOUL IN CHRIST. Moreover, our Lord Jesus Christ did not have a soul bereft of sense and reason, as Apollinaris thought, nor flesh without a soul, as Eunomius taught, but a soul with its reason, and flesh with its senses, by which in the time of his passion he sustained real bodily pain, as he himself testified when he said: "My soul is very sorrowful, even to death" (Matt. 26:38). And, "Now is my soul troubled" (John 12:27).   5.065

TWO NATURES IN CHRIST. We therefore acknowledge two natures or substances, the divine and the human, in one and the same Jesus Christ our Lord (Heb., ch. 2). And we say that these are bound and united with one another in such a way that they are not absorbed, or confused, or mixed, but are united or joined together in one person—the properties of the natures being unimpaired and permanent.   5.066

5.067   NOT TWO BUT ONE CHRIST. Thus we worship not two but one Christ the Lord. We repeat: one true God and man. With respect to his divine nature he is consubstantial with the Father, and with respect to the human nature he is consubstantial with us men, and like us in all things, sin excepted (Heb. 4:15).

5.068   THE SECTS. And indeed we detest the dogma of the Nestorians who make two of the one Christ and dissolve the unity of the Person. Likewise we thoroughly execrate the madness of Eutyches and of the Monothelites or Monophysites who destroy the property of the human nature.

5.069   THE DIVINE NATURE OF CHRIST IS NOT PASSIBLE, AND THE HUMAN NATURE IS NOT EVERYWHERE. Therefore, we do not in anyway teach that the divine nature in Christ has suffered or that Christ according to his human nature is still in this world and thus is everywhere. For neither do we think or teach that the body of Christ ceased to be a true body after his glorification, or was deified, and deified in such a way that it laid aside its properties as regards body and soul, and changed entirely into a divine nature and began to be merely one substance.

5.070   THE SECTS. Hence we by no means approve of or accept the strained, confused and obscure subtleties of Schwenkfeldt and of similar sophists with their self-contradictory arguments; neither are we Schwenkfeldians.

5.071   OUR LORD TRULY SUFFERED. We believe, moreover, that our Lord Jesus Christ truly suffered and died for us in the flesh, as Peter says (I Peter 4:1). We abhor the most impious madness of the Jacobites and all the Turks who execrate the suffering of the Lord. At the same time we do not deny that the Lord of glory was crucified for us, according to Paul's words (I Cor. 2:8).

5.072   IMPARTATION OF PROPERTIES. We piously and reverently accept and use the impartation of properties which is derived from Scripture and which has been used by all antiquity in explaining and reconciling apparently contradictory passages.

5.073   CHRIST IS TRULY RISEN FROM THE DEAD. We believe and teach that the same Jesus Christ our Lord, in his true flesh in which he was crucified and died, rose again from the dead, and that not another flesh was raised other than the one buried, or that a spirit was taken up instead of the flesh, but that he retained his true body. Therefore, while his disciples thought they saw the spirit of the Lord, he showed them his hands and feet which were marked by the prints of the nails and wounds, and added: "See my hands and my feet, that it is I myself; handle me, and see, for a spirit has not flesh and bones as you see that I have" (Luke 24:39).

5.074   CHRIST IS TRULY ASCENDED INTO HEAVEN. We believe that our Lord Jesus Christ, in his same flesh, ascended above all visible heavens into the highest heaven, that is, the dwelling-place of God and the blessed ones, at the right hand of God the Father. Although it signifies an equal participation in glory and majesty, it is also taken to be a certain place about which the Lord, speaking in the Gospel, says: "I go to prepare a place for you" (John 14:2). The apostle Peter also says: "Heaven must receive Christ until the time of restoring all things" (Acts 3:21). And from heaven the same Christ will return in judgment, when wickedness will then be at its greatest in the world and when the Antichrist, having corrupted true religion, will fill up all things with superstition and impiety and will cruelly lay waste the Church with bloodshed and flames (Dan., ch. 11). But Christ will come again to claim his own, and by his coming to destroy the Antichrist, and to judge the living and the dead (Acts 17:31). For the dead will rise again (I Thess. 4:14 ff.), and those who on that day (which is unknown to all creatures [Mark 13:32]) will be alive will be changed "in the twinkling of an eye," and all the faithful will be caught up to meet Christ in the air, so that then they may enter with him into the blessed dwelling-places to live forever (I Cor. 15:51 f.). But the unbelievers and ungodly will descend with the devils into hell to burn forever and never to be redeemed from torments (Matt. 25:46).

THE SECTS. We therefore condemn all who deny a real resurrection   5.075
of the flesh (II Tim. 2:18), or who with John of Jerusalem, against whom Jerome wrote, do not have a correct view of the glorification of bodies. We also condemn those who thought that the devil and all the ungodly would at some time be saved, and that there would be an end to punishments. For the Lord has plainly declared: "Their fire is not quenched, and their worm does not die" (Mark 9:44). We further condemn Jewish dreams that there will be a golden age on earth before the Day of Judgment, and that the pious, having subdued all their godless enemies, will possess all the kingdoms of the earth. For evangelical truth in Matt., chs. 24 and 25, and Luke, ch. 18, and apostolic teaching in II Thess., ch. 2, and II Tim., chs. 3 and 4, present something quite different.

THE FRUIT OF CHRIST'S DEATH AND RESURRECTION. Further by his   5.076
passion and death and everything which he did and endured for our sake by his coming in the flesh, our Lord reconciled all the faithful to the heavenly Father, made expiation for sins, disarmed death, overcame damnation and hell, and by his resurrection from the dead brought again and restored life and immortality. For he is our righteousness, life and resurrection, in a word, the fulness and perfection of all the faithful, salvation and all sufficiency. For the apostle says: "In him all the fulness of God was pleased to dwell," and, "You have come to fulness of life in him" (Col., chs. 1 and 2).

JESUS CHRIST IS THE ONLY SAVIOR OF THE WORLD, AND THE TRUE   5.077
AWAITED MESSIAH. For we teach and believe that this Jesus Christ our Lord is the unique and eternal Savior of the human race, and thus of the whole world, in whom by faith are saved all who before the law, under the law, and under the Gospel were saved, and however many will be saved at the end of the world. For the Lord himself says in the Gospel: "He who does not enter the sheepfold by the door but climbs in by another way, that man is a thief and a robber. . . . I am the door

of the sheep" (John 10:1 and 7). And also in another place in the same Gospel he says: "Abraham saw my day and was glad" (ch. 8:56). The apostle Peter also says: "There is salvation in no one else, for there is no other name under heaven given among men by which we must be saved." We therefore believe that we will be saved through the grace of our Lord Jesus Christ, as our fathers were (Acts 4:12, 10:43; 15:11). For Paul also says: "All our fathers ate the same spiritual food, and all drank the same spiritual drink. For they drank from the spiritual Rock which followed them, and the Rock was Christ" (I Cor. 10:3 f.). And thus we read that John says: "Christ was the Lamb which was slain from the foundation of the world" (Rev. 13:8), and John the Baptist testified that Christ is that "Lamb of God, who takes away the sin of the world" (John 1:29). Wherefore, we quite openly profess and preach that Jesus Christ is the sole Redeemer and Savior of the world, the King and High Priest, the true and awaited Messiah, that holy and blessed one whom all the types of the law and predictions of the prophets prefigured and promised; and that God appointed him before-hand and sent him to us, so that we are not now to look for any other. Now there only remains for all of us to give all glory to Christ, believe in him, rest in him alone, despising and rejecting all other aids in life. For however many seek salvation in any other than in Christ alone, have fallen from the grace of God and have rendered Christ null and void for themselves (Gal. 5:4).

5.078   THE CREEDS OF FOUR COUNCILS RECEIVED. And, to say many things with a few words, with a sincere heart we believe, and freely confess with open mouth, whatever things are defined from the Holy Scriptures concerning the mystery of the incarnation of our Lord Jesus Christ, and are summed up in the Creeds and decrees of the first four most excellent synods convened at Nicaea, Constantinople, Ephesus and Chalcedon—together with the Creed of blessed Athanasius,[5] and all similar symbols; and we condemn everything contrary to these.

5.079   THE SECTS. And in this way we retain the Christian, orthodox and catholic faith whole and unimpaired; knowing that nothing is contained in the aforesaid symbols which is not agreeable to the Word of God, and does not altogether make for a sincere exposition of the faith.

CHAPTER XII

Of the Law of God

5.080   THE WILL OF GOD IS EXPLAINED FOR US IN THE LAW OF GOD. We teach that the will of God is explained for us in the law of God, what he wills or does not will us to do, what is good and just, or what is evil and unjust. Therefore, we confess that the law is good and holy.

---

[5]The so-called Athanasian Creed was not written by Athanasius but dates from the ninth century. It is also called the "Quicunque" from the opening word of the Latin text.

THE LAW OF NATURE. And this law was at one time written in the **5.081** hearts of men by the finger of God (Rom. 2:15), and is called the law of nature (*the law of Moses is in two Tables*), and at another it was inscribed by his finger on the two Tables of Moses, and eloquently expounded in the books of Moses (Ex. 20:1 ff.; Deut. 5:6 ff.). For the sake of clarity we distinguish the moral law which is contained in the Decalogue or two Tables and expounded in the books of Moses, the ceremonial law which determines the ceremonies and worship of God, and the judicial law which is concerned with political and domestic matters.

THE LAW IS COMPLETE AND PERFECT. We believe that the whole **5.082** will of God and all necessary precepts for every sphere of life are taught in this law. For otherwise the Lord would not have forbidden us to add or to take away anything from this law; neither would he have commanded us to walk in a straight path before this law, and not to turn aside from it by turning to the right or to the left (Deut. 4:2; 12:32).

WHY THE LAW WAS GIVEN. We teach that this law was not given to **5.083** men that they might be justified by keeping it, but that rather from what it teaches we may know (our) weakness, sin and condemnation, and, despairing of our strength, might be converted to Christ in faith. For the apostle openly declares: "The law brings wrath," and, "Through the law comes knowledge of sin" (Rom. 4:15; 3:20), and, "If a law had been given which could justify or make alive, then righteousness would indeed be by the law. But the Scripture (that is, the law) has concluded all under sin, that the promise which was of the faith of Jesus might be given to those who believe . . . Therefore, the law was our schoolmaster unto Christ, that we might be justified by faith" (Gal. 3:21 ff.).

THE FLESH DOES NOT FULFIL THE LAW. For no flesh could or can **5.084** satisfy the law of God and fulfil it, because of the weakness in our flesh which adheres and remains in us until our last breath. For the apostle says again: "God has done what the law, weakened by the flesh, could not do: sending his own Son in the likeness of sinful flesh and for sin" (Rom. 8:3). Therefore, Christ is the perfecting of the law and our fulfilment of it (Rom. 10:4), who, in order to take away the curse of the law, was made a curse for us (Gal. 3:13). Thus he imparts to us through faith his fulfilment of the law, and his righteousness and obedience are imputed to us.

HOW FAR THE LAW IS ABROGATED. The law of God is therefore **5.085** abrogated to the extent that it no longer condemns us, nor works wrath in us. For we are under grace and not under the law. Moreover, Christ has fulfilled all the figures of the law. Hence, with the coming of the body, the shadows ceased, so that in Christ we now have the truth and all fulness. But yet we do not on that account contemptuously reject the law. For we remember the words of the Lord when he said: "I have not come to abolish the law and the prophets but to fulfil them" (Matt. 5:17). We know that in the law is delivered to us the patterns of virtues and vices. We know that the written law when explained by the Gospel is useful to the Church, and that therefore its reading is not to be banished from the Church. For although Moses' face was covered with a veil, yet the apostle says that the veil has been taken away and abolished by Christ. THE SECTS. We condemn everything that heretics old and new have taught against the law.

CHAPTER XIII

Of the Gospel of Jesus Christ, of the Promises, and of the Spirit and Letter

5.086   THE ANCIENTS HAD EVANGELICAL PROMISES. The Gospel is, indeed, opposed to the law. For the law works wrath and announces a curse, whereas the Gospel preaches grace and blessing. John says: "For the law was given through Moses; grace and truth came through Jesus Christ" (John 1:17). Yet notwithstanding it is most certain that those who were before the law and under the law, were not altogether destitute of the Gospel. For they had extraordinary evangelical promises such as these are: "The seed of the woman shall bruise the serpent's head" (Gen. 3:15). "In thy seed shall all the nations of the earth be blessed" (Gen. 22:18). "The scepter shall not depart from Judah . . . until he comes" (Gen. 49:10). "The Lord will raise up a prophet from among his own brethren" (Deut. 18:15; Acts 3:22), etc.

5.087   THE PROMISES TWOFOLD. And we acknowledge that two kinds of promises were revealed to the fathers, as also to us. For some were of present or earthly things, such as the promises of the Land of Canaan and of victories, and as the promise today still of daily bread. Others were then and are still now of heavenly and eternal things, namely, divine grace, remission of sins, and eternal life through faith in Jesus Christ.

5.088   THE FATHERS ALSO HAD NOT ONLY CARNAL BUT SPIRITUAL PROMISES. Moreover, the ancients had not only external and earthly but also spiritual and heavenly promises in Christ. Peter says: "The prophets who prophesied of the grace that was to be yours searched and inquired about this salvation" (I Peter 1:10). Wherefore the apostle Paul also said: "The Gospel of God was promised beforehand through his prophets in the holy scriptures" (Rom. 1:2). Thereby it is clear that the ancients were not entirely destitute of the whole Gospel.

5.089   WHAT IS THE GOSPEL PROPERLY SPEAKING? And although our fathers had the Gospel in this way in the writings of the prophets by which they attained salvation in Christ through faith, yet the Gospel is properly called glad and joyous news, in which, first by John the Baptist, then by Christ the Lord himself, and afterwards by the apostles and their successors, is preached to us in the world that God has now performed what he promised from the beginning of the world, and has sent, nay more, has given us his only Son and in him reconciliation with the Father, the remission of sins, all fulness and everlasting life. Therefore, the history delineated by the four Evangelists and explaining how these things were done or fulfilled by Christ, what things Christ taught and did, and that those who believe in him have all fulness, is rightly called the Gospel. The preaching and writings of the apostles, in which the apostles explain for us how the Son was given to us by the Father, and in him everything that has to do with life and salvation, is also rightly called evangelical doctrine, so that not even today, if sincerely preached, does it lose its illustrious title.

OF THE SPIRIT AND THE LETTER. That same preaching of the Gospel   5.090
is also called by the apostle "the spirit" and "the ministry of the spirit" because by faith it becomes effectual and living in the ears, nay more, in the hearts of believers through the illumination of the Holy Spirit (II Cor. 3:6). For the letter, which is opposed to the Spirit, signifies everything external, but especially the doctrine of the law which, without the Spirit and faith, works wrath and provokes sin in the minds of those who do not have a living faith. For this reason the apostle calls it "the ministry of death." In this connection the saying of the apostle is pertinent: "The letter kills, but the Spirit gives life." And false apostles preached a corrupted Gospel, having combined it with the law, as if Christ could not save without the law.

THE SECTS. Such were the Ebionites said to be, who were   5.091
descended from Ebion the heretic, and the Nazarites who were formerly called Mineans. All these we condemn, while preaching the pure Gospel and teaching that believers are justified by the Spirit[6] alone, and not by the law. A more detailed exposition of this matter will follow presently under the heading of justification.

THE TEACHING OF THE GOSPEL IS NOT NEW, BUT MOST ANCIENT   5.092
DOCTRINE. And although the teaching of the Gospel, compared with the teaching of the Pharisees concerning the law, seemed to be a new doctrine when first preached by Christ (which Jeremiah also prophesied concerning the New Testament), yet actually it not only was and still is an old doctrine (even if today it is called new by the Papists when compared with the teaching now received among them), but is the most ancient of all in the world. For God predestinated from eternity to save the world through Christ, and he has disclosed to the world through the Gospel this his predestination and eternal counsel (II Tim. 2:9 f.). Hence it is evident that the religion and teaching of the Gospel among all who ever were, are and will be, is the most ancient of all. Wherefore we assert that all who say that the religion and teaching of the Gospel is a faith which has recently arisen, being scarcely thirty years old, err disgracefully and speak shamefully of the eternal counsel of God. To them applies the saying of Isaiah the

---

[6]The original manuscript has "Christ" instead of "Spirit."

prophet: "Woe to those who call evil good and good evil, who put darkness for light and light for darkness, who put bitter for sweet and sweet for bitter!" (Isa. 5:20).

CHAPTER XIV

Of Repentance and the Conversion of Man

5.093   The doctrine of repentance is joined with the Gospel. For so has the Lord said in the Gospel: "Repentance and forgiveness of sins should be preached in my name to all nations" (Luke 24:47). WHAT IS REPENTANCE? By repentance we understand (1) the recovery of a right mind in sinful man awakened by the Word of the Gospel and the Holy Spirit, and received by true faith, by which the sinner immediately acknowledges his innate corruption and all his sins accused by the Word of God; and (2) grieves for them from his heart, and not only bewails and frankly confesses them before God with a feeling of shame, but also (3) with indignation abominates them; and (4) now zealously considers the amendment of his ways and constantly strives for innocence and virtue in which conscientiously to exercise himself all the rest of his life.

5.094   TRUE REPENTANCE IS CONVERSION TO GOD. And this is true repentance, namely, a sincere turning to God and all good, and earnest turning away from the devil and all evil. 1. REPENTANCE IS A GIFT OF GOD. Now we expressly say that this repentance is a sheer gift of God and not a work of our strength. For the apostle commands a faithful minister diligently to instruct those who oppose the truth, if "God may perhaps grant that they will repent and come to know the truth" (II Tim. 2:25). 2. LAMENTS SINS COMMITTED. Now that sinful woman who washed the feet of the Lord with her tears, and Peter who wept bitterly and bewailed his denial of the Lord (Luke 7:38; 22:62) show clearly how the mind of a penitent man ought to be seriously lamenting the sins he has committed. 3. CONFESSES SINS TO GOD. Moreover, the prodigal son and the publican in the Gospel, when compared with the Pharisee, present us with the most suitable pattern of how our sins are to be confessed to God. The former said: " 'Father, I have sinned against heaven and before you; I am no longer worthy to be called your son; treat me as one of your hired servants' " (Luke 15:8 ff.). And the latter, not daring to raise his eyes to heaven, beat his breast, saying, "God be merciful to me a sinner" (ch. 18:13). And we do not doubt that they were accepted by God into grace. For the apostle John says: "If we confess our sins, he is faithful and just, and will forgive our sins and cleanse us from all unrighteousness. If we say we have not sinned, we make him a liar, and his word is not in us" (I John 1:9 f.).

5.095   SACERDOTAL CONFESSION AND ABSOLUTION. But we believe that this sincere confession which is made to God alone, either privately between God and the sinner, or publicly in the Church where the general confession of sins is said, is sufficient, and that in order to obtain forgiveness of sins it is not necessary for anyone to confess his sins to a priest, murmuring them in his ears, that in turn he might receive absolution from the priest with his laying on of hands, because there is neither a commandment nor an example of this in Holy Scriptures. David testifies and says: "I acknowledged my sin to thee, and did not hide my iniquity; I said, 'I will confess my transgressions to the Lord'; then thou didst forgive the guilt of my sin" (Ps. 32:5). And the Lord who taught us to pray and at the same time to confess our sins said: "Pray then like this: Our Father, who art in heaven, . . . forgive us our debts, as we also forgive our debtors" (Matt. 6:12). Therefore it is necessary that we confess our sins to God our Father, and be reconciled with our neighbor if we have offended him. Concerning this kind of confession, the Apostle James says: "Confess your sins to one another" (James 5:16). If, however, anyone is overwhelmed by the burden of his sins and by perplexing temptations, and will seek counsel, instruction and comfort privately, either from a minister of the Church, or from any other brother who is instructed in God's law, we do not disapprove; just as we also fully approve of that general and public confession of sins which is usually said in Church and in meetings for worship, as we noted above, inasmuch as it is agreeable to Scripture.

OF THE KEYS OF THE KINGDOM OF HEAVEN. Concerning the keys   5.096
of the Kingdom of Heaven which the Lord gave to the apostles, many babble many astonishing things, and out of them forge swords, spears, scepters and crowns, and complete power over the greatest kingdoms, indeed, over souls and bodies. Judging simply according to the Word of the Lord, we say that all properly called ministers possess and exercise the keys or the use of them when they proclaim the Gospel; that is, when they teach, exhort, comfort, rebuke, and keep in discipline the people committed to their trust.

OPENING AND SHUTTING (THE KINGDOM). For in this way they open   5.097
the Kingdom of Heaven to the obedient and shut it to the disobedient. The Lord promised these keys to the apostles in Matt., ch. 16, and gave them in John, ch. 20, Mark, ch. 16, and Luke, ch. 24, when he sent out his disciples and commanded them to preach the Gospel in all the world, and to remit sins.

THE MINISTRY OF RECONCILIATION. In the letter to the Corinthians   5.098
the apostle says that the Lord gave the ministry of reconciliation to his ministers (II Cor. 5:18 ff.). And what this is he then explains, saying that it is the preaching or teaching of reconciliation. And explaining his words still more clearly he adds that Christ's ministers discharge the office of an ambassador in Christ's name, as if God himself through ministers exhorted the people to be reconciled to God, doubtless by faithful obedience. Therefore, they exercise the keys when they persuade [men] to believe and repent. Thus they reconcile men to God.

MINISTERS REMIT SINS. Thus they remit sins. Thus they open the   5.099
Kingdom of Heaven, and bring believers into it: very different from

those of whom the Lord said in the Gospel, "Woe to you lawyers! for you have taken away the key of knowledge; you did not enter yourselves, and you hindered those who were entering."

5.100   HOW MINISTERS ABSOLVE. Ministers, therefore, rightly and effectually absolve when they preach the Gospel of Christ and thereby the remission of sins, which is promised to each one who believes, just as each one is baptized, and when they testify that it pertains to each one peculiarly. Neither do we think that this absolution becomes more effectual by being murmured in the ear of someone or by being murmured singly over someone's head. We are nevertheless of the opinion that the remission of sins in the blood of Christ is to be diligently proclaimed, and that each one is to be admonished that the forgiveness of sins pertains to him.

5.101   DILIGENCE IN THE RENEWAL OF LIFE. But the examples in the Gospel teach us how vigilant and diligent the penitent ought to be in striving for newness of life and in mortifying the old man and quickening the new. For the Lord said to the man he healed of palsy: "See, you are well! Sin no more, that nothing worse befall you" (John 5:14). Likewise to the adulteress whom he set free he said: "Go, and sin no more" (ch. 8:11). To be sure, by these words he did not mean that any man, as long as he lived in the flesh, could not sin; he simply recommends diligence and a careful devotion, so that we should strive by all means, and beseech God in prayers lest we fall back into sins from which, as it were, we have been resurrected, and lest we be overcome by the flesh, the world and the devil. Zacchaeus the publican, whom the Lord had received back into favor, exclaims in the Gospel: "Behold, Lord, the half of my goods I give to the poor; and if I have defrauded any one of anything, I restore it fourfold" (Luke 19:8). Therefore, in the same way we preach that restitution and compassion, and even almsgiving, are necessary for those who truly repent, and we exhort all men everywhere in the words of the apostle: "Let not sin therefore reign in your mortal bodies, to make you obey their passions. Do not yield your members to sin as instruments of wickedness, but yield yourselves to God as men who have been brought from death to life, and your members to God as instruments of righteousness" (Rom. 6:12 f.).

5.102   ERRORS. Wherefore we condemn all impious utterances of some who wrongly use the preaching of the Gospel and say that it is easy to return to God. Christ has atoned for all sins. Forgiveness of sins is easy. Therefore, what harm is there in sinning? Nor need we be greatly concerned about repentance, etc. Notwithstanding we always teach that an access to God is open to all sinners, and that he forgives all sinners of all sins except the one sin against the Holy Spirit (Mark 3:29).

5.103   THE SECTS. Wherefore we condemn both old and new Novatians and Catharists.

5.104   PAPAL INDULGENCES. We especially condemn the lucrative doctrine of the Pope concerning penance, and against his simony and his simoniacal indulgences we avail ourselves of Peter's judgment concerning Simon: "Your silver perish with you, because you thought you could obtain the gift of God with money! You have neither part nor lot in this matter, for your heart is not right before God" (Acts 8:20 f.).

SATISFACTIONS. We also disapprove of those who think that by their own satisfactions they make amends for sins committed. For we teach that Christ alone by his death or passion is the satisfaction, propitiation or expiation of all sins (Isa., ch. 53; I Cor. 1:30). Yet as we have already said, we do not cease to urge the mortification of the flesh. We add, however, that this mortification is not to be proudly obtruded upon God as a satisfaction for sins, but is to be performed humbly, in keeping with the nature of the children of God, as a new obedience out of gratitude for the deliverance and full satisfaction obtained by the death and satisfaction of the Son of God.   5.105

CHAPTER XV

Of the True Justification of the Faithful

WHAT IS JUSTIFICATION? According to the apostle in his treatment of justification, to justify means to remit sins, to absolve from guilt and punishment, to receive into favor, and to pronounce a man just. For in his epistle to the Romans the apostle says: "It is God who justifies; who is to condemn?" (Rom. 8:33). To justify and to condemn are opposed. And in The Acts of the Apostles the apostle states: "Through Christ forgiveness of sins is proclaimed to you, and by him everyone that believes is freed from everything from which you could not be freed by the law of Moses" (Acts 13:38 f.). For in the Law and also in the Prophets we read: "If there is a dispute between men, and they come into court . . . the judges decide between them, acquitting the innocent and condemning the guilty" (Deut. 25:1). And in Isa., ch. 5: "Woe to those . . . who acquit the guilty for a bribe."   5.106

WE ARE JUSTIFIED ON ACCOUNT OF CHRIST. Now it is most certain that all of us are by nature sinners and godless, and before God's judgment-seat are convicted of godlessness and are guilty of death, but that, solely by the grace of Christ and not from any merit of ours or consideration for us, we are justified, that is, absolved from sin and death by God the Judge. For what is clearer than what Paul said: "Since all have sinned and fall short of the glory of God, they are justified by his grace as a gift, through the redemption which is in Christ Jesus" (Rom. 3:23 f.).   5.107

IMPUTED RIGHTEOUSNESS. For Christ took upon himself and bore the sins of the world, and satisfied divine justice. Therefore, solely on account of Christ's sufferings and resurrection God is propitious with respect to our sins and does not impute them to us, but imputes Christ's righteousness to us as our own (II Cor. 5:19 ff.; Rom. 4:25), so that now we are not only cleansed and purged from sins or are holy,   5.108

but also, granted the righteousness of Christ, and so absolved from sin, death and condemnation, are at last righteous and heirs of eternal life. Properly speaking, therefore, God alone justifies us, and justifies only on account of Christ, not imputing sins to us but imputing his righteousness to us.

5.109   WE ARE JUSTIFIED BY FAITH ALONE. But because we receive this justification, not through any works, but through faith in the mercy of God and in Christ, we therefore teach and believe with the apostle that sinful man is justified by faith alone in Christ, not by the law or any works. For the apostle says: "We hold that a man is justified by faith apart from works of law" (Rom. 3:28). Also: "If Abraham was justified by works, he has something to boast about, but not before God. For what does the scripture say? Abraham believed God, and it was reckoned to him as righteousness. . . . And to one who does not work but believes in him who justifies the ungodly, his faith is reckoned as righteousness" (Rom. 4:2 ff.; Gen. 15:6). And again: "By grace you have been saved through faith; and this is not your own doing, it is the gift of God—not because of works, lest any man should boast," etc. (Eph. 2:8 f.). Therefore, because faith receives Christ our righteousness and attributes everything to the grace of God in Christ, on that account justification is attributed to faith, chiefly because of Christ and not therefore because it is our work. For it is the gift of God.

5.110   WE RECEIVE CHRIST BY FAITH. Moreover, the Lord abundantly shows that we receive Christ by faith, in John, ch. 6, where he puts eating for believing, and believing for eating. For as we receive food by eating, so we participate in Christ by believing. JUSTIFICATION IS NOT ATTRIBUTED PARTLY TO CHRIST OR TO FAITH, PARTLY TO US. Therefore, we do not share in the benefit of justification partly because of the grace of God or Christ, and partly because of ourselves, our love, works or merit, but we attribute it wholly to the grace of God in Christ through faith. For our love and our works could not please God if performed by unrighteous men. Therefore, it is necessary for us to be righteous before we may love and do good works. We are made truly righteous, as we have said, by faith in Christ purely by the grace of God, who does not impute to us our sins, but the righteousness of Christ, or rather, he imputes faith in Christ to us for righteousness. Moreover, the apostle very clearly derives love from faith when he says: "The aim of our command is love that issues from a pure heart, a good conscience, and a sincere faith" (I Tim. 1:5).

5.111   JAMES COMPARED WITH PAUL. Wherefore, in this matter we are not speaking of a fictitious, empty, lazy and dead faith, but of a living, quickening faith. It is and is called a living faith because it apprehends Christ who is life and makes alive, and shows that it is alive by living works. And so James does not contradict anything in this doctrine of ours. For he speaks of an empty, dead faith of which some boasted but who did not have Christ living in them by faith (James 2:14 ff.). James said that works justify, yet without contradicting the apostle (otherwise he would have to be rejected) but showing that Abraham proved his living and justifying faith by works. This all the pious do, but they trust in Christ alone and not in their own works. For again the apostle said: "It is no longer I who live, but Christ who lives in me; and the life I now live in the flesh I live by faith in the Son of God,[7] who loved me and gave himself for me. I do not reject the grace of God; for if justification were through the law, then Christ died to no purpose," etc. (Gal. 2:20 f.).

CHAPTER XVI

Of Faith and Good Works, and of Their Reward, and of Man's Merit

WHAT IS FAITH? Christian faith is not an opinion or human convic-   5.112
tion, but a most firm trust and a clear and steadfast assent of the mind, and then a most certain apprehension of the truth of God presented in the Scriptures and in the Apostles' Creed, and thus also of God himself, the greatest good, and especially of God's promise and of Christ who is the fulfilment of all promises.

FAITH IS THE GIFT OF GOD. But this faith is a pure gift of God   5.113
which God alone of his grace gives to his elect according to his measure when, to whom and to the degree he wills. And he does this by the Holy Spirit by means of the preaching of the Gospel and steadfast prayer. THE INCREASE OF FAITH. This faith also has its increase, and unless it were given by God, the apostles would not have said: "Lord, increase our faith" (Luke 17:5). And all these things which up to this point we have said concerning faith, the apostles have taught before us. For Paul said: "For faith is the ὑπόστασις or sure subsistence, of things hoped for, and the ἔλεγχος, that is, the clear and certain apprehension" (Heb. 11:1). And again he says that all the promises of God are Yes through Christ and through Christ are Amen (II Cor. 1:20). And to the Philippians he said that it has been given to them to believe in Christ (Phil. 1:29). Again, God assigned to each the measure of faith (Rom. 12:3). Again: "Not all have faith" and, "Not all obey the Gospel" (II Thess. 3:2; Rom. 10:16). But Luke also bears witness, saying: "As many as were ordained to life believed" (Acts 13:48). Wherefore Paul also calls faith "the faith of God's elect" (Titus 1:1), and again: "Faith comes from hearing, and hearing comes by the Word of God" (Rom. 10:17). Elsewhere he often commands men to pray for faith.

FAITH EFFICACIOUS AND ACTIVE. The same apostle calls faith   5.114
efficacious and active through love (Gal. 5:6). It also quiets the conscience and opens a free access to God, so that we may draw near

---

[7]The Latin reads: "by the faith of the Son of God."

to him with confidence and may obtain from him what is useful and necessary. The same [faith] keeps us in the service we owe to God and our neighbor, strengthens our patience in adversity, fashions and makes a true confession, and in a word, brings forth good fruit of all kinds, and good works.

5.115   CONCERNING GOOD WORKS. For we teach that truly good works grow out of a living faith by the Holy Spirit and are done by the faithful according to the will or rule of God's Word. Now the apostle Peter says: "Make every effort to supplement your faith with virtue, and virtue with knowledge, and knowledge with self-control," etc. (II Peter 1:5 ff.). But we have said above that the law of God, which is his will, prescribes for us the pattern of good works. And the apostle says: "This is the will of God, your sanctification, that you abstain from immorality . . . that no man transgress, and wrong his brother in business" (I Thess. 4:3 ff.).

5.116   WORKS OF HUMAN CHOICE. And indeed works and worship which we choose arbitrarily are not pleasing to God. These Paul calls θλεὲοθρησκεὶας (Col. 2:23—"self-devised worship"). Of such the Lord says in the Gospel: "In vain do they worship me, teaching as doctrines the precepts of men" (Matt. 15:9). Therefore, we disapprove of such works, and approve and urge those that are of God's will and commission.

5.117   THE END OF GOOD WORKS. These same works ought not to be done in order that we may earn eternal life by them, for, as the apostle says, eternal life is the gift of God. Nor are they to be done for ostentation which the Lord rejects in Matt., ch. 6, nor for gain which he also rejects in Matt., ch. 23, but for the glory of God, to adorn our calling, to show gratitude to God, and for the profit of the neighbor. For our Lord says again in the Gospel: "Let your light so shine before men, that they may see your good works and give glory to your Father who is in heaven" (Matt. 5:16). And the apostle Paul says: "Lead a life worthy of the calling to which you have been called" (Eph. 4:1). Also: "And whatever you do, in word or deed, do everything in the name of the Lord Jesus, giving thanks to God and to the Father through him" (Col. 3:17), and, "Let each of you look not to his own interests, but to the interests of others" (Phil. 2:4), and, "Let our people learn to apply themselves to good deeds, so as to help cases of urgent need, and not to be unfruitful" (Titus 3:14).

5.118   GOOD WORKS NOT REJECTED. Therefore, although we teach with the apostle that a man is justified by grace through faith in Christ and not through any good works, yet we do not think that good works are of little value and condemn them. We know that man was not created or regenerated through faith in order to be idle, but rather that without ceasing he should do those things which are good and useful. For in the Gospel the Lord says that a good tree brings forth good fruit (Matt. 12:33), and that he who abides in me bears much fruit (John 15:5). The apostle says: "For we are his workmanship, created in Christ Jesus for good works, which God prepared beforehand, that we should walk in them" (Eph. 2:10), and again: "Who gave himself for us to redeem us from all iniquity and to purify for himself a people of his own who are zealous for good deeds" (Titus 2:14). We therefore condemn all who despise good works and who babble that they are useless and that we do not need to pay attention to them.

WE ARE NOT SAVED BY GOOD WORKS. Nevertheless, as was said **5.119** above, we do not think that we are saved by good works, and that they are so necessary for salvation that no one was ever saved without them. For we are saved by grace and the favor of Christ alone. Works necessarily proceed from faith. And salvation is improperly attributed to them, but is most properly ascribed to grace. The apostle's sentence is well known: "If it is by grace, then it is no longer of works; otherwise grace would no longer be grace. But if it is of works, then it is no longer grace, because otherwise work is no longer work" (Rom. 11:6).

GOOD WORKS PLEASE GOD. Now the works which we do by faith **5.120** are pleasing to God and are approved by him. Because of faith in Christ, those who do good works which, moreover, are done from God's grace through the Holy Spirit, are pleasing to God. For St. Peter said: "In every nation any one who fears God and does what is right is acceptable to him" (Acts 10:35). And Paul said: "We have not ceased to pray for you . . . that you may walk worthily of the Lord, fully pleasing to him, bearing fruit in every good work" (Col. 1:9 f.).

WE TEACH TRUE, NOT FALSE AND PHILOSOPHICAL VIRTUES. And **5.121** so we diligently teach true, not false and philosophical virtues, truly good works, and the genuine service of a Christian. And as much as we can we diligently and zealously press them upon all men, while censuring the sloth and hypocrisy of all those who praise and profess the Gospel with their lips and dishonor it by their disgraceful lives. In this matter we place before them God's terrible threats and then his rich promises and generous rewards—exhorting, consoling and rebuking.

GOD GIVES A REWARD FOR GOOD WORKS. For we teach that God **5.122** gives a rich reward to those who do good works, according to that saying of the prophet: "Keep your voice from weeping, . . . for your work shall be rewarded" (Jer. 31:16; Isa., ch. 4). The Lord also said in the Gospel: "Rejoice and be glad, for your reward is great in heaven" (Matt. 5:12), and, "Whoever gives to one of these my little ones a cup of cold water, truly, I say to you, he shall not lose his reward" (ch. 10:42). However, we do not ascribe this reward, which the Lord gives, to the merit of the man who receives it, but to the goodness, generosity and truthfulness of God who promises and gives it, and who, although he owes nothing to anyone, nevertheless promises that he will give a reward to his faithful worshippers; meanwhile he also gives them that they may honor him. Moreover, in the works even of the saints there is much that is unworthy of God and very much that is imperfect. But because God receives into favor and embraces those who do works for Christ's sake, he grants to them the promised reward. For in other respects our righteousnesses are compared to a filthy wrap (Isa. 64:6). And the Lord says in the Gospel: "When you have done all that is commanded you, say, 'We are unworthy servants; we have only done what was our duty' " (Luke 17:10).

5.123   THERE ARE NO MERITS OF MEN. Therefore, although we teach that God rewards our good deeds, yet at the same time we teach, with Augustine, that God does not crown in us our merits but his gifts. Accordingly we say that whatever reward we receive is also grace, and is more grace than reward, because the good we do, we do more through God than through ourselves, and because Paul says: "What have you that you did not receive? If then you received it, why do you boast as if you had not received it?" (I Cor. 4:7). And this is what the blessed martyr Cyprian concluded from this verse: We are not to glory in anything in us, since nothing is our own. We therefore condemn those who defend the merits of men in such a way that they invalidate the grace of God.

CHAPTER XVII

Of the Catholic and Holy Church of God, and of the One Only Head of the Church

5.124   THE CHURCH HAS ALWAYS EXISTED AND IT WILL ALWAYS EXIST. But because God from the beginning would have men to be saved, and to come to the knowledge of the truth (I Tim. 2:4), it is altogether necessary that there always should have been, and should be now, and to the end of the world, a Church.

5.125   WHAT IS THE CHURCH? The Church is an assembly of the faithful called or gathered out of the world; a communion, I say, of all saints, namely, of those who truly know and rightly worship and serve the true God in Christ the Savior, by the Word and Holy Spirit, and who by faith are partakers of all benefits which are freely offered through Christ. CITIZENS OF ONE COMMONWEALTH. They are all citizens of the one city, living under the same Lord, under the same laws, and in the same fellowship of all good things. For the apostle calls them "fellow citizens with the saints and members of the household of God" (Eph. 2:19), calling the faithful on earth saints (I Cor. 4:1), who are sanctified by the blood of the Son of God. The article of the Creed, "I believe in the holy catholic Church, the communion of saints," is to be understood wholly as concerning these saints.

5.126   ONLY ONE CHURCH FOR ALL TIMES. And since there is always but one God, and there is one mediator between God and men, Jesus the Messiah, and one Shepherd of the whole flock, one Head of this body, and, to conclude, one Spirit, one salvation, one faith, one Testament or covenant, it necessarily follows that there is only one Church. THE CATHOLIC CHURCH. We, therefore, call this Church catholic because it is universal, scattered through all parts of the world, and extended unto all times, and is not limited to any times or places. Therefore, we condemn the Donatists who confined the Church to I know not what corners of Africa. Nor do we approve of the Roman clergy who have recently passed off only the Roman Church as catholic.

PARTS OR FORMS OF THE CHURCH. The Church is divided into **5.127** different parts or forms; not because it is divided or rent asunder in itself, but rather because it is distinguished by the diversity of the numbers that are in it. MILITANT AND TRIUMPHANT. For the one is called the Church Militant, the other the Church Triumphant. The former still wages war on earth, and fights against the flesh, the world, and the prince of this world, the devil; against sin and death. But the latter, having been now discharged, triumphs in heaven immediately after having overcome all those things and rejoices before the Lord. Notwithstanding both have fellowship and union one with another.

THE PARTICULAR CHURCH. Moreover, the Church Militant upon the **5.128** earth has always had many particular churches. Yet all these are to be referred to the unity of the catholic Church. This [Militant] Church was set up differently before the Law among the patriarchs; otherwise under Moses by the Law; and differently by Christ through the Gospel.

THE TWO PEOPLES. Generally two peoples are usually counted, **5.129** namely, the Israelites and Gentiles, or those who have been gathered from among Jews and Gentiles into the Church. There are also two Testaments, the Old and the New. THE SAME CHURCH FOR THE OLD AND THE NEW PEOPLE. Yet from all these people there was and is one fellowship, one salvation in the one Messiah; in whom, as members of one body under one Head, all united together in the same faith, partaking also of the same spiritual food and drink. Yet here we acknowledge a diversity of times, and a diversity in the signs of the promised and delivered Christ; and that now the ceremonies being abolished, the light shines unto us more clearly, and blessings are given to us more abundantly, and a fuller liberty.

THE CHURCH THE TEMPLE OF THE LIVING GOD. This holy Church **5.130** of God is called the temple of the living God, built of living and spiritual stones and founded upon a firm rock, upon a foundation which no other can lay, and therefore it is called "the pillar and bulwark of the truth" (I Tim. 3:15). THE CHURCH DOES NOT ERR. It does not err as long as it rests upon the rock Christ, and upon the foundation of the prophets and apostles. And it is no wonder if it errs, as often as it deserts him who alone is the truth. THE CHURCH AS BRIDE AND VIRGIN. This Church is also called a virgin and the Bride of Christ, and even the only Beloved. For the apostle says: "I betrothed you to Christ to present you as a pure bride to Christ" (II Cor. 11:2). THE CHURCH AS A FLOCK OF SHEEP. The Church is called a flock of sheep under the one shepherd, Christ, according to Ezek., ch. 34, and John, ch. 10. THE CHURCH AS THE BODY. It is also called the body of Christ because the faithful are living members of Christ under Christ the Head.

5.131   CHRIST THE SOLE HEAD OF THE CHURCH. It is the head which has the preeminence in the body, and from it the whole body receives life; by its spirit the body is governed in all things; from it, also, the body receives increase, that it may grow up. Also, there is one head of the body, and it is suited to the body. Therefore the Church cannot have any other head besides Christ. For as the Church is a spiritual body, so it must also have a spiritual head in harmony with itself. Neither can it be governed by any other spirit than by the Spirit of Christ. Wherefore Paul says: "He is the head of the body, the church; he is the beginning, the firstborn from the dead, that in everything he might be pre-eminent" (Col. 1:18). And in another place: "Christ is the head of the church, his body, and is himself its Savior" (Eph. 5:23). And again: he is "the head over all things for the church, which is his body, the fulness of him who fills all in all" (Eph. 1:22 f.). Also: "We are to grow up in every way into him who is the head, into Christ, from whom the whole body, joined and knit together, makes bodily growth" (Eph. 4:15 f.). And therefore we do not approve of the doctrine of the Roman clergy, who make their Pope at Rome the universal shepherd and supreme head of the Church Militant here on earth, and so the very vicar of Jesus Christ, who has (as they say) all fulness of power and sovereign authority in the Church. CHRIST THE ONLY PASTOR OF THE CHURCH. For we teach that Christ the Lord is, and remains the only universal pastor, the highest Pontiff before God the Father; and that in the Church he himself performs all the duties of a bishop or pastor, even to the world's end; *[Vicar]* and therefore does not need a substitute for one who is absent. For Christ is present with his Church, and is its life-giving Head. NO PRIMACY IN THE CHURCH. He has strictly forbidden his apostles and their successors to have any primacy and dominion in the Church. Who does not see, therefore, that whoever contradicts and opposes this plain truth is rather to be counted among the number of those of whom Christ's apostles prophesied: Peter in II Peter, ch. 2, and Paul in Acts 20:2; II Cor. 11:2; II Thess., ch. 2, and also in other places?

5.132   NO DISORDER IN THE CHURCH. However, by doing away with a Roman head we do not bring any confusion or disorder into the Church, since we teach that the government of the Church which the apostles handed down is sufficient to keep the Church in proper order. In the beginning when the Church was without any such Roman head as is now said to keep it in order, the Church was not disordered or in confusion. The Roman head does indeed preserve his tyranny and the corruption that has been brought into the Church, and meanwhile he hinders, resists, and with all the strength he can muster cuts off the proper reformation of the Church.

5.133   DISSENSIONS AND STRIFE IN THE CHURCH. We are reproached because there have been manifold dissensions and strife in our churches since they separated themselves from the Church of Rome, and therefore cannot be true churches. As though there were never in the Church of Rome any sects, nor contentions and quarrels concerning religion, and indeed, carried on not so much in the schools as from pulpits in the midst of the people. We know, to be sure, that the apostle said: "God is not a God of confusion but of peace" (I Cor. 14:33), and, "While there is jealousy and strife among you, are you not of the flesh?" Yet we cannot deny that God was in the apostolic Church and that it was a true Church, even though there were wranglings and dissensions in it. The apostle Paul reprehended Peter, an apostle (Gal. 2:11 ff.), and Barnabas dissented from Paul. Great contention arose in the Church of Antioch between them that preached the one Christ, as Luke records in The Acts of the Apostles, ch. 15. And there have at all times been great contentions in the Church, and the most excellent teachers of the Church have differed among themselves about important matters without meanwhile the Church ceasing to be the Church because of these contentions. For thus it pleases God to use the dissensions that arise in the Church to the glory of his name, to illustrate the truth, and in order that those who are in the right might be manifest (I Cor. 11:19).

OF THE NOTES OR SIGNS OF THE TRUE CHURCH. Moreover, as we   **5.134** acknowledge no other head of the Church than Christ, so we do not acknowledge every church to be the true Church which vaunts herself to be such; but we teach that the true Church is that in which the signs or marks of the true Church are to be found, especially the lawful and sincere preaching of the Word of God as it was delivered to us in the books of the prophets and the apostles, which all lead us unto Christ, who said in the Gospel: "My sheep hear my voice, and I know them, and they follow me; and I give unto them eternal life. A stranger they do not follow, but they flee from him, for they do not know the voice of strangers" (John 10:5, 27, 28).

And those who are such in the Church have one faith and one spirit;   **5.135** and therefore they worship but one God, and him alone they worship in spirit and in truth, loving him alone with all their hearts and with all their strength, praying unto him alone through Jesus Christ, the only Mediator and Intercessor; and they do not seek righteousness and life outside Christ and faith in him. Because they acknowledge Christ the only head and foundation of the Church, and, resting on him, daily renew themselves by repentance, and patiently bear the cross laid upon them. Moreover, joined together with all the members of Christ by an unfeigned love, they show that they are Christ's disciples by persevering in the bond of peace and holy unity. At the same time they participate in the Sacraments instituted by Christ, and delivered unto us by his apostles, using them in no other way than as they received them from the Lord. That saying of the apostle Paul is well known to all: "I received from the Lord what I also delivered to you" (I Cor. 11:23 ff.). Accordingly, we condemn all such churches as strangers from the true Church of Christ, which are not such as we have heard they ought to be, no matter how much they brag of a succession of bishops, of unity, and of antiquity. Moreover, we have a charge from the apostles of Christ "to shun the worship of idols" (I Cor. 10:14;

I John 5:21), and "to come out of Babylon," and to have no fellowship with her, unless we want to be partakers with her of all God's plagues (Rev. 18:4; II Cor. 6:17).

5.136   OUTSIDE THE CHURCH OF GOD THERE IS NO SALVATION. But we esteem fellowship with the true Church of Christ so highly that we deny that those can live before God who do not stand in fellowship with the true Church of God, but separate themselves from it. For as there was no salvation outside Noah's ark when the world perished in the flood; so we believe that there is no certain salvation outside Christ, who offers himself to be enjoyed by the elect in the Church; and hence we teach that those who wish to live ought not to be separated from the true Church of Christ.

5.137   THE CHURCH IS NOT BOUND TO ITS SIGNS. Nevertheless, by the signs [of the true Church] mentioned above, we do not so narrowly restrict the Church as to teach that all those are outside the Church who either do not participate in the Sacraments, at least not willingly and through contempt, but rather, being forced by necessity, unwillingly abstain from them or are deprived of them; or in whom faith sometimes fails, though it is not entirely extinguished and does not wholly cease; or in whom imperfections and errors due to weakness are found. For we know that God had some friends in the world outside the commonwealth of Israel. We know what befell the people of God in the captivity of Babylon, where they were deprived of their sacrifices for seventy years. We know what happened to St. Peter, who denied his Master, and what is wont to happen daily to God's elect and faithful people who go astray and are weak. We know, moreover, what kind of churches the churches in Galatia and Corinth were in the apostles' time, in which the apostle found fault with many serious offenses; yet he calls them holy churches of Christ (I Cor. 1:2; Gal. 1:2).

5.138   THE CHURCH APPEARS AT TIMES TO BE EXTINCT. Yes, and it sometimes happens that God in his just judgment allows the truth of his Word, and the catholic faith, and the proper worship of God to be so obscured and overthrown that the Church seems almost extinct, and no more to exist, as we see to have happened in the days of Elijah (I Kings 19:10, 14), and at other times. Meanwhile God has in this world and in this darkness his true worshippers, and those not a few, but even seven thousand and more (I Kings 19:18; Rev. 7:3 ff.). For the apostle exclaims: "God's firm foundation stands, bearing this seal, 'The Lord knows those who are his,' " etc. (II Tim. 2:19). Whence the Church of God may be termed invisible; not because the men from whom the Church is gathered are invisible, but because, being hidden from our eyes and known only to God, it often secretly escapes human judgment.

5.139   NOT ALL WHO ARE IN THE CHURCH ARE OF THE CHURCH. Again, not all that are reckoned in the number of the Church are saints, and living and true members of the Church. For there are many hypocrites, who outwardly hear the Word of God, and publicly receive the

Sacraments, and seem to pray to God through Christ alone, to confess Christ to be their only righteousness, and to worship God, and to exercise the duties of charity, and for a time to endure with patience in misfortune. And yet they are inwardly destitute of true illumination of the Spirit, of faith and sincerity of heart, and of perseverance to the end. But eventually the character of these men, for the most part, will be disclosed. For the apostle John says: "They went out from us, but they were not of us; for if they had been of us, they would indeed have continued with us" (I John 2:19). And although while they simulate piety they are not of the Church, yet they are considered to be in the Church, just as traitors in a state are numbered among its citizens before they are discovered; and as the tares or darnel and chaff are found among the wheat, and as swellings and tumors are found in a sound body, when they are rather diseases and deformities than true members of the body. And therefore the Church of God is rightly compared to a net which catches fish of all kinds, and to a field, in which both wheat and tares are found (Matt. 13:24 ff., 47 ff.).

WE MUST NOT JUDGE RASHLY OR PREMATURELY. Hence we must **5.140** be very careful not to judge before the time, nor undertake to exclude, reject or cut off those whom the Lord does not want to have excluded or rejected, and those whom we cannot eliminate without loss to the Church. On the other hand, we must be vigilant lest while the pious snore the wicked gain ground and do harm to the Church.

THE UNITY OF THE CHURCH IS NOT IN EXTERNAL RITES. Further- **5.141** more, we diligently teach that care is to be taken wherein the truth and unity of the Church chiefly lies, lest we rashly provoke and foster schisms in the Church. Unity consists not in outward rites and ceremonies, but rather in the truth and unity of the catholic faith. The catholic faith is not given to us by human laws, but by Holy Scriptures, of which the Apostles' Creed is a compendium. And, therefore, we read in the ancient writers that there was a manifold diversity of rites, but that they were free, and no one ever thought that the unity of the Church was thereby dissolved. So we teach that the true harmony of the Church consists in doctrines and in the true and harmonious preaching of the Gospel of Christ, and in rites that have been expressly delivered by the Lord. And here we especially urge that saying of the apostle: "Let those of us who are perfect have this mind; and if in any thing you are otherwise minded, God will reveal that also to you. Nevertheless let us walk by the same rule according to what we have attained, and let us be of the same mind" (Phil. 3:15 f.).

CHAPTER XVIII

Of the Ministers of the Church,
Their Institution and Duties

GOD USES MINISTERS IN THE BUILDING OF THE CHURCH. God has **5.142** always used ministers for the gathering or establishing of a Church for himself, and for the governing and preservation of the same; and still he does, and always will, use them so long as the Church remains on earth. Therefore, the first beginning, institution, and office of ministers is a most ancient arrangement of God himself, and not a new one of men. INSTITUTION AND ORIGIN OF MINISTERS. It is true that God can, by his power, without any means join to himself a Church from among men; but he preferred to deal with men by the ministry of men. Therefore ministers are to be regarded, not as ministers by themselves alone, but as the ministers of God, inasmuch as God effects the salvation of men through them.

5.143   THE MINISTRY IS NOT TO BE DESPISED. Hence we warn men to beware lest we attribute what has to do with our conversion and instruction to the secret power of the Holy Spirit in such a way that we make void the ecclesiastical ministry. For it is fitting that we always have in mind the words of the apostle: "How are they to believe in him of whom they have not heard? And how are they to hear without a preacher? So faith comes from hearing, and hearing comes by the word of God" (Rom. 10:14, 17). And also what the Lord said in the Gospel: "Truly, truly, I say to you, he who receives any one whom I send receives me; and he who receives me receives him who sent me" (John 13:20). Likewise a man of Macedonia, who appeared to Paul in a vision while he was in Asia, secretly admonished him, saying: "Come over to Macedonia and help us" (Acts 16:9). And in another place the same apostle said: "We are fellow workmen for God; you are God's tillage, God's building" (I Cor. 3:9).

5.144   Yet, on the other hand, we must beware that we do not attribute too much to ministers and the ministry; remembering here also the words of the Lord in the Gospel: "No one can come to me unless my Father draws him" (John 6:44), and the words of the apostle: "What then is Paul? What is Apollos? Servants through whom you believed, as the Lord assigned to each. I planted, Apollos watered, but only God gives the growth" (I Cor. 3:5 ff.). GOD MOVES THE HEARTS OF MEN. Therefore, let us believe that God teaches us by his word, outwardly through his ministers, and inwardly moves the hearts of his elect to faith by the Holy Spirit; and that therefore we ought to render all glory unto God for this whole favor. But this matter has been dealt with in the first chapter of this Exposition.

5.145   WHO THE MINISTERS ARE AND OF WHAT SORT GOD HAS GIVEN TO THE WORLD. And even from the beginning of the world God has used the most excellent men in the whole world (even if many of them were simple in worldly wisdom or philosophy, but were outstanding in true theology), namely, the patriarchs, with whom he frequently spoke by angels. For the patriarchs were the prophets or teachers of their age whom God for this reason wanted to live for several centuries, in order that they might be, as it were, fathers and lights of the world. They were followed by Moses and the prophets renowned throughout all the world.

CHRIST THE TEACHER. After these the heavenly Father even sent his   **5.146**
only-begotten Son, the most perfect teacher of the world; in whom is
hidden the wisdom of God, and which has come to us through the
most holy, simple, and most perfect doctrine of all. For he chose
disciples for himself whom he made apostles. These went out into the
whole world, and everywhere gathered together churches by the
preaching of the Gospel, and then throughout all the churches in the
world they appointed pastors or teachers[8] according to Christ's command; through their successors he has taught and governed the Church
unto this day. Therefore, as God gave unto his ancient people the
patriarchs, together with Moses and the prophets, so also to his people
of the New Testament he sent his only-begotten Son, and, with him,
the apostles and teachers of the Church.

MINISTERS OF THE NEW TESTAMENT. Furthermore, the ministers of   **5.147**
the new people are called by various names. For they are called
apostles, prophets, evangelists, bishops, elders, pastors, and teachers
(I Cor. 12:28; Eph. 4:11). THE APOSTLES. The apostles did not stay in
any particular place, but throughout the world gathered together different churches. When they were once established, there ceased to be
apostles, and pastors took their place, each in his church. PROPHETS.
In former times the prophets were seers, knowing the future; but they
also interpreted the Scriptures. Such men are also found still today.
EVANGELISTS. The writers of the history of the Gospel were called
Evangelists; but they also were heralds of the Gospel of Christ; as Paul
also commended Timothy: "Do the work of an evangelist" (II Tim.
4:5). BISHOPS. Bishops are the overseers and watchmen of the Church,
who administer the food and needs of the life of the Church. PRES-
BYTERS. The presbyters are the elders and, as it were, senators and
fathers of the Church, governing it with wholesome counsel. PASTORS.
The pastors both keep the Lord's sheepfold, and also provide for its
needs. TEACHERS. The teachers instruct and teach the true faith and
godliness. Therefore, the ministers of the churches may now be called
bishops, elders, pastors, and teachers.

PAPAL ORDERS. Then in subsequent times many more names of   **5.148**
ministers in the Church were introduced into the Church of God. For
some were appointed patriarchs, others archbishops, others suffragans;
also, metropolitans, archdeacons, deacons, subdeacons, acolytes,
exorcists, cantors, porters, and I know not what others, as cardinals,
provosts, and priors; greater and lesser fathers, greater and lesser
orders. But we are not troubled about all these about how they once
were and are now. For us the apostolic doctrine concerning ministers
is sufficient.

CONCERNING MONKS. Since we assuredly know that monks, and   **5.149**
the orders or sects of monks, are instituted neither by Christ nor by the
apostles, we teach that they are of no use to the Church of God, nay

---

[8]*Ordinarunt pastores, atque doctores.*

rather, are pernicious. For, although in former times they were tolerable (when they were hermits, earning their living with their own hands, and were not a burden to anyone, but like the laity were everywhere obedient to the pastors of the churches), yet now the whole world sees and knows what they are like. They formulate I know not what vows; but they lead a life quite contrary to their vows, so that the best of them deserves to be numbered among those of whom the apostle said: "We hear that some of you are living an irregular life, mere busybodies, not doing any work" etc. (II Thess. 3:11). Therefore, we neither have such in our churches, nor do we teach that they should be in the churches of Christ.

5.150   MINISTERS ARE TO BE CALLED AND ELECTED. Furthermore, no man ought to usurp the honor of the ecclesiastical ministry; that is, to seize it for himself by bribery or any deceits, or by his own free choice. But let the ministers of the Church be called and chosen by lawful and ecclesiastical election; that is to say, let them be carefully chosen by the Church or by those delegated from the Church for that purpose in a proper order without any uproar, dissension and rivalry. Not any one may be elected, but capable men distinguished by sufficient consecrated learning, pious eloquence, simple wisdom, lastly, by moderation and an honorable reputation, according to that apostolic rule which is compiled by the apostle in I Tim., ch. 3, and Titus, ch. 1.

5.151   ORDINATION. And those who are elected are to be ordained by the elders with public prayer and laying on of hands. Here we condemn all those who go off of their own accord, being neither chosen, sent, nor ordained (Jer., ch. 23). We condemn unfit ministers and those not furnished with the necessary gifts of a pastor.

5.152   In the meantime we acknowledge that the harmless simplicity of some pastors in the primitive Church sometimes profited the Church more than the many-sided, refined and fastidious, but a little too esoteric learning of others. For this reason we do not reject even today the honest, yet by no means ignorant, simplicity of some.

5.153   PRIESTHOOD OF ALL BELIEVERS. To be sure, Christ's apostles call all who believe in Christ "priests," but not on account of an office, but because, all the faithful having been made kings and priests, we are able to offer up spiritual sacrifices to God through Christ (Ex. 19:6; I Peter 2:9; Rev. 1:6). Therefore, the priesthood and the ministry are very different from one another. For the priesthood, as we have just said, is common to all Christians; not so is the ministry. Nor have we abolished the ministry of the Church because we have repudiated the papal priesthood from the Church of Christ.

5.154   PRIESTS AND PRIESTHOOD. Surely in the new covenant of Christ there is no longer any such priesthood as was under the ancient people; which had an external anointing, holy garments, and very many ceremonies which were types of Christ, who abolished them all by his coming and fulfilling them. But he himself remains the only priest forever, and lest we derogate anything from him, we do not impart the name of priest to any minister. For the Lord himself did not appoint any priests in the Church of the New Testament who, having received authority from the suffragan, may daily offer up the sacrifice, that is, the very flesh and blood of the Lord, for the living and the dead, but ministers who may teach and administer the Sacraments.

THE NATURE OF THE MINISTERS OF THE NEW TESTAMENT. Paul **5.155** explains simply and briefly what we are to think of the ministers of the New Testament or of the Christian Church, and what we are to attribute to them. "This is how one should regard us, as servants of Christ and stewards of the mysteries of God" (I Cor. 4:1). Therefore, the apostle wants us to think of ministers as ministers. Now the apostle calls them ὑπηρέτας, rowers, who have their eyes fixed on the coxswain, and so men who do not live for themselves or according to their own will, but for others—namely, their masters, upon whose command they altogether depend. For in all his duties every minister of the Church is commanded to carry out only what he has received in commandment from his Lord, and not to indulge his own free choice. And in this case it is expressly declared who is the Lord, namely, Christ; to whom the ministers are subject in all the affairs of the ministry.

MINISTERS AS STEWARDS OF THE MYSTERIES OF GOD. Moreover, to **5.156** the end that he might expound the ministry more fully, the apostle adds that ministers of the Church are administrators and stewards of the mysteries of God. Now in many passages, especially in Eph., ch. 3, Paul called the mysteries of God the Gospel of Christ. And the Sacraments of Christ are also called mysteries by the ancient writers. Therefore for this purpose are the ministers of the Church called— namely, to preach the Gospel of Christ to the faithful, and to administer the Sacraments. We read, also, in another place in the Gospel, of "the faithful and wise steward," whom "his master will set over his household, to give them their portion of food at the proper time" (Luke 12:42). Again, elsewhere in the Gospel a man takes a journey in a foreign country and, leaving his house, gives his substance and authority over it to his servants, and to each his work.

THE POWER OF MINISTERS OF THE CHURCH. Now, therefore, it is **5.157** fitting that we also say something about the power and duty of the ministers of the Church. Concerning this power some have argued industriously, and to it have subjected everything on earth, even the greatest things, and they have done so contrary to the commandment of the Lord who has prohibited dominion for his disciples and has highly commended humility (Luke 22:24 ff.; Matt. 18:3 f.; 20:25 ff.). There is, indeed, another power that is pure and absolute, which is called the power of right. According to this power all things in the whole world are subject to Christ, who is Lord of all, as he himself has testified when he said: "All authority in heaven and on earth has been given to me" (Matt. 28:18), and again, "I am the first and the last, and behold I am alive for evermore, and I have the keys of Hades and Death"

(Rev. 1:18); also, "He has the key of David, which opens and no one shall shut, who shuts and no one opens" (Rev. 3:7).

5.158 THE LORD RESERVES TRUE POWER FOR HIMSELF. This power the Lord reserves to himself, and does not transfer it to any other, so that he might stand idly by as a spectator while his ministers work. For Isaiah says, "I will place on his shoulder the key of the house of David" (Isa. 22:22), and again, "The government will be upon his shoulders" (Isa. 9:6). For he does not lay the government on other men's shoulders, but still keeps and uses his own power, governing all things.

5.159 THE POWER OF THE OFFICE AND OF THE MINISTER. Then there is another power of an office or of ministry limited by him who has full and absolute power. And this is more like a service than a dominion. THE KEYS. For a lord gives up his power to the steward in his house, and for that cause gives him the keys, that he may admit into or exclude from the house those whom his lord will have admitted or excluded. In virtue of this power the minister, because of his office, does that which the Lord has commanded him to do; and the Lord confirms what he does, and wills that what his servant has done will be so regarded and acknowledged, as if he himself had done it. Undoubtedly, it is to this that these evangelical sentences refer: "I will give you the keys of the kingdom of heaven, and whatever you bind on earth shall be bound in heaven, and whatever you loose on earth shall be loosed in heaven" (Matt. 16:19). Again, "If you forgive the sins of any, they are forgiven; if you retain the sins of any, they are retained" (John 20:23). But if the minister does not carry out everything as the Lord has commanded him, but transgresses the bounds of faith, then the Lord certainly makes void what he has done. Wherefore the ecclesiastical power of the ministers of the Church is that function whereby they indeed govern the Church of God, but yet so do all things in the Church as the Lord has prescribed in his Word. When those things are done, the faithful esteem them as done by the Lord himself. But mention has already been made of the keys above.

5.160 THE POWER OF MINISTERS IS ONE AND THE SAME, AND EQUAL. Now the one and an equal power or function is given to all ministers in the Church. Certainly, in the beginning, the bishops or presbyters governed the Church in common; no man lifted up himself above another, none usurped greater power or authority over his fellow-bishops. For remembering the words of the Lord: "Let the leader among you become as one who serves" (Luke 22:26), they kept themselves in humility, and by mutual services they helped one another in the governing and preserving of the Church.

5.161 ORDER TO BE PRESERVED. Nevertheless, for the sake of preserving order some one of the ministers called the assembly together, proposed matters to be laid before it, gathered the opinions of the others, in short, to the best of man's ability took precaution lest any confusion should arise. Thus did St. Peter, as we read in The Acts of the

Apostles, who nevertheless was not on that account preferred to the others, nor endowed with greater authority than the rest. Rightly then does Cyprian the Martyr say, in his *De Simplicitate Clericorum:* "The other apostles were assuredly what Peter was, endowed with a like fellowship of honor and power; but [his] primacy proceeds from unity in order that the Church may be shown to be one."

WHEN AND HOW ONE WAS PLACED BEFORE THE OTHERS. St.   5.162
Jerome also in his commentary upon The Epistle of Paul to Titus, says something not unlike this: "Before attachment to persons in religion was begun at the instigation of the devil, the churches were governed by the common consultation of the elders; but after every one thought that those whom he had baptized were his own, and not Christ's, it was decreed that one of the elders should be chosen, and set over the rest, upon whom should fall the care of the whole Church, and all schismatic seeds should be removed." Yet St. Jerome does not recommend this decree as divine; for he immediately adds: "As the elders knew from the custom of the Church that they were subject to him who was set over them, so the bishops knew that they were above the elders, more from custom than from the truth of an arrangement by the Lord, and that they ought to rule the Church in common with them." Thus far St. Jerome. Hence no one can rightly forbid a return to the ancient constitution of the Church of God, and to have recourse to it before human custom.

THE DUTIES OF MINISTERS. The duties of ministers are various; yet   5.163
for the most part they are restricted to two, in which all the rest are comprehended: to the teaching of the Gospel of Christ, and to the proper administration of the Sacraments. For it is the duty of the ministers to gather together an assembly for worship in which to expound God's Word and to apply the whole doctrine to the care and use of the Church, so that what is taught may benefit the hearers and edify the faithful. It falls to ministers, I say, to teach the ignorant, and to exhort; and to urge the idlers and lingerers to make progress in the way of the Lord. Moreover, they are to comfort and to strengthen the fainthearted, and to arm them against the manifold temptations of Satan; to rebuke offenders; to recall the erring into the way; to raise the fallen; to convince the gainsayers to drive the wolf away from the sheepfold of the Lord; to rebuke wickedness and wicked men wisely and severely; not to wink at nor to pass over great wickedness. And, besides, they are to administer the Sacraments, and to commend the right use of them, and to prepare all men by wholesome doctrine to receive them; to preserve the faithful in a holy unity; and to check schisms; to catechize the unlearned, to commend the needs of the poor to the Church, to visit, instruct, and keep in the way of life the sick and those afflicted with various temptations. In addition, they are to attend to public prayers or supplications in times of need, together with common fasting, that is, a holy abstinence; and as diligently as possible to see to everything that pertains to the tranquility, peace and welfare of the churches.

5.164 But in order that the minister may perform all these things better and more easily, it is especially required of him that he fear God, be constant in prayer, attend to spiritual reading, and in all things and at all times be watchful, and by a purity of life to let his light to shine before all men.

5.165 DISCIPLINE. And since discipline is an absolute necessity in the Church and excommunication was once used in the time of the early fathers, and there were ecclesiastical judgments among the people of God, wherein this discipline was exercised by wise and godly men, it also falls to ministers to regulate this discipline for edification, according to the circumstances of the time, public state, and necessity. At all times and in all places the rule is to be observed that everything is to be done for edification, decently and honorably, without oppression and strife. For the apostle testifies that authority in the Church was given to him by the Lord for building up and not for destroying (II Cor. 10:8). And the Lord himself forbade the weeds to be plucked up in the Lord's field, because there would be danger lest the wheat also be plucked up with it (Matt. 13:29 f.).

5.166 EVEN EVIL MINISTERS ARE TO BE HEARD. Moreover, we strongly detest the error of the Donatists who esteem the doctrine and administration of the Sacraments to be either effectual or not effectual, according to the good or evil life of the ministers. For we know that the voice of Christ is to be heard, though it be out of the mouths of evil ministers; because the Lord himself said: "Practice and observe whatever they tell you, but not what they do" (Matt. 23:3). We know that the Sacraments are sanctified by the institution and the word of Christ, and that they are effectual to the godly, although they be administered by unworthy ministers. Concerning this matter, Augustine, the blessed servant of God, many times argued from the Scriptures against the Donatists.

5.167 SYNODS. Nevertheless, there ought to be proper discipline among ministers. In synods the doctrine and life of ministers is to be carefully examined. Offenders who can be cured are to be rebuked by the elders and restored to the right way, and if they are incurable, they are to be deposed, and like wolves driven away from the flock of the Lord by the true shepherds. For, if they be false teachers, they are not to be tolerated at all. Neither do we disapprove of ecumenical councils, if they are convened according to the example of the apostles, for the welfare of the Church and not for its destruction.

5.168 THE WORKER IS WORTHY OF HIS REWARD. All faithful ministers, as good workmen, are also worthy of their reward, and do not sin when they receive a stipend, and all things that be necessary for themselves and their family. For the apostle shows in I Cor., ch. 9, and in I Tim., ch. 5, and elsewhere that these things may rightly be given by the Church and received by ministers. The Anabaptists, who condemn and defame ministers who live from their ministry are also refuted by the apostolic teaching.

CHAPTER XIX

Of the Sacraments of the Church of Christ

THE SACRAMENTS [ARE] ADDED TO THE WORD AND WHAT THEY ARE. From the beginning, God added to the preaching of his Word in his Church Sacraments or sacramental signs. For thus does all Holy Scripture clearly testify. Sacraments are mystical symbols, or holy rites, or sacred actions, instituted by God himself, consisting of his Word, of signs and of things signified, whereby in the Church he keeps in mind and from time to time recalls the great benefits he has shown to men; whereby also he seals his promises, and outwardly represents, and, as it were, offers unto our sight those things which inwardly he performs for us, and so strengthens and increases our faith through the working of God's Spirit in our hearts. Lastly, he thereby distinguishes us from all other people and religions, and consecrates and binds us wholly to himself, and signifies what he requires of us. **5.169**

SOME ARE SACRAMENTS OF THE OLD, OTHERS OF THE NEW, TESTAMENTS. Some Sacraments are of the old, others of the new, people. The Sacraments of the ancient people were circumcision, and the Paschal Lamb, which was offered up; for that reason it is referred to the sacrifices which were practiced from the beginning of the world. **5.170**

THE NUMBER OF SACRAMENTS OF THE NEW PEOPLE. The Sacraments of the new people are Baptism and the Lord's Supper. There are some who count seven Sacraments of the new people. Of these we acknowledge that repentance, the ordination of ministers (not indeed the papal but apostolic ordination), and matrimony are profitable ordinances of God, but not Sacraments. Confirmation and extreme unction are human inventions which the Church can dispense with without any loss, and indeed, we do not have them in our churches. For they contain some things of which we can by no means approve. Above all we detest all the trafficking in which the Papists engage in dispensing the Sacraments. **5.171**

THE AUTHOR OF THE SACRAMENTS. The author of all Sacraments is not any man, but God alone. Men cannot institute Sacraments. For they pertain to the worship of God, and it is not for man to appoint and prescribe a worship of God, but to accept and preserve the one he has received from God. Besides, the symbols have God's promises annexed to them, which require faith. Now faith rests only upon the Word of God; and the Word of God is like papers or letters, and the Sacraments are like seals which only God appends to the letters. **5.172**

CHRIST STILL WORKS IN SACRAMENTS. And as God is the author of the Sacraments, so he continually works in the Church in which they are rightly carried out; so that the faithful, when they receive them from the ministers, know that God works in his own ordinance, and therefore they receive them as from the hand of God; and the minister's faults (even if they be very great) cannot affect them, since they acknowledge the integrity of the Sacraments to depend upon the institution of the Lord. **5.173**

5.174   THE AUTHOR AND THE MINISTERS OF THE SACRAMENTS TO BE DISTINGUISHED. Hence in the administration of the Sacraments they also clearly distinguish between the Lord himself and the ministers of the Lord, confessing that the substance of the Sacraments is given them by the Lord, and the outward signs by the ministers of the Lord.

5.175   THE SUBSTANCE OR CHIEF THING IN THE SACRAMENTS. But the principle thing which God promises in all Sacraments and to which all the godly in all ages direct their attention (some call it the substance and matter of the Sacraments) is Christ the Savior—that only sacrifice, and the Lamb of God slain from the foundation of the world; that rock, also, from which all our fathers drank, by whom all the elect are circumcised without hands through the Holy Spirit, and are washed from all their sins, and are nourished with the very body and blood of Christ unto eternal life.

5.176   THE SIMILARITY AND DIFFERENCE IN THE SACRAMENTS OF OLD AND NEW PEOPLES. Now, in respect of that which is the principal thing and the matter itself in the Sacraments, the Sacraments of both peoples are equal. For Christ, the only Mediator and Savior of the faithful, is the chief thing and very substance of the Sacraments in both; for the one God is the author of them both. They were given to both peoples as signs and seals of the grace and promises of God, which should call to mind and renew the memory of God's great benefits, and should distinguish the faithful from all the religions in the world; lastly, which should be received spiritually by faith, and should bind the receivers to the Church, and admonish them of their duty. In these and similar respects, I say, the Sacraments of both people are not dissimilar, although in the outward signs they are different. And, indeed, with respect to the signs we make a great difference. For ours are more firm and lasting, inasmuch as they will never be changed to the end of the world. Moreover, ours testify that both the substance and the promise have been fulfilled or perfected in Christ; the former signified what was to be fulfilled. Ours are also more simple and less laborious, less sumptuous and involved with ceremonies. Moreover, they belong to a more numerous people, one that is dispersed throughout the whole earth. And since they are more excellent, and by the Holy Spirit kindle greater faith, a greater abundance of the Spirit also ensues.

5.177   OUR SACRAMENTS SUCCEED THE OLD WHICH ARE ABROGATED. But now since Christ the true Messiah is exhibited unto us, and the abundance of grace is poured forth upon the people of The New Testament, the Sacraments of the old people are surely abrogated and have ceased; and in their stead the symbols of the New Testament are placed—Baptism in the place of circumcision, the Lord's Supper in place of the Paschal Lamb and sacrifices.

5.178   IN WHAT THE SACRAMENTS CONSIST. And as formerly the Sacraments consisted of the word, the sign, and the thing signified; so even now they are composed, as it were, of the same parts. For the

Word of God makes them Sacraments, which before they were not.
THE CONSECRATION OF THE SACRAMENTS. For they are consecrated by
the Word, and shown to be sanctified by him who instituted them. To
sanctify or consecrate anything to God is to dedicate it to holy uses;
that is, to take it from the common and ordinary use, and to appoint it
to a holy use. For the signs in the Sacraments are drawn from common
use, things external and visible. For in baptism the sign is the element
of water, and that visible washing which is done by the minister; but
the thing signified is regeneration and the cleansing from sins. Likewise, in the Lord's Supper, the outward sign is bread and wine, taken
from things commonly used for meat and drink; but the thing signified
is the body of Christ which was given, and his blood which was shed
for us, or the communion of the body and blood of the Lord.
Wherefore, the water, bread, and wine, according to their nature and
apart from the divine institution and sacred use, are only that which
they are called and we experience. But when the Word of God is added
to them, together with invocation of the divine name, and the renewing
of their first institution and sanctification, then these signs are consecrated, and shown to be sanctified by Christ. For Christ's first
institution and consecration of the Sacraments remains always effectual
in the Church of God, so that those who do not celebrate the Sacraments in any other way than the Lord himself instituted from the
beginning still today enjoy that first and all-surpassing consecration.
And hence in the celebration of the Sacraments the very words of
Christ are repeated.

SIGNS TAKE NAME OF THINGS SIGNIFIED. And as we learn out of   **5.179**
the Word of God that these signs were instituted for another purpose
than the usual use, therefore we teach that they now, in their holy use,
take upon them the names of things signified, and are no longer called
mere water, bread or wine, but also regeneration or the washing of
water, and the body and blood of the Lord or symbols and Sacraments
of the Lord's body and blood. Not that the symbols are changed into
the things signified, or cease to be what they are in their own nature.
For otherwise they would not be Sacraments. If they were only the
thing signified, they would not be signs.

THE SACRAMENTAL UNION. Therefore the signs acquire the names   **5.180**
of things because they are mystical signs of sacred things, and because
the signs and the things signified are sacramentally joined together;
joined together, I say, or united by a mystical signification, and by the
purpose or will of him who instituted the Sacraments. For the water,
bread, and wine are not common, but holy signs. And he that
instituted water in baptism did not institute it with the will and
intention that the faithful should only be sprinkled by the water of
baptism; and he who commanded the bread to be eaten and the wine to
be drunk in the supper did not want the faithful to receive only bread
and wine without any mystery as they eat bread in their homes; but
that they should spiritually partake of the things signified, and by faith
be truly cleansed from their sins, and partake of Christ.

5.181   THE SECTS. And, therefore, we do not at all approve of those who attribute the sanctification of the Sacraments to I know not what properties and formula or to the power of words pronounced by one who is consecrated and who has the intention of consecrating, and to other accidental things which neither Christ or the apostles delivered to us by word or example. Neither do we approve of the doctrine of those who speak of the Sacraments just as common signs, not sanctified and effectual. Nor do we approve of those who despise the visible aspect of the Sacraments because of the invisible, and so believe the signs to be superfluous because they think they already enjoy the thing themselves, as the Messalians are said to have held.

5.182   THE THING SIGNIFIED IS NEITHER INCLUDED IN OR BOUND TO THE SACRAMENTS. We do not approve of the doctrine of those who teach that grace and the things signified are so bound to and included in the signs that whoever participate outwardly in the signs, no matter what sort of persons they be, also inwardly participate in the grace and things signified.

5.183   However, as we do not estimate the value of the Sacraments by the worthiness or unworthiness of the ministers, so we do not estimate it by the condition of those who receive them. For we know that the value of the Sacraments depends upon faith and upon the truthfulness and pure goodness of God. For as the Word of God remains the true Word of God, in which, when it is preached, not only bare words are repeated, but at the same time the things signified or announced in words are offered by God, even if the ungodly and unbelievers hear and understand the words yet do not enjoy the things signified, because they do not receive them by true faith; so the Sacraments, which by the Word consist of signs and the things signified, remain true and inviolate Sacraments, signifying not only sacred things, but, by God offering, the things signified, even if unbelievers do not receive the things offered. This is not the fault of God who gives and offers them, but the fault of men who receive them without faith and illegitimately; but whose unbelief does not invalidate the faithfulness of God (Rom. 3:3 f.)

5.184   THE PURPOSE FOR WHICH SACRAMENTS WERE INSTITUTED. Since the purpose for which Sacraments were instituted was also explained in passing when right at the beginning of our exposition it was shown what Sacraments are, there is no need to be tedious by repeating what once has been said. Logically, therefore, we now speak severally of the Sacraments of the new people.

CHAPTER XX

Of Holy Baptism

5.185   THE INSTITUTION OF BAPTISM. Baptism was instituted and consecrated by God. First John baptized, who dipped Christ in the water in Jordan. From him it came to the apostles, who also baptized with water. The Lord expressly commanded them to preach the Gospel and to baptize "in the name of the Father and of the Son and of the Holy Spirit" (Matt. 28:19). And in The Acts, Peter said to the Jews who inquired what they ought to do: "Be baptized every one of you in the name of Jesus Christ for the forgiveness of your sins; and you shall receive the gift of the Holy Spirit" (Acts 2:37 f.). Hence by some baptism is called a sign of initiation for God's people, since by it the elect of God are consecrated to God.

ONE BAPTISM. There is but one baptism in the Church of God; and 5.186 it is sufficient to be once baptized or consecrated unto God. For baptism once received continues for all of life, and is a perpetual sealing of our adoption.

WHAT IT MEANS TO BE BAPTIZED. Now to be baptized in the name 5.187 of Christ is to be enrolled, entered, and received into the covenant and family, and so into the inheritance of the sons of God; yes, and in this life to be called after the name of God; that is to say, to be called a son of God; to be cleansed also from the filthiness of sins, and to be granted the manifold grace of God, in order to lead a new and innocent life. Baptism, therefore, calls to mind and renews the great favor God has shown to the race of mortal men. For we are all born in the pollution of sin and are the children of wrath. But God, who is rich in mercy, freely cleanses us from our sins by the blood of his Son, and in him adopts us to be his sons, and by a holy covenant joins us to himself, and enriches us with various gifts, that we might live a new life. All these things are assured by baptism. For inwardly we are regenerated, purified, and renewed by God through the Holy Spirit; and outwardly we receive the assurance of the greatest gifts in the water, by which also those great benefits are represented, and, as it were, set before our eyes to be beheld.

WE ARE BAPTIZED WITH WATER. And therefore we are baptized, 5.188 that is, washed or sprinkled with visible water. For the water washes dirt away, and cools and refreshes hot and tired bodies. And the grace of God performs these things for souls, and does so invisibly or spiritually.

THE OBLIGATION OF BAPTISM. Moreover, God also separates us 5.189 from all strange religions and peoples by the symbol of baptism, and consecrates us to himself as his property. We, therefore, confess our faith when we are baptized, and obligate ourselves to God for obedience, mortification of the flesh, and newness of life. Hence, we are enlisted in the holy military service of Christ that all our life long we should fight against the world, Satan, and our own flesh. Moreover, we are baptized into one body of the Church, that with all members of the Church we might beautifully concur in the one religion and in mutual services.

THE FORM OF BAPTISM. We believe that the most perfect form of 5.190 baptism is that by which Christ was baptized, and by which the apostles baptized. Those things, therefore, which by man's device were added afterwards and used in the Church we do not consider necessary to the perfection of baptism. Of this kind is exorcism, the use of burning lights, oil, salt, spittle, and such other things as that baptism is to be celebrated twice every year with a multitude of ceremonies. For we believe that one baptism of the Church has been sanctified in God's first institution, and that it is consecrated by the Word and is also effectual today in virtue of God's first blessing.

5.191   THE MINISTER OF BAPTISM. We teach that baptism should not be administered in the Church by women or midwives. For Paul deprived women of ecclesiastical duties, and baptism has to do with these.

5.192   ANABAPTISTS. We condemn the Anabaptists, who deny that newborn infants of the faithful are to be baptized. For according to evangelical teaching, of such is the Kingdom of God, and they are in the covenant of God. Why, then, should the sign of God's covenant not be given to them? Why should those who belong to God and are in his Church not be initiated by holy baptism? We condemn also the Anabaptists in the rest of their peculiar doctrines which they hold contrary to the Word of God. We therefore are not Anabaptists and have nothing in common with them.

CHAPTER XXI

Of the Holy Supper of the Lord

5.193   THE SUPPER OF THE LORD. The Supper of the Lord (which is called the Lord's Table, and the Eucharist, that is, a Thanksgiving), is, therefore, usually called a supper, because it was instituted by Christ at his last supper, and still represents it, and because in it the faithful are spiritually fed and given drink.

5.194   THE AUTHOR AND CONSECRATOR OF THE SUPPER. For the author of the Supper of the Lord is not an angel or any man, but the Son of God himself, our Lord Jesus Christ, who first consecrated it to his Church. And the same consecration or blessing still remains among all those who celebrate no other but that very Supper which the Lord instituted, and at which they repeat the words of the Lord's Supper, and in all things look to the one Christ by a true faith, from whose hands they receive, as it were, what they receive through the ministry of the ministers of the Church.

5.195   A MEMORIAL OF GOD'S BENEFITS. By this sacred rite the Lord wishes to keep in fresh remembrance that greatest benefit which he showed to mortal men, namely, that by having given his body and shed his blood he has pardoned all our sins, and redeemed us from eternal death and the power of the devil, and now feeds us with his flesh, and gives us his blood to drink, which, being received spiritually by true faith, nourish us to eternal life. And this so great a benefit is renewed as often as the Lord's Supper is celebrated. For the Lord said: "Do this in remembrance of me." This holy Supper also seals to us that the very body of Christ was truly given for us, and his blood shed for the remission of our sins, lest our faith should in any way waver.

THE SIGN AND THING SIGNIFIED. And this is visibly represented by this Sacrament outwardly through the ministers, and, as it were, presented to our eyes to be seen, which is invisibly wrought by the Holy Spirit inwardly in the soul. Bread is outwardly offered by the minister, and the words of the Lord are heard: "Take, eat; this is my body"; and, "Take and divide among you. Drink of it, all of you; this is my blood." Therefore the faithful receive what is given by the ministers of the Lord, and they eat the bread of the Lord and drink of the Lord's cup. At the same time by the work of Christ through the Holy Spirit they also inwardly receive the flesh and blood of the Lord, and are thereby nourished unto life eternal. For the flesh and blood of Christ is the true food and drink unto life eternal; and Christ himself, since he was given for us and is our Savior, is the principal thing in the Supper, and we do not permit anything else to be substituted in his place.

5.196

But in order to understand better and more clearly how the flesh and blood of Christ are the food and drink of the faithful, and are received by the faithful unto eternal life, we would add these few things. There is more than one kind of eating. There is corporeal eating whereby food is taken into the mouth, is chewed with the teeth, and swallowed into the stomach. In times past the Capernaites thought that the flesh of the Lord should be eaten in this way, but they are refuted by him in John, ch. 6. For as the flesh of Christ cannot be eaten corporeally without infamy and savagery, so it is not food for the stomach. All men are forced to admit this. We therefore disapprove of that canon in the Pope's decrees, *Ego Berengarius (De Consecrat.,* Dist. 2). For neither did godly antiquity believe, nor do we believe, that the body of Christ is to be eaten corporeally and essentially with a bodily mouth.

5.197

SPIRITUAL EATING OF THE LORD. There is also a spiritual eating of Christ's body; not such that we think that thereby the food itself is to be changed into spirit, but whereby the body and blood of the Lord, while remaining in their own essence and property, are spiritually communicated to us, certainly not in a corporeal but in a spiritual way, by the Holy Spirit, who applies and bestows upon us these things which have been prepared for us by the sacrifice of the Lord's body and blood for us, namely, the remission of sins, deliverance, and eternal life; so that Christ lives in us and we live in him, and he causes us to receive him by true faith to this end that he may become for us such spiritual food and drink, that is, our life.

5.198

CHRIST AS OUR FOOD SUSTAINS US IN LIFE. For even as bodily food and drink not only refresh and strengthen our bodies, but also keeps them alive, so the flesh of Christ delivered for us, and his blood shed for us, not only refresh and strengthen our souls, but also preserve them alive, not in so far as they are corporeally eaten and drunken, but in so far as they are communicated unto us spiritually by the Spirit of God, as the Lord said: "The bread which I shall give for

5.199

the life of the world is my flesh" (John 6:51), and "the flesh" (namely what is eaten bodily) "is of no avail; it is the spirit that gives life" (v. 63). And: "The words that I have spoken to you are spirit and life."

5.200   CHRIST RECEIVED BY FAITH. And as we must by eating receive food into our bodies in order that it may work in us, and prove its efficacy in us—since it profits us nothing when it remains outside us—so it is necessary that we receive Christ by faith, that he may become ours, and he may live in us and we in him. For he says: "I am the bread of life; he who comes to me shall not hunger, and he who believes in me shall never thirst" (John 6:35); and also, "He who eats me will live because of me . . . he abides in me, I in him" (vs. 57, 56).

5.201   SPIRITUAL FOOD. From all this it is clear that by spiritual food we do not mean some imaginary food I know not what, but the very body of the Lord given to us, which nevertheless is received by the faithful not corporeally, but spiritually by faith. In this matter we follow the teaching of the Savior himself, Christ the Lord, according to John, ch. 6.

5.202   EATING NECESSARY FOR SALVATION. And this eating of the flesh and drinking of the blood of the Lord is so necessary for salvation that without it no man can be saved. But this spiritual eating and drinking also occurs apart from the Supper of the Lord, and as often and wherever a man believes in Christ. To which that sentence of St. Augustine's perhaps applies: "Why do you provide for your teeth and your stomach? Believe, and you have eaten."

5.203   SACRAMENTAL EATING OF THE LORD. Besides the higher spiritual eating there is also a sacramental eating of the body of the Lord by which not only spiritually and internally the believer truly participates in the true body and blood of the Lord, but also, by coming to the Table of the Lord, outwardly receives the visible Sacrament of the body and blood of the Lord. To be sure, when the believer believed, he first received the life-giving food, and still enjoys it. But therefore, when he now receives the Sacrament, he does not receive nothing. For he progresses in continuing to communicate in the body and blood of the Lord, and so his faith is kindled and grows more and more, and is refreshed by spiritual food. For while we live, faith is continually increased. And he who outwardly receives the Sacrament by true faith, not only receives the sign, but also, as we said, enjoys the thing itself. Moreover, he obeys the Lord's institution and commandment, and with a joyful mind gives thanks for his redemption and that of all mankind, and makes a faithful memorial to the Lord's death, and gives a witness before the Church, of whose body he is a member. Assurance is also given to those who receive the Sacrament that the body of the Lord was given and his blood shed, not only for men in general, but particularly for every faithful communicant, to whom it is food and drink unto eternal life.

5.204   UNBELIEVERS TAKE THE SACRAMENT TO THEIR JUDGMENT. But he who comes to this sacred Table of the Lord without faith, communicates only in the Sacrament and does not receive the substance of the

Sacrament whence comes life and salvation; and such men unworthily eat of the Lord's Table. Whoever eats the bread or drinks the cup of the Lord in an unworthy manner will be guilty of the body and blood of the Lord, and eats and drinks judgment upon himself (I Cor. 11:26–29). For when they do not approach with true faith, they dishonor the death of Christ, and therefore eat and drink condemnation to themselves.

THE PRESENCE OF CHRIST IN THE SUPPER. We do not, therefore, so **5.205** join the body of the Lord and his blood with the bread and wine as to say that the bread itself is the body of Christ except in a sacramental way; or that the body of Christ is hidden corporeally under the bread, so that it ought to be worshipped under the form of bread; or yet that whoever receives the sign, receives also the thing itself. The body of Christ is in heaven at the right hand of the Father; and therefore our hearts are to be lifted up on high, and not to be fixed on the bread, neither is the Lord to be worshipped in the bread. Yet the Lord is not absent from his Church when she celebrates the Supper. The sun, which is absent from us in the heavens, is notwithstanding effectually present among us. How much more is the Sun of Righteousness, Christ, although in his body he is absent from us in heaven, present with us, not corporeally, but spiritually, by his vivifying operation, and as he himself explained at his Last Supper that he would be present with us (John, chs. 14; 15; and 16). Whence it follows that we do not have the Supper without Christ, and yet at the same time have an unbloody and mystical Supper, as it was universally called by antiquity.

OTHER PURPOSES OF THE LORD'S SUPPER. Moreover, we are **5.206** admonished in the celebration of the Supper of the Lord to be mindful of whose body we have become members, and that, therefore, we may be of one mind with all the brethren, live a holy life, and not pollute ourselves with wickedness and strange religions; but, persevering in the true faith to the end of our life, strive to excel in holiness of life.

PREPARATION FOR THE SUPPER. It is therefore fitting that when we **5.207** would come to the Supper, we first examine ourselves according to the commandment of the apostle, especially as to the kind of faith we have, whether we believe that Christ has come to save sinners and to call them to repentance, and whether each man believes that he is in the number of those who have been delivered by Christ and saved; and whether he is determined to change his wicked life, to lead a holy life, and with the Lord's help to persevere in the true religion and in harmony with the brethren, and to give due thanks to God for his deliverance.

THE OBSERVANCE OF THE SUPPER WITH BOTH BREAD AND WINE. **5.208** We think that rite, manner, or form of the Supper to be the most simple and excellent which comes nearest to the first institution of the Lord and to the apostles' doctrine. It consists in proclaiming the Word of God, in godly prayers, in the action of the Lord himself, and its repetition, in the eating of the Lord's body and drinking of his blood;

in a fitting remembrance of the Lord's death, and a faithful thanksgiving; and in a holy fellowship in the union of the body of the Church.

5.209   We therefore disapprove of those who have taken from the faithful one species of the Sacrament, namely, the Lord's cup. For these seriously offend against the institution of the Lord who says: "Drink ye all of this"; which he did not so expressly say of the bread.

5.210   We are not now discussing what kind of mass once existed among the fathers, whether it is to be tolerated or not. But this we say freely that the mass which is now used throughout the Roman Church has been abolished in our churches for many and very good reasons which, for brevity's sake, we do not now enumerate in detail. We certainly could not approve of making a wholesome action into a vain spectacle and a means of gaining merit, and of celebrating it for a price. Nor could we approve of saying that in it the priest is said to effect the very body of the Lord, and really to offer it for the remission of the sins of the living and the dead, and in addition, for the honor, veneration and remembrance of the saints in heaven, etc.

CHAPTER XXII

Of Religious and Ecclesiastical Meetings

5.211   WHAT OUGHT TO BE DONE IN MEETINGS FOR WORSHIP. Although it is permitted all men to read the Holy Scriptures privately at home, and by instruction to edify one another in the true religion, yet in order that the Word of God may be properly preached to the people, and prayers and supplication publicly made, also that the Sacraments may be rightly administered, and that collections may be made for the poor and to pay the cost of all the Church's expenses, and in order to maintain social intercourse, it is most necessary that religious or Church gatherings be held. For it is certain that in the apostolic and primitive Church, there were such assemblies frequented by all the godly.

5.212   MEETINGS FOR WORSHIP NOT TO BE NEGLECTED. As many as spurn such meetings and stay away from them, despise true religion, and are to be urged by the pastors and godly magistrates to abstain from stubbornly absenting themselves from sacred assemblies.

5.213   MEETINGS ARE PUBLIC. But Church meetings are not to be secret and hidden, but public and well attended, unless persecution by the enemies of Christ and the Church does not permit them to be public. For we know how under the tyranny of the Roman emperors the meetings of the primitive Church were held in secret places.

5.214   DECENT MEETING PLACES. Moreover, the places where the faithful meet are to be decent, and in all respects fit for God's Church. Therefore, spacious buildings or temples are to be chosen, but they are to be purged of everything that is not fitting for a church. And everything is to be arranged for decorum, necessity, and godly decency, lest anything be lacking that is required for worship and the necessary works of the Church.

MODESTY AND HUMILITY TO BE OBSERVED IN MEETINGS. And as we believe that God does not dwell in temples made with hands, so we know that on account of God's Word and sacred use places dedicated to God and his worship are not profane, but holy, and that those who are present in them are to conduct themselves reverently and modestly, seeing that they are in a sacred place, in the presence of God and his holy angels.   5.215

THE TRUE ORNAMENTATION OF SANCTUARIES. Therefore, all luxurious attire, all pride, and everything unbecoming to Christian humility, discipline and modesty, are to be banished from the sanctuaries and places of prayer of Christians. For the true ornamentation of churches does not consist in ivory, gold, and precious stones, but in the frugality, piety, and virtues of those who are in the Church. Let all things be done decently and in order in the church, and finally, let all things be done for edification.   5.216

WORSHIP IN THE COMMON LANGUAGE. Therefore, let all strange tongues keep silence in gatherings for worship, and let all things be set forth in a common language which is understood by the people gathered in that place.   5.217

CHAPTER XXIII

Of the Prayers of the Church, of Singing,
and of Canonical Hours

COMMON LANGUAGE. It is true that a man is permitted to pray privately in any language that he understands, but public prayers in meetings for worship are to be made in the common language known to all. PRAYER. Let all the prayers of the faithful be poured forth to God alone, through the mediation of Christ only, out of faith and love. The priesthood of Christ the Lord and true religion forbid the invocation of saints in heaven or to use them as intercessors. Prayer is to be made for magistracy, for kings, and all that are placed in authority, for ministers of the Church, and for all needs of churches. In calamities, especially of the Church, unceasing prayer is to be made both privately and publicly.   5.218

FREE PRAYER. Moreover, prayer is to be made voluntarily, without constraint or for any reward. Nor is it proper for prayer to be superstitiously restricted to one place, as if it were not permitted to pray anywhere except in a sanctuary. Neither is it necessary for public prayers to be the same in all churches with respect to form and time. Each Church is to exercise its own freedom. Socrates, in his history, says, "In all regions of the world you will not find two churches which wholly agree in prayer" (*Hist. ecclesiast.* V.22, 57). The authors of this difference, I think, were those who were in charge of the   5.219

Churches at particular times. Yet if they agree, it is to be highly commended and imitated by others.

5.220 THE METHOD TO BE EMPLOYED IN PUBLIC PRAYERS. As in everything, so also in public prayers there is to be a standard lest they be excessively long and irksome. The greater part of meetings for worship is therefore to be given to evangelical teaching, and care is to be taken lest the congregation is wearied by too lengthy prayers and when they are to hear the preaching of the Gospel they either leave the meeting or, having been exhausted, want to do away with it altogether. To such people the sermon seems to be overlong, which otherwise is brief enough. And therefore it is appropriate for preachers to keep to a standard.

5.221 SINGING. Likewise moderation is to be exercised where singing is used in a meeting for worship. That song which they call the Gregorian Chant has many foolish things in it; hence it is rightly rejected by many of our churches. If there are churches which have a true and proper sermon[9] but no singing, they ought not to be condemned. For all churches do not have the advantage of singing. And it is well known from testimonies of antiquity that the custom of singing is very old in the Eastern Churches whereas it was late when it was at length accepted in the West.

5.222 CANONICAL HOURS. Antiquity knew nothing of canonical hours, that is, prayers arranged for certain hours of the day, and sung or recited by the Papists, as can be proved from their breviaries and by many arguments. But they also have not a few absurdities, of which I say nothing else; accordingly they are rightly omitted by churches which substitute in their place things that are beneficial for the whole Church of God.

CHAPTER XXIV

Of Holy Days, Fasts and the Choice of Foods

5.223 THE TIME NECESSARY FOR WORSHIP. Although religion is not bound to time, yet it cannot be cultivated and exercised without a proper distribution and arrangement of time. Every Church, therefore, chooses for itself a certain time for public prayers, and for the preaching of the Gospel, and for the celebration of the Sacraments; and no one is permitted to overthrow this appointment of the Church at his own pleasure. For unless some due time and leisure is given for the outward exercise of religion, without doubt men would be drawn away from it by their own affairs.

5.224 THE LORD'S DAY. Hence we see that in the ancient churches there were not only certain set hours in the week appointed for meetings, but

---

[9]The Latin has *orationem* which has been rendered as "prayer." But from the context it would seem that the word should be given its usual classical meaning of a "speech."

that also the Lord's Day itself, ever since the apostles' time, was set aside for them and for a holy rest, a practice now rightly preserved by our Churches for the sake of worship and love.

SUPERSTITION. In this connection we do not yield to the Jewish observance and to superstitions. For we do not believe that one day is any holier than another, or think that rest in itself is acceptable to God. Moreover, we celebrate the Lord's Day and not the Sabbath as a free observance. 5.225

THE FESTIVALS OF CHRIST AND THE SAINTS. Moreover, if in Christian liberty the churches religiously celebrate the memory of the Lord's nativity, circumcision, passion, resurrection, and of his ascension into heaven, and the sending of the Holy Spirit upon his disciples, we approve of it highly. But we do not approve of feasts instituted for men and for saints. Holy days have to do with the first Table of the Law and belong to God alone. Finally, holy days which have been instituted for the saints and which we have abolished, have much that is absurd and useless, and are not to be tolerated. In the meantime, we confess that the remembrance of saints, at a suitable time and place, is to be profitably commended to the people in sermons, and the holy examples of the saints set forth to be imitated by all. 5.226

FASTING. Now, the more seriously the Church of Christ condemns surfeiting, drunkenness, and all kinds of lust and intemperance, so much the more strongly does it commend to us Christian fasting. For fasting is nothing else than the abstinence and moderation of the godly, and a discipline, care and chastisement of our flesh undertaken as a necessity for the time being, whereby we are humbled before God, and we deprive the flesh of its fuel so that it may the more willingly and easily obey the Spirit. Therefore, those who pay no attention to such things do not fast, but imagine that they fast if they stuff their stomachs once a day, and at a certain or prescribed time abstain from certain foods, thinking that by having done this work they please God and do something good. Fasting is an aid to the prayers of the saints and for all virtues. But as is seen in the books of the prophets, the fast of the Jews who fasted from food but not from wickedness did not please God. 5.227

PUBLIC AND PRIVATE FASTING. Now there is a public and a private fasting. In olden times they celebrated public fasts in calamitous times and in the affliction of the Church. They abstained altogether from food till the evening, and spent all that time in holy prayers, the worship of God, and repentance. These differed little from mourning, and there is frequent mention of them in the Prophets and especially by Joel in Ch. 2. Such a fast should be kept at this day, when the Church is in distress. Private fasts are undertaken by each one of us, as he feels himself withdrawn from the Spirit. For in this manner he withdraws the flesh from its fuel. 5.228

CHARACTERISTICS OF FASTING. All fasts ought to proceed from a free and willing spirit, and from genuine humility, and not feigned to gain the applause or favor of men, much less that a man should wish to merit righteousness by them. But let every one fast to this end, that he 5.229

149

may deprive the flesh of its fuel in order that he may the more zealously serve God.

5.230   LENT. The fast of Lent is attested by antiquity but not at all in the writings of the apostles. Therefore it ought not, and cannot, be imposed on the faithful. It is certain that formerly there were various forms and customs of fasting. Hence, Irenaeus, a most ancient writer, says: "Some think that a fast should be observed one day only, others two days, but others more, and some forty days. This diversity in keeping this fast did not first begin in our times, but long before us by those, as I suppose, who did not simply keep to what had been delivered to them from the beginning, but afterwards fell into another custom either through negligence or ignorance" (*Fragm. 3,* ed. Stieren, I. 824 f.). Moreover, Socrates, the historian, says: "Because no ancient text is found concerning this matter, I think the apostles left this to every man's own judgment, that every one might do what is good without fear or constraint" (*Hist. ecclesiast.* V.22, 40).

5.231   CHOICE OF FOOD. Now concerning the choice of foods, we think that in fasting all things should be denied to the flesh whereby the flesh is made more insolent, and by which it is greatly pleased, and by which it is inflamed with desire whether by fish or meat or spices or delicacies and excellent wines. Moreover, we know that all the creatures of God were made for the use and service of men. All things which God made are good, and without distinction are to be used in the fear of God and with proper moderation (Gen. 2:15 f.). For the apostle says: "To the pure all things are pure" (Titus 1:15), and also: "Eat whatever is sold in the meat market without raising any question on the ground of conscience" (I Cor. 10:25). The same apostle calls the doctrine of those who teach to abstain from meats "the doctrine of demons"; for "God created fools to be received with thanksgiving by those who believe and know this truth that everything created by God is good, and nothing is to be rejected if it is received with thanksgiving" (I Tim. 4:1 ff.). The same apostle, in the epistle to the Colossians, reproves those who want to acquire a reputation for holiness by excessive abstinence (Col. 2:18 ff.).

5.232   SECTS. Therefore we entirely disapprove of the Tatians and the Encratites, and all the disciples of Eustathius, against whom the Gangrian Synod was called.

CHAPTER XXV

Of Catechizing and of Comforting and Visiting the Sick

5.233   YOUTH TO BE INSTRUCTED IN GODLINESS. The Lord enjoined his ancient people to exercise the greatest care that young people, even from infancy, be properly instructed. Moreover, he expressly commanded in his law that they should teach them, and that the mysteries of the Sacraments should be explained. Now since it is well known from the writings of the Evangelists and apostles that God has no less concern for the youth of his new people, when he openly testifies and says: "Let the children come to me; for to such belongs the kingdom of heaven" (Mark 10:14), the pastors of the churches act most wisely when they early and carefully catechize the youth, laying the first grounds of faith, and faithfully teaching the rudiments of our religion by expounding the Ten Commandments, the Apostles' Creed, the Lord's Prayer, and the doctrine of the Sacraments, with other such principles and chief heads of our religion. Here let the Church show her faith and diligence in bringing the children to be catechized, desirous and glad to have her children well instructed.

THE VISITATION OF THE SICK. Since men are never exposed to more   5.234
grievous temptations than when they are harassed by infirmities, are sick and are weakened by diseases of both soul and body, surely it is never more fitting for pastors of churches to watch more carefully for the welfare of their flocks than in such diseases and infirmities. Therefore let them visit the sick soon, and let them be called in good time by the sick, if the circumstance itself would have required it. Let them comfort and confirm them in the true faith, and then arm them against the dangerous suggestions of Satan. They should also hold prayer for the sick in the home and, if need be, prayers should also be made for the sick in the public meeting; and they should see that they happily depart this life. We said above that we do not approve of the Popish visitation of the sick with extreme unction because it is absurd and is not approved by canonical Scriptures.

CHAPTER XXVI

Of the Burial of the Faithful,
and of the Care to Be Shown for the Dead;
of Purgatory, and the Appearing of Spirits

THE BURIAL OF BODIES. As the bodies of the faithful are the   5.235
temples of the Holy Spirit which we truly believe will rise again at the Last Day, Scriptures command that they be honorably and without superstition committed to the earth, and also that honorable mention be made of those saints who have fallen asleep in the Lord, and that all duties of familial piety be shown to those left behind, their widows and orphans. We do not teach that any other care be taken for the dead. Therefore, we greatly disapprove of the Cynics, who neglected the bodies of the dead or most carelessly and disdainfully cast them into the earth, never saying a good word about the deceased, or caring a bit about those whom they left behind them.

THE CARE FOR THE DEAD. On the other hand, we do not approve of   5.236
those who are overly and absurdly attentive to the deceased; who, like the heathen, bewail their dead (although we do not blame that moderate mourning which the apostle permits in I Thess. 4:13, judging it to

be inhuman not to grieve at all); and who sacrifice for the dead, and mumble certain prayers for pay, in order by such ceremonies to deliver their loved ones from the torments in which they are immersed by death, and then think they are able to liberate them by such incantations.

5.237   THE STATE OF THE SOUL DEPARTED FROM THE BODY. For we believe that the faithful, after bodily death, go directly to Christ, and, therefore, do not need the eulogies and prayers of the living for the dead and their services. Likewise we believe that unbelievers are immediately cast into hell from which no exit is opened for the wicked by any services of the living.

5.238   PURGATORY. But what some teach concerning the fire of purgatory is opposed to the Christian faith, namely, "I believe in the forgiveness of sins, and the life everlasting," and to the perfect purgation through Christ, and to these words of Christ our Lord: "Truly, truly, I say to you, he who hears my word and believes him who sent me, has eternal life; he shall not come into judgment, but has passed from death to life" (John 5:24). Again: "He who has bathed does not need to wash, except for his feet, but he is clean all over, and you are clean" (John 13:10).

5.239   THE APPARITION OF SPIRITS. Now what is related of the spirits or souls of the dead sometimes appearing to those who are alive, and begging certain duties of them whereby they may be set free, we count those apparitions among the laughingstocks, crafts, and deceptions of the devil, who, as he can transform himself into an angel of light, so he strives either to overthrow the true faith or to call it into doubt. In the Old Testament the Lord forbade the seeking of the truth from the dead, and any sort of commerce with spirits (Deut. 18:11). Indeed, as evangelical truth declares, the glutton, being in torment, is denied a return to his brethren, as the divine oracle declares in the words: "They have Moses and the prophets; let them hear them. If they hear not Moses and the prophets, neither will they be convinced if some one should rise from the dead" (Luke 16:29 ff.).

CHAPTER XXVII

Of Rites, Ceremonies and Things Indifferent

5.240   CEREMONIES AND RITES. Unto the ancient people were given at one time certain ceremonies, as a kind of instruction for those who were kept under the law, as under a schoolmaster or tutor. But when Christ, the Deliverer, came and the law was abolished, we who believe are no more under the law (Rom. 6:14), and the ceremonies have disappeared; hence the apostles did not want to retain or to restore them in Christ's Church to such a degree that they openly testified that they did not wish to impose any burden upon the Church. Therefore, we would seem to be bringing in and restoring Judaism if we were to increase ceremonies and rites in Christ's Church according to the custom in the ancient Church. Hence, we by no means approve of the opinion of those who think that the Church of Christ must be held in check by many different rites, as if by some kind of training. For if the apostles did not want to impose upon Christian people ceremonies or rites which were appointed by God, who, I pray, in his right mind would obtrude upon them the inventions devised by man? The more the mass of rites is increased in the Church, the more is detracted not only from Christian liberty, but also from Christ, and from faith in him, as long as the people seek those things in ceremonies which they should seek in the only Son of God, Jesus Christ, through faith. Wherefore a few moderate and simple rites, that are not contrary to the Word of God, are sufficient for the godly.

DIVERSITY OF RITES. If different rites are found in churches, no one   5.241
should think that for this reason the churches disagree. Socrates says: "It would be impossible to put together in writing all the rites of churches throughout cities and countries. No religion observes the same rites, even though it embraces the same doctrine concerning them. For those who are of the same faith disagree among themselves about rites" (*Hist. ecclesiast.* V.22, 30, 62). This much says Socrates. And we, today, having in our churches different rites in the celebration of the Lord's Supper and in some other things, nevertheless do not disagree in doctrine and faith; nor is the unity and fellowship of our churches thereby rent asunder. For the churches have always used their liberty in such rites, as being things indifferent. We also do the same thing today.

THINGS INDIFFERENT. But at the same time we admonish men to be   5.242
on guard lest they reckon among things indifferent what are in fact not indifferent, as some are wont to regard the mass and the use of images in places of worship as things indifferent. "Indifferent," wrote Jerome to Augustine, "is that which is neither good nor bad, so that, whether you do it or not, you are neither just nor unjust." Therefore, when things indifferent are wrested to the confession of faith, they cease to be free; as Paul shows that it is lawful for a man to eat flesh if someone does not remind him that it was offered to idols; for then it is unlawful, because he who eats it seems to approve idolatry by eating it (I Cor. 8:9 ff.; 10:25 ff.).

CHAPTER XXVIII

Of the Possessions of the Church

THE POSSESSIONS OF THE CHURCH AND THEIR PROPER USE. The   5.243
Church of Christ possesses riches through the munificence of princes and the liberality of the faithful who have given their means to the Church. For the Church has need of such resources and from ancient time has had resources for the maintenance of things necessary for the Church. Now the true use of the Church's wealth was, and is now, to

maintain teaching in schools and in religious meetings, along with all the worship, rites, and buildings of the Church; finally, to maintain teachers, scholars, and ministers, with other necessary things, and especially for the succor and relief of the poor. MANAGEMENT. Moreover, God-fearing and wise men, noted for the management of domestic affairs, should be chosen to administer properly the Church's possessions.

5.244 THE MISUSE OF THE CHURCH'S POSSESSIONS. But if through misfortune or through the audacity, ignorance or avarice of some persons the Church's wealth is abused, it is to be restored to a sacred use by godly and wise men. For neither is an abuse, which is the greatest sacrilege, to be winked at. Therefore, we teach that schools and institutions which have been corrupted in doctrine, worship and morals must be reformed, and that the relief of the poor must be arranged dutifully, wisely, and in good faith.

CHAPTER XXIX

Of Celibacy, Marriage and the Management of Domestic Affairs

5.245 SINGLE PEOPLE. Those who have the gift of celibacy from heaven, so that from the heart or with their whole soul are pure and continent and are not aflame with passion, let them serve the Lord in that calling, as long as they feel endued with that divine gift; and let them not lift up themselves above others, but let them serve the Lord continuously in simplicity and humility (I Cor. 7:7 ff.). For such are more apt to attend to divine things than those who are distracted with the private affairs of a family. But if, again, the gift be taken away, and they feel a continual burning, let them call to mind the words of the apostle: "It is better to marry than to be aflame" (I Cor. 7:9).

5.246 MARRIAGE. For marriage (which is the medicine of incontinency, and continency itself) was instituted by the Lord God himself, who blessed it most bountifully, and willed man and woman to cleave one to the other inseparably, and to live together in complete love and concord (Matt. 19:4 ff.). Whereupon we know that the apostle said: "Let marriage be held in honor among all, and let the marriage bed be undefiled" (Heb. 13:4). And again: "If a girl marries, she does not sin" (I Cor. 7:28). THE SECTS. We therefore condemn polygamy, and those who condemn second marriages.

5.247 HOW MARRIAGES ARE TO BE CONTRACTED. We teach that marriages are to be lawfully contracted in the fear of the Lord, and not against the laws which forbid certain degrees of consanguinity, lest the marriages should be incestuous. Let marriages be made with consent of the parents, or of those who take the place of parents, and above all for that purpose for which the Lord instituted marriages. Moreover, let them be kept holy with the utmost faithfulness, piety, love and purity of those joined together. Therefore let them guard against quarrels, dissensions, lust and adultery.

MATRIMONIAL FORUM. Let lawful courts be established in the Church, and holy judges who may care for marriages, and may repress all unchastity and shamefulness, and before whom matrimonial disputes may be settled.   **5.248**

THE REARING OF CHILDREN. Children are to be brought up by the parents in the fear of the Lord; and parents are to provide for their children, remembering the saying of the apostle: "If anyone does not provide for his relatives, he has disowned the faith and is worse than an unbeliever" (I Tim. 5:8). But especially they should teach their children honest trades or professions by which they may support themselves. They should keep them from idleness and in all these things instill in them true faith in God, lest through a lack of confidence or too much security or filthy greed they become dissolute and achieve no success.   **5.249**

And it is most certain that those works which are done by parents in true faith by way of domestic duties and the management of their households are in God's sight holy and truly good works. They are no less pleasing to God than prayers, fasting and almsgiving. For thus the apostle has taught in his epistles, especially in those to Timothy and Titus. And with the same apostle we account the doctrine of those who forbid marriage or openly castigate or indirectly discredit it, as if it were not holy and pure, among the doctrine of demons.   **5.250**

We also detest an impure single life, the secret and open lusts and fornications of hypocrites pretending to be continent when they are the most incontinent of all. All these God will judge. We do not disapprove of riches or rich men, if they be godly and use their riches well. But we reject the sect of the Apostolicals, etc.[10]   **5.251**

CHAPTER XXX

Of the Magistracy

THE MAGISTRACY IS FROM GOD. Magistracy of every kind is instituted by God himself for the peace and tranquillity of the human race, and thus it should have the chief place in the world. If the magistrate is opposed to the Church, he can hinder and disturb it very much; but if he is a friend and even a member of the Church, he is a most useful and excellent member of it, who is able to benefit it greatly, and to assist it best of all.   **5.252**

THE DUTY OF THE MAGISTRATE. The chief duty of the magistrate is to secure and preserve peace and public tranquillity. Doubtless he will   **5.253**

---

[10] The Apostolicals were followers of a religious fanatic, Gherardo Segarelli, of Parma, who in the thirteenth century wanted to restore the poverty of the apostolic life.

never do this more successfully than when he is truly God-fearing and religious; that is to say, when, according to the example of the most holy kings and princes of the people of the Lord, he promotes the preaching of the truth and sincere faith, roots out lies and all superstition, together with all impiety and idolatry, and defends the Church of God. We certainly teach that the care of religion belongs especially to the holy magistrate.

5.254 Let him, therefore, hold the Word of God in his hands, and take care lest anything contrary to it is taught. Likewise let him govern the people entrusted to him by God with good laws made according to the Word of God, and let him keep them in discipline, duty and obedience. Let him exercise judgment by judging uprightly. Let him not respect any man's person or accept bribes. Let him protect widows, orphans and the afflicted. Let him punish and even banish criminals, impostors and barbarians. For he does not bear the sword in vain (Rom. 13:4).

5.255 Therefore, let him draw this sword of God against all malefactors, seditious persons, thieves, murderers, oppressors, blasphemers, perjured persons, and all those whom God has commanded him to punish and even to execute. Let him suppress stubborn heretics (who are truly heretics), who do not cease to blaspheme the majesty of God and to trouble, and even to destroy the Church of God.

5.256 WAR. And if it is necessary to preserve the safety of the people by war, let him wage war in the name of God; provided he has first sought peace by all means possible, and cannot save his people in any other way except by war. And when the magistrate does these things in faith, he serves God by those very works which are truly good, and receives a blessing from the Lord.

5.257 We condemn the Anabaptists, who, when they deny that a Christian may hold the office of a magistrate, deny also that a man may be justly put to death by the magistrate, or that the magistrate may wage war, or that oaths are to be rendered to a magistrate, and such like things.

5.258 THE DUTY OF SUBJECTS. For as God wants to effect the safety of his people by the magistrate, whom he has given to the world to be, as it were, a father, so all subjects are commanded to acknowledge this favor of God in the magistrate. Therefore let them honor and reverence the magistrate as the minister of God; let them love him, favor him, and pray for him as their father; and let them obey all his just and fair commands. Finally, let them pay all customs and taxes, and all other such dues faithfully and willingly. And if the public safety of the country and justice require it, and the magistrate of necessity wages war, let them even lay down their life and pour out their blood for the public safety and that of the magistrate. And let them do this in the name of God willingly, bravely and cheerfully. For he who opposes the magistrate provokes the severe wrath of God against himself.

5.259 SECTS AND SEDITIONS. We, therefore, condemn all who are contemptuous of the magistrate—rebels, enemies of the state, seditious villains, finally, all who openly or craftily refuse to perform whatever duties they owe.

We beseech God, our most merciful Father in heaven, that he will   **5.260**
bless the rulers of the people, and us, and his whole people, through
Jesus Christ, our only Lord and Savior; to whom be praise and glory
and thanksgiving, for all ages. Amen.

THE WESTMINSTER CONFESSION OF FAITH

- Introduction to the Westminster Standards
- The Westminster Confession of Faith
- The Shorter Catechism
- The Larger Catechism

Introduction to the Westminster Standards

The Westminster Standards developed in the unique context of the English Reformation. On the Continent, reformation of religion normally led to a national Protestant church. A prime example is the Lutheran Church in Germany. In England the pattern was different. In 1531, Henry VIII, denied a divorce by the Pope, unilaterally created the Church of England by declaring himself its Supreme Head. England had a national church without having had a prior reformation.

The history of reformation in England is marked by the desire to purify, or reform, the existing state church from within while remaining loyal to it. The people who sought that reformation were called Puritans. They wanted a church that was Calvinistic in theology, and more Presbyterian in polity, but distinctively English in character. They wished to be faithful to Scripture and also loyal to their earthly king. The Westminster Confession and catechisms were their final, though futile, achievement. They produced theological documents that shaped Calvinism and Presbyterianism worldwide. The Church of England, however, remained unreformed according to their wishes.

During the reign of Edward VI, Archbishop of Canterbury Thomas Cranmer developed a theological statement in Forty-two Articles. They were referred to an ecumenical committee of six, including John Knox. Their dual thrust against Rome on the one side and Anabaptism on the other carried over into the later Thirty-nine Articles and the Westminster Confession.

After Edward's death, Mary I took the throne determined to restore the Roman Catholic faith to England. Many Protestants were martyred, and others fled into exile, principally to Frankfurt. There the group divided. The conflict between Nonconformist Puritans, who sought to reform all according to Scripture, and the Conformist Anglicans, who insisted on maintaining the forms of the official state church, marked subsequent English history.

Elizabeth I came to the throne a Protestant. She insisted, however, that she was "supreme governor" in matters spiritual, as well as temporal, and demanded conformity to the Prayer Book of 1552, including a rubric requiring vestments. Puritans, so named in this period, rejected vestments as a symbol of surviving "popery" in the English Church. In this conflict over church order some Puritan leaders formed embryonic presbyteries for mutual support.

When James VI of Scotland ascended the English throne as James I, in 1603, Puritan hopes were high. They had a king raised as a Presbyterian. In 1604 at Hampton Court the king received many petitions from the Puritans. The sole request James granted was authorization for a new translation of the Bible that later bore his name. For the rest, James threw down the gauntlet and set the course for future conflict. His motto was "No Bishop, no King." He feared that allowing leaders in the church to be elected by the people might foster a desire for representative government in the state. Efforts toward and resistance to ecclesiastical and political reform remained intertwined in seventeenth-century England.

James's son, Charles I, was crowned in 1625. His acting on the principle of divine right to rule brought together middle-class Parliamentarians and aggrieved Puritans in opposition to him. The king dismissed Parliament and attempted to suppress religious nonconformity. His great mistake was the attempt to force bishops and the *Book of Common Prayer* on Scotland. When Charles used military force to impose his will, the Scots twice soundly defeated the English. Charles was forced to convene a new Parliament to raise money to pay off the invading Scottish army. What was later called the Long Parliament convened in November 1640, and demanded political and religious reforms. Civil war broke out in the summer of 1642. It was a religious and class conflict pitting Nonconformist middle-class Parliamentarians against High Church Royalists. This was the context in which the Westminster Standards came into being.

THE WESTMINSTER ASSEMBLY

The House of Commons presented the king a "Grand Remonstrance" in December 1641. It stated an intention to assemble "a General Synod of the most grave, pious, learned and judicious Divines of this Island, assisted by some from foreign parts professing the same Religion with us," to consult with the Parliament on its reform of religion. The general opinion of the dominantly Presbyterian Puritan parliamentarians was that the doctrine of the Church of England was basically Reformed and needed only to be protected from misinterpretation. The government and liturgy of the English Church, however, needed much amendment to harmonize with Scripture and the example of other Reformed churches.

Elected parliamentarians selected two ministers, or Divines, from their districts, one each from Oxford and Cambridge Universities, and four from London. On five occasions the Parliament sent bills implementing the assembly to the king only to have him refuse to sign them. The sixth bill was passed as an ordinance agreed to by both Houses of Parliament and put into effect without the king's assent. One hundred and twenty-one ministers were named in the ordinance along with twenty members of the House of Commons and ten members of the House of Lords. Representatives of the Churches of New England were invited, but declined to attend. Presumably they hoped by noninvolvement to preserve their Independent, or Congregational, form of church government.

Members of the assembly represented four differing ideologies regarding church government. There were establishment Episcopalians; Independents or Congregationalists; Erastians who, following Thomas

Erastus, believed that final authority in ecclesiastical matters rested with the civil authorities; and Presbyterians. Few of the establishment Episcopalians attended since the king had forbidden the proceedings. A small group of Independents was led by members who had just returned from exile in Holland. Their influence grew as time passed with support from the Parliamentary army and its General, Oliver Cromwell. The Presbyterians initially held a sizable majority.

These differences over church polity were internal ones among ministers and laypersons who were loyal ministers and members of the Church of England. They shared a generally Reformed, or Calvinistic, theological perspective. The "Grand Debate" in the assembly was not over theology but whether the polity of the one State Church of England would become Congregational or Presbyterian. In the end, historical circumstances defeated the efforts of both parties.

The Divines met initially on Saturday, July 1, 1643, in Westminster Abbey, from which location the name Westminster Assembly derived. The Parliament's appointed moderator, Dr. Twisse, preached to the assembled Divines, both Houses of Parliament, and a large congregation on John 14:18, "I will not leave you comfortless; I will come unto you," a text pertinent to those troubled times of "Popish wars and combustions." The assembly continued to have days of worship and fasting in concert with the Parliament. These occurred regularly once each month and at other times when the Parliament's forces were being defeated in battle or they had particular reason to rejoice. Services typically lasted from nine A.M. to four P.M. with prayers of two hours in length and sermons of an hour duration. The Divines were consistent in confessing their own faults and, as good state churchmen, in preaching against all sects, especially Anabaptists, who wanted complete separation of church and state, and Antinomians, who believed that there was no need for the law of God in the Christian life.

Initially, the Parliament had assigned the assembly the task of revising the Anglican Thirty-nine Articles. After two months and the revision of sixteen articles, this work was interrupted and never completed. The Parliament had appealed to the General Assembly of the Church of Scotland and the Scottish Convention of Estates, asking for military aid. The price for Scottish cooperation was a Solemn League and Covenant to bind together England, Scotland, and Ireland with a common Confession of Faith, Directory for Worship, Form of Church Government, and Catechism. Despite some initial reluctance by the English Parliamentary representatives, and its denunciation by the king, the Covenant was subscribed, not only by official representatives but widely by the British people.

The Scottish State Church sent representatives to the English Parliament to oversee implementing the religious uniformity called for in the Solemn League and Covenant. At the request of Parliament the Scots commissioners sat in the assembly and participated in the debates. Although technically not members, the Scots exercised considerable influence in the committees of the assembly and spoke in its plenary sessions. The chief differences with the Scots were over matters of church government. Many of the English Divines initially hoped for some form of episcopacy with Presbyterian modifications. In matters of theology, however, there seemed to be no significant differences. The Scots commissioners participated fully in the preparation of the Confession of Faith.

The assembly was organized into numerous committees to carry on its work. In addition to work on the Thirty-nine Articles, the assembly had been busy with questions of ordination, discipline, government, and worship. With the arrival of the Scots commissioners, and at their urging, the assembly, in August 1644, took up the matter of writing a confession of faith. The House of Commons gave its official order to prepare a Confession of Faith on April 17, 1645. Numerous committees dealt with the confession and the whole assembly was given the opportunity to debate each word in it on three separate occasions. On May 12, 1645, a drafting committee was chosen. Eleven men, therefore, became the chief authors of the Confession of Faith. Seven were English Divines: Cornelius Burges, Thomas Gataker, Robert Harris, Charles Herle, Joshua Hoyle, Edward Reynolds, and Thomas Temple. They were assisted by the four Scots clergy: Robert Baillie, George Gillespie, Alexander Henderson, and Samuel Rutherford.

After the assembly as a whole had reviewed the draft of the confession in its parts and in the whole, a committee was appointed to reword the draft, incorporating changes voted by the assembly and preparing it for final review by the body. The entire process lasted a year and a half. One man, Edward Reynolds, sat on every committee that dealt with the confession and supplied continuity during its development. Cornelius Burges acted as secretary and transcriber throughout the process.

On December 4, 1646, the assembly deemed its work on the Confession of Faith done and resolved to go as a whole body and present it to the Houses of Parliament. Copies were delivered to the Parliament on December 14, 1646. The Parliament, however, was not satisfied. It had ordered that proofs from Scripture should be annexed to the confession and that had not been done. The assembly over time had given numerous practical reasons for its reluctance to attach specific texts from Scripture for each article. The assembly reported that it regarded its propositions as received truths among all the (Reformed) churches. Its debates had not been over the truth or falsehood of any article, but rather about the most appropriate manner of expression. The House, nonetheless, insisted on Scripture proofs and the assembly complied by setting up a committee of three to work on it. In the end, the proof texts received the same careful process as the confession itself. For example, Scripture proofs for Chapter 1 of the confession were debated for six days. On April 29, 1647, the Confession of Faith with Scriptures was delivered to the Parliament.

That should complete the story of the Westminster Standards. By the end of 1647 the assembly had delivered to Parliament the Westminster Confession of Faith as its guide in doctrine, a Shorter Catechism for teaching the faith to children, a Larger Catechism to aid ministers in their preaching, a Directory for Public Worship, a form for Presbyterian church government, and a Psalter to provide biblical psalms to be sung in public worship. A large body of loyal ministers of the Church of England, with Scottish assistance, had achieved the internal reform of the State Church, in a more Calvinistic direction theologically and a more Presbyterian manner governmentally. That had been the goal of the Puritan members of the Church of England for a century. Historical circumstances, however, prevented the work of the assembly from ever being fully implemented in England. The last numbered sitting of the Westminster Assembly was February 22, 1649. It had sat for five and one-half years, meeting on average about four times a week.

In the fifteen years following the completion of the Westminster Standards Presbyterianism was weakened and finally defeated as a political and social force in England. Cromwell's army of Independents and sectarians defeated the Royalist forces and then beheaded the king. Cromwell's Protectorate was followed by anarchy and then a restoration of the monarchy. Elizabethan standards of theology, polity, and worship were then enforced in England.

Before the collapse of Presbyterianism in England, the Scottish commissioners had returned home bearing the fruits of the Westminster Assembly's labors. The Act of the Scottish General Assembly on August 27, 1647, made the Westminster Confession the public Confession of Faith of the Church of Scotland. History subsequent to the actual creation of the Westminster Standards therefore determined that its transmission to other countries was primarily via Scots' influence. This circumstance has also largely conditioned people mistakenly to interpret the Confession of Faith as a Scottish product rather than the work of Presbyterian Puritans in the Church of England.

SIXTEENTH-CENTURY BRITISH THEOLOGY AND PHILOSOPHY

The Augustinian/Calvinist tradition was strong in sixteenth-century England. Peter Martyr Vermigli taught theology at Oxford and Martin Bucer taught at Cambridge. When the Thirty-nine Articles were adopted in 1563, Calvin's *Institutes* was an acknowledged textbook in the English universities and Calvin's catechism was officially mandated for use in the universities. More of Calvin's works were published in England between 1548 and 1600 than the works of any other writer. Puritans therefore, on the one side, viewed the increasingly Arminian theology, which emphasized human response rather than God's initiative, and the Aristotelian rationalism practiced by the High Church Royalists as unwanted innovations. Presbyterian Puritans also, on the other side, rejected what they perceived as the subjective enthusiasm of the Anabaptists, who advocated a return to the primitive church, that in their view only baptized adults. They were equally offended by the Quakers, who claimed a revelatory inner light that bypassed the need for Scripture.

The period of modern science and thought began in England in the 1660s. That is well after the work of the Westminster Assembly was finished. The Westminster Assembly came at the end of the Age of Faith that extended from the Middle Ages through the Protestant Reformation. The Westminster Divines were neither as skeptical as the free thinkers nor as rationalist as Protestant Scholasticism that developed in subsequent decades. The Age of Reason, with its stress on the independent power of the human mind, came, unexpectedly, soon after the assembly had finished its work.

THE IRISH ARTICLES

In its specific formulations the Westminster Confession of Faith does not draw on Continental creeds but on its distinctively English Reformed background. The immediate source of the Westminster Confession was the Irish Articles of 1615. The principal author of the Irish Articles was James Ussher, then professor of divinity at the University of Dublin and later Archbishop of Armagh and Primate of Ireland. Headings of chapters in the Westminster Confession that cannot be traced to the Irish Articles can generally be found in a compilation of Reformed theology, prepared by Ussher and issued during the Westminster Assembly, entitled A Body of Divinitie. Ussher's opening question, "What is that which all men especially desire?" is similar in style to the first question of the Westminster Shorter Catechism. Its answer is also characteristic of English Reformed theology since it identifies a relationship to God rather than reason as what is essential to a person's humanity.

THE THEOLOGICAL STRUCTURE OF THE WESTMINSTER CONFESSION

Having begun with the doctrine of Scripture, on July 16, 1645, the main topics or heads of the confession were distributed among the three main committees. The minutes record the topics given to each of three committees. Ordered—The First Committee to prepare the Confession of Faith upon these heads: God and the Holy Trinity; God's decrees, Predestination, Election, etc.; the works of Creation and Providence; Man's Fall. Ordered—The Second Committee: Sin, and the punishment thereof; Freewill; the Covenant of Grace; Christ our Mediator. Ordered—The Third Committee: Effectual Vocation; Justification; Adoption; Sanctification.

The Westminster Confession of Faith is composed of thirty-three chapters. It begins with Chapter I on Scripture, which is the source from which all other truths are derived. A second section, Chapters II through V, declares the sovereignty of God. It speaks of God's decrees, or plans, or purposes, displayed in the creation of the world and in the providential care of God's people. A central section, Chapters VI through XX, addresses the working out of God's purposes in human history. Chapters VI and VII describe the fall of humanity into sin and God's covenant to redeem them. In Chapter VIII, Jesus Christ the mediator of God's covenant is presented as the pinnacle of God's purposeful work on behalf of humanity. Then Chapters XI through XX describe the way of salvation in Christ and how it becomes effective in the lives of believers. A fourth section of the confession, Chapters XXI through XXVI, deals with ethical dimensions of the Christian life. It treats topics such as the law of God, liberty of conscience, church and state, and marriage and divorce. The final section, Chapters XXVII through XXXV, treats the church, the sacraments, and last things.

The confession provides a concise system of theology in the form used in mid-seventeenth-century Britain. The functional concern of these Puritan Divines was, however, that theology be a practical rather than a theoretical discipline. This is manifested by the fact that nearly two-thirds of the confession deals with practical matters of the Christian life in its personal and social dimensions.

THE CATECHISMS

In December 1643, the assembly put the task of preparing a catechism into the hands of Herbert Palmer, considered the best catechist in England. Months and even years passed with little apparent progress. Numerous other members of the assembly were added to a committee to "hasten" the catechism. The breakthrough came when the assembly finally came to the idea of having two catechisms, one larger and one more brief. Both were to follow the order and expound the content of the Confession of Faith which by then was completed.

The Larger Catechism became even longer than the Confession of Faith. The purpose of the Larger Catechism was to provide guidance for preachers in giving a plain exposition of the doctrines articulated in the confession. The practical orientation to Christian living is evidenced in the extensive detail given in the Larger Catechism. Questions 1–5 expound what the Scriptures principally teach; Questions 6–90 deal with the practical duties of living the Christian life.

When the Larger Catechism neared completion in August 1647, the assembly resolved to proceed with the Shorter Catechism. It appointed a committee, chaired by Palmer, to prepare a draft. In October, Palmer died at age forty-six. The assembly then appointed a small committee of Dr. Anthony Tuckney, Marshall, and Ward, assisted by the one remaining Scots commissioner, Rutherford. John Wallis was added at the end of the process to transcribe the catechism for transmission to the

Parliament. Because the Shorter Catechism is in his handwriting, and because he later wrote a commentary on it, many incorrectly assumed that it was his work. The assembly as a whole spent many days debating the wording of the catechism, and later its Scripture proofs, so it became a distillation of the best thought of the whole body.

The function of the Shorter Catechism was to provide a simple summary statement for young people of what was contained in the Larger Catechism and the Confession of Faith. The Larger Catechism states the policy of the church. The Shorter Catechism is a statement of personal religion. Much of the material in the Confession of Faith from Chapter XXI to the end is omitted. Civil and ecclesiastical matters and adult issues such as divorce and remarriage are left to the Larger Catechism for explanation. The structure of the Shorter Catechism parallels that of the Larger Catechism. Questions 1–38 deal with what Christians are to believe. Questions 39–107 concern the duties of the Christian life. The members of the assembly were divided over how the catechism was to be used. The prevailing view was that it was not for rote memory, but best used simply as a guide for teacher and pupil to deepen their discussion of the Christian faith.

THEMES AND CHARACTERISTICS OF THE WESTMINSTER STANDARDS THAT REMAIN IMPORTANT FOR THEOLOGY, CHRISTIAN LIFE, AND MINISTRY

Scripture

The Westminster Divines began their theological inquiry with the written Word of God which reveals the living Word of God, Jesus Christ. Chapter I of the confession has ten subsections. The first five are an ascending development on the theme of the Holy Spirit's relationship to Scripture. The last five sections deal with the interpretation of Scripture in light of its purpose of bringing us to salvation in Christ.

Chapter I begins with the phrase "the light of nature." In the context of British Reformed theology and illumined by the writings of the Westminster Divines themselves, this is an assertion of the Augustinian/Calvinist understanding of revelation. "Nature" refers not to "the works of creation and providence," which are mentioned next, but to the implanting of the knowledge of God in the human heart. This sense of the divine is suppressed by human sin but can never be wholly eradicated. The "works of creation and providence" only reinforce in people what they already know in their hearts. God's Word is like prescription lenses that focus, reinforce, and make clear what was previously only dimly perceived. For the Westminster Divines, there were not two sources of revelation, nature and Scripture, but only one: God's Word. Christ and Scripture were both known as the Word of God for the Divines. As Edward Reynolds declared, "Preaching of the Word is called preaching of Christ."

The final section on Scripture in the Confession of Faith concludes that the "Supreme Judge, by which all controversies of religion are to be determined . . . can be no other but the Holy Spirit speaking in the Scripture." This is an assertion of the Reformed balance of Word and Spirit that the Westminster Divines displayed. On the one side they rejected the independent role of reason and church tradition that was accepted by Roman Catholics and the High Church Anglicans. On the other side they resisted the independent role given to experience and inner light by various sectarians and the Quakers. For the Westminster Divines, the final judge was the living Word of God, the Spirit of Christ, leading persons to the truth through the central witness of Scripture to Christ.

The Sovereignty of God

Many have contended that the central theme of Reformed theology and especially the theology of the Westminster Divines is the sovereignty of God. To modern people that has an uncongenial ring. It implies harshness, arbitrariness, and injustice. We must remember that these are the very qualities that the Westminster Divines were protesting in their king, who claimed divine right for his actions.

The Westminster Divines lived and wrote in a world prior to the advent of modern science. They were not trying to define ultimate chains of cause and effect. They were giving heartfelt expression to their trust in God's ultimate care. The meaning of the sovereignty of God is that human beings are, at every moment of our lives, in relationship to the living God. The thrust of Reformed theology is that we glorify God by living lives of obedient activity. That is the concept embodied in the beginning of the Westminster Shorter Catechism when it says that the "chief end," or goal, of human beings is "to glorify God and enjoy him forever." By living in the spirit of Christ, obedient to God, we will reap a byproduct, not of grim servitude, but of a freeing enjoyment.

Election and Predestination

For some people, the first word that comes into their minds after they hear Presbyterian is "predestination." We rightly resist a concept of God who arbitrarily predetermines every action in a way that denies free will. So did the Westminster Divines. Again, they must be understood as living in a prescientific world.

Election is the concept from which predestination comes. Election is the Reformed way of saying that we are saved by grace alone. Election means choice. In the theology of the Westminster Divines, God chooses us before we do anything to deserve that choice. That is a doctrine of comfort for believers. If God has chosen us we cannot slip out of God's care, even on our worst days.

Predestination is the seventeenth-century corollary of election. It is a way of saying that God will always be with us, caring for us, and empowering us. We cannot sort out the precise relationship between God's choice and our freedom any more than we can fully understand the influence of heredity and environment on our choices. While we can be sure that we are free and morally responsible, it is also comforting to know that God is at work in history and in our lives for good.

Presbyterians in twentieth-century America dealt with this issue through additions to the Westminster Confession. Chapters entitled "Of the Holy Spirit" and "Of the Gospel of the Love of God and Missions" were added to the confession in the Northern church in 1903 and in the Southern church in 1942. Their purpose was to show that God's sovereignty and God's infinite love for all persons are not contradictory but are rather coherent twin principles of the Reformed faith. A Declaratory Statement was also added in 1903 by the Presbyterian Church U.S.A. to formally disavow "certain inferences drawn from statements in the Confession of Faith." Contrary to the implication that Christ had died only for some, and that others were foreordained to damnation, the Declaratory Statement made clear that Christ's sacrifice for sin was sufficient for all and offered to all. A second declaration affirmed that children dying in infancy are "saved by Christ through the Spirit."

Willing to Be Reformed

This willingness to be further reformed "according to the Word of God and the call of the Spirit" has been characteristic of American Presbyterianism. The first Synod, in what was called the Adopting Act of 1729, stated that all ministers were to subscribe to the Westminster Confession and Catechisms "in all essential and necessary articles." The same day they agreed that parts of Chapters XX and XXIII of the confession, giving the civil magistrate authority over the church or power to persecute people for their religion, were not essential for the church in America. In the 1950s, both the Northern and Southern branches of American Presbyterianism amended the Westminster Confession to remove the prohibition of divorce and remarriage except on grounds of adultery or desertion. Instead, Presbyterians emphasized human weakness and God's forgiveness by stating that "remarriage of divorced persons may be sanctioned by the Church, in keeping with the redemptive gospel of Christ, when sufficient penitence for sin and failure is evident, and a firm purpose of and endeavor after Christian marriage is manifested."

Presbyterian Polity

The principal struggle in the Westminster Assembly was over the government of the church. It was so important because the English Parliament and the human community in that time and place were seeking to develop a representative democracy that guaranteed both individual freedom and liberty of conscience on the one side, and order and responsibility in human affairs on the other. Presbyterian polity has the same goal. Thus, the Presbyterian General Assembly remains, in the words of one of its Stated Clerks, one of the last great parliamentary bodies in the Western world. Parliamentary procedure, for all of the joking about it, remains useful and necessary as a way to guarantee free expression, and the rights of both the majority and the minority, in public debate. Parliamentary procedure and Presbyterian polity only work well, however, when there is a trust among people and a valuing of the institution of the church. The Westminster Divines provide a solid example of people who, in the midst of exceptional stress, continued to rely on democratic institutions and procedures as essential for human well-being and the service of God.

We honor the remarkable achievements of the Westminster Divines by understanding their work in its historical context and utilizing themes relevant to our own situation. We must radically respect their caution that confessions are subordinate standards to Scripture. "All synods or councils since the apostles' times, whether general or particular, may err, and many have erred; therefore they are not to be made the rule of faith or practice, but to be used as a help in both" (6.175).

QUESTIONS FOR STUDY

1. How did the social context of the Westminster Assembly influence its work and how does our social context influence the church today?

2. What were the defining characteristics of the Puritan movement in the Church of England? How does it compare with various movements for reform in the contemporary church?

3. What potential value do the distinctive theological emphases of the Westminster Standards have for Christians in the twenty-first century?

THE WESTMINSTER CONFESSION OF FAITH[a]

Presbyterian Church in the United States	The United Presbyterian Church in the United States of America
CHAPTER I	CHAPTER I

Of the Holy Scripture

1. Although the light of nature, and the works of creation and providence, do so far manifest the goodness, wisdom, and power of God, as to leave men inexcusable;[1] yet are they[b] not sufficient to give that knowledge of God, and of his will, which is necessary unto salvation;[2] therefore it pleased the Lord, at sundry times, and in divers manners, to reveal himself, and to declare that his will unto his Church;[3] and afterwards for the better preserving and propagating of the truth, and for the more sure establishment and comfort of the Church against the corruption of the flesh, and the malice of Satan and of the world, to commit the same wholly unto writing;[4] which maketh the Holy Scripture to be most necessary;[5] those former ways of God's revealing his will unto his people being now ceased.[6]   **6.001**

2. Under the name of Holy Scripture, or the Word of God written, are now contained all the books of the Old and New Testaments, which are these: **6.002**

Of the Old Testament

Genesis	Numbers	Judges
Exodus	Deuteronomy	Ruth
Leviticus	Joshua	I Samuel

---

[a]The text of the Westminster Confession of Faith is that adopted by The United Presbyterian Church in the United States of America in 1958. Footnotes have been added to show how the text of 1958 differs from that of the 1647 edition of the Confession published under the title *The Humble Advice of the Assembly of Divines, Now by Authority of Parliament Sitting at Westminster, Concerning a Confession of Faith: with the Quotations and Text of Scripture Annexed. Presented by Them Lately to Both Houses of Parliament.* No attempt is made to trace the various amendments leading to the text of 1958. The footnotes use the punctuation, spelling, and capitalization of 1647.

On the organization of the Presbyterian Church in the United States in 1861, it adopted the Standards of the Presbyterian Church in the United States of America from which its constituents had withdrawn. The only amendment in the Confession since 1861, by this Church, has been in striking out the clause in Chapter XXIV, Section 4, making it unlawful to marry a deceased wife's sister.

[b]UPCUSA ed. reads: "they are."

Presbyterian Church in the United States		The United Presbyterian Church in the United States of America
II Samuel	Proverbs	Amos
I Kings	Ecclesiastes	Obadiah
II Kings	The Song of Songs	Jonah
I Chronicles	Isaiah	Micah
II Chronicles	Jeremiah	Nahum
Ezra	Lamentations	Habakkuk
Nehemiah	Ezekiel	Zephaniah
Esther	Daniel	Haggai
Job	Hosea	Zechariah
Psalms	Joel	Malachi

Of the New Testament

Matthew	Ephesians	Hebrews
Mark	Philippians	James
Luke	Colossians	I Peter
John	I Thessalonians	II Peter
Acts of the Apostles	II Thessalonians	I John
Romans	I Timothy	II John
I Corinthians	II Timothy	III John
II Corinthians	Titus	Jude
Galatians	Philemon	Revelation[c]

All which are given by inspiration of God, to be the rule of faith and life.

6.003   3. The books commonly called Apocrypha, not being of divine inspiration, are no part of the canon of the Scripture; and therefore are of no authority in the Church of God, nor to be any otherwise approved, or made use of, than other human writings.[7]

6.004   4. The authority of the Holy Scripture, for which it ought to be believed and obeyed, dependeth not upon the testimony of any man or church, but wholly upon God (who is truth itself), the author thereof; and therefore it is to be received, because it is the Word of God.[8]

6.005   5. We may be moved and induced by the testimony of the Church to an high and reverent esteem for[d] the Holy Scripture; and the heavenliness of the matter, the efficacy of the doctrine, the majesty of the style, the consent of all the parts, the scope of the whole (which is to give all glory to God), the full discovery it makes of the only way of man's

---

[c]Ed. 1647 includes "of John."

[d]UPCUSA ed. reads: "of."

174

Presbyterian Church
in the United States

The United Presbyterian Church
in the United States of America

salvation, the many other incomparable excellencies, and the entire perfection thereof, are arguments whereby it doth abundantly evidence itself to be the Word of God; yet, notwithstanding, our full persuasion and assurance of the infallible truth and divine authority thereof, is from the inward work of the Holy Spirit, bearing witness by and with the Word in our hearts.[9]

6. The whole counsel of God, concerning all things necessary for his own glory, man's salvation, faith, and life, is either expressly set down in Scripture, or by good and necessary consequence may be deduced from Scripture:[10] unto which nothing at any time is to be added, whether by new revelations of the Spirit, or traditions of men.[11] Nevertheless we acknowledge the inward illumination of the Spirit of God to be necessary for the saving understanding of such things as are revealed in the Word;[12] and that[e] there are some circumstances concerning the worship of God, and government of the Church, common to human actions and societies, which are to be ordered by the light of nature and Christian prudence, according to the general rules of the Word, which are always to be observed.[13]   **6.006**

7. All things in Scripture are not alike plain in themselves, nor alike clear unto all;[14] yet those things which are necessary to be known, believed, and observed, for salvation, are so clearly propounded and opened in some place of Scripture or other, that not only the learned, but the unlearned, in a due use of the ordinary means, may attain unto a sufficient understanding of them.[15]   **6.007**

8. The Old Testament in Hebrew (which was the native language of the people of God of old), and the New Testament in Greek (which at the time of the writing of it was most generally known to the nations), being immediately inspired by God,[16] and by his singular care and providence kept pure in all ages, are therefore authentical; so as in all controversies of religion the Church is finally to appeal unto them.[17] But because these original tongues are not known to all the people of God who have right unto, and interest in, the Scriptures, and are commanded, in the fear of God, to read and search them,[18] therefore they are to be translated into the[f] language of every people unto which they come, that the Word of God dwelling plentifully in all, they may worship him in an acceptable manner, and, through patience and comfort of the Scriptures, may have hope.[19]   **6.008**

9. The infallible rule of interpretation of Scripture, is the Scripture itself; and therefore, when there is a question about the true and full   **6.009**

---

[e]UPCUSA ed. reads: "and there are."

[f]Ed. 1647 reads: "the vulgar language of every nation."

sense of any scripture (which is not manifold, but one), it may be searched and known by other places that speak more clearly.[20]

6.010   10. The Supreme Judge, by which[g] all controversies of religion are to be determined, and all decrees of councils, opinions of ancient writers, doctrines of men, and private spirits, are to be examined, and in whose sentence we are to rest, can be no other but the Holy Spirit speaking in the Scripture.[21]

CHAPTER II

CHAPTER II

Of God, and of the Holy Trinity

6.011   1. There is but one only living and true God,[1] who is infinite in being and perfection,[2] a most pure spirit,[3] invisible,[4] without body, parts, or passions,[5] immutable,[6] immense,[7] eternal,[8] incomprehensible,[9] almighty;[10] most wise,[11] most holy,[12] most free,[13] most absolute,[14] working all things according to the counsel of his own immutable and most righteous will;[15] for his own glory;[16] most loving,[17] gracious, merciful, long-suffering, abundant in goodness and truth, forgiving iniquity, transgression, and sin;[18] the rewarder of them that diligently seek him;[19] and withal[h] most just and terrible in his judgments;[20] hating all sin,[21] and who will by no means clear the guilty.[22]

6.012   2. God hath all life, glory, goodness, blessedness, in and of himself;[23] and is alone in and unto himself all-sufficient, not standing in need of any creatures which he hath made, nor deriving any glory from them, but only manifesting his own glory in, by, unto, and upon them:[24] he is the alone fountain of all being, of whom, through whom, and to whom, are all things;[25] and hath most sovereign dominion over them, to do by them, for them, or[i] upon them, whatsoever himself pleaseth.[26] In his sight all things are open and manifest;[27] his knowledge is infinite, infallible, and independent upon the creature;[28] so as nothing is to him contingent or uncertain.[29] He is most holy in all his counsels, in all his works, and in all his commands.[30] To him is due from angels and men, and every other creature, whatsoever worship, service, or obedience he is pleased to require of them.[31]

6.013   3. In the unity of the Godhead there be three Persons of one substance, power, and eternity: God the Father, God the Son, and God

---

[g]UPCUSA ed. reads: "whom."

[h]Ed. 1647 reads: "with all."

[i]UPCUSA ed. reads: "and."

Presbyterian Church in the United States	The United Presbyterian Church in the United States of America

the Holy Ghost.[32] The Father is of none, neither begotten nor proceeding; the Son is eternally begotten of the Father;[33] the Holy Ghost eternally proceeding from the Father and the Son.[34]

CHAPTER III	CHAPTER III[j]

Of God's Eternal Decrees[k]

1. God from all eternity did by the most wise and holy counsel of his own will, freely and unchangeably ordain whatsoever comes to pass;[1] yet so as thereby neither is God the author of sin;[2] nor is violence offered to the will of the creatures, nor is the liberty or contingency of second causes taken away, but rather established.[3]   **6.014**

2. Although God knows whatsoever may or can come to pass, upon all supposed conditions;[4] yet hath he not decreed anything because he foresaw it as future, or as that which would come to pass, upon such conditions.[5]   **6.015**

3. By the decree of God, for the manifestation of his glory, some men and angels are predestinated unto everlasting life,[6] and others fore-ordained to everlasting death.[7]   **6.016**

4. These angels and men, thus predestinated and fore-ordained, are particularly and unchangeably designed; and their number is so certain and definite that it cannot be either increased or diminished.[8]   **6.017**

5. Those of mankind that are predestinated unto life, God, before the foundation of the world was laid,[9] according to his eternal and immutable purpose,[10] and the secret counsel and good pleasure of his will,[11] hath chosen in Christ,[12] unto everlasting glory,[13] out of his[m] free grace and love alone, without any foresight of faith or good works, or perseverance in either of them, or any other thing in the creature, as conditions, or causes moving him thereunto;[14] and all to the praise of his glorious grace.[15]   **6.018**

6. As God hath appointed the elect unto glory, so hath he, by the eternal and most free purpose of his will, fore-ordained all the means thereunto.[16] Wherefore they who are elected being fallen in Adam are redeemed by Christ,[17] are effectually called unto faith in Christ by his Spirit working in due season;[18] are justified,[19] adopted,[20] sanctified,[21] and kept by his power through faith unto salvation.[22] Neither are any   **6.019**

---

[j]See Declaratory Statement at end of Confession of Faith. The Declaratory Statement is the authoritative interpretation of Chapter III.

[k]UPCUSA ed. reads: "Decree."

[m]Ed. 1647 reads: "his meer grace and love."

other redeemed by Christ, effectually called, justified, adopted, sanctified, and saved, but the elect only.[23]

6.020   7. The rest of mankind, God was pleased, according to the unsearchable counsel of his own will, whereby he extendeth or withholdeth mercy as he pleaseth, for the glory of his sovereign power over his creatures, to pass by,[24] and to ordain them to dishonour and wrath for their sin,[25] to the praise of his glorious justice.[26]

6.021   8. The doctrine of this high mystery of predestination is to be handled with special prudence and care, that men attending the will of God revealed in his Word, and yielding obedience thereunto, may, from the certainty of their effectual vocation, be assured of their eternal election. So shall this doctrine afford matter of praise, reverence, and admiration of God; and of humility, diligence, and abundant consolation to all that sincerely obey the gospel.[27]

CHAPTER IV   CHAPTER IV

Of Creation

6.022   1. It pleased God the Father, Son, and Holy Ghost, for the manifestation of the glory of his eternal power, wisdom, and goodness, in the beginning, to create or make of nothing the world, and all things therein, whether visible or invisible, in the space of six days, and all very good.[1]

6.023   2. After God had made all other creatures, he created man, male and female,[2] with reasonable and immortal souls,[3] endued with knowledge, righteousness, and true holiness after his own image,[4] having the law of God written in their hearts,[5] and power to fulfill it; and yet under a possibility of transgressing, being left to the liberty of their own will, which was subject unto change.[6] Besides this law written in their hearts, they received a command not to eat of the tree of the knowledge of good and evil;[7] which while they kept they were happy in their communion with God,[8] and had dominion over the creatures.[9]

CHAPTER V   CHAPTER V

Of Providence

6.024   1. God, the great Creator of all things, doth uphold, direct, dispose, and govern all creatures, actions, and things, from the greatest even to the least,[1] by his most wise and holy providence,[2] according to his infallible foreknowledge,[3] and the free and immutable counsel of his own will,[4] to the praise of the glory of his wisdom, power, justice, goodness, and mercy.[5]

2. Although in relation to the foreknowledge and decree of God, the first cause, all things come to pass immutably and infallibly,[6] yet, by the same providence, he ordereth them to fall out according to the nature of second causes, either necessarily,[7] freely, or contingently.[8]   **6.025**

3. God, in his ordinary providence, maketh use of means,[9] yet is free to work without,[10] above,[11] and against them, at his pleasure.[12]   **6.026**

4. The almighty power, unsearchable wisdom, and infinite goodness of God, so far manifest themselves in his providence, that it extendeth itself even to the first Fall,[13] and all other sins of angels and men,[14] and that not by a bare permission, but such as hath joined with it a most wise and powerful bounding,[15] and otherwise ordering and governing of them, in a manifold dispensation, to his own holy ends;[16] yet so, as the sinfulness thereof proceedeth only from the creature, and not from God; who being most holy and righteous, neither is nor can be the author or approver of sin.[17]   **6.027**

5. The most wise, righteous, and gracious God, doth often-times leave for a season his own children to manifold temptations and the corruption of their own hearts, to chastise them for their former sins, or to discover unto them the hidden strength of corruption and deceitfulness of their hearts, that they[n] be humbled;[18] and to raise them to a more close and constant dependence for their support upon himself, and to make them more watchful against all future occasions of sin, and for sundry other just and holy ends.[19]   **6.028**

6. As for those wicked and ungodly men whom God, as a righteous judge, for former sins, doth blind and harden;[20] from them he not only withholdeth his grace, whereby they might have been enlightened in their understandings, and wrought upon in their hearts,[21] but sometimes also withdraweth the gifts which they had;[22] and exposeth them to such objects as their corruption makes occasion of sin;[23] and withal, giveth[o] them over to their own lusts, the temptations of the world, and the power of Satan;[24] whereby it cometh[p] to pass that they harden themselves, even under those means which God useth for the softening of others.[25]   **6.029**

7. As the providence of God doth, in general, reach to all creatures; so, after a most special manner, it taketh care of his Church, and disposeth all things to the good thereof.[26]   **6.030**

---

[n]UPCUSA ed. reads: "they may be."

[o]UPCUSA ed. reads: "gives."

[p]UPCUSA ed. reads: "comes."

Presbyterian Church
in the United States

The United Presbyterian Church
in the United States of America

CHAPTER VI

CHAPTER VI

Of the Fall of Man, of Sin, and of the Punishment Thereof

6.031   1. Our first parents, being seduced by the subtilty and temptation of Satan, sinned in eating the forbidden fruit.[1] This their sin God was pleased, according to his wise and holy counsel, to permit, having purposed to order it to his own glory.[2]

6.032   2. By this sin they fell from their original righteousness and communion with God,[3] and so became dead in sin,[4] and wholly defiled in all the faculties and parts of soul and body.[5]

6.033   3. They being the root of all mankind, the guilt of this sin was imputed,[6] and the same death in sin and corrupted nature conveyed to all their posterity, descending from them by ordinary generation.[7]

6.034   4. From this original corruption, whereby we are utterly indisposed, disabled, and made opposite to all good, and wholly inclined to all evil,[8] do proceed all actual transgressions.[9]

6.035   5. This corruption of nature, during this life, doth remain in those that are regenerated:[10] and although it be through Christ pardoned and mortified, yet both itself, and all the motions thereof, are truly and properly sin.[11]

6.036   6. Every sin, both original and actual, being a transgression of the righteous law of God, and contrary thereunto, doth, in its own nature, bring guilt upon the sinner,[12] whereby he is bound over to the wrath of God,[13] and curse of the law,[14] and so made subject to death,[15] with all miseries spiritual, temporal, and eternal.[16]

CHAPTER VII

CHAPTER VII

Of God's Covenant with Man

6.037   1. The distance between God and the creature is so great, that although reasonable creatures do owe obedience unto him as their Creator, yet they could never have any fruition of him, as their blessedness and reward, but by some voluntary condescension on God's part, which he hath been pleased to express by way of covenant.[1]

6.038   2. The first covenant made with man was a covenant of works,[2] wherein life was promised to Adam, and in him to his posterity, upon condition of perfect and personal obedience.[3]

6.039   3. Man, by his Fall, having made himself incapable of life by that covenant, the Lord was pleased to make a second, commonly called

Presbyterian Church
in the United States

The United Presbyterian Church
in the United States of America

the covenant of grace:[4] wherein he freely offered[q] unto sinners life and salvation by Jesus Christ, requiring of them faith in him, that they may be saved,[5] and promising to give unto all those that are ordained unto life, his Holy Spirit, to make them willing and able to believe.[6]

4. This covenant of grace is frequently set forth in the Scripture by the name of a testament, in reference to the death of Jesus Christ, the testator, and to the everlasting inheritance, with all things belonging to it, therein bequeathed.   6.040

5. This covenant was differently administered in the time of the law, and in the time of the gospel:[7] under the law it was administered by promises, prophecies, sacrifices, circumcision, the paschal lamb, and other types and ordinances delivered to the people of the Jews, all fore-signifying Christ to come,[8] which were for that time sufficient and efficacious, through the operation of the Spirit, to instruct and build up the elect in faith in the promised Messiah,[9] by whom they had full remission of sins, and eternal salvation; and is called the Old Testament.[10]   6.041

6. Under the gospel, when Christ the substance was exhibited, the ordinances in which this covenant is dispensed, are the preaching of the Word, and the administration of the sacraments of Baptism and the Lord's Supper;[11] which, though fewer in number, and administered with more simplicity and less outward glory, yet in them it is held forth in more fullness, evidence, and spiritual efficacy,[12] to all nations, both Jews and Gentiles;[13] and is called the New Testament. There are not, therefore, two covenants of grace differing in substance, but one and the same under various dispensations.[14]   6.042

CHAPTER VIII   CHAPTER VIII

Of Christ the Mediator

1. It pleased God, in his eternal purpose, to choose and ordain the Lord Jesus, his only begotten Son, to be the Mediator between God and man,[1] the prophet,[2] priest,[3] and king;[4] the head and Savior of his Church,[5] the heir of all things,[6] and judge of the world;[7] unto whom he did, from all eternity, give a people to be his seed,[8] and to be by him in time redeemed, called, justified, sanctified, and glorified.[9]   6.043

2. The Son of God, the second Person in the Trinity, being very and eternal God, of one substance, and equal with the Father, did, when the fullness of time was come, take upon him man's nature,[10] with all the essential properties and common infirmities thereof; yet without   6.044

---

[q]UPCUSA ed. reads: "offereth."

sin:[11] being conceived by the power of the Holy Ghost, in the womb of the Virgin Mary, of her substance.[12] So that two whole, perfect, and distinct natures, the Godhead and the manhood, were inseparably joined together in one person, without conversion, composition, or confusion.[13] Which person is very God and very man, yet one Christ, the only Mediator between God and man.[14]

6.045   3. The Lord Jesus in his human nature thus united to the divine, was sanctified and anointed with the Holy Spirit above measure;[15] having in him all the treasures of wisdom and knowledge,[16] in whom it pleased the Father that all fullness should dwell:[17] to the end that being holy, harmless, undefiled, and full of grace and truth, he might be thoroughly furnished to execute the office of a Mediator and Surety.[18] Which office he took not unto himself, but was thereunto called by his Father;[19] who put all power and judgment into his hand, and gave him commandment to execute the same.[20]

6.046   4. This office the Lord Jesus did most willingly undertake,[21] which, that he might discharge, he was made under the law,[22] and did perfectly fulfill it;[23] endured most grievous torments immediately in his soul,[24] and most painful sufferings in his body;[25] was crucified and died,[26] was buried, and remained under the power of death, yet saw no corruption.[27] On the third day he arose from the dead,[28] with the same body in which he suffered;[29] with which also he ascended into heaven, and there sitteth at the right hand of his Father,[30] making intercession;[31] and shall return to judge men and angels, at the end of the world.[32]

6.047   5. The Lord Jesus, by his perfect obedience and sacrifice of himself, which he through the eternal Spirit once offered up unto God, hath fully satisfied the justice of his Father;[33] and purchased not only reconciliation, but an everlasting inheritance in the kingdom of heaven, for all those whom the Father hath given unto him.[34]

6.048   6. Although the work of redemption was not actually wrought by Christ till after his incarnation, yet the virtue, efficacy, and benefits thereof were communicated unto the elect, in all ages successively from the beginning of the world, in and by those promises, types, and sacrifices wherein he was revealed, and signified to be the seed of the woman, which should bruise the serpent's head, and the Lamb slain from the beginning of the world, being yesterday and today the same and for ever.[35]

6.049   7. Christ, in the work of mediation, acteth according to both natures; by each nature doing that which is proper to itself;[36] yet by reason of the unity of the person, that which is proper to one nature is sometimes, in Scripture, attributed to the person denominated by the other nature.[37]

6.050   8. To all those for whom Christ hath purchased redemption, he doth certainly and effectually apply and communicate the same;[38]

making intercession for them,[39] and revealing unto them, in and by the Word, the mysteries of salvation;[40] effectually persuading them by his Spirit to believe and obey; and governing their hearts by his Word and Spirit;[41] overcoming all their enemies by his almighty power and wisdom, in such manner and ways as are most consonant to his wonderful and unsearchable dispensation.[42]

CHAPTER IX

Of the Holy Spirit

1. The Holy Spirit, the third Person in the Trinity, proceeding from the Father and the Son, of the same substance and equal in power and glory, is, together with the Father and the Son, to be believed in, loved, obeyed, and worshipped throughout all ages.[1]

6.051

2. He is the Lord and Giver of life, everywhere present, and is the source of all good thoughts, pure desires, and holy counsels in men. By him the prophets were moved to speak the Word of God, and all the writers of the Holy Scriptures inspired to record infallibly the mind and will of God. The dispensation of the gospel is especially committed to him. He prepares the way for it, accompanies it with his persuasive power, and urges its message upon the reason and conscience of men, so that they who reject its merciful offer are not only without excuse, but are also guilty of resisting the Holy Spirit.[2]

6.052

3. The Holy Spirit, whom the Father is ever willing to give to all who ask him, is the only efficient agent in the application of

6.053

Presbyterian Church
in the United States

The United Presbyterian Church
in the United States of America

redemption. He regenerates men by his grace, convicts them of sin, moves them to repentance, and persuades and enables them to embrace Jesus Christ by faith. He unites all believers to Christ, dwells in them as their Comforter and Sanctifier, gives to them the spirit of Adoption and Prayer, and performs all those gracious offices by which they are sanctified and sealed unto the day of redemption.[3]

6.054   4. By the indwelling of the Holy Spirit all believers being vitally united to Christ, who is the Head, are thus united one to another in the Church, which is his body. He calls and anoints ministers for their holy office, qualifies all other officers in the Church for their special work, and imparts various gifts and graces to its members. He gives efficacy to the Word and to the ordinances of the gospel. By him the Church will be preserved, increased, purified, and at last made perfectly holy in the presence of God.[4]

CHAPTER X
Of the Gospel

6.055   1. God in infinite and perfect love, having provided in the covenant of grace, through the mediation and sacrifice of the Lord Jesus Christ, a way of life and salvation, sufficient for and adapted to the whole lost race of man, doth freely offer this salvation to all men in the gospel.[1]

6.056   2. In the gospel God declares his love for the world and his

Presbyterian Church
in the United States

The United Presbyterian Church
in the United States of America

desire that all men should be saved; reveals fully and clearly the only way of salvation; promises eternal life to all who truly repent and believe in Christ; invites and commands all to embrace the offered mercy; and by his Spirit accompanying the Word pleads with men to accept his gracious invitation.[2]

3. It is the duty and privilege of everyone who hears the gospel immediately to accept its merciful provisions; and they who continue in impenitence and unbelief incur aggravated guilt and perish by their own fault.[3]

6.057

4. Since there is no other way of salvation than that revealed in the gospel, and since in the divinely established and ordinary method of grace faith cometh by hearing the Word of God, Christ hath commissioned his Church to go into all the world and to make disciples of all nations. All believers are, therefore, under obligation to sustain the ordinances of the Christian religion where they are already established, and to contribute by their prayers, gifts, and personal efforts to the extension of the Kingdom of Christ throughout the whole earth.[4]

6.058

CHAPTER XI

CHAPTER IX

Of Free Will

1. God hath endued the will of man with that natural liberty, that it is neither forced, nor by any absolute necessity of nature determined to[r] good or evil.[1]

6.059

---

[r]Ed. 1647 includes: "do."

Presbyterian Church in the United States	The United Presbyterian Church in the United States of America

6.060   2. Man, in his state of innocency, had freedom and power to will and to do that which is[s] good and well-pleasing to God;[2] but yet mutably, so that he might fall from it.[3]

6.061   3. Man, by his Fall into a state of sin, hath wholly lost all ability of will to any spiritual good accompanying salvation;[4] so as a natural man, being altogether averse from that good,[5] and dead in sin,[6] is not able, by his own strength, to convert himself, or to prepare himself thereunto.[7]

6.062   4. When God converteth[t] a sinner and translateth[u] him into the state of grace, he freeth him from his natural bondage under sin, and, by his grace alone, enableth[v] him freely to will and to do that which is spiritually good;[8] yet so as that, by reason of his remaining corruption, he doth not perfectly, nor only, will that which is good, but doth also will that which is evil.[9]

6.063   5. The will of man is made perfectly and immutably free to good alone, in the state of glory[10] only.[11]

CHAPTER XII   CHAPTER X

Of Effectual Calling

6.064   1. All those whom God hath predestinated unto life, and those only, he is pleased, in his appointed and accepted time, effectually to call, by his Word and Spirit, out of that state of sin and death in which they are by nature, to grace and salvation by Jesus Christ:[1] enlightening their minds, spiritually and savingly, to understand the things of God,[2] taking away their heart of stone, and giving unto them an heart of flesh;[3] renewing their wills, and by his almighty power determining them to that which is good;[4] and effectually drawing them to Jesus Christ;[5] yet so as they come most freely, being made willing by his grace.[6]

6.065   2. This effectual call is of God's free and special grace alone, not from anything at all foreseen in man,[7] who is altogether passive therein, until, being quickened and renewed by the Holy Spirit,[8] he is thereby enabled to answer this call, and to embrace the grace offered and conveyed in it.[9]

---

[s]Ed. 1647 reads: "was."

[t]UPCUSA ed. reads: "converts."

[u]UPCUSA ed. reads: "translates."

[v]UPCUSA ed. reads: "enables."

Presbyterian Church in the United States	The United Presbyterian Church in the United States of America

3.[a] Elect infants, dying in infancy, are regenerated and saved by   **6.066**
Christ through the Spirit, who worketh when, and where, and how he
pleaseth. So also are all other elect persons who are incapable of being
outwardly called by the ministry of the Word.[10]

4. Others, not elected, although they may be called by the ministry   **6.067**
of the Word, and may have some common operations of the Spirit, yet
they never truly come to Christ, and therefore cannot be saved:[11] much
less can men, not professing the Christian religion, be saved in any
other way whatsoever,[b] [12]be they never so diligent to frame their lives
according to the light of nature, and the law of that religion they do
profess; and to assert and maintain that they may[c] is without warrant of
the Word of God.[13]

CHAPTER XIII	CHAPTER XI

Of Justification

1. Those whom God effectually calleth, he also freely justifieth:[1]   **6.068**
not by infusing righteousness into them, but by pardoning their sins,
and by accounting and accepting their persons as righteous; not for
anything wrought in them, or done by them, but for Christ's sake
alone; not[d] by imputing faith itself, the act of believing, or any other
evangelical obedience to them, as their righteousness; but by imputing
the obedience and satisfaction of Christ unto them,[2] they receiving and
resting on him and his righteousness by faith; which faith they have not
of themselves, it is the gift of God.[3]

2. Faith, thus receiving and resting on Christ and his righteousness,   **6.069**
is the alone instrument of justification;[4] yet is it not alone in the person
justified, but is ever accompanied with all other saving graces, and is
no dead faith, but worketh by love.[5]

3. Christ, by his obedience and death, did fully discharge the debt   **6.070**
of all those that are thus justified, and did make a proper, real, and full
satisfaction to his Father's justice in their behalf.[6] Yet inasmuch as he
was given by the Father for them,[7] and his obedience and satisfaction
accepted in their stead,[8] and both freely, not for anything in them, their

---

[a]See Declaratory Statement at end of the Confession of Faith. The Declaratory Statement is the
authoritative interpretation of Chapter X, Section 3, in the UPCUSA ed.

[b]UPCUSA ed. includes: "than by Christ." Ed. 1647 lacks: "than by Christ."

[c]Ed. 1647 reads "is very pernicious, and to be detested."

[d]Ed. 1647 reads: "nor."

Presbyterian Church
in the United States

The United Presbyterian Church
in the United States of America

justification is only of free grace;[9] that both the exact justice and rich grace of God might be glorified in the justification of sinners.[10]

6.071   4. God did, from all eternity, decree to justify all the elect;[11] and Christ did, in the fullness of time, die for their sins and rise again for their justification:[12] nevertheless they are not justified until the Holy Spirit doth, in due time, actually apply Christ unto them.[13]

6.072   5. God doth continue to forgive the sins of those that are justified;[14] and although they can never fall from the state of justification,[15] yet they may by their sins fall under God's Fatherly displeasure, and not have the light of his countenance restored unto them, until they humble themselves, confess their sins, beg pardon, and renew their faith and repentance.[16]

6.073   6. The justification of believers under the Old Testament was, in all these respects, one and the same with the justification of believers under the New Testament.[17]

CHAPTER XIV   CHAPTER XII

Of Adoption

6.074   1. All those that are justified, God vouchsafeth, in and for his only Son Jesus Christ, to make partakers of the grace of adoption:[1] by which they are taken into the number, and enjoy the liberties and privileges of the children of God;[2] have his name put upon them;[3] receive the Spirit of adoption;[4] have access to the throne of grace with boldness;[5] are enabled to cry, Abba, Father;[6] are pitied,[7] protected,[8] provided for,[9] and chastened by him as by a father;[10] yet never cast off,[11] but sealed to the day of redemption,[12] and inherit the promises,[13] as heirs of everlasting salvation.[14]

CHAPTER XV   CHAPTER XIII

Of Sanctification

6.075   1. They who are effectually called and regenerated, having a new heart and a new spirit created in them, are further sanctified, really and personally, through the virtue of Christ's death and resurrection, by his Word and Spirit dwelling in them;[1] the dominion of the whole body of sin is destroyed,[2] and the several lusts thereof are more and more weakened and mortified,[3] and they more and more quickened and strengthened, in all saving graces,[4] to the practice of true holiness, without which no man shall see the Lord.[5]

Presbyterian Church
in the United States

The United Presbyterian Church
in the United States of America

2. This sanctification is throughout in the whole man,[6] yet imperfect in this life: there abideth still some remnants of corruption in every part, whence ariseth a continual and irreconcilable war, the flesh lusting against the Spirit, and the Spirit against the flesh.[7]   6.076

3. In which war, although the remaining corruption for a time may much prevail,[8] yet, through the continual supply of strength from the sanctifying Spirit of Christ, the regenerate part doth overcome:[9] and so the saints grow in grace,[10] perfecting holiness in the fear of God.[11]   6.077

CHAPTER XVI   CHAPTER XIV

Of Saving Faith

1. The grace of faith, whereby the elect are enabled to believe to the saving of their souls, is the work of the Spirit of Christ in their hearts;[1] and is ordinarily wrought by the ministry of the Word:[2] by which also, and by the administration of the sacraments, and prayer, it is increased and strengthened.[3]   6.078

2. By this faith, a Christian believeth to be true whatsoever is revealed in the Word, for the authority of God himself speaking therein;[4] and acteth differently, upon that which each particular passage thereof containeth; yielding obedience to the commands, trembling at the threatenings, and embracing the promises of God for this life, and that which is to come. But the principal acts of saving faith are, accepting, receiving, and resting upon Christ alone for justification, sanctification, and eternal life, by virtue of the covenant of grace.   6.079

3. This faith is different in degrees, weak or strong;[5] may be often and many ways assailed and weakened, but gets the victory;[6] growing up in many to the attainment of a full assurance through Christ,[7] who is both the author and finisher of our faith.[8]   6.080

CHAPTER XVII   CHAPTER XV

Of Repentance Unto Life

1. Repentance unto life is an evangelical grace,[1] the doctrine whereof is to be preached by every minister of the gospel, as well as that of faith in Christ.[2]   6.081

2. By it a sinner, out of the sight and sense, not only of the danger, but also of the filthiness and odiousness of his sins, as contrary to the holy nature and righteous law of God, and upon the apprehension of his mercy in Christ to such as are penitent, so grieves for, and hates his   6.082

sins, as to turn from them all unto God,[3] purposing and endeavoring to walk with him in all the ways of his commandments.[4]

6.083   3. Although repentance be not to be rested in as any satisfaction for sin, or any cause of the pardon thereof,[5] which is the act of God's free grace in Christ;[6] yet is it of such necessity to all sinners, that none may expect pardon without it.[7]

6.084   4. As there is no sin so small but it deserves damnation;[8] so there is no sin so great that it can bring damnation upon those who truly repent.[9]

6.085   5. Men ought not to content themselves with a general repentance, but it is every man's duty to endeavor to repent of his particular sins, particularly.[10]

6.086   6. As every man is bound to make private confession of his sins to God, praying for the pardon thereof,[11] upon which, and the forsaking of them, he shall find mercy:[12] so he that scandalizeth his brother, or the church of Christ, ought to be willing, by a private or public confession and sorrow for his sin, to declare his repentance to those that are offended;[13] who are thereupon to be reconciled to him, and in love to receive him.[14]

CHAPTER XVIII   CHAPTER XVI

Of Good Works

6.087   1. Good works are only such as God hath commanded in his holy Word,[1] and not such as, without the warrant thereof, are devised by men out of blind zeal, or upon any pretense of good intention.[2]

6.088   2. These good works, done in obedience to God's commandments, are the fruits and evidences of a true and lively faith:[3] and by them believers manifest their thankfulness,[4] strengthen their assurance,[5] edify their brethren,[6] adorn the profession of the gospel,[7] stop the mouths of the adversaries,[8] and glorify God,[9] whose workmanship they are, created in Christ Jesus thereunto,[10] that, having their fruit unto holiness, they may have the end, eternal life.[11]

6.089   3. Their ability to do good works is not at all of themselves, but wholly from the Spirit of Christ.[12] And that they may be enabled thereunto, besides the graces they have already received, there is required an actual influence of the same Holy Spirit to work in them to will and to do of his good pleasure;[13] yet are they not hereupon to grow negligent, as if they were not bound to perform any duty unless upon a special motion of the Spirit; but they ought to be diligent in stirring up the grace of God that is in them.[14]

4. They, who in their obedience, attain to the greatest height which   **6.090**
is possible in this life, are so far from being able to supererogate and
to do more than God requires, that they fall short of much which in
duty they are bound to do.[15]

5. We cannot, by our best works, merit pardon of sin, or eternal   **6.091**
life, at the hand of God, because[e] of the great disproportion that is
between them and the glory to come, and the infinite distance that is
between us and God, whom by them we can neither profit, nor satisfy
for the debt of our former sins;[16] but when we have done all we can,
we have done but our duty, and are unprofitable servants:[17] and
because, as they are good, they proceed from his Spirit;[18] and as they
are wrought by us, they are defiled and mixed with so much weakness
and imperfection that they cannot endure the severity of God's judgment.[19]

6. Yet notwithstanding, the persons of believers being accepted   **6.092**
through Christ, their good works also are accepted in him,[20] not as
though they were in this life wholly unblamable and unreprovable in
God's sight;[21] but that he, looking upon them in his Son, is pleased to
accept and reward that which is sincere, although accompanied with
many weaknesses and imperfections.[22]

7. Works done by unregenerate men, although for the matter of them they may be things which God commands, and of good use both to themselves and others;[23] yet because they proceed not from a heart purified by faith;[24] nor are done in a right manner, according to the Word;[25] nor to a right end, the glory of God;[26] they are therefore sinful, and cannot please God, or make a man meet to receive grace from God.[27] And yet their neglect of them is more sinful, and displeasing unto God.[28]	7. [f]Works done by unregenerate men, although for the matter of them they may be things which God commands, and in themselves praiseworthy and useful, and although the neglect of such things is sinful and displeasing unto God; yet, because they proceed not from a heart purified by faith; nor are done in a right manner, according to his Word; nor to a right end, the glory of God; they come short of what God requires, and do not make any man meet to receive the grace of God.

6.093

---

[e]UPCUSA ed. reads: "by reason."

[f]Ed. 1647 reads: "VII. Works done by unregenerate men, although, for the matter of them, they
may bee things which God commands, and of good use both to themselves, and others: yet, because
they proceed not from an heart purified by faith; nor are done in a right manner, according to the
Word; nor, to a right end, the glory of God; they are therefore sinfull, and cannot please God, or
make a man meet to receive grace from God. And yet, their neglect of them is more sinfull, and
displeasing unto God."

Presbyterian Church
in the United States

The United Presbyterian Church
in the United States of America

CHAPTER XIX

CHAPTER XVII

Of the Perseverance of the Saints

6.094   1. They whom God hath accepted in his Beloved, effectually called and sanctified by his Spirit, can neither totally nor finally fall away from the state of grace: but shall certainly persevere therein to the end, and be eternally saved.[1]

6.095   2. This perseverance of the saints depends, not upon their own free-will, but upon the immutability of the decree of election, flowing from the free and unchangeable love of God the Father;[2] upon the efficacy of the merit and intercession of Jesus Christ;[3] the abiding of the Spirit and of the seed of God within them;[4] and the nature of the covenant of grace;[5] from all which ariseth also the certainty and infallibility thereof.[6]

6.096   3. Nevertheless they may, through the temptations of Satan and of the world, the prevalency of corruption remaining in them, and the neglect of the means of their preservation, fall into grievous sins; and for a time continue therein:[7] whereby they incur God's displeasure,[8] and grieve his Holy Spirit;[9] come to be deprived of some measure of their graces and comforts;[10] have their hearts hardened,[11] and their consciences wounded;[12] hurt and scandalize others,[13] and bring temporal judgments upon themselves.[14]

CHAPTER XX

CHAPTER XVIII

Of the Assurance of Grace and Salvation

6.097   1. Although hypocrites, and other unregenerate men, may vainly deceive themselves with false hopes and carnal presumptions: of being in the favor of God and estate of salvation;[1] which hope of theirs shall perish:[2] yet such as truly believe in the Lord Jesus, and love him in sincerity, endeavoring to walk in all good conscience before him, may in this life be certainly assured that they are in a state of grace,[3] and may rejoice in the hope of the glory of God: which hope shall never make them ashamed.[4]

6.098   2. This certainty is not a bare conjectural and probable persuasion, grounded upon a fallible hope; but an infallible assurance of faith,[5] founded upon the divine truth of the promises of salvation,[6] the inward evidence of those graces unto which these promises are made,[7] the testimony of the Spirit of adoption witnessing with our spirits that we are the children of God;[8] which Spirit is the earnest of our inheritance, whereby we are sealed to the day of redemption.[9]

Presbyterian Church
in the United States

The United Presbyterian Church
in the United States of America

3. This infallible assurance doth not so belong to the essence of   **6.099**
faith but that a true believer may wait long and conflict with many
difficulties before he be partaker of it:[10] yet, being enabled by the Spirit
to know the things which are freely given him of God, he may, without
extraordinary revelation, in the right use of ordinary means, attain
thereunto.[11] And therefore it is the duty of everyone to give all
diligence to make his calling and election sure; that thereby his heart
may be enlarged in peace and joy in the Holy Ghost, in love and
thankfulness to God, and in strength and cheerfulness in the duties of
obedience, the proper fruits of this assurance: so far is it from
inclining men to looseness.[12]

4. True believers may have the assurance of their salvation divers   **6.100**
ways shaken, diminished, and intermitted; as, by negligence in preserving of it; by falling into some special sin, which woundeth the
conscience, and grieveth the Spirit; by some sudden or vehement
temptation; by God's withdrawing the light of his countenance and
suffering even such as fear him to walk in darkness and to have no
light:[13] yet are they never utterly destitute of that seed of God, and life
of faith, that love of Christ and the brethren, that sincerity of heart and
conscience of duty, out of which, by the operation of the Spirit, this
assurance may in due time be revived,[14] and by the which, in the
meantime, they are supported from utter despair.[15]

CHAPTER XXI   CHAPTER XIX

Of the Law of God

1. God gave to Adam a law, as a covenant of works, by which he   **6.101**
bound him and all his posterity to personal, entire, exact, and perpetual obedience; promised life upon the fulfilling, and threatened death
upon the breach of it; and endued him with power and ability to keep
it.

2. This law, after his Fall, continued to be a perfect rule of   **6.102**
righteousness; and, as such, was delivered by God upon mount Sinai
in ten commandments, and written in two tables:[1] the first four
commandments containing our duty toward God, and the other six our
duty to man.[2]

3. Besides this law, commonly called moral, God was pleased to   **6.103**
give to the people of Israel, as a Church under age, ceremonial laws,
containing several typical ordinances, partly of worship, prefiguring
Christ, his graces, actions, sufferings, and benefits;[3] and partly

Presbyterian Church
in the United States

The United Presbyterian Church
in the United States of America

holding forth divers instructions of moral duties.[4] All which ceremonial laws are now abrogated under the New Testament.[5]

6.104 4. To them also, as a body politic, he gave sundry judicial laws,
which expired together with the state of that people, not obliging any
other, now, further than the general equity thereof may require.[6]

6.105 5. The moral law doth forever bind all, as well justified persons as
others, to the obedience thereof; and that not only in regard of the
matter contained in it, but also in respect of the authority of God the
Creator who gave it.[7] Neither doth Christ in the gospel any way
dissolve, but much strengthen, this obligation.[8]

6.106 6. Although true believers be not under the law as a covenant of
works, to be thereby justified or condemned;[9] yet is it of great use to
them, as well as to others; in that, as a rule of life, informing them of
the will of God and their duty, it directs and binds them to walk
accordingly;[10] discovering also the sinful pollutions of their nature,
hearts, and lives;[11] so as, examining themselves thereby, they may
come to further conviction of, humiliation for, and hatred against sin;[12]
together with a clearer sight of the need they have of Christ, and the
perfection of his obedience.[13] It is likewise of use to the regenerate, to
restrain their corruptions, in that it forbids sin,[14] and the threatenings
of it serve to show what even their sins deserve, and what afflictions in
this life they may expect for them, although freed from the curse
thereof threatened in the law.[15] The promises of it, in like manner,
show them God's approbation of obedience, and what blessings they
may expect upon the performance thereof;[16] although not as due to
them by the law as a covenant of works: so as a man's doing good, and
refraining from evil, because the law encourageth to the one, and
deterreth from the other, is no evidence of his being under the law, and
not under grace.[17]

6.107 7. Neither are the forementioned uses of the law contrary to the
grace of the gospel, but do sweetly comply with it:[18] the Spirit of
Christ subduing and enabling the will of man to do that freely and
cheerfully, which the will of God, revealed in the law, requireth to be
done.[19]

CHAPTER XXII   CHAPTER XX

Of Christian Liberty,
and Liberty of Conscience

6.108 1. The liberty which Christ hath purchased for believers under the
gospel consists in their freedom from the guilt of sin, the condemning
wrath of God, the curse of the moral law;[1] and in their being delivered

Presbyterian Church
in the United States

The United Presbyterian Church
in the United States of America

from this present evil world, bondage to Satan, and dominion of sin,[2] from the evil of afflictions, the sting of death, the victory of the grave, and everlasting damnation;[3] as also in their free access to God,[4] and their yielding obedience unto him, not out of slavish fear, but a childlike love, and a willing mind.[5] All which were common also to believers under the law;[6] but under the New Testament, the liberty of Christians is further enlarged in their freedom from the yoke of the ceremonial law, to which the Jewish church was subjected;[7] and in greater boldness of access to the throne of grace,[8] and in fuller[a] communications of the free Spirit of God, than believers under the law did ordinarily partake of.[9]

2. God alone is Lord of the conscience, and hath left it free from the doctrines and commandments of men which are in anything contrary to his Word, or beside it in matters of faith or worship.[10] So that to believe such doctrines, or to obey such commandments out of conscience, is to betray true liberty of conscience;[11] and the requiring an implicit faith, and an absolute and blind obedience, is to destroy liberty of conscience, and reason also.[12]   **6.109**

3. They who, upon pretense of Christian liberty, do practice any sin, or cherish any lust, do thereby destroy the end of Christian liberty; which is, that, being delivered out of the hands of our enemies, we might serve the Lord without fear, in holiness and righteousness before him, all the days of our life.[13]   **6.110**

4. And because the powers which God hath ordained, and the liberty which Christ hath purchased, are not intended by God to destroy, but mutually to uphold and preserve one another; they who, upon pretense of Christian liberty, shall oppose any lawful power, or the lawful exercise of it, whether it be civil or ecclesiastical, resist the ordinance of God.[14] And for their publishing of such opinions, or maintaining of such practices, as are contrary to the light of nature, or to the known principles of Christianity, whether concerning faith, worship, or conversation; or to the power of godliness; or such erroneous opinions or practices as, either in their own nature, or in the manner of publishing or maintaining them, are destructive to the external peace and order which Christ hath established in the church; they may lawfully be called to account, and proceeded against by the censures of the Church.[b][15]   **6.111**

---

[a]UPCUSA ed. reads; "full."

[b]Ed. 1647 includes: "and by the Power of the Civill Magistrate."

195

Presbyterian Church
in the United States

The United Presbyterian Church
in the United States of America

CHAPTER XXIII

CHAPTER XXI

Of Religious Worship
and the Sabbath Day

6.112   1. The light of nature showeth that there is a God, who hath lordship and sovereignty over all; is good, and doeth good unto all; and is therefore to be feared, loved, praised, called upon, trusted in, and served with all the heart, and with all the soul, and with all the might.[1] But the acceptable way of worshipping the true God is instituted by himself, and so limited by his own revealed will, that he may not be worshipped according to the imaginations and devices of men, or the suggestions of Satan, under any visible representation or any other way not prescribed in the Holy Scripture.[2]

6.113   2. Religious worship is to be given to God, the Father, Son, and Holy Ghost; and to him alone:[3] not to angels, saints, or any other creature:[4] and since the Fall, not without a Mediator; nor in the mediation of any other but of Christ alone.[5]

6.114   3. Prayer with thanksgiving, being one special part of religious worship,[6] is by God required of all men;[7] and that it may be accepted, it is to be made in the name of the Son,[8] by the help of his Spirit,[9] according to his will,[10] with understanding, reverence, humility, fervency, faith, love, and perseverance;[11] and, if vocal, in a known tongue.[12]

6.115   4. Prayer is to be made for things lawful,[13] and for all sorts of men living, or that shall live hereafter,[14] but not for the dead.[i][15]

6.116   5. The reading of the Scriptures with godly fear;[17] the sound preaching,[18] and conscionable hearing of the Word, in obedience unto God with understanding, faith, and reverence;[19] singing of psalms with grace in the heart;[20] as, also, the due administration and worthy receiving of the sacraments instituted by Christ; are all parts of the ordinary religious worship of God:[21] besides religious oaths,[22] and[j] vows,[23] solemn fastings,[24] and thanksgivings upon special occasion;[25] which are, in their several times and seasons, to be used in an holy and religious manner.[26]

6.117   6. Neither prayer, nor any other part of religious worship, is now, under the gospel, either tied unto, or made more acceptable by, any place in which it is performed, or towards which it is directed:[27] but

---

[i]Ed. 1647 includes: "nor for those of whom it may be known, that they have sinned the sin unto death."

[j]Ed. 1647 lacks: "and."

Presbyterian Church
in the United States

The United Presbyterian Church
in the United States of America

God is to be worshipped everywhere[28] in spirit and in[k] truth;[29] as in private families[30] daily,[31] and in secret each one by himself,[32] so more solemnly in the public assemblies, which are not carelessly or willfully to be neglected or forsaken, when God, by his Word or providence, calleth thereunto.[33]

7. As it is of the law of nature that, in general, a due proportion of time be set apart for the worship of God; so, in his Word, by a positive, moral, and perpetual commandment, binding all men in all ages, he hath particularly appointed one day in seven for a Sabbath, to be kept holy unto him:[34] which, from the beginning of the world to the resurrection of Christ, was the last day of the week; and, from the resurrection of Christ, was changed into the first day of the week, which in Scripture is called the Lord's Day, and is to be continued to the end of the world as the Christian Sabbath.[35]

6.118

8. This Sabbath is then kept holy unto the Lord when men, after a due preparing of their hearts, and ordering of their common affairs beforehand, do not only observe an holy rest all the day from their own works, words, and thoughts about their worldly employments and recreations;[36] but also are taken up the whole time in the public and private exercises of his worship, and in the duties of necessity and mercy.[37]

6.119

CHAPTER XXIV   CHAPTER XXII

Of Lawful Oaths and Vows

1. A lawful oath is a part of religious worship,[1] wherein upon just occasion, the person swearing solemnly calleth God to witness what he asserteth or promiseth; and to judge him according to the truth or falsehood of what he sweareth.[2]

6.120

2. The name of God only is that by which men ought to swear, and therein it is to be used with all holy fear and reverence,[3] therefore to swear vainly or rashly by that glorious and dreadful name, or to swear at all by any other thing, is sinful, and to be abhorred.[4] Yet, as, in matters of weight and moment, an oath is warranted by the Word of God, under the New Testament, as well as under the Old, so a lawful oath, being imposed by lawful authority, in such matters ought to be taken.[5]

6.121

---

[k]Ed. 1647 lacks: "in."

Presbyterian Church
in the United States

The United Presbyterian Church
in the United States of America

6.122 3. Whosoever taketh an oath ought duly to consider the weightiness of so solemn an act, and therein to avouch nothing but what he is fully persuaded is the truth. Neither may any man bind himself by oath to anything but what is good and just, and what he believeth so to be, and what he is able and resolved to perform. Yet it is a sin to refuse an oath touching anything that is good and just, being imposed by lawful authority.[6]

3. Whosoever taketh an oath ought duly to consider the weightiness of so solemn an act, and therein to avouch nothing but what he is fully persuaded is the truth. Neither may any man bind himself by oath to anything but what is good and just, and what he believeth so to be, and what he is able and resolved to perform.[m]

6.123 4. An oath is to be taken in the plain and common sense of the words, without equivocation or mental reservation.[7] It cannot oblige to sin; but in anything not sinful, being taken, it binds to performance, although to a man's own hurt:[8] nor is it to be violated, although made to heretics or infidels.[9]

6.124 5. A vow is of the like nature with a promissory oath, and ought to be made with the like religious care, and to be performed with the like faithfulness.[10]

6.125 6. It is not to be made to any creature, but to God alone:[11] and that it may be accepted, it is to be made voluntarily, out of faith and conscience of duty, in way of thankfulness for mercy received, or for obtaining of what we want; whereby we more strictly bind ourselves to necessary duties, or to other things, so far and so long as they may fitly conduce thereunto.[12]

6.126 7. No man may vow to do anything forbidden in the Word of God, or what would hinder any duty therein commanded, or which is not in his own power, and for the performance whereof he hath no promise or ability from God.[13] In which respects,[n] monastical vows of perpetual single life, professed poverty, and regular obedience, are so far from being degrees of higher perfection, that they are superstitious and sinful snares, in which no Christian may entangle himself.

---

[m]Ed. 1647 continues: "Yet is it a sin, to refuse an Oath touching any thing that is good and just, being imposed by lawfull Authority."

[n]Ed. 1647 includes: "Popish."

Presbyterian Church
in the United States

The United Presbyterian Ch
in the United States of America

CHAPTER XXV

CHAPTER XXIII

Of the Civil Magistrate

1. God, the Supreme Lord and King of all the world, hath ordained civil magistrates to be under him over the people, for his own glory and the public good; and to this end, hath armed them with the power of the sword, for the defense and encouragement of them that are good, and for the punishment of evildoers.[1]   6.127

2. It is lawful for Christians to accept and execute the office of a magistrate, when called thereunto;[2] in the managing whereof, as they ought especially to maintain piety, justice, and peace, according to the wholesome laws of each commonwealth,[3] so, for that end, they may lawfully, now under the New Testament, wage war upon just and necessary occasions.[4]   6.128

3. °Civil magistrates may not assume to themselves the administration of the Word and Sacraments; or the power of the keys of the kingdom of heaven; or, in the least, interfere in matters of faith.[5] Yet, as nursing fathers, it is the duty of civil magistrates to protect the church of our common Lord, without giving the preference to any denomination of Christians above the rest, in such a manner that all ecclesiastical persons whatever shall enjoy the full, free, and unquestioned liberty of discharging every part of their sacred functions, without violence or danger. And, as Jesus Christ hath appointed a regular government and discipline in his church, no law of any commonwealth should interfere with, let, or hinder, the due exercise thereof, among the voluntary members of any denomination of Christians, according to their own profession and belief. It is the duty of civil magistrates to protect the person and good name of all their people, in such an effectual manner as that no person be suffered, either upon pretense of religion or infidelity, to offer any indignity, violence, abuse, or injury to any other person whatsoever: and to take order, that all religious and ecclesiastical assemblies be held without molestation or disturbance.[6]   6.129

°Ed. 1647 reads: "III. The Civill Magistrate may not assume to himself the administration of the Word and Sacraments, or the power of the Keyes of the Kingdome of Heaven: yet, he hath Authoritie, and it is his duetie, to take order, that Unitie and Peace be preserved in the Church, that the Truth of God be kept pure, and intire, and that all Blasphemies and Heresies be suppressed, all corruptions and abuses in Worship and Discipline prevented, or reformed; and all the Ordinances of God duely settled, administered, and observed. For the better effecting whereof, he hath power to call Synods, to be present at them, and to provide that whatsoever is transacted in them, be according to the minde of God."

Presbyterian Church
in the United States

6.130 4. It is the duty of the people to pray for magistrates,[7] to honor their persons,[8] to pay them tribute and other dues,[9] to obey their lawful commands, and to be subject to their authority, for conscience' sake.[10] Infidelity, or difference in religion, doth not make void the magistrate's just and legal authority, nor free the people from their due obedience to him:[11] from which ecclesiastical persons are not exempted;[12] much less hath the Pope any power or[P] jurisdiction over them in their dominions, or over any of their people; and least of all to deprive them of their dominions or lives, if he shall judge them to be heretics, or upon any other pretense whatsoever.[13]

CHAPTER XXIV [q]

Of Marriage and Divorce

6.131 1. Christian marriage is an institution ordained of God, blessed by our Lord Jesus Christ, established and sanctified for the happiness and welfare of mankind, into which spiritual and

---

[P]Ed. 1647 reads: "and."

[q]Ed. 1647, Chapter XXIV reads: "I. Marriage is to be between one Man and one Woman: neither is it lawfull for any Man to have more then one Wife, nor for any Woman to have more then one Husband, at the same time.

"II. Marriage was ordained for the mutuall help of Husband and Wife, for the increase of man-kinde with a legitimate issue, and of the Church with an holy seed and, for preventing of uncleannesse.

"III. It is lawful for all sorts of people to marry, who are able with judgement, to give their consent. Yet, is it the duty of Christians to marry onely in the Lord: And therefore such as professe the true reformed Religion, should not marry with Infidels, Papists or other Idolaters: Neither should such as are godly be unequally yoked, by marrying with such as are notoriously wicked in their life, or maintaine damnable Heresies. (Continued next page.)

Presbyterian Church
in the United States

The United Presbyterian Church
in the United States of America

physical union one man and one woman enter, cherishing a mutual esteem and love, bearing with each other's infirmities and weaknesses, comforting each other in trouble, providing in honesty and industry for each other and for their household, praying for each other, and living together the length of their days as heirs of the grace of life.

2. Because the corruption of **6.132** man is apt unduly to put asunder those whom God hath joined together in marriage, and because the Church is concerned with the establishment of marriage in the Lord as Scripture

---

"IV. Marriage ought not to be within the degrees of Consanguinity or Affinity forbidden in the Word: Nor can such incestuous marriages ever be made lawfull by any Law of man, or consent of Parties, so as those persons may live together as man and wife. The man may not marry any of his wives kindred, nearer in blood, then he may of his own: nor the woman of her husbands kindred, nearer in blood, then of her own.

"V. Adultery, or fornication committed after a Contract, being detected before marriage, giveth just occasion to the innocent party to dissolve that Contract. In the case of Adultery after marriage, it is lawfull for the innocent party to sue out a Divorce: And after the Divorce, to marry another, as if the offending party were dead.

"VI. Although the corruption of man be such as is apt to study arguments, unduely to put asunder those whom God hath joyned together in marriage: yet, nothing but Adultery, or such wilfull desertion as can no way be remedied, by the Church, or Civil Magistrate, is cause sufficient of dissolving the bond of Marriage: Wherein, a publicke and orderly course of proceeding is to be observed: And the Persons concerned in it, not left to their own wills and discretion, in their owne case."

Presbyterian Church
in the United States

The United Presbyterian Church
in the United States of America

sets it forth, and with the present penitence as well as with the past innocence or guilt of those whose marriage has been broken; therefore as a breach of that holy relation may occasion divorce, so remarriage after a divorce granted on grounds explicitly stated in Scripture or implicit in the gospel of Christ may be sanctioned in keeping with his redemptive gospel, when sufficient penitence for sin and failure is evident, and a firm purpose of and endeavor after Christian marriage is manifest.

CHAPTER XXVI

Of Marriage and Divorce

6.133   1. Marriage is a union between one man and one woman, designed of God to last so long as they both shall live.[1]

6.134   2. Marriage is designed for the mutual help of husband and wife;[2] for the safeguarding, undergirding, and development of their moral and spiritual character;[3] for the propagation of children and the rearing of them in the discipline and instruction of the Lord.[4]

6.135   3. All persons who are able with judgment to give their consent may marry,[5] except within the limits of blood relationship forbidden by Scripture,[6] and such marriages are valid before God in the eyes of the church.[7] But no marriage can be fully and securely Christian in spirit or in

Presbyterian Church
in the United States

The United Presbyterian Church
in the United States of America

purpose unless both partners are committed to a common Christian faith and to a deeply shared intention of building a Christian home. Evangelical Christians should seek as partners in marriage only persons who hold in common a sound basis of evangelical faith.[8]

4. Marriage for the Christian has religious as well as civil significance.[9] The distinctive contribution of the church in performing the marriage ceremony is to affirm the divine institution of marriage;[10] to invoke God's blessing upon those who enter into the marital relationship in accordance with his word;[11] to hear the vows of those who desire to be married; and to assure the married partners of God's grace within their new relationship.[12]

5. It is the divine intention that persons entering the marriage covenant become inseparably united, thus allowing for no dissolution save that caused by the death of either husband or wife.[13] However, the weaknesses of one or both partners may lead to gross and persistent denial of the marriage vows so that marriage dies at the heart and the union becomes intolerable; yet only in cases of extreme, unrepented-of, and irremediable unfaithfulness (physical or spiritual) should separation or divorce be considered. Such separation or divorce is accepted as permissible only because of the failure of one or both of the

6.136

6.137

Presbyterian Church
in the United States

The United Presbyterian Church
in the United States of America

partners, and does not lessen in any way the divine intention for indissoluble union.[14]

6.138   6. The remarriage of divorced persons may be sanctioned by the church, in keeping with the redemptive gospel of Christ, when sufficient penitence for sin and failure is evident, and a firm purpose of and endeavor after Christian marriage is manifested.[15]

6.139   7. Divorced persons should give prayerful thought to discover if God's vocation for them is to remain unmarried, since one failure in this realm raises serious question as to the rightness and wisdom of undertaking another union.[16]

CHAPTER XXVII   CHAPTER XXV

Of the Church

6.140   1. The catholic or universal church, which is invisible, consists of the whole number of the elect, that have been, are, or shall be gathered into one, under Christ the head thereof; and is the spouse, the body, the fullness of Him that filleth all in all.[1]

6.141   2. The visible Church, which is also catholic or universal under the gospel (not confined to one nation as before under the law), consists of all those throughout the world that profess the true religion,[r 2] together with their children;[3] and is the Kingdom of the Lord Jesus Christ;[4] the house and family of God,[s 5] through which men are ordinarily saved and union with which is essential to their best growth and service.[6]

6.142   3. Unto this catholic visible Church, Christ hath given the ministry, oracles, and ordinances of God, for the gathering and perfecting of the saints, in this life, to the end of the world: and doth by his own

---

[r]Ed. 1647 reads: "and of their children."

[s]Ed. 1647 reads: "out of which, there is no ordinary possibility of Salvation."

Presbyterian Church in the United States	The United Presbyterian Church in the United States of America

presence and Spirit, according to his promise, make them effectual thereunto.[7]

4. This catholic Church hath been sometimes more, sometimes less, visible.[8] And particular churches, which are members thereof, are more or less pure, according as the doctrine of the gospel is taught and embraced, ordinances administered, and public worship performed more or less purely in them.[9] **6.143**

5. The purest churches under heaven are subject both to mixture and error:[10] and some have so degenerated as to become[t] apparently no churches of Christ.[11] Nevertheless, there shall be always a Church on earth, to worship God according to his will.[12] **6.144**

		6.145
6. The Lord Jesus Christ is the only head of the Church,[13] and the claim of any man to be the vicar of Christ and the head of the Church, is without warrant in fact or in Scripture, even anti-Christian, a usurpation dishonoring to the Lord Jesus Christ.	6.[u] The Lord Jesus Christ is the only head of the Church, and the claim of any man to be the vicar of Christ and the head of the Church is unscriptural, without warrant in fact, and is a usurpation dishonoring to the Lord Jesus Christ.	

CHAPTER XXVIII	CHAPTER XXVI

Of the Communion of Saints

1. All saints being[v] united to Jesus Christ their head, by his Spirit and by faith, have fellowship with him in his graces, sufferings, death, resurrection, and glory:[1] and, being united to one another in love, they have communion in each other's gifts and graces,[2] and are obliged to the performance of such duties, public and private, as to conduce to their mutual good, both in the inward and outward man.[3] **6.146**

2. Saints by their[w] profession are bound to maintain an holy fellowship and communion in the worship of God, and in performing such other spiritual services as tend to their mutual edification;[4] as also in relieving each other in outward things, according to their several **6.147**

---

[t]Ed. 1647 reads: "no Churches of Christ, but Synagogues of Satan."

[u]Ed. 1647 reads: "VI. There is no other Head of the Church, but the Lord Jesus Christ: Nor can the Pope of Rome, in any sense be head thereof: but is, that Antichrist, that Man of sin and Son of Perdition, that exalteth himself, in the Church, against Christ, and all that is called God."

[v]UPCUSA ed. reads: "that are."

[w]UPCUSA ed. reads: "by profession."

Presbyterian Church in the United States	The United Presbyterian Church in the United States of America

abilities and necessities. Which communion, as God offereth opportunity, is to be extended unto all those who, in every place, call upon the name of the Lord Jesus.[5]

6.148   3. This communion which the saints have with Christ, doth not make them in any wise partakers of the substance of his Godhead, or to be equal with Christ in any respect: either of which to affirm, is impious and blasphemous.[6] Nor doth their communion one with another as saints, take away or infringe the title or property which each man hath in his goods and possessions.[7]

CHAPTER XXIX	CHAPTER XXVII

Of the Sacraments

6.149   1. Sacraments are holy signs and seals of the covenant of grace, immediately instituted by God,[1] to represent Christ and his benefits, and to confirm our interest in him:[2] as also to put a visible difference between those that belong unto the church, and the rest of the world;[3] and solemnly to engage them to the service of God in Christ, according to his Word.[4]

6.150   2. There is in every sacrament a spiritual relation, or sacramental union, between the sign and the thing signified; whence it comes to pass that the names and effects of the one are attributed to the other.[5]

6.151   3. The grace which is exhibited in or by the sacraments, rightly used, is not conferred by any power in them; neither doth the efficacy of a sacrament depend upon the piety or intention of him that doth administer it, but upon the work of the Spirit,[6] and the word of institution, which contains, together with a precept authorizing the use thereof, a promise of benefit to worthy receivers.[7]

6.152   4. There be only two sacraments ordained by Christ our Lord in the gospel, that is to say, baptism and the supper of the Lord:[8] neither of which may be dispensed by any but by a minister of the Word, lawfully ordained.[9]

6.153   5. The sacraments of the Old Testament, in regard of the spiritual things thereby signified and exhibited, were, for substance, the same with those of the New.[10]

CHAPTER XXX	CHAPTER XXVIII

Of Baptism

6.154   1. Baptism is a sacrament of the New Testament, ordained by Jesus Christ,[1] not only for the solemn admission of the party baptized into the visible Church,[2] but also to be unto him a sign and seal of the covenant of grace,[3] of his ingrafting into Christ,[4] of regeneration,[5] of remission of sins,[6] and of his giving up unto God, through Jesus Christ, to walk in newness of life:[7] which sacrament is, by Christ's own appointment, to be continued in his church until the end of the world.[8]

2. The outward element to be used in this sacrament is water, wherewith the party is to be baptized in the name of the Father, and of the Son, and of the Holy Ghost,[9] by a minister of the gospel, lawfully called thereunto.[10]   **6.155**

3. Dipping of the person into the water is not necessary, but baptism is rightly administered by pouring or sprinkling water upon the person.[11]   **6.156**

4. Not only those that do actually profess faith in and obedience unto Christ,[12] but also the infants of one or both believing parents are to be baptized.[13]   **6.157**

5. Although it be a great sin to contemn or neglect this ordinance,[14] yet grace and salvation are not so inseparably annexed unto it as that no person can be regenerated or saved without it,[15] or that all that are baptized are undoubtedly regenerated.[16]   **6.158**

6. The efficacy of Baptism is not tied to that moment of time wherein it is administered;[17] yet, notwithstanding, by the right use of this ordinance the grace promised is not only offered, but really exhibited and conferred by the Holy Ghost, to such (whether of age or infants) as that grace belongeth unto, according to the counsel of God's own will, in his appointed time.[18]   **6.159**

7. The sacrament of Baptism is but once to be administered to any person.[19]   **6.160**

CHAPTER XXXI   CHAPTER XXIX

Of the Lord's Supper

1. Our Lord Jesus, in the night wherein he was betrayed, instituted the sacrament of his body and blood, called the Lord's Supper, to be observed in his Church unto the end of the world; for the perpetual remembrance of the sacrifice of himself in his death, the sealing all benefits thereof unto true believers, their spiritual nourishment and growth in him, their further engagement in and to all duties which they owe unto him; and to be a bond and pledge of their communion with him, and with each other, as members of his mystical body.[1]   **6.161**

2. In this sacrament Christ is not offered up to his Father, nor any real sacrifice made at all for remission of sins of the quick or dead,   **6.162**

but[x] a commemoration of that one[y] offering up of himself, by himself, upon the cross, once for all, and a spiritual oblation of all possible praise unto God for the same; so that the so-called sacrifice of the mass is most contradictory to Christ's one[z] sacrifice, the only propitiation for all the sins of the elect.[2]

6.163

3. The Lord Jesus hath, in this ordinance, appointed his ministers to declare his word of institution to the people, to pray, and bless the elements of bread and wine, and thereby to set them apart from a common to an holy use; and to take and break the bread, to take the cup, and (they communicating also themselves) to give both to the communicants.[3]

3. The Lord Jesus hath, in this ordinance, appointed his ministers to declare his word of institution to the people, to pray, and bless the elements of bread and wine, and thereby to set them apart from a common to an holy use; and to take and break the bread, to take the cup, and (they communicating also themselves) to give both to the communicants; but to none who are not then present in the congregation.

6.164

4. Private masses, or receiving this sacrament by a priest, or any other, alone; as likewise the denial of the cup to the people; worshipping the elements, the lifting them up, or carrying them about for adoration, and the reserving them for any pretended religious use, are all contrary to the nature of this sacrament, and to the institution of Christ.[4]

6.165

5. The outward elements in this sacrament, duly set apart to the uses ordained by Christ, have such relation to him crucified, as that truly, yet sacramentally only, they are sometimes called by the name of the things they represent, to wit, the body and blood of Christ;[5] albeit, in substance and nature, they still remain truly, and only, bread and wine, as they were before.[6]

6.166

6. That doctrine which maintains a change of the substance of bread and wine, into the substance of Christ's body and blood (commonly called transubstantiation) by consecration of a priest, or by any other way, is repugnant, not to Scripture alone, but even to common sense and reason; overthroweth the nature of the sacrament; and hath been, and is, the cause of manifold superstitions, yea, of gross idolatries.[7]

---

[x]Ed. 1647 reads: ". . . but onely a Commemoration of that one offering up of Himselfe, by Himselfe, upon the Crosse, once for all: and, a spirituall Oblation of all possible praise unto God, for the same: So that, the Popish Sacrifice of the masse (as they call it) is most abominably injurious to Christs one, onely Sacrifice, the alone Propitiation for all the sins of the Elect."

[y]UPCUSA ed. reads: "once."

[z]UPCUSA ed. reads: "own."

Presbyterian Church
in the United States

The United Presbyterian Church
in the United States of America

7. Worthy receivers, outwardly partaking of the visible elements in   **6.167**
this sacrament, do then also inwardly by faith, really and indeed, yet
not carnally and corporally, but spiritually, receive and feed upon
Christ crucified, and all benefits of his death: the body and blood of
Christ being then not corporally or carnally in, with, or under the
bread and wine; yet as really, but spiritually, present to the faith of
believers in that ordinance, as the elements themselves are to their
outward senses.[8]

8. Although ignorant and wicked men receive the outward elements in this sacrament, yet they receive not the thing signified thereby; but by their unworthy coming thereunto are guilty of the body and blood of the Lord, and bring judgement on themselves.[9]	8. Although ignorant and wicked men receive the outward elements in this sacrament, yet they receive not the thing signified thereby; but by their unworthy coming thereunto are guilty of the body and blood of the Lord,[a] and bring judgment on themselves. Wherefore all ignorant and ungodly persons, as they are unfit to enjoy communion with him, so are they unworthy of the Lord's Table, and cannot, without great sin against Christ, while they remain such, partake of these holy mysteries, or be admitted thereunto.	**6.168**

CHAPTER XXXII

CHAPTER XXX

Of Church Censures

1. The Lord Jesus, as king and head of his Church, hath therein   **6.169**
appointed a government in the hand of Church officers, distinct from
the civil magistrate.[1]

2. To these officers the keys of the Kingdom of Heaven are commit-   **6.170**
ted, by virtue whereof they have power respectively to retain and remit
sins, to shut that kingdom against the impenitent, both by the word and
censures; and to open it unto penitent sinners, by the ministry of the
gospel, and by absolution from censures, as occasion shall require.[2]

---

[a]Ed. 1647 reads: ". . . to their own damnation."

Presbyterian Church
in the United States

The United Presbyterian Church
in the United States of America

6.171   3. Church censures are necessary for the reclaiming and gaining of offending brethren; for deterring of others from like offenses; for purging out of that leaven which might infect the whole lump; for vindicating the honor of Christ, and the holy profession of the gospel; and for preventing the wrath of God, which might justly fall upon the Church, if they should suffer his covenant, and the seals thereof, to be profaned by notorious and obstinate offenders.[3]

6.172   4. For the better attaining of these ends, the officers of the church are to proceed by admonition, suspension from the sacrament of the Lord's Supper for a season, and by excommunication from the Church, according to the nature of the crime, and demerit of the person.[4]

CHAPTER XXXIII   CHAPTER XXXI

Of Synods and Councils

6.173   1. For the better government and further edification of the Church, there ought to be such assemblies as are commonly called synods or councils:[b] and it belongeth to the overseers and other rulers of the particular churches, by virtue of their office, and the power which Christ hath given them for edification, and not for destruction, to appoint such assemblies; and to convene together in them, as often as they shall judge it expedient for the good of the Church.[1]

6.174   2.[c] It belongeth to synods and councils, ministerially, to determine controversies of faith, and cases of conscience; to set down rules and directions for the better ordering of the public worship of God, and government of his Church; to receive complaints in cases of mal-administration, and authoritatively to determine the same: which decrees and determinations, if consonant to the Word of God, are to be received with reverence and submission, not only for their agreement with the Word, but also for the power whereby they are made, as being an ordinance of God, appointed thereunto in his Word.[2]

6.175   3. All synods or councils since the apostles' times, whether general or particular, may err, and many have erred; therefore they are not to be made the rule of faith or practice, but to be used as a help in both.[3]

---

[b]Remainder of this section added in 1788.

[c]Ed. 1647 reads: "II. As Magistrates may lawfully call a Synod of Ministers, and other fit Persons, to consult and advise with, about matters of Religion: So, if Magistrates be open Enemies to the Church, the Ministers of Christ, of themselves, by vertue of their Office, or, they, with other fit persons, upon delegation from their Churches, may meet together in such Assemblies." Sections 3–5 renumbered as 2–4 in 1788.

Presbyterian Church
in the United States

The United Presbyterian Church
in the United States of America

4. Synods and councils are to handle or conclude nothing but that **6.176** which is ecclesiastical; and are not to intermeddle with civil affairs which concern the commonwealth unless by way of humble petition in cases extraordinary; or by way of advice for satisfaction of conscience, if they be thereunto required by the civil magistrate.[4]

CHAPTER XXXIV

CHAPTER XXXII

Of the State of Man After Death, and of the Resurrection of the Dead

1. The bodies of men, after death, return to dust, and see corrup- **6.177** tion;[1] but their souls (which neither die nor sleep), having an immortal subsistence, immediately return to God who gave them.[2] The souls of the righteous, being then made perfect in holiness, are received into the highest heavens, where they behold the face of God in light and glory, waiting for the full redemption of their bodies;[3] and the souls of the wicked are cast into hell, where they remain in torments and utter darkness, reserved to the judgment of the great day.[4] Besides these two places for souls separated from their bodies, the Scripture acknowledgeth none.

2. At the last day, such as are found alive shall not die, but be **6.178** changed:[5] and all the dead shall be raised up with the self-same bodies, and none other, although with different qualities, which shall be united again to their souls for ever.[6]

3. The bodies of the unjust shall, by the power of Christ, be raised **6.179** to dishonor; the bodies of the just, by his Spirit, unto honor, and be made conformable to his own glorious body.[7]

CHAPTER XXXV

CHAPTER XXXIII

Of the Last Judgment

1. God hath appointed a day, wherein he will judge the world in **6.180** righteousness by Jesus Christ,[1] to whom all power and judgment is given of the Father.[2] In which day, not only the apostate angels shall be judged; but likewise all persons, that have lived upon earth, shall appear before the tribunal of Christ, to give an account of their thoughts, words, and deeds; and to receive according to what they have done in the body, whether good or evil.[3]

2. The end of God's appointing this day, is for the manifestation of **6.181** the glory of his mercy in the eternal salvation of the elect;[4] and of his

justice in the damnation of the reprobate, who are wicked and disobedient.[5] For then shall the righteous go into everlasting life, and receive that fullness of joy and refreshing which shall come from the presence of the Lord:[6] but the wicked, who know not God, and obey not the gospel of Jesus Christ, shall be cast into eternal torments, and punished with everlasting destruction from the presence of the Lord, and from the glory of his power.[7]

6.182   3. As Christ would have us to be certainly persuaded that there shall be a day of judgment, both to deter all men from sin, and for the greater consolation of the godly in their adversity;[8] so will he have that day unknown to men, that they may shake off all carnal security, and be always watchful, because they know not at what hour the Lord will come; and may be ever prepared to say, Come, Lord Jesus, come quickly.[9] Amen.

CHAPTER XXXIV [d]

Of the Holy Spirit

6.183   1. The Holy Spirit, the third Person in the Trinity, proceeding from the Father and the Son, of the same substance and equal in power and glory, is, together with the Father and the Son, to be believed in, loved, obeyed, and worshiped throughout all ages.

6.184   2. He is the Lord and Giver of life, everywhere present, and is the source of all good thoughts, pure desires, and holy counsels in men. By him the prophets were moved to speak the Word of God, and all the writers of the Holy Scriptures inspired to record infallibly the mind and will of God. The dispensation of the gospel is especially committed to him. He

---

[d] Added 1903.

prepares the way for it, accompanies it with his persuasive power, and urges its message upon the reason and conscience of men, so that they who reject its merciful offer are not only without excuse, but are also guilty of resisting the Holy Spirit.

3. The Holy Spirit, whom the **6.185** Father is ever willing to give to all who ask him, is the only efficient agent in the application of redemption. He regenerates men by his grace, convicts them of sin, moves them to repentance, and persuades and enables them to embrace Jesus Christ by faith. He unites all believers to Christ, dwells in them as their Comforter and Sanctifier, gives to them the Spirit of adoption and prayer, and performs all these gracious offices by which they are sanctified and sealed unto the day of redemption.

4. By the indwelling of the **6.186** Holy Spirit all believers being vitally united to Christ, who is the head, are thus united one to another in the Church, which is his body. He calls and anoints ministers for their holy office, qualifies all other officers in the Church for their special work, and imparts various gifts and graces to its members. He gives efficacy to the Word and to the ordinances of the gospel. By him the Church will be preserved, increased, purified, and at last made perfectly holy in the presence of God.

Presbyterian Church
in the United States

The United Presbyterian Church
in the United States of America

CHAPTER XXXV[*]

Of the Gospel of
the Love of God
and Missions

6.187

1. God in infinite and perfect love, having provided in the covenant of grace, through the mediation and sacrifice of the Lord Jesus Christ, a way of life and salvation, sufficient for and adapted to the whole lost race of man, doth freely offer this salvation to all men in the gospel.

6.188

2. In the gospel God declares his love for the world and his desire that all men should be saved; reveals fully and clearly the only way of salvation; promises eternal life to all who truly repent and believe in Christ; invites and commands all to embrace the offered mercy; and by his Spirit accompanying the Word pleads with men to accept his gracious invitation.

6.189

3. It is the duty and privilege of everyone who hears the gospel immediately to accept its merciful provisions; and they who continue in impenitence and unbelief incur aggravated guilt and perish by their own fault.

6.190

4. Since there is no other way of salvation than that revealed in the gospel, and since in the divinely established and ordinary method of grace faith cometh by hearing the Word of God, Christ

---

[*]Added 1903.

214

Presbyterian Church
in the United States

The United Presbyterian Church
in the United States of America

hath commissioned his Church to go into all the world and to make disciples of all nations. All believers are, therefore, under obligation to sustain the ordinances of the Christian religion where they are already established, and to contribute by their prayers, gifts, and personal efforts to the extension of the Kingdom of Christ throughout the whole earth.

Declaratory Statement[f]

6.191 While the ordination vow of ministers, ruling elders, and deacons, as set forth in the Form of Government, requires the reception and adoption of the Confession of Faith only as containing the system of doctrine taught in the Holy Scriptures, nevertheless, seeing that the desire has been formally expressed for a disavowal by the Church of certain inferences drawn from statements in the Confession of Faith, and also for a declaration of certain aspects of revealed truth which appear at the present time to call for more explicit statement, therefore The United Presbyterian Church in the United States of America does authoritatively declare as follows:

6.192 *First*, with reference to Chapter III of the Confession of Faith: that concerning those who are saved in Christ, the doctrine of God's eternal decree is held in harmony with the doctrine of

---

[f]Added 1903.

215

Presbyterian Church
in the United States

The United Presbyterian Church
in the United States of America

his love to all mankind, his gift of his Son to be the propitiation for the sins of the whole world, and his readiness to bestow his saving grace on all who seek it; that concerning those who perish, the doctrine of God's eternal decree is held in harmony with the doctrine that God desires not the death of any sinner, but has provided in Christ a salvation sufficient for all, adapted to all, and freely offered in the gospel to all; that men are fully responsible for their treatment of God's gracious offer; that his decree hinders no man from accepting that offer; and that no man is condemned except on the ground of his sin.

6.193

Second, with reference to Chapter X, Section 3, of the Confession of Faith, that it is not to be regarded as teaching that any who die in infancy are lost. We believe that all dying in infancy are included in the election of grace, and are regenerated and saved by Christ through the Spirit, who works when and where and how he pleases.

GENERAL NOTE: At several points the Confession of Faith is more specific in its statements than the Scriptures. These statements are inferences drawn from the Scriptures or from statements based on the Scriptures, or from the experience and observation of the Church. In such cases no texts are cited, but reference is made to this General Note.

Chapter I
1. Rom. 1:19, 20; 2:14, 15; 1:32.
2. I Cor. 1:21; 2:13, 14; 2:9–12; Acts 4:12; Rom. 10:13, 14.
3. Heb. 1:1, 2; Gal. 1:11, 12; Deut. 4:12–14.
4. Luke 24:27; II Tim. 3:16; Rom. 15:4; II Peter 3:15, 16.
5. Luke 16:29–31; Heb. 2:1–3; II Tim. 3:15, 16: II Peter 1:10.
6. See General Note.
7. The Canon of Scripture is not established by explicit passages, but by the testimony of Jesus and His Apostles; of ancient manuscripts and versions; of ancient Christian writers and church councils, and by the internal evidence exhibited in the separate books.
8. I Thess. 2:13; II Tim. 3:16; II Peter 1:21; Gal. 1:11, 12.
9. I Cor. 2:10, 11; John 16: 13, 14; I Cor. 2:6–9.
10. Mark 7:5–7.
11. This statement is an inference from the sufficiency of the Scriptures.
12. John 6:45; I Cor. 2:9, 10, 12.
13. I Cor. 14:26, 40; 11:13, 14.
14. II Peter 3:16; John 16:17; 6:60.
15. Ps. 119:105, 130; Acts 17:11, 12.
16. See Note under Section 3, figure 9 above.
17. Isaiah 8:20; Acts 15:14–18.
18. John 5:39; II Tim. 3:14, 15; II Peter 1:19.
19. I Cor. 14:6, 9, 11, 12, 24, 27, 28; Matt. 28:19, 20; Col. 3:16; Rom. 15:4.
20. Matt. 4:5–7; 12:1–7.
21. Matt. 22:29, 31; Acts 28:25; Luke 10:26.

Chapter II
1. Deut. 6:4; I Cor. 8:4, 6; I Thess. 1:9; Jer. 10:10.
2. Jer. 23:24; Ps. 147:5; I Kings 8:27; Ps. 139.

3. John 4:24.
4. I Tim. 1:17.
5. Luke 24:39; Deut. 4:15, 16.
6. James 1:17; Mal. 3:6.
7. I Kings 8:27; Jer. 23:23, 24.
8. Ps. 90:2; I Tim. 1:17.
9. Rom. 11:33; Ps. 145:3.
10. Rev. 4:8.
11. Rom. 16:27.
12. Isa. 6:3; Rev. 4:8.
13. Ps. 115:3.
14. Isa. 44:6; Acts 17:24, 25.
15. Eph. 1:11.
16. Rom. 11:36; Rev. 4:11.
17. I John 4:8–10.
18. Exod. 34:6, 7.
19. Heb. 11:6.
20. Neh. 9:32, 33.
21. Hab. 1:13; Ps. 5:5, 6.
22. Exod. 34:7; Nahum 1:2, 3.
23. John 5:26; Acts 7:2; Ps. 119:68; I Tim. 6:15; Rom. 9:5.
24. Acts 17:24, 25.
25. Rom. 11:36; Isa. 40:12–17.
26. Dan. 4:25; Eph. 1:11.
27. Heb. 4:13.
28. Rom. 11:33; Ps. 147:5.
29. Isa. 46:9–11; Acts 15:18; Ezek. 11:5.
30. Ps. 145:17; Rom. 7:12.
31. Rev. 7:11, 12; Rev. 5:12–14.
32. Matt. 28:19; II Cor. 13:14; Matt. 3:16, 17.
33. John 1:14, 18; 17:24.
34. Gal. 4:6; John 15:26.

Chapter III
1. Eph. 1:11; Acts 4:27, 28; Matt. 10:29, 30; Eph. 2:10.
2. James 1:13; I John 1:5.
3. Acts 2:23; Matt. 17:12; Acts 4:27, 28; John 19:11; Prov. 16:33; Acts 27:23, 24, 34, 44.
4. I Sam. 23:11, 12; Matt. 11:21, 23; Ps. 139:1–4.
5. Rom. 9:11, 13, 16, 18; II Tim. 1:9; Eph. 1:4, 5.
6. I Tim. 5:21; Acts 13:48; Rom. 8:29, 30; John 10:27–29.
7. Matt. 25:41; Rom. 9:22, 23; Jude 4.
8. John 10:14–16, 27–29; 6:37–39; 13:18; Acts 13:48; II Tim. 2:19.
9. Eph. 1:4.
10. Eph. 1:11.
11. Eph. 1:9.
12. II Tim. 1:9.
13. Rom. 8:30; I Peter 5:10.
14. II Tim. 1:9; Eph. 1:6, 2:8, 9.

217

15. Eph. 1:5, 6, 12.
16. Eph. 2:10; II Thess. 2:13; I Peter 1:2; Eph. 1:4.
17. Rom. 5:19; I Thess. 5:9, 10; Titus 2:14.
18. Rom. 9:11; II Thess. 2:13, 14; I Cor. 1:9.
19. Rom. 8:30.
20. Eph. 1:5.
21. Eph. 1:4; I Thess. 4:3; II Thess. 2:13.
22. I Peter 1:5; John 10:28.
23. John 17:9; 6:64, 65; 8:47; 10:26; Acts 13:48; I John 2:19.
24. Matt. 11:25, 26.
25. Rom. 2:8, 9; II Thess. 2:10–12; Rom. 9:14–22.
26. Rev. 15:3, 4.
27. See General Note.

Chapter IV
1. Gen. 1:1–3; Exod. 20:11; Jer. 10:12; Col. 1:16; John 1:2, 3; Heb. 1:2; 11:3; Ps. 104:24; Gen. 1.
2. Gen. 1:27.
3. Ps. 8:5, 6; Gen. 2:19, 20; Luke 23:43; Matt. 10:28.
4. Gen. 1:26; Col. 3:10; Eph. 4:24.
5. Rom.. 2:14, 15.
6. Gen. 2:16, 17, 3:6, 17.
7. Gen. 2:16, 17.
8. Gen. 2:17; 3:8–11, 23.
9. Gen. 1:28; Ps. 8:6–8.

Chapter V
1. Neh. 9:6; Heb. 1:3; Ps. 135:6; Matt. 10:29–31; Acts 17:25, 28; Matt. 6:26, 30; Job, Chapters 38–41.
2. Prov. 15:3; II Chron. 16:9; Ps. 145:17; 104:24.
3. Acts 15:18.
4. Eph. 1:11; Ps. 33:11.
5. Eph. 3:10; Rom.. 9:17; Ps. 145.
6. Acts 2:23. See under figures 3 and 4 above.
7. Gen. 8:22; Jer. 31–35.
8. Exod. 21:13; Gen. 50:19, 20; I Kings 22:34; Isa. 10:6–7.
9. Acts 27:24, 31, 44; Isa. 55:10, 11.
10. Hos. 1:7.
11. Rom.. 4:19–21.
12. II Kings 6:6; Dan. 3:27.
13. This statement is sustained by the doctrines of God's decrees and providence. See citations under Chapter III and Chapter V. Sections 1, 2, 3.
14. Rom. 11:32, 33; II Sam. 24:1; Acts 4:27, 28. See citations under Chapter III and Chapter V, Sections 1, 2, 3.
15. II Kings 19:28; Isa. 10:5–7, 12, 15.
16. Gen. 50:20. See under figure 15 above.
17. I John 2:16; Ps. 50:21; James 1:13, 14.
18. Deut. 8:2; II Chron. 32:25, 26, 31.
19. II Cor. 12:7–9; Ps. 73; 77:1–12; Mark 14:66–72; John 21:15–17.
20. Rom. 1:24, 26, 28; 11:7, 8; II Thess. 2:11, 12.
21. Deut. 29:4; Mark 4:11, 12.
22. Matt. 13:12; 25:29.
23. II Kings 8:12, 13.
24. Ps. 81:11, 12; II Thess. 2:10–12.
25. Exod. 8:15, 32; II Cor. 2:15, 16; Isa. 8:14; Exod. 7:3; I Peter 2:7, 8; Isa. 6:9, 10; Acts 28:26, 27.
26. Amos 9:8, 9; Rom. 8:28; Eph. 1:22.

Chapter VI
1. Gen. 3:13; II Cor. 11:3; Gen. 3:1–14.
2. Rom. 5:19–21.
3. Gen. 3:7, 8; 2:17.
4. Rom. 5:12; Eph. 2:3.
5. Gen. 6:5; Jer. 17:9; Rom. 3:10–19; 8:6–8; Ps. 58:1–5.
6. Acts 17:26. Compare Gen. 2:16, 17, with Rom. 5:12, 15–19; I Cor. 15:21, 22, 45, 49.
7. Ps. 51:5; Gen. 5:3; John 3:6; Rom. 3:10–18.
8. Rom. 5:6; 8:7; John 3:6; Rom. 7:18; Gen. 8:21; Rom. 8:7.
9. James 1:14, 15; Matt. 15:19.
10. Rom. 7:14, 17, 18, 23.
11. Rom. 7:5, 7, 8, 25.
12. Rom. 3:19; 2:15; I John 3:4.
13. Eph. 2:3; Rom. 5:12.
14. Gal. 3:10.
15. Rom. 6:23; Gen. 2:17.
16. Eph. 4:18; Matt. 25:41; II Thess. 1:9; Rom. 1:21–28; Lev. 26:14ff.; Deut. 28:15ff.

Chapter VII
1. See General Note.

2. Gen. 2:16, 17; Gal. 3:10; Hosea 6:7; Rom. 5:12, 19; I Cor. 15:22, 47.
3. Compare Gen. 2:16, 17, with Rom. 5:12–14; Rom. 10:5; Luke 10:25–28; and with the covenants made with Noah and Abraham.
4. Matt. 26:28; Gal. 3:21; Rom. 8:3; Isa. 42:6; Gen. 3:15; Heb. 10:5–10.
5. John 3:16; Acts 16:30, 31.
6. John 3:5–8; 6:37–44; Ezek. 36:26, 27.
7. Heb. 1:1, 2; II Cor. 3:6–9.
8. Rom. 4:11; Heb., Chapters 8, 9, 10.
9. Heb. 11:13; John 8:56, Gal. 3:6–8.
10. Acts 15:11; Rom. 3:30; Gal. 3:8, 9, 14.
11. Matt. 28:19, 20; I Cor. 11:23–25.
12. Heb. 8:6–13; II Cor. 3:9–11.
13. Eph. 2:15–19. See under figure 11 above.
14. Gal. 3:17, 29. See context and citations under figure 10 above.

Chapter VIII
1. Isa. 42:1; I Peter 1:19, 20; I Tim. 2:5; John 3:16.
2. Acts 3:22; Deut. 18:15.
3. Heb. 5:5, 6.
4. Ps. 2:6; Luke 1:33; Isa 9:6, 7.
5. Eph. 5:23.
6. Heb. 1:2.
7. Acts 17:31; II Cor. 5:10.
8. John 17:6; Eph. 1:4; John 6:37, 39; Isa. 53:10.
9. I Tim. 2:5, 6; Mark 10:45; I Cor. 1:30; Rom. 8:30.
10. John 1:1, 14; I John 5:20; Phil. 2:6; Gal. 4:4; Heb. 2:14.
11. Heb. 2:17; 4:15.
12. Luke 1:27, 31, 35; Gal. 4:4. See under figure 10 above.
13. Col. 2:9; Rom. 9:5. See under figure 12 above.
14. Rom. 1:3, 4; I Tim 2:5.
15. Luke 4:18, 19, 21; Acts 10:38.
16. Col. 2:3.
17. Col. 1:19.
18. Heb. 7:26; John 1:14; Luke 4:18–21.
19. Heb. 5:4, 5.
20. John 5:22, 27; Matt 28:18.
21. Ps. 40:7, 8; Phil. 2:5–8.
22. Gal. 4:4.
23. Matt. 3:15; John 17:4.

24. Matt. 26:37, 38; Luke 22:44; Matt. 27:46.
25. Matt., Chapters 26 and 27.
26. Phil. 2:8.
27. Acts 2:24, 27; 13:37.
28. I Cor. 15:4.
29. John 20:25, 27.
30. Luke 24:50, 51; Acts 1:9; Acts 2:33–36.
31. Rom. 8:34; Heb. 7:25.
32. Acts 10:42; Matt. 13:40–42; 16:27; 25:31–33; II Tim. 4:1.
33. Rom. 5:19; Heb. 9:14; Rom. 3:25, 26; Heb. 10:14; Eph. 5:2.
34. Eph. 1:11, 14; John 17:2; Rom. 5:10, 11; Heb. 9:12, 15.
35. Gen. 3:15; Rev. 13:8; Heb. 13:8.
36. I Peter 3:18; Heb. 9:14; John 10:17, 18.
37. Acts 20:28; John 3:13; I John 3:16.
38. John 6:37, 39; 10:16.
39. I John 2:1; Rom. 8:34.
40. John 15:15; 17:6; Gal. 1:11, 12; Eph. 1:7–9.
41. Rom. 8:9, 14; Titus 3:4, 5; Rom. 15:18, 19; John 17:17.
42. Ps. 110:1; I Cor. 15:25, 26; Mal. 4:2, 3; Col. 2:15.

Chapter IX (PCUS)
1. *Paragraph 1:* II Cor. 13:14; John 15:26; Matt. 28:19; 3:16; Luke 1:35; Eph. 4:30; Heb. 10:29; I Cor. 10:10, 11; Rev. 22:17; Eph. 2:18–20, 22; John 14:26; 16:7; Gal. 4:6; Acts 5:3, 4; 16:6, 7; Mark 3:29; Rom. 8:26, 27; I John 2:20–27.
2. *Paragraph 2:* Eph. 4:30; 5:9; Gen. 1:2; John 3:5; Acts 2:1–21; Gal. 5:22–25; John 16:8–11; II Peter 1:21; II Tim. 3:16; I Cor. 2:10; I Peter 1:11; John 16:13–15; Acts 7:51; I Thess. 5:19; Eph. 4:30; Ps. 104:30.
3. *Paragraph 3:* John 3:1–8; Acts 2:38; Luke 11:13; I Cor. 12:3; John 7:37–39; 16:13; 16:7–11; Rev. 22:17; Titus 3:5–7; II Thess. 2:13; Gal. 4:6; I John 4:2; Rom. 8:14, 17, 26, 27; Eph. 4:30; I Cor. 2:13, 14.
4. *Paragraph 4:* Eph. 2:14–18; 4:1–6; 5:18; Acts 2:4; 13:2; I Cor. 12; II Peter 1:19–21; I Thess. 1:5, 6; John 20:22, 23; Matt. 28:19, 20.

Chapter X (PCUS)
1. *Paragraph 1:* Rev. 22:17; John 3:16; I John 2:1, 2; Acts 2:38, 39; Matt. 11:28–30; II Cor. 5:14–19; Titus 2:11; Heb. 2:9; Luke 24:46, 47.
2. *Paragraph 2:* Matt. 28:19, 20; Acts 4:12; John 6:37–40; 17:3; Acts 16:31; 2:38; Gal. 2:16–20; Rom. 1:16, 17; 4:5; Acts 13:38, 39, 48; II Peter 3:9; Matt. 11:28–30; Mark 1:14, 15; Acts 17:30; Rev. 22:17; Ezek. 33:11; Isa. 1:18; Luke 13:34.
3. *Paragraph 3:* Heb. 2:3; 12:25; Acts 13:46; Matt. 10:32, 33; Luke 12:47, 48; Heb. 10:29.
4. *Paragraph 4:* Acts 4:12; Matt. 28:19, 20; Acts 1:8; Rom. 10:13–15; Heb. 10:19–25; Gal. 3:28; I Cor. 16:1, 2; Matt. 9:36–38; Acts 13:2–4; Col. 3:16; Rev. 22:17; Col. 1:28, 29.

Chapter XI (PCUS)
1. Deut. 30:19; John 7:17; Rev. 22:17; James 1:14; John 5:40.
2. Gen. 1:26. See under figure 1 above.
3. Gen 2:16, 17; 3:6.
4. Rom. 5:6, 8:7; John 15:5.
5. Rom. 3:10, 12; 8:7.
6. Eph. 2:1, 5; Col. 2:13.
7. John 6:44, 65; I Cor. 2:14; Rom. 8:8; Eph. 2:2–5; Titus 3:3–5.
8. Col. 1:13; John 8:34, 36; Phil 2:13; Rom. 6:18, 22.
9. Gal. 5:17; Rom. 7:15.
10. I John 3:2; Rev. 22:3, 4.
11. II Chron. 6:36; I John 1:8–10; 2:1–6; Ps. 17:15.

Chapter XII (PCUS)
1. Rom. 11:7; 8:30; II Thess. 2:13, 14; Rom. 8:2; II Tim. 1:9, 10.
2. Acts 26:18; I Cor. 2:10, 12.
3. Ezek. 36:26.
4. Ezek. 11:19; 36:27; Phil. 2:13; 4:13; Deut. 30:6.
5. John 6:44, 45.
6. John 6:37. See under figure 5 above.
7. II Tim. 1:9; Titus 3:4, 5; Rom. 9:11; Eph. 2:4, 5, 8, 9.
8. I Cor. 2:14; Rom. 8:7; Eph. 2:5.
9. John 6:37; Ezek. 36:27; John 5:25.
10. Acts 4:12; John 3:8.

11. Matt. 22:14; 13:20, 21; John 6:64–66; 8:24; I John 2:19; Heb. 6:4–6.
12. Acts 4:12; John 14:6; John 17:3.
13. II John 9:11; Gal. 1:8.

Chapter XIII (PCUS)
1. Rom. 8:30; 3:24.
2. Rom. 4:5–8; II Cor. 5:19, 21; Titus 3:5, 7; Eph. 1:7; Jer. 23:6; Rom. 3:22, 24, 25, 27, 28; I Cor. 1:30, 31; Rom. 5:17–19.
3. Phil. 3:9; Eph. 2:8; Acts 13:38, 39.
4. John 1:12; Rom. 3:28; 5:1.
5. James 2:17, 22, 26; Gal. 5:6.
6. Rom. 5:8–10, 19; I Cor. 15:3; II Cor. 5:21; I Peter 2:24; 3:18; Heb. 10:10, 14; Isa. 53.
7. Rom. 8:32; John 3:16.
8. II Cor. 5:21; Isa. 53:6.
9. Rom. 3:24; 6:23; Eph. 1:7; 2:6–9.
10. Rom. 3:26; Eph. 2:7.
11. I Peter 1:2, 19, 20; Rom. 8:30.
12. Gal. 4:4; I Tim. 2:6; Rom. 4:25.
13. John 3:5, 18, 36; Gal. 2:16; Titus 3:4–7.
14. Matt. 6:12; I John 1:9; 2:1.
15. Luke 22:32; John 10:28; Heb. 10:14; Phil. 1:6; I John 2:19.
16. Ps. 89:31–33; 32:5; Matt. 26:75; Ps. 51:7–12; I Cor. 11:30, 32.
17. Heb. 11:13; John 8:56; Gal. 3:6–8; Acts 15:11; Rom. 3:30; Gal. 3:8, 9, 14.

Chapter XIV (PCUS)
1. Eph. 1:5; Gal. 4:4, 5.
2. John 1:12; Rom. 8:17.
3. Rev. 3:12.
4. Rom. 8:15.
5. Eph. 3:12; Heb. 4:16; Rom. 5:2.
6. Gal. 4:6.
7. Ps. 103:13.
8. Prov. 14:26; Ps. 27:1–3.
9. Matt. 6:30, 32; I Peter 5:7.
10. Heb. 12:6.
11. Lam. 3:31; Heb. 13:5.
12. Eph. 4:30.
13. Heb. 6:12.
14. I Peter 1:4; Heb. 1:14.

Chapter XV (PCUS)
1. Acts 20:32; Rom. 6:5, 6; John 17:17; Eph. 5:26; II Thess. 2:13.

2. Rom. 6:6, 14.
3. Rom. 8:13; Gal. 5:24; Col. 3:5.
4. Col. 1:11; II Peter 3:13, 14;
   Eph. 3:16–19.
5. II Cor. 7:1; Heb. 12:14.
6. I Thess. 5:23.
7. I John 1:10; Phil. 3:12;
   Gal. 5:17; Rom. 7:18, 23.
8. Rom. 7:23.
9. Rom. 6:14, I John 5:4;
   Eph. 4:16.
10. II Peter 3:18; I Cor. 3:18.
11. II Cor. 7:1.

Chapter XVI (PCUS)
1. I Cor. 12:3; Eph. 2:8;
   Heb. 12:2.
2. Rom. 10:14, 17.
3. I Peter 2:2, Acts 20:32;
   Matt. 28:19; I Cor. 11:23–29;
   II Cor. 12:8–10.
4. I Thess. 2:13; I John 5:10;
   Acts 24:14.
5. Matt. 6:30; Matt. 8:10;
   Rom. 4:19, 20.
6. Luke 22:31, 32; I Cor. 10:13.
7. Heb. 6:11, 12; Heb. 10:22;
   II Tim. 1:12.
8. Heb. 12:2.

Chapter XVII (PCUS)
1. Acts 11:18.
2. Luke 24:47; Mark 1:15;
   Acts 20:21.
3. Ezek. 18:30, 31; Ezek. 36:31;
   Ps. 51:4; Jer. 31:18, 19;
   II Cor. 7:11.
4. Ps. 119:59, 106; John 14:23.
5. Titus 3:5; Acts 5:31.
6. Rom. 3:24; Eph. 1:7.
7. Luke 13:3; Acts 17:30.
8. Rom. 6:23; Matt. 12:36;
   James 2:10.
9. Isa. 55:7; Rom. 8:1; Isa. 1:18.
10. Ps. 19:13; Luke 19:8; I Tim.
   1:13, 15; Dan. 9; Neh. 9.
11. Ps. 32:5, 6; Ps. 51:4, 5, 7, 9,
   14.
12. Prov. 28:13; I John 1:9.
13. James 5:16; Luke 17:3, 4;
   Josh. 7:19; Ps. 51.
14. II Cor. 2:7, 8; Gal. 6:1, 2.

Chapter XVIII (PCUS)
1. Deut. 12:32; Ps. 119:9;
   Matt. 28:20; Luke 10:25, 26;
   II Peter 1:19.
2. Matt. 15:9; Isa. 29:13;
   John 16:2; I Sam. 15:22, 23;
   Col. 2:20–23.
3. James 2:18, 22.

4. Ps. 116:12, 13; Col. 3:17;
   I Chron. 29:6–9.
5. I John 2:3, 5; II Peter 1:5–10.
6. II Cor. 9:2; Matt. 5:16.
7. Titus 2:5; I Tim. 6:1;
   Titus 2:9–12.
8. I Peter 2:15.
9. I Peter 2:12; Phil. 1:11;
   John 15:8.
10. Eph. 2:10.
11. Rom. 6:22.
12. John 15:5, 6; Ezek. 36:26, 27.
13. Phil. 2:13; Phil. 4:13;
   II Cor. 3:5.
14. Phil. 2:12; Heb. 6:11, 12;
   Isa. 64:7; II Peter 1:3, 5, 10,
   11; II Tim. 1:6; Jude 20, 21.
15. Luke 17:10; Gal. 5:17.
16. Rom. 3:20; Rom. 4:2, 4, 6;
   Eph. 2:8, 9; Titus 3:5–7;
   Rom. 8:18.
17. See citations under 15 above.
18. Gal. 5:22, 23.
19. Isa. 64:6; Ps. 143:2; Ps. 130:3;
   Gal. 5:17; Rom. 7:15, 18.
20. Eph. 1:6; I Peter 2:5; Gen. 4:4;
   Heb. 11:4.
21. I Cor. 4:3, 4; Ps. 143:2.
22. II Cor. 8:12; Heb. 6:10.
23. II Kings 10:30, 31; Phil. 1:15,
   16, 18.
24. Heb. 11:4, 6; Gen. 4:3–5.
25. I Cor. 13:3; Isa. 1:12.
26. Matt. 6:2, 5, 16; Rom. 14:23.
27. Titus 1:15; Prov. 15:8;
   Prov. 28:9.
28. Matt. 25:24–28; Matt. 25:41–45;
   Matt. 23:23.

Chapter XIX (PCUS)
1. Phil. 1:6; John 10:28, 29; Jer.
   32:40; I John 3:9; I Peter 1:5,
   9.
2. II Tim. 2:19; Jer. 31:3;
   Eph. 1:4, 5; John 13:1;
   Rom. 8:35–39.
3. Heb. 10:10, 14; John 17:11, 24;
   Heb. 7:25; Heb. 9:12–15;
   Rom. 8:32–39; Luke 22:32.
4. John 14:16, 17; I John 2:27;
   I John 3:9.
5. Jer. 32:40; Heb. 8:10–12.
6. II Thess. 3:3; I John 2:19;
   John 10:28; I Thess. 5:23, 24;
   Heb. 6:17–20.
7. Matt. 26:70, 72, 74;
   II Sam. 12:9, 13.
8. Isa. 64:7, 9; II Sam. 11:27.
9. Eph. 4:30.

10. Ps. 51:8, 10, 12; Rev. 2:4.
11. Mark 6:52; Ps. 95:8.
12. Ps. 32:3, 4; Ps. 51:8.
13. II Sam. 12:14; Ezek. 16:54.
14. II Sam. 12:10; Ps. 89:31, 32; I Cor. 11:32.

Chapter XX (PCUS)
1. Deut. 29:19; John 8:41.
2. Matt. 7:22, 23.
3. II Tim. 1:12; I John 2:3; I John 5:13; I John 3:14, 18, 19, 21, 24.
4. Rom. 5:2, 5. See citations under 3 above.
5. Heb. 6:11, 12. See citations under 3 and 4 above.
6. Heb. 6:17, 18; II Peter 1:4, 5.
7. II Peter 1:10, 11; I John 3:14.
8. Rom. 8:15, 16.
9. Eph. 1:13, 14; II Cor. 1:21, 22.
10. Isa. 50:10; I John 5:13; Ps. 73; 77; 88.
11. I Cor. 2:12; I John 4:13; Ps. 77:10–20; Ps. 73. See citations under Section 2 above.
12. II Peter 1:10; Rom. 6:1, 2; Titus 2:11, 12, 14.
13. Ps. 51:8, 12, 14; Eph. 4:30; Ps. 77:1–10; Matt. 26:69–72; Ps. 31:22; Ps. 88; Isa. 50:10.
14. I John 3:9; Luke 22:32; Ps. 73:15; Ps. 51:8, 12; Isa. 50:10.
15. Micah 7:7–9.

Chapter XXI (PCUS)
1. Gal. 3:12; Hos. 6:7 (A.S.V.); Gen. 2:16, 17. Compare Rom. 5:12–14; I Cor. 15:22; Luke 10:25–28, and the covenants made with Noah and Abraham; Gen. 1:26; Deut. 30:19; John 7:17; Rev. 22:17; James 1:14; James 1:25; James 2:8, 10; Rom. 3:19; Deut. 5:32; Deut. 10:4; Exod. 34:1; Rom. 13:8, 9.
2. Matt. 22:37–40; Exod. 20:3–18.
3. Heb. 10:1; Gal. 4:1–3; Col. 2:17; Heb. 9.
4. See Lev. 5:1–6; 6:1–7, and similar passages.
5. Mark 7:18, 19 (A.S.V.); Gal. 2:4; Col. 2:17; Eph. 2:15, 16.
6. Matt. 5:38, 39; I Cor. 9:8–10; Exod. Chapters 21 and 22.
7. Rom. 13:8, 9; I John 2:3, 4, 7; Rom. 3:31; Rom. 6:15. See citations under Section 2 above.
8. Matt. 5:18, 19; James 2:8; Rom. 3:31.

9. Rom. 6:14; Rom. 8:1; Gal. 4:4, 5; Acts 13:39.
10. Rom. 7:12; Ps. 119:5; I Cor. 7:19; Gal. 5:14, 18, 23.
11. Rom. 7:7; Rom. 3:20.
12. Rom. 7:9, 14, 24.
13. Gal. 3:24; Rom. 8:3, 4; Rom. 7:24, 25.
14. James 2:11; Ps. 119:128.
15. Ezra 9:13, 14; Ps. 89:30–34.
16. Ps. 37:11; Ps. 19:11; Lev. 26:3–13; Eph. 6:2; Matt. 5:5.
17. Rom. 6:12, 14; Heb. 12:28, 29; I Peter 3:8–12; Ps. 34:12–16.
18. See citations under Section 6 above.
19. See citations under Chapter X, Section 1; Gal. 3:13.

Chapter XXII (PCUS)
1. Titus 2:14; I Thess. 1:10.
2. Gal. 1:4; Acts 26:18; Col. 1:13; Rom. 6:14.
3. Ps. 119:71; I Cor. 15:56, 57; Rom. 8:1.
4. Rom. 5:2.
5. Rom. 8:14, 15; Eph. 2:18; Gal. 4:6; Heb. 10:19; I John 4:18.
6. Gal. 3:9, 14. See citations under Chapter VIII, Section 6.
7. Gal. 5:1; Acts 15:10; Gal. 4:1–3, 6.
8. Heb. 4:14, 16; Heb. 10:19, 20.
9. John 7:38, 39; II Cor. 3:13, 17, 18.
10. Rom. 14:4; Acts 4:19; Acts 5:29; I Cor. 7:23; Matt. 23:8–10; II Cor. 1:24; Matt. 15:19.
11. Gal. 2:3, 4; Col. 2:20, 22, 23; Gal. 5:1.
12. Hosea 5:11; Rev. 13:12, 16, 17.
13. Gal. 5:13; I Peter 2:16; Luke 1:74, 75; II Peter 2:19; John 8:34.
14. I Peter 2:13, 14, 16; Heb. 13:17; Rom. 13:1–8.
15. I Cor. 5:1, 5, 11, 13; Titus 1:13; Matt. 18:17, 18; II Thess. 3:14; Titus 3:10.

Chapter XXIII (PCUS)
1. Rom. 1:19, 20; Jer. 10:7; Ps. 19:1–6.
2. Deut. 12:32; Matt. 15:9; Matt. 4:9, 10; Acts 17:24, 25; Exod. 20:4–6; Deut. 4:15–20; Col. 2:20–23.
3. John 5:23; II Cor. 13:14; Matt. 4:10; Rev. 5:11–13.

4. Col. 2:18; Rev. 19:10; Rom. 1:25.
5. John 14:6; I Tim. 2:5; Eph. 2:18.
6. Phil. 4:6.
7. Luke 18:1; I Tim. 2:8.
8. John 14:13, 14.
9. Rom. 8:26.
10. I John 5:14.
11. Ps. 47:7; Heb. 12:28; Gen. 18:27; James 5:16; Eph. 6:18; James 1:6, 7; Mark 11:24; Matt. 6:12, 14, 15; Col. 4:2.
12. I Cor. 14:14.
13. I John 5:14.
14. I Tim. 2:1, 2; John 17:20; II Sam. 7:29.
15. This statement is based on the absence of any command to pray for the dead, and of any example in the Scripture of such prayer. I John 5:14.
16. Original note 16 removed by amendment enacted by the General Assembly in 1939.
17. Acts 15:21; Acts 17:11; Rev. 1:3.
18. II Tim. 4:2.
19. James 1:22; Acts 10:33; Heb. 4:2; Matt. 13:19; Isa. 66:2.
20. Col. 3:16; Eph. 5:19; James 5:13.
21. Matt. 28:19; Acts 2:42; I Cor. 11:23–29.
22. Deut. 6:13.
23. Ps. 116:14; Isa. 19:21; Neh. 10:29.
24. Joel 2:12; Matt. 9:15; I Cor. 7:5; Esther 4:16.
25. Ps. 107.
26. John 4:24; Heb. 10:22.
27. John 4:21.
28. Mal. 1:11; I Tim. 2:8.
29. John 4:23, 24.
30. Deut. 6:7; Job 1:5; Acts 10:2.
31. Matt. 6:11.
32. Matt. 6:6; Eph. 6:18.
33. Isa. 56:7; Heb. 10:25; Acts 2:42; Luke 4:16; Acts 13:42.
34. Exod. 20:8–11; Isa. 56:2, 4, 6.
35. I Cor. 16:1, 2; Acts 20:7. These texts are cited in connection with the example of the apostles and the early church.
36. Exod. 16:23, 25, 26, 29, 30; Exod. 31:15, 16; Isa. 58:13; Neh. 13:15–22; Luke 23:56.
37. Isa. 58:13; Matt. 12:1–13.

Chapter XXIV (PCUS)
1. Deut. 10:20.
2. II Cor. 1:23; II Chron. 6:22, 23; Exod. 20:7.
3. Deut. 6:13.
4. Jer. 5:7; James 5:12; Matt. 5:37; Exod. 20:7.
5. I Kings 8:31; Ezra 10:5; Matt. 26:63, 64.
6. See citations under Section 2, above.
7. Ps. 24:4; Jer. 4:2.
8. Ps. 15:4.
9. Ezek. 17:16, 18; Josh. 9:18, 19; II Sam. 21:1.
10. Ps. 66:13, 14; Ps. 61:8; Deut. 23:21, 23.
11. Ps. 76:11; Jer. 44:25, 26.
12. Ps. 50:14; Gen. 28:20–22. Compare with the above I Sam. 1:11; Ps. 132:2–5.
13. Num. 30:5, 8, 12, 13.

Chapter XXV (PCUS)
1. Rom. 13:1, 3, 4; I Peter 2:13, 14.
2. Prov. 8:15, 16. See citations under Section 1, above.
3. Ps. 82:3, 4; I Peter 2:13. See citations under Section 1, above.
4. Rom. 13:1–4; Luke 3:14, Matt. 8:9; Acts 10:1, 2.
5. Matt. 16:19; I Cor. 4:1; John 18:36; Eph. 4:11, 12; II Chron. 26:18.
6. See General Note.
7. I Tim. 2:1, 2.
8. I Peter 2:17.
9. Rom. 13:6, 7.
10. Rom. 13:5; Titus 3:1.
11. This is an inference from the duties just stated.
12. Rom. 13:1; Acts 25:10, 11.
13. This is an inference from the doctrine of the civil magistrate, and from duties incumbent on believers with respect to him.

Chapter XXVI (PCUS)
1. Gen. 2:23, 24; I Cor. 7:2, 39; Matt. 19:4–6; Eph. 5:28, 31, 33; I Cor. 13:8, 13; Matt. 5:31, 32; Mark 10:5–9; Rom. 7:2, 3.
2. Gen. 2:18, 24.
3. Gen. 1:27, 28; Eph. 5:22, 23; Col. 3:18, 19; Gen. 2:18–25; I Cor. 7:3–5, 9, 36.
4. Gen. 1:27, 28; Gen. 9:1; Mal. 2:15; Matt. 18:5, 6, 10, 14; Matt. 19:14; Eph. 6:1–4;

Col. 3:20, 21; Mark 10:13–16;
Luke 18:15–17.
5. Gen. 1:27, 28.
6. Mark 6:18; I Cor. 5:1;
Lev. 18:6–18.
7. Mark 1:30; John 2:1, 2;
I Tim. 5:14; Heb. 13:4;
I Cor. 7:7, 36; I Cor. 9:5;
I Tim. 4:3.
8. I Cor. 7 especially v. 39;
II Cor. 6:14, 15.
9. Prov. 18:22; Matt. 19:6;
Eph. 5:29, 30, 32; Mark 10:9,
11, 12.
10. Gen. 1:27, 28.
11. Mark 10:9.
12. Eph. 5:22, 23.
13. Gen. 2:23, 24; Matt. 5:31, 32;
Mark 10:5–9; Rom. 7:2, 3;
I Cor. 7:2, 10, 11, 39;
Eph. 5:28, 31, 33;
Matt. 19:4–9; I Cor. 13:4–13.
14. Mark 10:4–9; I Cor. 7:12, 13,
15; Matt. 19:7–9.
15. II Sam. 12:13; Neh. 9:17; Ps.
32:5; Ps. 130:4; Matt. 12:31a;
Matt. 21:31, 32; John 8:3, 11;
Rom. 3:23; Gal. 6:1; I Tim. 2:4;
Heb. 7:25; I John 1:9; I John 2:1,
2; Luke 7:36–50; Luke 15:11–32;
John 3:16, 17; Rom. 10:9, 10.
16. Matt. 5:31, 32; I Cor. 7:10, 11,
20, 32–35; Mark 10:11;
Luke 16:18.

Chapter XXVII (PCUS)
1. Eph. 1:22, 23; Col. 1:18;
Eph. 5:23, 27, 32.
2. I Cor. 1:2; I Cor. 12:12, 13;
Rom. 15:9–12.
3. Gen. 17:7. See context. Compare Gal. 3:7, 9, 14; Rom. 4;
Acts 2:39; I Cor. 7:14;
Mark 10:13–16.
4. Matt. 13:47; Col. 1:13;
Isa. 9:7.
5. Eph. 2:19.
6. Matt. 28:19; Acts 2:38;
I Cor. 12:13; Matt. 26:26–28.
7. Eph. 4:11–13; Isa. 59:21;
Matt. 28:19, 20.
8. Rom. 11:3, 4; Acts 9:31.
9. I Cor. 5:6, 7; Rev. 2, 3.
10. Matt. 13:24–30, 47, 48.
11. Rom. 11:18–22; Rev. 18:2.
12. Matt. 16:18; Ps. 102:28;
Matt. 28:19, 20.
13. Col. 1:18.

Chapter XXVIII (PCUS)
1. I John 1:3; Eph. 3:16–19; John
1:16; Phil. 3:10; Rom. 6:5, 6;
Rom. 8:17.
2. Eph. 4:15, 16; I John 1:3, 7.
3. I Thess. 5:11, 14; Gal. 6:10;
I John 3:16–18.
4. Heb. 10:24, 25; Acts 2:42, 46;
I Cor. 11:20.
5. I John 3:17; Acts 11:29, 30;
II Cor., Chapters 8 and 9.
6. Col. 1:18; I Cor. 8:6; Ps. 14:7.
7. Acts 5:4.

Chapter XXIX (PCUS)
1. Gen. 17:9–11; Exod. 13:9, 10;
Rom. 4:11; Exod. 12:3–20.
2. I Cor. 10:16; I Cor. 11:25, 26;
Gal. 3:27.
3. Exod. 12:48; Heb. 13:10;
I Cor. 11:27–29.
4. Rom. 6:3, 4; I Cor. 10:14–16.
See context.
5. Gen. 17:10; Matt. 26:27, 28;
Titus 3:5.
6. Rom. 2:28, 29; I Cor. 3:7;
I Cor. 6:11; John 3:5;
Acts 8:13–23.
7. John 6:63.
8. Matt. 28:19; I Cor. 11:20, 23.
9. See General Note.
10. Col. 2:11, 12; I Cor. 5:7, 8.

Chapter XXX (PCUS)
1. Matt. 28:19.
2. Acts 2:41; Acts 10:47.
3. Rom. 4:11. Compare with
Gal. 3:29; Col. 2:11, 12.
4. Gal. 3:27; Rom. 6:3, 4.
5. Titus 3:5.
6. Acts 2:38; Mark 1:4;
Acts 22:16.
7. Rom. 6:3, 4.
8. Matt. 28:19, 20.
9. Acts 10:47; Acts 8:36, 38;
Matt. 28:19; Eph. 4:11–13.
10. See General Note.
11. Mark 7:4; Acts 1:5; Acts 2:3,
4, 17; Acts 11:15, 16;
Heb. 9:10, 19–21.
12. See citations under Section 1
above.
13. Gen. 17:7, 9–10; Gal. 3:9, 14;
Rom. 4:11, 12; Acts 2:38, 39;
Acts 16:14, 15, 33; Col. 2:11,
12; I Cor. 7:14; Mark 10:13–16;
Luke 18:15, 16.
14. Luke 7:30; Gen. 17:14.
15. Rom. 4:11; Luke 23:40–43;
Acts 10:45–47.

16. Acts 8:13, 23.
17. John 3:5, 8; Rom. 4:11.
18. Gal. 3:27, Eph. 1:4, 5;
    Eph. 5:25, 26; Acts 2:38–41;
    Acts 16:31, 33.
19. There is no command, and no adequate example for the repetition of baptism.

Chapter XXXI (PCUS)
1. I Cor. 11:23–26; Matt. 26:26, 27; Luke 22:19, 20; I Cor. 10:16, 17, 21; I Cor. 12:13.
2. Heb. 9:22, 25, 26, 28; Matt. 26:26, 27; Luke 22:19, 20; Heb. 10:11, 12, 14, 18.
3. See citations under Sections 1, 2.
4. Matt. 15:9. Note – There is not the least appearance of a warrant for any of these things, either in precept or example, in any part of the Word of God. See all the places in which the ordinance is mentioned.
5. Matt. 26:26–28.
6. I Cor. 11:26, 27.
7. These statements are inferences from the doctrine of the sacraments, and do not require specific Scripture proofs.
8. I Cor. 10:16; John 6:53–58. See Note under Section 6, above.
9. I Cor. 11:27, 29; I Cor. 10:21; I Cor. 5:6, 7, 13; II Thess. 3:6, 14, 15.

Chapter XXXII (PCUS)
1. John 18:36; Isa. 9:6, 7; I Cor. 12:28; I Tim. 5:17.
2. Matt. 16:19; Matt. 18:17, 18; John 20:21–23; II Cor. 2:6–8.
3. I Tim. 5:20; I Tim. 1:20; Jude 23; I Cor. 5; I Cor. 11:27–34; II Sam. 12:14.

4. I Thess. 5:12; II Thess. 3:6, 14; I Cor. 5:4, 5, 13; Matt. 18:17; Titus 3:10.

Chapter XXXIII (PCUS)
1. Acts 15.
2. Acts 16:4; Acts 15:15, 19, 24, 27–31; Matt. 18:17–20.
3. See General Note.
4. Luke 12:13, 14; John 18:36; Matt. 22:21.

Chapter XXXIV (PCUS)
1. Gen. 3:19; Acts 13:36.
2. Luke 23:43; Phil. 1:23; II Cor. 5:6–8.
3. Luke 16:23; Rom. 8:23. See under figure 2 above.
4. Luke 16:23, 24; II Peter 2:9.
5. I Thess. 4:17; I Cor. 15:51, 52.
6. I Cor. 15:42–44. See preceding context.
7. Acts 24:15; John 5:28, 29; Phil. 3:21.

Chapter XXXV (PCUS)
1. Acts 17:31; Matt. 25:31–34.
2. John 5:22, 27.
3. Jude 6; II Peter 2:4; II Cor. 5:10; Rom. 2:16; Rom. 14:10, 12; Matt. 12:36, 37; I Cor. 3:13–15.
4. Rom. 9:23; Eph. 2:4–7.
5. Rom. 2:5, 6; II Thess. 1:7, 8.
6. Matt. 25:31–34; II Thess. 1:7; Ps. 16:11.
7. Matt. 25:41, 46; II Thess. 1:9; Mark 9:47, 48.
8. II Cor. 5:11; I Thess. 1:5–7; Luke 21:27, 28; II Peter 3:11, 14.
9. Mark 13:35–37; Luke 12:35, 36; Rev. 22:20. See Matt. 24:36, 42–44.

The
SHORTER CATECHISM

THE SHORTER CATECHISM

Q. 1. What is the chief end of man?
A. Man's chief end is to glorify God,[1] and to enjoy him forever.[2]

Q. 2. What rule hath God given to direct us how we may glorify and enjoy him?
A. The Word of God which is contained in the Scriptures of the Old and New Testaments is the only rule to direct us how we may glorify and enjoy him.[1]

Q. 3. What do the Scriptures principally teach?
A. The Scriptures principally teach what man is to believe concerning God, and what duty God requires of man.[1]

Q. 4. What is God?
A. God is a Spirit,[1] infinite, eternal, and unchangeable, in his being,[2] wisdom,[3] power,[4] holiness,[5] justice,[6] goodness,[7] and truth.[8]

Q. 5. Are there more Gods than one?
A. There is but one only, the living and true God.[1]

Q. 6. How many Persons are there in the Godhead?
A. There are three Persons in the Godhead: the Father, the Son, and the Holy Ghost; and these three are one God, the same in substance, equal in power and glory.[1]

Q. 7. What are the decrees of God?
A. The decrees of God are his eternal purpose, according to the counsel of his will, whereby, for his own glory, he hath foreordained whatsoever comes to pass.[1]

Q. 8. How doth God execute his decrees?
A. God executeth his decrees in the works of creation and providence.[1]

Q. 9. What is the work of creation?
A. The work of creation is God's making all things of nothing, by the word of his power, in the space of six days, and all very good.[1]

Q. 10. How did God create man?
A. God created man male and female, after his own image,[1] in knowledge, righteousness, and holiness,[2] with dominion over the creatures.[3]

Q. 11. What are God's works of providence?
A. God's works of providence are his most holy,[1] wise,[2] and powerful preserving[3] and governing all his creatures, and all their actions.[4]

7.012   **Q. 12. What special act of providence did God exercise towards man, in the estate wherein he was created?**
A. When God created man, he entered into a covenant of life with him, upon condition of perfect obedience;[1] forbidding him to eat of the tree of knowledge of good and evil, upon the pain of death.[2]

7.013   **Q. 13. Did our first parents continue in the estate wherein they were created?**
A. Our first parents, being left to the freedom of their own will, fell from the estate wherein they were created, by sinning against God.[1]

7.014   **Q. 14. What is sin?**
A. Sin is any want of conformity unto, or transgression of, the law of God.[1]

7.015   **Q. 15. What was the sin whereby our first parents fell from the estate wherein they were created?**
A. The sin whereby our first parents fell from the estate wherein they were created was their eating the forbidden fruit.[1]

7.016   **Q. 16. Did all mankind fall in Adam's first transgression?**
A. The covenant being made with Adam, not only for himself, but for his posterity,[1] all mankind, descending from him by ordinary generation, sinned in him, and fell with him, in his first transgression.[2]

7.017   **Q. 17. Into what estate did the Fall bring mankind?**
A. The Fall brought mankind into an estate of sin and misery.[1]

7.018   **Q. 18. Wherein consists the sinfulness of that estate whereinto man fell?**
A. The sinfulness of that estate whereinto man fell consists in: the guilt of Adam's first sin,[1] the want of original righteousness, and the corruption of his whole nature, which is commonly called original sin;[2] together with all actual transgressions which proceed from it.[3]

7.019   **Q. 19. What is the misery of that estate whereinto man fell?**
A. All mankind, by their fall, lost communion with God,[1] are under his wrath and curse,[2] and so made liable to all miseries of this life, to death itself, and to the pains of hell forever.[3]

7.020   **Q. 20. Did God leave all mankind to perish in the estate of sin and misery?**
A. God, having out of his mere good pleasure, from all eternity, elected some to everlasting life,[1] did enter into a covenant of grace, to deliver them out of the estate of sin and misery, and to bring them into an estate of salvation by a Redeemer.[2]

7.021   **Q. 21. Who is the Redeemer of God's elect?**
A. The only Redeemer of God's elect is the Lord Jesus Christ,[1] who, being the eternal Son of God, became man,[2] and so was, and

continueth to be, God and man, in two distinct natures, and one Person forever.[3]

Q. 22. How did Christ, being the Son of God, become man?   7.022
A. Christ, the Son of God, became man, by taking to himself a true body and a reasonable soul,[1] being conceived by the power of the Holy Ghost, in the womb of the Virgin Mary, and born of her,[2] yet without sin.[3]

Q. 23. What offices doth Christ execute as our Redeemer?   7.023
A. Christ, as our Redeemer, executeth the offices of a prophet,[1] of a priest,[2] and of a king, both in his estate of humiliation and exaltation.[3]

Q. 24. How doth Christ execute the office of a prophet?   7.024
A. Christ executeth the office of a prophet in revealing to us,[1] by his Word and Spirit, the will of God for our salvation.[2]

Q. 25. How doth Christ execute the office of a priest?   7.025
A. Christ executeth the office of a priest in his once offering up of himself a sacrifice to satisfy divine justice,[1] and reconcile us to God,[2] and in making continual intercession for us.[3]

Q. 26. How doth Christ execute the office of a king?   7.026
A. Christ executeth the office of a king in subduing us to himself,[1] in ruling and defending us,[2] and in restraining and conquering all his and our enemies.[3]

Q. 27. Wherein did Christ's humiliation consist?   7.027
A. Christ's humiliation consisted in his being born, and that in a low condition,[1] made under the law,[2] undergoing the miseries of this life,[3] the wrath of God,[4] and the cursed death of the cross;[5] in being buried, and continuing under the power of death for a time.[6]

Q. 28. Wherein consisteth Christ's exaltation?   7.028
A. Christ's exaltation consisteth in his rising again from the dead on the third day,[1] in ascending up into heaven, in sitting at the right hand of God the Father,[2] and in coming to judge the world at the last day.[3]

Q. 29. How are we made partakers of the redemption purchased by Christ?   7.029
A. We are made partakers of the redemption purchased by Christ by the effectual application of it to us by his Holy Spirit.[1]

Q. 30. How doth the Spirit apply to us the redemption purchased by Christ?   7.030
A. The Spirit applieth to us the redemption purchased by Christ by working faith in us,[1] and thereby uniting us to Christ in our effectual calling.[2]

Q. 31. What is effectual calling?   7.031
A. Effectual calling is the work of God's Spirit,[1] whereby, convincing us of our sin and misery,[2] enlightening our minds in the knowledge

of Christ,[3] and renewing our wills,[4] he doth persuade and enable us to embrace Jesus Christ, freely offered to us in the gospel.[5]

7.032   **Q. 32. What benefits do they that are effectually called partake of in this life?**
A. They that are effectually called do in this life partake of justification,[1] adoption,[2] sanctification, and the several benefits which, in this life, do either accompany or flow from them.[3]

7.033   **Q. 33. What is justification?**
A. Justification is an act of God's free grace, wherein he pardoneth all our sins,[1] and accepteth us as righteous in his sight,[2] only for the righteousness of Christ imputed to us,[3] and received by faith alone.[4]

7.034   **Q. 34. What is adoption?**
A. Adoption is an act of God's free grace,[1] whereby we are received into the number, and have a right to all the privileges, of the sons of God.[2]

7.035   **Q. 35. What is sanctification?**
A. Sanctification is the work of God's free grace,[1] whereby we are renewed in the whole man after the image of God,[2] and are enabled more and more to die unto sin and live unto righteousness.[3]

7.036   **Q. 36. What are the benefits which in this life do accompany or flow from justification, adoption, and sanctification?**
A. The benefits which in this life do accompany or flow from justification, adoption, and sanctification are: assurance of God's love, peace of conscience, joy in the Holy Ghost,[1] increase of grace,[2] and perseverance therein to the end.[3]

7.037   **Q. 37. What benefits do believers receive from Christ at death?**
A. The souls of believers are at their death made perfect in holiness, and do immediately pass into glory;[1] and their bodies, being still united to Christ,[2] do rest in their graves till the resurrection.[3]

7.038   **Q. 38. What benefits do believers receive from Christ at the resurrection?**
A. At the resurrection, believers, being raised up in glory,[1] shall be openly acknowledged and acquitted in the Day of Judgment,[2] and made perfectly blessed in the full enjoying of God[3] to all eternity.[4]

7.039   **Q. 39. What is the duty which God requireth of man?**
A. The duty which God requireth of man is obedience to his revealed will.[1]

7.040   **Q. 40. What did God at first reveal to man for the rule of his obedience?**
A. The rule which God at first revealed to man for his obedience was the moral law.[1]

Q. 41. Where is the moral law summarily comprehended?   7.041
A. The moral law is summarily comprehended in the Ten Commandments.[1]

Q. 42. What is the sum of the Ten Commandments?   7.042
A. The sum of the Ten Commandments is: to love the Lord our God with all our heart, with all our soul, with all our strength, and with all our mind; and our neighbor as ourselves.[1]

Q. 43. What is the preface to the Ten Commandments?   7.043
A. The preface to the Ten Commandments is in these words: "I am the Lord thy God, which have brought thee out of the land of Egypt, out of the house of bondage."[1]

Q. 44. What doth the preface to the Ten Commandments teach us?   7.044
A. The preface to the Ten Commandments teacheth us that because God is the Lord, and our God and Redeemer, therefore we are bound to keep all his commandments.

Q. 45. Which is the First Commandment?   7.045
A. The First Commandment is, "Thou shalt have no other gods before me."[1]

Q. 46. What is required in the First Commandment?   7.046
A. The First Commandment requireth us[1] to know and acknowledge God to be the only true God, and our God;[2] and to worship and glorify him accordingly.[3]

Q. 47. What is forbidden in the First Commandment?   7.047
A. The First Commandment forbiddeth the denying,[1] or not worshiping and glorifying, the true God as God,[2] and our God;[3] and the giving of that worship and glory to any other which is due to him alone.[4]

Q. 48. What are we specially taught by these words, "before me," in the First Commandment?   7.048
A. These words, "before me," in the First Commandment teach us that God, who seeth all things, taketh notice of, and is much displeased with, the sin of having any other god.[1]

Q. 49. Which is the Second Commandment?   7.049
A. The Second Commandment is, "Thou shalt not make unto thee any graven image, or any likeness of any thing that is in heaven above, or that is in the earth beneath, or that is in the water under the earth: thou shalt not bow down thyself to them, nor serve them: for I the Lord thy God am a jealous God, visiting the iniquity of the fathers upon the children unto the third and fourth generation of them that hate me; and showing mercy unto thousands of them that love me, and keep my commandments."[1]

7.050   **Q. 50. What is required in the Second Commandment?**
A. The Second Commandment requireth the receiving, observing, and keeping pure and entire all such religious worship and ordinances as God hath appointed in his Word.[1]

7.051   **Q. 51. What is forbidden in the Second Commandment?**
A. The Second Commandment forbiddeth the worshiping of God by images,[1] or any other way not appointed in his Word.[2]

7.052   **Q. 52. What are the reasons annexed to the Second Commandment?**
A. The reasons annexed to the Second Commandment are: God's sovereignty over us,[1] his propriety in us,[2] and the zeal he hath to his own worship.[3]

7.053   **Q. 53. Which is the Third Commandment?**
A. The Third Commandment is, "Thou shalt not take the name of the Lord thy God in vain: for the Lord will not hold him guiltless that taketh his name in vain."[1]

7.054   **Q. 54. What is required in the Third Commandment?**
A. The Third Commandment requireth the holy and reverent use of God's names,[1] titles, attributes,[2] ordinances,[3] Word,[4] and works.[5]

7.055   **Q. 55. What is forbidden in the Third Commandment?**
A. The Third Commandment forbiddeth all profaning or abusing of anything whereby God maketh himself known.[1]

7.056   **Q. 56. What is the reason annexed to the Third Commandment?**
A. The reason annexed to the Third Commandment is that, however the breakers of this commandment may escape punishment from men, yet the Lord our God will not suffer them to escape his righteous judgment.[1]

7.057   **Q. 57. Which is the Fourth Commandment?**
A. The Fourth Commandment is, "Remember the Sabbath day, to keep it holy. Six days shalt thou labor, and do all thy work: but the seventh day is the Sabbath of the Lord thy God: in it thou shalt not do any work, thou, nor thy son, nor thy daughter, thy manservant, nor thy maidservant, nor thy cattle, nor thy stranger that is within thy gates: for in six days the Lord made heaven and earth, the sea, and all that in them is, and rested the seventh day: wherefore the Lord blessed the Sabbath day, and hallowed it."[1]

7.058   **Q. 58. What is required in the Fourth Commandment?**
A. The Fourth Commandment requireth the keeping holy to God such set times as he hath appointed in his Word; expressly one whole day in seven, to be a holy Sabbath to himself.[1]

Q. 59. Which day of the seven hath God appointed to be the   7.059
weekly Sabbath?
A. From the beginning of the world to the resurrection of Christ,
God appointed the seventh day of the week to be the weekly Sabbath;[1]
and the first day of the week ever since, to continue to the end of the
world, which is the Christian Sabbath.[2]

Q. 60. How is the Sabbath to be sanctified?   7.060
A. The Sabbath is to be sanctified by a holy resting all that day,
even from such worldly employments and recreations as are lawful on
other days;[1] and spending the whole time in the public and private
exercises of God's worship,[2] except so much as is to be taken up in the
works of necessity and mercy.[3]

Q. 61. What is forbidden in the Fourth Commandment?   7.061
A. The Fourth Commandment forbiddeth the omission, or careless
performance, of the duties required,[1] and the profaning the day by
idleness, or doing that which is in itself sinful,[2] or by unnecessary
thoughts, words, or works, about our worldly employments or recreations.[3]

Q. 62. What are the reasons annexed to the Fourth Command-   7.062
ment?
A. The reasons annexed to the Fourth Commandment are: God's
allowing us six days of the week for our own employments,[1] his
challenging a special propriety in the seventh,[2] his own example,[3] and
his blessing the Sabbath Day.[4]

Q. 63. Which is the Fifth Commandment?   7.063
A. The Fifth Commandment is, "Honor thy father and thy mother:
that thy days may be long upon the land which the Lord thy God giveth
thee."[1]

Q. 64. What is required in the Fifth Commandment?   7.064
A. The Fifth Commandment requireth the preserving the honor,
and performing the duties, belonging to everyone in their several
places and relations, as superiors, inferiors, or equals.[1]

Q. 65. What is forbidden in the Fifth Commandment?   7.065
A. The Fifth Commandment forbiddeth the neglecting of, or doing
anything against, the honor and duty which belongeth to everyone in
their several places and relations.[1]

Q. 66. What is the reason annexed to the Fifth Command-   7.066
ment?
A. The reason annexed to the Fifth Commandment is a promise of
long life and prosperity (as far as it shall serve for God's glory, and
their own good) to all such as keep this commandment.[1]

Q. 67. Which is the Sixth Commandment?   7.067
A. The Sixth Commandment is, "Thou shall not kill."[1]

7.068   **Q. 68. What is required in the Sixth Commandment?**
A. The Sixth Commandment requireth all lawful endeavors to preserve our own life,[1] and the life of others.[2]

7.069   **Q. 69. What is forbidden in the Sixth Commandment?**
A. The Sixth Commandment forbiddeth the taking away of our own life,[1] or the life of our neighbor unjustly,[2] or whatsoever tendeth thereunto.[3]

7.070   **Q. 70. Which is the Seventh Commandment?**
A. The Seventh Commandment is, "Thou shalt not commit adultery."[1]

7.071   **Q. 71. What is required in the Seventh Commandment?**
A. The Seventh Commandment requireth the preservation of our own[1] and our neighbor's chastity,[2] in heart,[3] speech,[4] and behavior.[5]

7.072   **Q. 72. What is forbidden in the Seventh Commandment?**
A. The Seventh Commandment forbiddeth all unchaste thoughts,[1] words,[2] and actions.[3]

7.073   **Q. 73. Which is the Eighth Commandment?**
A. The Eighth Commandment is, "Thou shalt not steal."[1]

7.074   **Q. 74. What is required in the Eighth Commandment?**
A. The Eighth Commandment requireth the lawful procuring and furthering the wealth and outward estate of ourselves[1] and others.[2]

7.075   **Q. 75. What is forbidden in the Eighth Commandment?**
A. The Eighth Commandment forbiddeth whatsoever doth, or may, unjustly hinder our own,[1] or our neighbor's, wealth or outward estate.[2]

7.076   **Q. 76. Which is the Ninth Commandment?**
A. The Ninth Commandment is, "Thou shalt not bear false witness against thy neighbor."[1]

7.077   **Q. 77. What is required in the Ninth Commandment?**
A. The Ninth Commandment requireth the maintaining and promoting of truth between man and man,[1] and of our own[2] and our neighbor's good name,[3] especially in witness-bearing.[4]

7.078   **Q. 78. What is forbidden in the Ninth Commandment?**
A. The Ninth Commandment forbiddeth whatsoever is prejudicial to truth,[1] or injurious to our own or our neighbor's good name.[2]

7.079   **Q. 79. Which is the Tenth Commandment?**
A. The Tenth Commandment is, "Thou shalt not covet thy neighbor's house, thou shalt not covet thy neighbor's wife, nor his manservant, nor his maidservant, nor his ox, nor his ass, nor any thing that is thy neighbor's."[1]

Q. 80. What is required in the Tenth Commandment?   7.080
A. The Tenth Commandment requireth full contentment with our own condition,[1] with a right and charitable frame of spirit toward our neighbor and all that is his.[2]

Q. 81. What is forbidden in the Tenth Commandment?   7.081
A. The Tenth Commandment forbiddeth all discontentment with our own estate,[1] envying or grieving at the good of our neighbor,[2] and all inordinate motions and affections to anything that is his.[3]

Q. 82. Is any man able perfectly to keep the commandments of God?   7.082
A. No mere man, since the Fall, is able, in this life, perfectly to keep the commandments of God,[1] but doth daily break them, in thought,[2] word,[3] and deed.[4]

Q. 83. Are all transgressions of the law equally heinous?   7.083
A. Some sins in themselves, and by reason of several aggravations, are more heinous in the sight of God than others.[1]

Q. 84. What doth every sin deserve?   7.084
A. Every sin deserveth God's wrath and curse, both in this life and that which is to come.[1]

Q. 85. What doth God require of us, that we may escape his wrath and curse, due to us for sin?   7.085
A. To escape the wrath and curse of God, due to us for sin, God requireth of us faith in Jesus Christ, repentance unto life,[1] with the diligent use of all the outward means whereby Christ communicateth to us the benefits of redemption.[2]

Q. 86. What is faith in Jesus Christ?   7.086
A. Faith in Jesus Christ is a saving grace,[1] whereby we receive[2] and rest upon him alone for salvation,[3] as he is offered to us in the gospel.[4]

Q. 87. What is repentance unto life?   7.087
A. Repentance unto life is a saving grace,[1] whereby a sinner, out of a true sense of his sin,[2] and apprehension of the mercy of God in Christ,[3] doth, with grief and hatred of his sin, turn from it unto God,[4] with full purpose of, and endeavor after, new obedience.[5]

Q. 88. What are the outward means whereby Christ communicateth to us the benefits of redemption?   7.088
A. The outward and ordinary means whereby Christ communicateth to us the benefits of redemption are his ordinances, especially the Word, sacraments, and prayer,[1] all which are made effectual to the elect for salvation.

Q. 89. How is the Word made effectual to salvation?   7.089
A. The Spirit of God maketh the reading, but especially the preaching, of the Word an effectual means of convincing and converting

sinners,[1] and of building them up in holiness and comfort, through faith unto salvation.[2]

7.090   **Q. 90. How is the Word to be read and heard, that it may become effectual to salvation?**
A. That the Word may become effectual to salvation we must attend thereunto with diligence,[1] preparation,[2] and prayer;[3] receive it with faith[4] and love;[5] lay it up in our hearts;[6] and practice it in our lives.[7]

7.091   **Q. 91. How do the sacraments become effectual means of salvation?**
A. The sacraments become effectual means of salvation, not from any virtue in them, or in him that doth administer them, but only by the blessing of Christ, and the working of his Spirit in them that by faith receive them.[1]

7.092   **Q. 92. What is a sacrament?**
A. A sacrament is a holy ordinance instituted by Christ, wherein, by sensible signs, Christ and the benefits of the new covenant are represented,[1] sealed, and applied to believers.[2]

7.093   **Q. 93. Which are the sacraments of the New Testament?**
A. The sacraments of the New Testament are Baptism[1] and the Lord's Supper.[2]

7.094   **Q. 94. What is Baptism?**
A. Baptism is a sacrament, wherein the washing with water, in the name of the Father, and of the Son, and of the Holy Ghost,[1] doth signify and seal our ingrafting into Christ, and partaking of the benefits of the covenant of grace,[2] and our engagement to be the Lord's.[3]

7.095   **Q. 95. To whom is Baptism to be administered?**
A. Baptism is not to be administered to any that are out of the visible Church, till they profess their faith in Christ and obedience to him;[1] but the infants of such as are members of the visible Church are to be baptized.[2]

7.096   **Q. 96. What is the Lord's Supper?**
A. The Lord's Supper is a sacrament, wherein by giving and receiving bread and wine, according to Christ's appointment, his death is showed forth;[1] and the worthy receivers are, not after a corporal and carnal manner, but by faith, made partakers of his body and blood, with all his benefits, to their spiritual nourishment and growth in grace.[2]

7.097   **Q. 97. What is required to the worthy receiving of the Lord's Supper?**
A. It is required of them that would worthily partake of the Lord's Supper that they examine themselves, of their knowledge to discern the Lord's body,[1] of their faith to feed upon him,[2] of their repentance,[3]

love,[4] and new obedience;[5] lest, coming unworthily, they eat and drink judgment to themselves.[6]

Q. 98. What is prayer? 7.098
A. Prayer is an offering up of our desires unto God,[1] for things agreeable to his will,[2] in the name of Christ,[3] with confession of our sins,[4] and thankful acknowledgment of his mercies.[5]

Q. 99. What rule hath God given for our direction in prayer? 7.099
A. The whole Word of God is of use to direct us in prayer;[1] but the special rule of direction is that form of prayer which Christ taught his disciples, commonly called "the Lord's Prayer."[2]

Q. 100. What doth the preface of the Lord's Prayer teach us? 7.100
A. The preface of the Lord's prayer, which is, "Our Father which art in heaven," teacheth us to draw near to God with all holy reverence and confidence, as children to a father, able and ready to help us;[1] and that we should pray with and for others.[2]

Q. 101. What do we pray for in the first petition? 7.101
A. In the first petition, which is, "Hallowed be thy name," we pray that God would enable us, and others, to glorify him in all that whereby he maketh himself known,[1] and that he would dispose all things to his own glory.[2]

Q. 102. What do we pray for in the second petition? 7.102
A. In the second petition, which is, "Thy kingdom come," we pray that Satan's kingdom may be destroyed,[1] and that the Kingdom of grace may be advanced, ourselves and others brought into it, and kept in it,[2] and that the Kingdom of glory may be hastened.[3]

Q. 103. What do we pray for in the third petition? 7.103
A. In the third petition, which is, "Thy will be done in earth, as it is in heaven," we pray that God, by his grace, would make us able and willing to know, obey, and submit to his will in all things,[1] as the angels do in heaven.[2]

Q. 104. What do we pray for in the fourth petition? 7.104
A. In the fourth petition, which is, "Give us this day our daily bread," we pray that, of God's free gift, we may receive a competent portion of the good things of this life,[1] and enjoy his blessing with them.[2]

Q. 105. What do we pray for in the fifth petition? 7.105
A. In the fifth petition, which is, "And forgive us our debts, as we forgive our debtors," we pray that God, for Christ's sake, would freely pardon all our sins;[1] which we are the rather encouraged to ask because by his grace we are enabled from the heart to forgive others.[2]

7.106   **Q. 106. What do we pray for in the sixth petition?**

A. In the sixth petition, which is, "And lead us not into temptation, but deliver us from evil," we pray that God would either keep us from being tempted to sin[1] or support and deliver us when we are tempted.[2]

7.107   **Q. 107. What doth the conclusion of the Lord's Prayer teach us?**

A. The conclusion of the Lord's Prayer, which is, "For thine is the kingdom, and the power, and the glory, forever. Amen," teacheth us to take our encouragement in prayer from God only,[1] and in our prayers to praise him, ascribing Kingdom, power, and glory to him;[2] and in testimony of our desire and assurance to be heard, we say, "Amen."[3]

7.108   THE TEN COMMANDMENTS

EXODUS, CH. 20

GOD spake all these words, saying, I am the Lord thy God, which have brought thee out of the land of Egypt, out of the house of bondage.

I. Thou shalt have no other gods before me.

II. Thou shalt not make unto thee any graven image, or any likeness of any thing that is in heaven above, or that is in the earth beneath, or that is in the water under the earth: thou shalt not bow down thyself to them, nor serve them: for I the Lord thy God am a jealous God, visiting the iniquity of the fathers upon the children unto the third and fourth generation of them that hate me; and showing mercy unto thousands of them that love me, and keep my commandments.

III. Thou shalt not take the name of the Lord thy God in vain: for the Lord will not hold him guiltless that taketh his name in vain.

IV. Remember the Sabbath day, to keep it holy. Six days shalt thou labor, and do all thy work: but the seventh day is the Sabbath of the Lord thy God: in it thou shalt not do any work, thou, nor thy son, nor thy daughter, thy manservant, nor thy maidservant, nor thy cattle, nor thy stranger that is within thy gates: for in six days the Lord made heaven and earth, and sea, and all that in them is, and rested the seventh day: wherefore the Lord blessed the Sabbath day, and hallowed it.

V. Honor thy father and thy mother: that thy days may be long upon the land which the Lord thy God giveth thee.

VI. Thou shalt not kill.

VII. Thou shalt not commit adultery.

VIII. Thou shalt not steal.

IX. Thou shalt not bear false witness against thy neighbor.

X. Thou shalt not covet thy neighbor's house, thou shalt not covet thy neighbor's wife, nor his manservant, nor his maidservant, nor his ox, nor his ass, nor any thing that is thy neighbor's.

THE LORD'S PRAYER 7.109

MATTHEW, CH. 6

Our Father which art in heaven, hallowed be thy name. Thy kingdom come. Thy will be done in earth, as it is in heaven. Give us this day our daily bread. And forgive us our debts, as we forgive our debtors. And lead us not into temptation, but deliver us from evil: For thine is the kingdom, and the power, and the glory, forever. Amen.

THE APOSTLES' CREED 7.110

I BELIEVE in God the Father Almighty, Maker of heaven and earth;

And in Jesus Christ his only Son our Lord; who was conceived by the Holy Ghost, born of the Virgin Mary, suffered under Pontius Pilate, was crucified, dead, and buried; he descended into hell;[1] the third day he rose again from the dead; he ascended into heaven, and sitteth on the right hand of God the Father Almighty; from thence he shall come to judge the quick and the dead.

I believe in the Holy Ghost; the holy catholic Church; the communion of saints; the forgiveness of sins; the resurrection of the body; and the life everlasting. Amen.

Q. 1.
1. I Cor. 10:31; Rom. 11:36.
2. Ps. 73:24–26; John 17:22, 24.

Q. 2.
1. Gal. 1:8, 9; Isa. 8:20; Luke 16:29, 31; II Tim. 3:15–17.

Q. 3.
1. Micah 6:8; John 20:31; John 3:16.

Q. 4.
1. John 4:24.
2. Ps. 90:2; Mal. 3:6; James 1:17; I Kings 8:27; Jer. 23:24; Isa. 40:22.
3. Ps. 147:5; Rom. 16:27.
4. Gen. 17:1; Rev. 19:16.
5. Isa. 57:15; John 17:11; Rev. 4:8.
6. Deut. 32:4.
7. Ps. 100:5; Rom. 2:4.
8. Exod. 34:6; Ps. 117:2.

Q. 5.
1. Deut. 6:4; Jer. 10:10.

Q. 6.
1. II Cor. 13:14; Matt. 28:19; Matt. 3:16, 17.

Q. 7.
1. Eph. 1:11; Acts 4:27, 28; Ps. 33:11; Eph. 2:10; Rom. 9:22, 23; 11:33.

Q. 8.
1. Rev. 4:11; Eph. 1:11.

Q. 9.
1. Heb. 11:3; Rev. 4:11; Gen. 1:1–31.

Q. 10.
1. Gen. 1:27.
2. Col. 3:10; Eph. 4:24.
3. Gen. 1:28.

Q. 11.
1. Ps. 145:17.
2. Ps. 104:24.
3. Heb. 1:3.
4. Ps. 103:19; Matt. 10:29, 30; Job, Chapters 38–41.

Q. 12.
1. Compare Gen. 2:16, 17 with Rom. 5:12–14; Rom. 10:5; Luke 10:25–28, and with the covenants made with Noah and Abraham.
2. Gen. 2:17.

Q. 13.
1. Gen. 3:6–8, 13; II Cor. 11:3.

Q. 14.
1. I John. 3:4; James 4:17; Rom. 3:23.

Q. 15.
1. See proof to Answer 13. Gen 3:6.

Q. 16.
1. Acts 17:26. See under Question 12.
2. Gen. 2:17. Compare Rom. 5:12–20; I Cor. 15:21, 22.

Q. 17.
1. Rom. 5:12; Gal. 3:10.

Q. 18.
1. Rom. 5:12, 19; I Cor. 15:22.
2. Rom. 5:6; Eph. 2:1–3; Rom 8:7, 8; Gen. 6:5; Rom. 3:10–20; Ps. 51:5; 58:3.
3. James 1:14, 15; Matt. 15:19.

Q. 19.
1. Gen. 3:8, 24.
2. Eph. 2:3.
3. Rom. 5:14; Rom. 6:23.

Q. 20.
1. Eph. 1:4–7.
2. Titus 3:4–7; Titus 1:2; Gal. 3:21; Rom. 3:20–22.

Q. 21.
1. I Tim. 2:5.
2. John 1:1, 14; John 10:30; Phil. 2:6; Gal. 4:4.
3. See texts just cited; also Phil. 2:5–11.

Q. 22.
1. John 1:14; Heb. 2:14; Matt. 26:38.
2. Luke 1:31, 35, 41, 42; Gal. 4:4.
3. Heb. 4:15; Heb. 7:26.

Q. 23.
1. Acts 3:22; Luke 4:18, 21.
2. Heb. 5:5, 6; Heb. 4:14, 15.
3. Rev. 19:16; Isa. 9:6, 7; Ps. 2:6.

Q. 24.
1. John 1:1, 4.
2. John 15:15; John 20:31; II Peter 1:21; John 14:26.

Q. 25.
1. Heb. 9:14, 28; Rom. 3:26; Rom. 10:4.
2. Heb. 2:17.
3. Heb. 7:25.

Q. 26.
1. Ps. 110:3.
2. Isa. 33:22.
3. I Cor. 15:25; Acts 12:17; 18:9, 10.

Q. 27.
1. Luke 2:7; Phil. 2:6–8; II Cor. 8:9.

2. Gal. 4:4.
3. Isa. 53:3.
4. Matt. 27:46; Luke 22:41–44.
5. Gal. 3:13; Phil. 2:8.
6. I Cor. 15:3, 4.

Q. 28.
1. See last quoted text.
2. Acts 1:9; Eph. 1:19, 20.
3. Acts 1:11; Acts 17:31.

Q. 29.
1. John 1:12, 13; John 3:5, 6; Titus 3:5, 6.

Q. 30.
1. Eph. 2:8.
2. John 15:5; I Cor. 6:17; I Cor. 1:9; I Peter 5:10.

Q. 31.
1. II Tim. 1:8, 9; Eph. 1:18–20.
2. Acts 2:37.
3. Acts 26:18.
4. Ezek. 11:19; Ezek. 36:26, 27.
5. John 6:44, 45; Phil. 2:13; Deut. 30:6; Eph. 2:5.

Q. 32.
1. Rom. 8:30.
2. Eph. 1:5.
3. I Cor. 1:30.

Q. 33.
1. Eph. 1:7.
2. II Cor. 5:19, 21; Rom. 4:5; Rom. 3:22, 24, 25.
3. Rom. 5:17–19; Rom. 4:6–8.
4. Rom. 5:1; Acts 10:43; Gal. 2:16; Phil. 3:9.

Q. 34.
1. I John. 3:1.
2. John 1:12; Rom. 8:17.

Q. 35.
1. II Thess. 2:13.
2. Eph. 4:23, 24.
3. Rom. 6:4, 6, 14; Rom. 8:4.

Q. 36.
1. Rom. 5:1, 2, 5; Rom. 14:17.
2. Col. 1:10, 11; Prov. 4:18; Eph. 3:16–18; II Peter 3:18.
3. Jer. 32:40; I John. 2:19, 27; Rev. 14:21; I Peter 1:5; I John. 5:13.

Q. 37.
1. Luke 23:43; Luke 16:23; Phil. 1:23; II Cor. 5:6–8.
2. I Thess. 4:14.
3. Rom. 8:23; I Thess. 4:14.

Q. 38.
1. I Cor. 15:42, 43.
2. Matt. 25:33, 34; Matt. 10:32.
3. Ps. 16:11; I Cor. 2:9.

4. I Thess. 4:17. See preceding context.

Q. 39.
1. Deut. 29:29; Micah 6:8; I Sam. 15:22.

Q. 40.
1. Rom. 2:14, 15; Rom. 10:5.

Q. 41.
1. Matt. 19:17–19.

Q. 42.
1. Matt. 22:37–40.

Q. 43.
1. Exod. 20:2.

Q. 45.
1. Exod. 20:3.

Q. 46.
1. The exposition of the Ten Commandments found in answers to Questions 46–81 are deductions from the commandments themselves and the rules set forth in the Larger Catechism, Q. 99. The texts under the specifications are given to show that they are in accord with the general teaching of the Scriptures.
2. I Chron. 28:9; Deut. 26:17.
3. Matt. 4:10; Ps. 95:6, 7; Ps. 29:2.

Q. 47.
1. Ps. 14:1.
2. Rom. 1:20, 21.
3. Ps. 81:11.
4. Rom. 1:25.

Q. 48.
1. I Chron. 28:9; Ps. 44:20, 21.

Q. 49.
1. Exod. 20:4–6.

Q. 50.
1. Deut. 12:32; Duet. 32:46; Matt. 28:20.

Q. 51.
1. Deut. 4:15, 16; See verses 17–19; Acts 17:29.
2. Deut. 12:30–32.

Q. 52.
1. Ps. 95:2, 3.
2. Ps. 45:11.
3. Exod. 34:14.

Q. 53.
1. Exod. 20:7.

Q. 54.
1. Ps. 29:2; Matt. 6:9.
2. Rev. 15:3, 4.
3. Mal. 1:14.

4. Ps. 138:2.
5. Ps. 107:21, 22.

Q. 55.
1. Mal. 2:2; Isa. 5:12.

Q. 56.
1. Deut. 28:58, 59.

Q. 57.
1. Exod. 20:8–11.

Q. 58.
1. Lev. 19:30; Deut. 5:12; Isa. 56:2–7.

Q. 59.
1. Gen. 2:3; Luke 23:56.
2. Acts 20:7; I Cor. 16:1, 2; John 20:19–26.

Q. 60.
1. Lev. 23:3; Exod. 16:25–29; Jer. 17:21, 22.
2. Ps. 92:1, 2. (A Psalm or Song for the sabbath day.) Luke 4:16; Isa. 58:13; Acts 20:7.
3. Matt. 12:11, 12. See context.

Q. 61.
1. Ezek. 22:26; Mal. 1:13; Amos 8:5.
2. Ezek. 23:38.
3. Isa. 58:13; Jer. 17:24, 27.

Q. 62.
1. Exod. 31:15, 16.
2. Lev. 23:3.
3. Exod. 31:17.
4. Gen. 2:3.

Q. 63.
1. Exod. 20:12.

Q. 64.
1. Eph. 5:21, 22; Eph. 6:1, 5, 9; Rom. 13:1; Rom. 12:10.

Q. 65.
1. Rom. 13:7, 8.

Q. 66.
1. Eph. 6:2, 3.

Q. 67.
1. Exod. 20:13.

Q. 68.
1. Eph. 5:29; Matt. 10:23.
2. Ps. 82:3, 4; Job 29:13; I Kings 18:4.

Q. 69.
1. Acts 16:28.
2. Gen. 9:6.
3. Matt. 5:22; I John. 3:15; Gal. 5:15; Prov. 24:11, 12; Exod. 21:18–32.

Q. 70.
1. Exod. 20:14.

Q. 71.
1. I Thess. 4:4, 5.
2. I Cor. 7:2; Eph. 5:11, 12.
3. Matt. 5:28.
4. Eph. 4:29; Col. 4:6.
5. I Peter 3:2.

Q. 72.
1. Matt. 5:28.
2. Eph. 5:4.
3. Eph. 5:3.

Q. 73.
1. Exod. 20:15.

Q. 74.
1. II Thess. 3:10–12; Rom. 12:17; Prov. 27:23.
2. Lev. 25:35; Phil. 2:4; Prov. 13:4; Prov. 20:4; Prov. 24:30–34.

Q. 75.
1. 1 Tim. 5:8.
2. Eph. 4:28; Prov. 21:16; II Thess. 3:7–10.

Q. 76.
1. Exod. 20:16.

Q. 77.
1. Zech. 8:16.
2. I Peter 3:16; Acts 25:10.
3. III John 12.
4. Prov. 14:5, 25.

Q. 78.
1. Prov. 19:5; Prov. 6:16–19.
2. Luke 3:14; Ps. 15:3.

Q. 79.
1. Exod. 20:17.

Q. 80.
1. Heb. 13:5.
2. Rom. 12:15; Phil. 2:4; I Cor. 13:4–6.

Q. 81.
1. I Cor. 10:10.
2. Gal. 5:26.
3. Col. 3:5.

Q. 82.
1. I Kings 8:46; I John. 1:8–2:6.
2. Gen. 8:21.
3. James 3:8.
4. James 3:2.

Q. 83.
1. Ps. 19:13; John 19:11.

Q. 84.
1. Gal. 3:10; Matt. 25:41.

Q. 85.
1. Acts 20:21; Mark 1:15; John 3:18.
2. See under Question 88 below.

Q. 86.
1. Heb. 10:39.
2. John 1:12.
3. Phil. 3:9.
4. John 6:40.

Q. 87.
1. Acts 11:18.
2. Acts 2:37.
3. Joel 2:13.
4. II Cor. 7:11; Jer. 31:18, 19; Acts 26:18.
5. Ps. 119:59.

Q. 88.
1. Matt. 28:19, 20; Acts 2:41, 42.

Q. 89.
1. Ps. 19:7, Ps. 119:130; Heb. 4:12.
2. I Thess. 1:6; Rom. 1:16; Rom. 16:25; Acts 20:32.

Q. 90.
1. Prov. 8:34.
2. Luke 8:18; I Peter 2:1, 2.
3. Ps. 119:18.
4. Heb. 4:2.
5. II Thess. 2:10.
6. Ps. 119:11.
7. Luke 8:15; James 1:25.

Q. 91.
1. I Peter 3:21; Acts 8:13, 23. See intervening context. I Cor. 3:7; I Cor. 6:11; I Cor. 12:13.

Q. 92.
1. Matt. 28:19; Matt. 26:26–28.
2. Rom. 4:11.

Q. 93.
1. Matt. 28:19.
2. I Cor. 11:23.

Q. 94.
1. See Matt. 28:19 cited under Question 93 above.
2. Gal. 3:27; Rom. 6:3.
3. Rom. 6:4.

Q. 95.
1. Acts 2:41.
2. Gen. 17:7, 10; Gal. 3:17, 18, 29; Acts 2:38, 39.

Q. 96.
1. Matt. 26:26, 27; I Cor. 11:26.
2. I Cor. 10:16; Eph. 3:17.

Q. 97.
1. I Cor. 11:28, 29.
2. John 6:53–56.

3. Zech. 12:10.
4. I John. 4:19; Gal. 5:6.
5. Rom. 6:4; Rom. 6:17–22.
6. I Cor. 11:27.

Q. 98.
1. Ps. 62:8; Ps. 10:17.
2. I John. 5:14; Matt. 26:39; John 6:38.
3. John 16:23.
4. Dan. 9:4.
5. Phil. 4:6.

Q. 99.
1. II Tim. 3:16, 17; I John. 5:14.
2. Matt. 6:9.

Q. 100.
1. Isa. 64:9; Luke 11:13; Rom. 8:15.
2. Eph. 6:18; Acts 12:5; Zech. 8:21.

Q. 101.
1. Ps. 67:1–3; II Thess. 3:1; Ps. 145.
2. Isa. 64:1, 2; Rom. 11:36.

Q. 102.
1. Ps. 68:1.
2. II Thess. 3:1; Ps. 51:18; 67:1–3; Rom. 10:1.
3. Rev. 22:20; II Peter 3:11–13.

Q. 103.
1. Ps. 119:35–36; Acts 21:14.
2. Ps. 103:20–22.

Q. 104.
1. Prov. 30:8.
2. I Tim. 4:4, 5; Prov. 10:22.

Q. 105.
1. Ps. 51:1; Rom 3:24, 25.
2. Luke 11:4; Matt. 18:35; Matt. 6:14, 15.

Q. 106.
1. Matt. 26:41; Ps. 19:13.
2. I Cor. 10:13; Ps. 51:10, 12.

Q. 107.
1. Dan. 9:18, 19.
2. I Chron. 29:11–13.
3. Rev. 22:20, 21; I Cor. 14:16.

THE APOSTLES' CREED

1. *I.e.* Continued in the state of the dead, and under the power of death, until the third day. See the answer to Question 50 in the Larger Catechism.

The
LARGER CATECHISM

THE LARGER CATECHISM

Q. 1. What is the chief and highest end of man? 7.111
A. Man's chief and highest end is to glorify God,[1] and fully to enjoy him forever.[2]

Q. 2. How doth it appear that there is a God? 7.112
A. The very light of nature in man, and the works of God, declare plainly that there is a God;[1] but his Word and Spirit only, do sufficiently and effectually reveal him unto men for their salvation.[2]

Q. 3. What is the Word of God? 7.113
A. The holy Scriptures of the Old and New Testaments are the Word of God, the only rule of faith and obedience.[1]

Q. 4. How doth it appear that the Scriptures are the Word of God? 7.114
A. The Scriptures manifest themselves to be the Word of God, by their majesty and purity; by the consent of all the parts, and the scope of the whole, which is to give all glory to God; by their light and power to convince and convert sinners, to comfort and build up believers unto salvation.[1] But the Spirit of God, bearing witness by and with the Scriptures in the heart of man, is alone able fully to persuade it that they are the very word of God.[2]

Q. 5. What do the Scriptures principally teach? 7.115
A. The Scriptures principally teach, what man is to believe concerning God, and what duty God requires of man.[1]

What Man Ought to Believe Concerning God

Q. 6. What do the Scriptures make known of God? 7.116
A. The Scriptures make known what God is,[1] the persons in the Godhead,[2] his decrees,[3] and the execution of his decrees.[4]

Q. 7. What is God? 7.117
A. God is a Spirit,[1] in and of himself infinite in being,[2] glory, blessedness, and perfection;[3] all-sufficient,[4] eternal,[5] unchangeable,[6] incomprehensible,[7] everywhere present,[8] almighty;[9] knowing all

things,[10] most wise,[11] most holy,[12] most just,[13] most merciful and gracious, long-suffering, and abundant in goodness and truth.[14]

7.118   Q.   8.   Are there more Gods than one?
A.   There is but one only, the living and true God.[1]

7.119   Q.   9.   How many persons are there in the Godhead?
A.   There be three persons in the Godhead: the Father, the Son, and the Holy Ghost; and these three are one true, eternal God, the same in substance, equal in power and glory; although distinguished by their personal properties.[1]

7.120   Q.   10.   What are the personal properties of the three persons in the Godhead?
A.   It is proper to the Father to beget his Son,[1] and to the Son to be begotten of the Father,[2] and to the Holy Ghost to proceed from the Father and the Son, from all eternity.[3]

7.121   Q.   11.   How doth it appear that the Son and the Holy Ghost are equal with the Father?
A.   The Scriptures manifest that the Son and the Holy Ghost are God equal with the Father, ascribing unto them such names,[1] attributes,[2] works,[3] and worship,[4] as are proper to God only.

7.122   Q.   12.   What are the decrees of God?
A.   God's decrees are the wise, free, and holy acts of the counsel of his will, whereby, from all eternity, he hath, for his own glory, unchangeably foreordained whatsoever comes to pass in time,[1] especially concerning angels and men.

7.123   Q.   13.   What hath God especially decreed concerning angels and men?
A.   God, by an eternal and immutable decree, out of his mere love, for the praise of his glorious grace, to be manifested in due time, hath elected some angels to glory;[1] and, in Christ, hath chosen some men to eternal life, and the means thereof;[2] and also, according to his sovereign power, and the unsearchable counsel of his own will (whereby he extendeth or withholdeth favor as he pleaseth) hath passed by, and foreordained the rest to dishonor and wrath, to be for their sin inflicted, to the praise of the glory of his justice.[3]

7.124   Q.   14.   How doth God execute his decrees?
A.   God executeth his decrees in the works of creation and providence, according to his infallible foreknowledge, and the free and immutable counsel of his own will.[1]

7.125   Q.   15.   What is the work of creation?
A.   The work of creation is that wherein God did in the beginning,

by the word of his power, make of nothing, the world and all things therein for himself, within the space of six days, and all very good.[1]

Q. 16. How did God create angels?

A. God created all the angels, spirits,[1] immortal,[2] holy,[3] excelling in knowledge,[4] mighty in power;[5] to execute his commandments, and to praise his name,[6] yet subject to change.[7]

7.126

Q. 17. How did God create man?

A. After God had made all other creatures, he created man, male and female;[1] formed the body of the man of the dust of the ground,[2] and the woman of the rib of man;[3] endued them with living, reasonable, and immortal souls;[4] made them after his own image,[5] in knowledge,[6] righteousness and holiness,[7] having the law of God written in their hearts,[8] and power to fulfill it, with dominion over the creatures;[9] yet subject to fall.[10]

7.127

Q. 18. What are God's works of providence?

A. God's works of providence are his most holy,[1] wise,[2] and powerful preserving,[3] and governing all his creatures;[4] ordering them, and all their actions,[5] to his own glory.[6]

7.128

Q. 19. What is God's providence toward the angels?

A. God by his providence permitted some of the angels, willfully and irrecoverably, to fall into sin and damnation,[1] limiting and ordering that, and all their sins, to his own glory;[2] and established the rest in holiness and happiness;[3] employing them all, at his pleasure, in the administrations of his power, mercy, and justice.[4]

7.129

Q. 20. What was the providence of God toward man in the estate in which he was created?

A. The providence of God toward man in the estate in which he was created was, the placing him in paradise, appointing him to dress it, giving him liberty to eat of the fruit of the earth,[1] putting the creatures under his dominion,[2] ordaining marriage for his help,[3] affording him communion with himself,[4] and instituting the Sabbath;[5] entering into a covenant of life with him, upon condition of personal, perfect, and perpetual obedience,[6] of which the tree of life was a pledge; and forbidding to eat of the tree of the knowledge of good and evil, upon pain of death.[7]

7.130

Q. 21. Did man continue in that estate wherein God at first created him?

A. Our first parents, being left to the freedom of their own will, through the temptation of Satan, transgressed the commandment of God, in eating the forbidden fruit, and thereby fell from the estate of innocency wherein they were created.[1]

7.131

7.132   **Q. 22. Did all mankind fall in that first transgression?**
A. The covenant being made with Adam, as a public person, not for himself only, but for his posterity, all mankind, descending from him by ordinary generation,[1] sinned in him, and fell with him in that first transgression.[2]

7.133   **Q. 23. Into what estate did the Fall bring mankind?**
A. The Fall brought mankind into an estate of sin and misery.[1]

7.134   **Q. 24. What is sin?**
A. Sin is any want of conformity unto, or transgression of, any law of God, given as a rule to the reasonable creature.[1]

7.135   **Q. 25. Wherein consists the sinfulness of that estate whereinto man fell?**
A. The sinfulness of that estate whereinto man fell, consisteth in the guilt of Adam's first sin,[1] the want of that righteousness wherein he was created, and the corruption of his nature, whereby he is utterly indisposed, disabled, and made opposite unto all that is spiritually good, and wholly inclined to all evil, and that continually;[2] which is commonly called original sin, and from which do proceed all actual transgressions.[3]

7.136   **Q. 26. How is original sin conveyed from our first parents unto their posterity?**
A. Original sin is conveyed from our first parents unto their posterity by natural generation, so as all that proceed from them in that way, are conceived and born in sin.[1]

7.137   **Q. 27. What misery did the Fall bring upon mankind?**
A. The Fall brought upon mankind the loss of communion with God,[1] his displeasure and curse; so as we are by nature children of wrath,[2] bondslaves to Satan,[3] and justly liable to all punishments in this world and that which is to come.[4]

7.138   **Q. 28. What are the punishments of sin in this world?**
A. The punishments of sin in this world, are either inward, as blindness of mind,[1] a reprobate sense,[2] strong delusions,[3] hardness of heart,[4] horror of conscience,[5] and vile affections:[6] or outward, as the curse of God upon the creatures for our sake,[7] and all other evils that befall us in our bodies, names, estates, relations, and employments;[8] together with death itself.[9]

7.139   **Q. 29. What are the punishments of sin in the world to come?**
A. The punishments of sin in the world to come are everlasting separation from the comfortable presence of God, and most grievous torments in soul and body, without intermission, in hell fire forever.[1]

Q. 30. Doth God leave all mankind to perish in the estate of 7.140
sin and misery?

A. God doth not leave all men to perish in the estate of sin and misery, into which they fell by the breach of the first covenant, commonly called the covenant of works;[1] but of his mere love and mercy delivereth his elect out of it, and bringeth them into an estate of salvation by the second covenant, commonly called the covenant of grace.[2]

Q. 31. With whom was the covenant of grace made? 7.141

A. The covenant of grace was made with Christ as the second Adam, and in him with all the elect as his seed.[1]

Q. 32. How is the grace of God manifested in the second 7.142
covenant?

A. The grace of God is manifested in the second covenant, in that he freely provideth and offereth to sinners a mediator,[1] and life and salvation by him;[2] and requiring faith as the condition to interest them in him,[3] promiseth and giveth his Holy Spirit to all his elect, to work in them that faith, with all other saving graces;[4] and to enable them unto all holy obedience,[5] as the evidence of the truth of their faith[6] and of their thankfulness to God,[7] and as the way which he hath appointed them to salvation.[8]

Q. 33. Was the covenant of grace always administered after 7.143
one and the same manner?

A. The covenant of grace was not always administered after the same manner, but the administrations of it under the Old Testament were different from those under the New.[1]

Q. 34. How was the covenant of grace administered under the 7.144
Old Testament?

A. The covenant of grace was administered under the Old Testament, by promises,[1] prophecies,[2] sacrifices,[3] circumcision,[4] the passover,[5] and other types and ordinances; which did all foresignify Christ then to come, and were for that time sufficient to build up the elect in faith in the promised Messiah,[6] by whom they then had full remission of sin and eternal salvation.[7]

Q. 35. How is the covenant of grace administered under the 7.145
New Testament?

A. Under the New Testament, when Christ the substance was exhibited, the same covenant of grace was, and still is to be, administered in the preaching of the Word,[1] and the administration of the sacraments of Baptism,[2] and the Lord's Supper;[3] in which grace and salvation are held forth in more fullness, evidence, and efficacy to all nations.[4]

Q. 36. Who is the Mediator of the covenant of grace? 7.146

A. The only Mediator of the covenant of grace is the Lord Jesus

Christ,[1] who being the eternal Son of God, of one substance and equal with the Father, in the fullness of time became man, and so was, and continues to be, God and man, in two entire distinct natures, and one person, forever.[2]

7.147   Q. 37. How did Christ, being the Son of God, become man?
A.   Christ, the Son of God, became man by taking to himself a true body, and a reasonable soul,[1] being conceived by the power of the Holy Ghost, in the womb of the Virgin Mary, of her substance, and born of her,[2] yet without sin.[3]

7.148   Q. 38. Why was it requisite that the Mediator should be God?
A.   It was requisite that the Mediator should be God; that he might sustain and keep the human nature from sinking under the infinite wrath of God, and the power of death; give worth and efficacy to his sufferings, obedience, and intercession; and to satisfy God's justice, procure his favor, purchase a peculiar people, give his Spirit to them, conquer all their enemies, and bring them to everlasting salvation.[1]

7.149   Q. 39. Why was it requisite that the Mediator should be man?
A.   It was requisite that the Mediator should be man; that he might advance our nature, perform obedience to the law,[1] suffer and make intercession for us in our nature,[2] have a fellow feeling of our infirmities;[3] that we might receive the adoption of sons,[4] and have comfort and access with boldness unto the throne of grace.[5]

7.150   Q. 40. Why was it requisite that the Mediator should be God and man in one person?
A.   It was requisite that the Mediator who was to reconcile God and man, should himself be both God and man, and this in one person; that the proper works of each nature might be accepted of God for us, and relied on by us, as the works of the whole person.[1]

7.151   Q. 41. Why was our Mediator called Jesus?
A.   Our Mediator was called Jesus, because he saveth his people from their sins.[1]

7.152   Q. 42. Why was our Mediator called Christ?
A.   Our Mediator was called Christ, because he was anointed with the Holy Ghost above measure;[1] and so set apart, and fully furnished with all authority and ability,[2] to execute the office of prophet,[3] priest,[4] and king of his church, in the estate both of his humiliation and exaltation.[5]

7.153   Q. 43. How doth Christ execute the office of a prophet?
A.   Christ executeth the office of a prophet, in his revealing to the church in all ages,[1] by his Spirit and Word,[2] in divers ways of

administration, the whole will of God, in all things concerning their edification and salvation.[3]

Q. 44. How doth Christ execute the office of a priest? 7.154
A. Christ executeth the office of a priest, in his once offering himself a sacrifice without spot to God,[1] to be a reconciliation for the sins of his people;[2] and in making continual intercession for them.[3]

Q. 45. How doth Christ execute the office of a king? 7.155
A. Christ executeth the office of a king, in calling out of the world a people to himself;[1] and giving them officers,[2] laws,[3] and censures, by which he visibly governs them;[4] in bestowing saving grace upon his elect,[5] rewarding their obedience,[6] and correcting them for their sins,[7] preserving and supporting them under all their temptations and sufferings;[8] restraining and overcoming all their enemies,[9] and powerfully ordering all things for his own glory,[10] and their good;[11] and also in taking vengeance on the rest, who know not God, and obey not the gospel.[12]

Q. 46. What was the estate of Christ's humiliation? 7.156
A. The estate of Christ's humiliation was that low condition, wherein he, for our sakes, emptying himself of his glory, took upon him the form of a servant, in his conception and birth, life, death, and after his death until his resurrection.[1]

Q. 47. How did Christ humble himself in his conception and 7.157
birth?
A. Christ humbled himself in his conception and birth, in that, being from all eternity the Son of God in the bosom of the Father, he was pleased in the fullness of time to become the Son of man, made of a woman of low estate, and to be born to her, with divers circumstances of more than ordinary abasement.[1]

Q. 48. How did Christ humble himself in his life? 7.158
A. Christ humbled himself in his life, by subjecting himself to the law,[1] which he perfectly fulfilled,[2] and by conflicting with the indignities of the world,[3] temptations of Satan,[4] and infirmities in his flesh; whether common to the nature of man, or particularly accompanying that his low condition.[5]

Q. 49. How did Christ humble himself in his death? 7.159
A. Christ humbled himself in his death, in that having been betrayed by Judas,[1] forsaken by his disciples,[2] scorned and rejected by the world,[3] condemned by Pilate, and tormented by his persecutors;[4] having also conflicted with the terrors of death and the powers of darkness, felt and borne the weight of God's wrath,[5] he laid down his life an offering for sin,[6] enduring the painful, shameful, and cursed death of the cross.[7]

7.160   **Q. 50. Wherein consisted Christ's humiliation after his death?**

A. Christ's humiliation after his death consisted in his being buried,[1] and continuing in the state of the dead, and under the power of death till the third day,[2] which hath been otherwise expressed in these words: "He descended into hell."

7.161   **Q. 51. What was the estate of Christ's exaltation?**

A. The estate of Christ's exaltation comprehendeth his resurrection,[1] ascension,[2] sitting at the right hand of the Father,[3] and his coming again to judge the world.[4]

7.162   **Q. 52. How was Christ exalted in his resurrection?**

A. Christ was exalted in his resurrection, in that, not having seen corruption in death (of which it was not possible for him to be held),[1] and having the very same body in which he suffered, with the essential properties thereof[2] (but without mortality and other common infirmities belonging to this life), really united to his soul,[3] he rose again from the dead the third day by his own power;[4] whereby he declared himself to be the Son of God,[5] to have satisfied divine justice,[6] to have vanquished death and him that had the power of it,[7] and to be Lord of quick and dead.[8] All which he did as a public person,[9] the head of his church,[10] for their justification,[11] quickening in grace,[12] support against enemies,[13] and to assure them of their resurrection from the dead at the last day.[14]

7.163   **Q. 53. How was Christ exalted in his ascension?**

A. Christ was exalted in his ascension, in that having, after his resurrection, often appeared unto, and conversed with his apostles, speaking to them of the things pertaining to the Kingdom of God,[1] and giving them commission to preach the gospel to all nations;[2] forty days after his resurrection, he, in our nature, and as our head, triumphing over enemies, visibly went up into the highest heavens,[3] there to receive gifts for men,[4] to raise up our affections thither,[5] and to prepare a place for us,[6] where himself is, and shall continue till his second coming at the end of the world.[7]

7.164   **Q. 54. How is Christ exalted in his sitting at the right hand of God?**

A. Christ is exalted in his sitting at the right hand of God, in that as God-man he is advanced to the highest favor with God the Father,[1] with all fullness of joy,[2] glory,[3] and power over all things in heaven and earth;[4] and doth gather and defend his church, and subdue their enemies; furnisheth his ministers and people with gifts and graces,[5] and maketh intercession for them.[6]

7.165   **Q. 55. How doth Christ make intercession?**

A. Christ maketh intercession, by his appearing in our nature continually before the Father in heaven,[1] in the merit of his obedience and sacrifice on earth;[2] declaring his will to have it applied to all believers;[3] answering all accusations against them;[4] and procuring for them quiet of conscience, notwithstanding daily failings,[5] access with boldness to the throne of grace,[6] and acceptance of their persons[7] and services.[8]

Q. 56. How is Christ to be exalted in his coming again to judge the world?   7.166

A. Christ is to be exalted in his coming again to judge the world, in that he, who was unjustly judged and condemned by wicked men, shall come again at the last day in great power, and in the full manifestation of his own glory, and of his Father's, with all his holy angels, with a shout, with the voice of the archangel, and with the trumpet of God, to judge the world in righteousness.[1]

Q. 57. What benefits hath Christ procured by his mediation?   7.167

A. Christ by his mediation hath procured redemption, with all other benefits of the covenant of grace.[1]

Q. 58. How do we come to be made partakers of the benefits which Christ hath procured?   7.168

A. We are made partakers of the benefits which Christ hath procured, by the application of them unto us, which is the work especially of God the Holy Ghost.[1]

Q. 59. Who are made partakers of redemption through Christ?   7.169

A. Redemption is certainly applied, and effectually communicated, to all those for whom Christ hath purchased it;[1] who are in time by the Holy Ghost enabled to believe in Christ, according to the gospel.[2]

Q. 60. Can they who have never heard the gospel, and so know not Jesus Christ nor believe in him, be saved by their living according to the light of nature?   7.170

A. They who having never heard the gospel, know not Jesus Christ, and believe not in him, cannot be saved,[1] be they never so diligent to frame their lives according to the light of nature,[2] or the laws of that religion which they profess;[3] neither is there salvation in any other, but in Christ alone,[4] who is the Saviour only of his body the church.[5]

Q. 61. Are all they saved who hear the gospel, and live in the church?   7.171

A. All that hear the gospel, and live in the visible Church, are not saved; but only they who are true members of the Church invisible.[1]

Q. 62. What is the visible church?   7.172

A. The visible church is a society made up of all such as in all ages and places of the world do profess the true religion,[1] and of their children.[2]

7.173   Q. 63. What are the special privileges of the visible church?

A. The visible church hath the privilege of being under God's special care and government;[1] of being protected and preserved in all ages, notwithstanding the opposition of all enemies;[2] and of enjoying the communion of saints, the ordinary means of salvation,[3] and offers of grace by Christ, to all members of it, in the ministry of the gospel, testifying that whosoever believes in him shall be saved,[4] and excluding none that will come unto him.[5]

7.174   Q. 64. What is the invisible church?

A. The invisible church is the whole number of the elect, that have been, are, or shall be gathered into one under Christ the head.[1]

7.175   Q. 65. What special benefits do the members of the invisible church enjoy by Christ?

A. The members of the invisible church, by Christ, enjoy union and communion with him in grace and glory.[1]

7.176   Q. 66. What is that union which the elect have with Christ?

A. The union which the elect have with Christ is the work of God's grace,[1] whereby they are spiritually and mystically, yet really and inseparably, joined to Christ as their head and husband;[2] which is done in their effectual calling.[3]

7.177   Q. 67. What is effectual calling?

A. Effectual calling is the work of God's almighty power and grace,[1] whereby (out of his free and especial love to his elect, and from nothing in them moving him thereunto)[2] he doth in his accepted time invite and draw them to Jesus Christ, by his Word and Spirit;[3] savingly enlightening their minds,[4] renewing and powerfully determining their wills,[5] so as they (although in themselves dead in sin) are hereby made willing and able, freely to answer his call, and to accept and embrace the grace offered and conveyed therein.[6]

7.178   Q. 68. Are the elect only effectually called?

A. All the elect, and they only, are effectually called;[1] although others may be, and often are, outwardly called by the ministry of the Word,[2] and have some common operations of the Spirit,[3] who, for their willful neglect and contempt of the grace offered to them, being justly left in their unbelief, do never truly come to Jesus Christ.[4]

7.179   Q. 69. What is the communion in grace, which the members of the invisible church have with Christ?

A. The communion in grace, which the members of the invisible church have with Christ, is their partaking of the virtue of his mediation, in their justification,[1] adoption,[2] sanctification, and whatever else in this life manifests their union with him.[3]

Q. 70. What is justification? 7.180

A. Justification is an act of God's free grace unto sinners, in which he pardoneth all their sin, accepteth and accounteth their persons righteous in his sight;[1] not for anything wrought in them, or done by them,[2] but only for the perfect obedience and full satisfaction of Christ, by God imputed to them[3] and received by faith alone.[4]

Q. 71. How is justification an act of God's free grace? 7.181

A. Although Christ by his obedience and death, did make a proper, real, and full satisfaction to God's justice in the behalf of them that are justified: yet inasmuch as God accepteth the satisfaction from a surety, which he might have demanded of them; and did provide this surety, his only Son, imputing his righteousness to them, and requiring nothing of them for their justification, but faith, which also is his gift, their justification is to them of free grace.[1]

Q. 72. What is justifying faith? 7.182

A. Justifying faith is a saving grace,[1] wrought in the heart of a sinner, by the Spirit and the Word of God;[2] whereby he, being convinced of his sin and misery, and of the disability in himself and all other creatures to recover him out of his lost condition,[3] not only assenteth to the truth of the promise of the gospel,[4] but receiveth and resteth upon Christ and his righteousness therein held forth, for pardon of sin,[5] and for the accepting and accounting of his person righteous in the sight of God for salvation.[6]

Q. 73. How doth faith justify a sinner in the sight of God? 7.183

A. Faith justifies a sinner in the sight of God, not because of those other graces which do always accompany it, or of good works that are the fruits of it;[1] nor as if the grace of faith, or any act thereof, were imputed to him for justification;[2] but only as it is an instrument, by which he receiveth and applieth Christ and his righteousness.[3]

Q. 74. What is adoption? 7.184

A. Adoption is an act of the free grace of God,[1] in and for his only Son Jesus Christ,[2] whereby all those that are justified are received into the number of his children,[3] have his name put upon them,[4] the Spirit of his Son given to them,[5] are under his Fatherly care and dispensations,[6] admitted to all the liberties and privileges of the sons of God, made heirs of all the promises, and fellow heirs with Christ in glory.[7]

Q. 75. What is sanctification? 7.185

A. Sanctification is a work of God's grace, whereby they, whom God hath, before the foundation of the world, chosen to be holy, are, in time, through the powerful operation of his Spirit, applying the death and resurrection of Christ unto them, renewed in their whole man after the image of God;[1] having the seeds of repentance unto life, and all other saving graces, put into their hearts,[2] and those graces so stirred up, increased and strengthened,[3] as that they more and more die unto sin, and rise into newness of life.[4]

7.186   Q. 76. What is repentance unto life?
A.   Repentance unto life is a saving grace,[1] wrought in the heart of a sinner by the Spirit and Word of God,[2] whereby out of the sight and sense, not only of the danger,[3] but also of the filthiness and odiousness of his sins,[4] and upon the apprehension of God's mercy in Christ to such as are penitent,[5] he so grieves for, and hates his sins,[6] as that he turns from them all to God,[7] purposing and endeavoring constantly to walk with him in all the ways of new obedience.[8]

7.187   Q. 77. Wherein do justification and sanctification differ?
A.   Although sanctification be inseparably joined with justification,[1] yet they differ in that God, in justification, imputeth the righteousness of Christ;[2] in sanctification, his Spirit infuseth grace, and enableth to the exercise thereof;[3] in the former, sin is pardoned;[4] in the other, it is subdued;[5] the one doth equally free all believers from the revenging wrath of God, and that perfectly in this life, that they never fall into condemnation;[6] the other is neither equal in all,[7] nor in this life perfect in any,[8] but growing up to perfection.[9]

7.188   Q. 78. Whence ariseth the imperfection of sanctification in believers?
A.   The imperfection of sanctification in believers ariseth from the remnants of sin abiding in every part of them, and the perpetual lusting of the flesh against the Spirit; whereby they are often foiled with temptations, and fall into many sins,[1] are hindered in all their spiritual service,[2] and their best works are imperfect and defiled in the sight of God.[3]

7.189   Q. 79. May not true believers, by reason of their imperfections, and the many temptations and sins they are overtaken with, fall away from the state of grace?
A.   True believers, by reason of the unchangeable love of God,[1] and his decree and covenant to give them perseverance,[2] their inseparable union with Christ,[3] his continual intercession for them,[4] and the Spirit and seed of God abiding in them,[5] can neither totally nor finally fall away from the state of grace, but are kept by the power of God through faith unto salvation.[6]

7.190   Q. 80. Can true believers be infallibly assured that they are in the estate of grace, and that they shall persevere therein unto salvation?
A.   Such as truly believe in Christ, and endeavor to walk in all good conscience before him, may, without extraordinary revelation, by faith grounded upon the truth of God's promises, and by the Spirit enabling them to discern in themselves those graces to which the

promises of life are made, and bearing witness with their spirits that they are the children of God, be infallibly assured that they are in the estate of grace, and shall persevere therein unto salvation.[1]

Q. 81. Are all true believers at all times assured of their present being in the estate of grace, and that they shall be saved?   7.191

A. Assurance of grace and salvation not being of the essence of faith, true believers may wait long before they obtain it;[1] and, after the enjoyment thereof, may have it weakened and intermitted, through manifold distempers, sins, temptations, and desertions;[2] yet are they never left without such a presence and support of the Spirit of God, as keeps them from sinking into utter despair.[3]

Q. 82. What is the communion in glory which the members of the invisible church have with Christ?   7.192

A. The communion in glory which the members of the invisible church have with Christ, is in this life,[1] immediately after death,[2] and at last perfected at the resurrection and day of judgment.[3]

Q. 83. What is the communion in glory with Christ, which the members of the invisible church enjoy in this life?   7.193

A. The members of the invisible church have communicated to them, in this life, the first fruits of glory with Christ, as they are members of him their head, and so in him are interested in that glory which he is fully possessed of;[1] and as an earnest thereof, enjoy the sense of God's love,[2] peace of conscience, joy in the Holy Ghost, and hope of glory.[3] As, on the contrary, the sense of God's revenging wrath, horror of conscience, and a fearful expectation of judgment, are to the wicked the beginning of the torment which they shall endure after death.[4]

Q. 84. Shall all men die?   7.194

A. Death being threatened as the wages of sin,[1] it is appointed unto all men once to die;[2] for that all have sinned.[3]

Q. 85. Death being the wages of sin, why are not the righteous delivered from death, seeing all their sins are forgiven in Christ?   7.195

A. The righteous shall be delivered from death itself at the last day, and even in death are delivered from the sting and curse of it;[1] so that although they die, yet it is out of God's love,[2] to free them perfectly from sin and misery,[3] and to make them capable of further communion with Christ in glory, which they then enter upon.[4]

Q. 86. What is the communion in glory with Christ, which the members of the invisible church enjoy immediately after death?   7.196

A. The communion in glory with Christ, which the members of the invisible church enjoy immediately after death, is in that their souls are then made perfect in holiness, and received into the highest heavens, where they behold the face of God in light and glory;[1] waiting for the full redemption of their bodies,[2] which even in death continue united to Christ,[3] and rest in their graves as in their beds, till at the last day they be again united to their souls.[4] Whereas the souls of the wicked are at their death cast into hell, where they remain in torments and utter darkness; and their bodies kept in their graves, as in their prisons, until the resurrection and judgment of the great day.[5]

7.197   Q. 87. What are we to believe concerning the resurrection?
A. We are to believe that, at the last day, there shall be a general resurrection of the dead, both of the just and unjust;[1] when they that are then found alive shall in a moment be changed; and the selfsame bodies of the dead which are laid in the grave, being then again united to their souls forever, shall be raised up by the power of Christ.[2] The bodies of the just, by the Spirit of Christ, and by virtue of his resurrection as their head, shall be raised in power, spiritual, and incorruptible, and made like to his glorious body;[3] and the bodies of the wicked shall be raised up in dishonor by him as an offended judge.[4]

7.198   Q. 88. What shall immediately follow after the resurrection?
A. Immediately after the resurrection shall follow the general and final judgment of angels and men,[1] the day and hour whereof no man knoweth, that all may watch and pray, and be ever ready for the coming of the Lord.[2]

7.199   Q. 89. What shall be done to the wicked at the day of judgment?
A. At the day of judgment, the wicked shall be set on Christ's left hand,[1] and upon clear evidence, and full conviction of their own consciences,[2] shall have the fearful but just sentence of condemnation pronounced against them;[3] and thereupon shall be cast out from the favorable presence of God, and the glorious fellowship with Christ, his saints, and all his holy angels, into hell, to be punished with unspeakable torments both of body and soul, with the devil and his angels forever.[4]

7.200   Q. 90. What shall be done to the righteous at the day of judgment?
A. At the day of judgment, the righteous, being caught up to Christ in the clouds,[1] shall be set on his right hand, and, there openly acknowledged and acquitted,[2] shall join with him in the judging of reprobate angels and men;[3] and shall be received into heaven,[4] where they shall be fully and forever freed from all sin and misery;[5] filled with inconceivable joy;[6] made perfectly holy and happy both in body and soul, in the company of innumerable saints and angels,[7] but especially in the immediate vision and fruition of God the Father, of our Lord Jesus Christ, and of the Holy Spirit, to all eternity.[8] And this

is the perfect and full communion, which the members of the invisible Church shall enjoy with Christ in glory, at the resurrection and day of judgment.

Having Seen What the Scriptures Principally Teach Us to Believe Concerning God, It Follows to Consider What They Require as the Duty of Man

Q. 91. What is the duty which God requireth of man?   7.201
A. The Duty which God requireth of man is obedience to his revealed will.[1]

Q. 92. What did God at first reveal unto man as the rule of   7.202
his obedience?
A. The rule of obedience revealed to Adam in the estate of innocence, and to all mankind in him, besides a special command, not to eat of the fruit of the tree of the knowledge of good and evil, was the moral law.[1]

Q. 93. What is the moral law?   7.203
A. The moral law is the declaration of the will of God to mankind, directing and binding everyone to personal, perfect, and perpetual conformity and obedience thereunto, in the frame and disposition of the whole man, soul and body, and in performance of all those duties of holiness and righteousness which he oweth to God and man:[1] promising life upon the fulfilling, and threatening death upon the breach of it.[2]

Q. 94. Is there any use of the moral law to man since the   7.204
Fall?
A. Although no man since the Fall can attain to righteousness and life by the moral law,[1] yet there is great use thereof, as well common to all men, as peculiar either to the unregenerate, or the regenerate.[2]

Q. 95. Of what use is the moral law to all men?   7.205
A. The moral law is of use to all men, to inform them of the holy nature and will of God,[1] and of their duty binding them to walk accordingly;[2] to convince them of their disability to keep it, and of the sinful pollution of their nature, hearts, and lives,[3] to humble them in the sense of their sin and misery,[4] and thereby help them to a clearer sight of the need they have of Christ,[5] and of the perfection of his obedience.

Q. 96. What particular use is there of the moral law to   7.206
unregenerate men?
A. The moral law is of use to unregenerate men, to awaken their consciences to flee from the wrath to come,[1] and to drive them to Christ;[2] or, upon their continuance in the estate and way of sin, to leave them inexcusable,[3] and under the curse thereof.[4]

263

7.207   Q. 97. What special use is there of the moral law to the regenerate?

A. Although they that are regenerate and believe in Christ be delivered from the moral law as a covenant of works, so as thereby they are neither justified nor condemned: yet, besides the general uses thereof common to them with all men, it is of special use to show them how much they are bound to Christ for his fulfilling it, and enduring the curse thereof, in their stead and for their good;[1] and thereby to provoke them to more thankfulness, and to express the same in their greater care to conform themselves thereunto as the rule of their obedience.[2]

7.208   Q. 98. Wherein is the moral law summarily comprehended?

A. The moral law is summarily comprehended in the Ten Commandments,[1] which were delivered by the voice of God upon Mount Sinai, and written by him on two tables of stone;[2] and are recorded in the twentieth chapter of Exodus; the first four commandments containing our duty to God, and the other six our duty to man.

7.209   Q. 99. What rules are to be observed for the right understanding of the Ten Commandments?

A. For the right understanding of the Ten Commandments, these rules are to be observed:

1. That the law is perfect, and bindeth everyone to full conformity in the whole man unto the righteousness thereof, and unto entire obedience forever; so as to require the utmost perfection of every duty, and to forbid the least degree of every sin.[1]

2. That it is spiritual, and so reacheth the understanding, will, affections, and all other powers of the soul; as well as words, works, and gestures.[1]

3. That one and the same thing, in divers respects, is required or forbidden in several commandments.[1]

4. That as, where a duty is commanded, the contrary sin is forbidden;[1] and where a sin is forbidden, the contrary duty is commanded;[2] so, where a promise is annexed, the contrary threatening is included;[3] and where a threatening is annexed, the contrary promise is included.[4]

5. That what God forbids, is at no time to be done;[1] what he commands is always our duty;[2] and yet every particular duty is not to be done at all times.[3]

6. That, under one sin or duty, all of the same kind are forbidden or commanded; together with all the causes, means, occasions, and appearances thereof, and provocations thereunto.[1]

7. That what is forbidden or commanded to ourselves, we are bound, according to our places, to endeavor that it may be avoided or performed by others, according to the duty of their places.[1]

8. That in what is commanded to others, we are bound, according to our places and callings, to be helpful to them:[1] and to take heed of partaking with others in what is forbidden them.[2]

Q. 100. What special things are we to consider in the Ten Commandments?   7.210
A. We are to consider in the Ten Commandments: the preface, the substances of the commandments themselves, and the several reasons annexed to some of them the more to enforce them.

Q. 101. What is the preface to the Ten Commandments?   7.211
A. The preface to the Ten Commandments is contained in these words: "I am the Lord thy God, which have brought thee out of the land of Egypt, out of the house of bondage."[1] Wherein God manifesteth his sovereignty, as being Jehovah, the eternal, immutable, and almighty God; having his being in and of himself, and giving being to all his words and works; and that he is a God in covenant, as with Israel of old, so with all his people; who as he brought them out of their bondage in Egypt, so he delivered us from our spiritual thralldom; and that therefore we are bound to take him for our God alone, and to keep all his commandments.

Q. 102. What is the sum of the four Commandments which contain our duty to God?   7.212
A. The sum of the four Commandments containing our duty to God is, to love the Lord our God with all our heart, and with all our soul, and with all our strength, and with all our mind.[1]

Q. 103. Which is the First Commandment?   7.213
A. The First Commandment is, "Thou shalt have no other gods before me."[1]

Q. 104. What are the duties required in the First Commandment?   7.214
A. The duties required in the First Commandment[1] are: the knowing and acknowledging of God to be the only true God, and our God;[2] and to worship and glorify him accordingly;[3] by thinking,[4] meditating,[5] remembering,[6] highly esteeming,[7] honoring,[8] adoring,[9] choosing,[10] loving,[11] desiring,[12] fearing of him;[13] believing him;[14] trusting,[15] hoping,[16] delighting,[17] rejoicing in him;[18] being zealous for him;[19] calling upon him, giving all praise and thanks,[20] and yielding all obedience and submission to him with the whole man;[21] being careful in all things to please him,[22] and sorrowful when in anything he is offended;[23] and walking humbly with him.[24]

Q. 105. What are the sins forbidden in the First Commandment?   7.215
A. The sins forbidden in the First Commandment are: atheism, in

denying or not having a God;[1] idolatry, in having or worshipping more gods than one, or any with, or instead of the true God;[2] the not having and vouching him for God, and our God;[3] the omission or neglect of anything due to him, required in this commandment;[4] ignorance,[5] forgetfulness,[6] misapprehensions, false opinions,[7] unworthy and wicked thoughts of him;[8] bold and curious searchings into his secrets;[9] all profaneness,[10] hatred of God,[11] self-love,[12] self-seeking,[13] and all other inordinate and immoderate setting of our mind, will, or affections upon other things, and taking them off from him in whole or in part;[14] vain credulity,[15] unbelief,[16] heresy,[17] misbelief,[18] distrust,[19] despair,[20] incorrigibleness, and insensibleness under judgments,[21] hardness of heart,[22] pride,[23] presumption,[24] carnal security,[25] tempting of God;[26] using unlawful means,[27] and trusting in lawful means;[28] carnal delights and joys,[29] corrupt, blind, and indiscreet zeal;[30] lukewarmness,[31] and deadness in the things of God;[32] estranging ourselves, and apostatizing from God;[33] praying or giving any religious worship to saints, angels, or any other creatures;[34] all compacts and consulting with the devil,[35] and hearkening to his suggestions;[36] making men the lords of our faith and conscience;[37] slighting and despising God, and his commands;[38] resisting and grieving of his Spirit,[39] discontent and impatience at his dispensations, charging him foolishly for the evils he inflicts on us;[40] and ascribing the praise of any good, we either are, have, or can do, to fortune, idols,[41] ourselves,[42] or any other creature.[43]

7.216   **Q. 106.   What are we especially taught by these words "before me," in the First Commandment?**
A.   These words "before me," or "before my face," in the First Commandment, teach us, that God, who seeth all things, taketh special notice of, and is much displeased with, the sin of having any other God; that so it may be an argument to dissuade from it, and to aggravate it as a most impudent provocation;[1] as also to persuade us to do as in his sight, whatever we do in his service.[2]

7.217   **Q. 107.   Which is the Second Commandment?**
A.   The Second Commandment is, "Thou shalt not make unto thee any graven image, or any likeness of any thing that is in heaven above, or that is in the earth beneath, or that is in the water under the earth: thou shalt not bow down thyself to them, nor serve them: for I the Lord thy God am a jealous God, visiting the iniquity of the fathers upon the children unto the third and fourth generation of them that hate me; and shewing mercy unto thousands of them that love me, and keep my commandments."[1]

7.218   **Q. 108.   What are the duties required in the Second Commandment?**
A.   The duties required in the Second Commandment are: the receiving, observing, and keeping pure and entire, all such religious worship and ordinances as God hath instituted in his Word;[1] particularly prayer and thanksgiving in the name of Christ;[2] the reading,

preaching, and hearing of the Word;[3] the administration and receiving of the sacraments;[4] church government and discipline;[5] the ministry and maintenance thereof;[6] religious fasting;[7] swearing by the name of God;[8] and vowing unto him:[9] as also the disapproving, detesting, opposing all false worship;[10] and, according to each one's place and calling, removing it, and all monuments of idolatry.[11]

Q. 109. What are the sins forbidden in the Second Commandment?   7.219

A. The sins forbidden in the Second Commandment are: all devising,[1] counseling,[2] commanding,[3] using,[4] and any wise approving any religious worship not instituted by God himself;[5] the making any representation of God, of all, or of any of the three Persons, either inwardly in our mind, or outwardly in any kind of image or likeness of any creature whatsoever;[6] all worshiping of it,[7] or God in it or by it;[8] the making of any representation of feigned deities,[9] and all worship of them, or service belonging to them;[10] all superstitious devices,[11] corrupting the worship of God,[12] adding to it, or taking from it,[13] whether invented and taken up of ourselves,[14] or received by tradition from others,[15] though under the title of antiquity,[16] custom,[17] devotion,[18] good intent, or any other pretense whatsoever;[19] simony,[20] sacrilege;[21] all neglect,[22] contempt,[23] hindering,[24] and opposing the worship and ordinances which God hath appointed.[25]

Q. 110. What are the reasons annexed to the Second Commandment, the more to enforce it?   7.220

A. The reasons annexed to the Second Commandment, the more to enforce it, contained in these words, "For I the Lord thy God am a jealous God, visiting the iniquity of the fathers upon the children unto the third and fourth generation of them that hate me; and shewing mercy unto thousands of them that love me, and keep my commandments;"[1] are, besides God's sovereignty over us, and propriety in us, his revengeful indignation against all false worship,[2] as being a spiritual whoredom;[3] accounting the breakers of this Commandment such as hate him, and threatening to punish them unto divers generations,[4] and esteeming the observers of it such as love him and keep his commandments, and promising mercy to them unto many generations.[5]

Q. 111. Which is the Third Commandment?   7.221

A. The Third Commandment is, "Thou shalt not take the name of the Lord thy God in vain; for the Lord will not hold him guiltless that taketh his name in vain."[1]

Q. 112. What is required in the Third Commandment?   7.222

A. The Third Commandment requires, that the name of God, his titles, attributes,[1] ordinances,[2] the word,[3] sacraments,[4] prayer,[5] oaths,[6] vows,[7] lots,[8] his works,[9] and whatsoever else there is whereby he makes himself known, be holily and reverently used in thought,[10] meditation,[11] word,[12] and writing;[13] by an holy profession,[14] and answerable conversation,[15] to the glory of God,[16] and the good of ourselves[17] and others.[18]

7.223   **Q. 113. What are the sins forbidden in the Third Commandment?**

A. The sins forbidden in the Third Commandment are: the not using of God's name as is required;[1] and the abuse of it in an ignorant,[2] vain,[3] irreverent, profane,[4] superstitious,[5] or wicked mentioning or otherwise using the titles, attributes,[6] ordinances,[7] or works;[8] by blasphemy;[9] perjury;[10] all sinful cursing,[11] oaths,[12] vows,[13] and lots;[14] violating our oaths and vows, if lawful;[15] and fulfilling them, if of things unlawful;[16] murmuring and quarreling at,[17] curious prying into,[18] and misapplying of God's decrees[19] and providence;[20] misinterpreting,[21] misapplying,[22] or any way perverting the Word, or any part of it,[23] to profane jests,[24] curious and unprofitable questions, vain janglings, or the maintaining of false doctrines;[25] abusing it, the creatures, or anything contained under the name of God, to charms,[26] or sinful lusts and practices;[27] the maligning,[28] scorning,[29] reviling,[30] or any way opposing of God's truth, grace, and ways;[31] making profession of religion in hypocrisy, or for sinister ends;[32] being ashamed of it,[33] or a shame to it, by uncomfortable,[34] unwise,[35] unfruitful,[36] and offensive walking[37] or backsliding from it.[38]

7.224   **Q. 114. What reasons are annexed to the Third Commandment?**

A. The reasons annexed to the Third Commandment, in these words, "the Lord thy God," and, "for the Lord will not hold him guiltless that taketh his name in vain,"[1] are because he is the Lord and our God, therefore his name is not to be profaned, or any way abused by us;[2] especially because he will be so far from acquitting and sparing the transgressors of this Commandment, as that he will not suffer them to escape his righteous judgment,[3] albeit many such escape the censures and punishments of men.[4]

7.225   **Q. 115. Which is the Fourth Commandment?**

A. The Fourth Commandment is, "Remember the sabbath day, to keep it holy. Six days shalt thou labour, and do all thy work: but the seventh day is the sabbath of the Lord thy God: in it thou shalt not do any work, thou, nor thy son, nor thy daughter, thy manservant, nor thy maidservant, nor thy cattle, nor thy stranger that is within thy gates; for in six days the Lord made heaven and earth, the sea, and all that in them is, and rested the seventh day: wherefore the Lord blessed the sabbath day, and hallowed it."[1]

7.226   **Q. 116. What is required in the Fourth Commandment?**

A. The Fourth Commandment requireth of all men the sanctifying or keeping holy to God such set times as he hath appointed in his

Word, expressly one whole day in seven;[1] which was the seventh from the beginning of the world to the resurrection of Christ,[2] and the first day of the week ever since, and so to continue to the end of the world; which is the Christian Sabbath,[3] and in the New Testament called "the Lord's Day."

Q. 117. How is the Sabbath or Lord's Day to be sanctified?   7.227

A. The Sabbath, or Lord's Day, is to be sanctified by an holy resting all that day,[1] not only from such works as are at all times sinful, but even from such worldly employments and recreations as are on other days lawful;[2] and making it our delight to spend the whole time (except so much of it as is to be taken up in works of necessity and mercy)[3] in the public and private exercise of God's worship.[4] And, to that end, we are to prepare our hearts, and with such foresight, diligence, and moderation, to dispose, and seasonably to dispatch our worldly business, that we may be the more free and fit for the duties of the day.[5]

Q. 118. Why is the charge of keeping the Sabbath more specially directed to governors of families and other superiors?   7.228

A. The charge of keeping the Sabbath is more specially directed to governors of families and other superiors, because they are bound not only to keep it themselves, but to see that it be observed by all those that are under their charge; and because they are prone ofttimes to hinder them by employments of their own.[1]

Q. 119. What are the sins forbidden in the Fourth Commandment?   7.229

A. The sins in the Fourth Commandment are: all omissions of the duties required,[1] all careless, negligent, and unprofitable performing of them, and being weary of them;[2] all profaning the day by idleness, and doing that which is in itself sinful;[3] and by all needless works, words, and thoughts about our worldly employments and recreations.[4]

Q. 120. What are the reasons annexed to the Fourth Commandment, the more to enforce it?   7.230

A. The reasons annexed to the Fourth Commandment, the more to enforce it, are taken from the equity of it, God allowing us six days of seven for our own affairs, and reserving but one for himself, in these words, "Six days shalt thou labour, and do all thy work;"[1] from God's challenging a special propriety in that day. "The seventh day is the sabbath of the Lord thy God;"[2] from the example of God who "in six days . . . made heaven and earth, the sea, and all that in them is, and rested the seventh day;" and from that blessing which God put upon that day, not only in sanctifying it to be a holy day for his service, but in ordaining it to be a means of blessing to us in our sanctifying it, "wherefore the Lord blessed the sabbath day, and hallowed it."[3]

7.231   **Q. 121. Why is the word "remember" set in the beginning of the Fourth Commandment?**

A. The word "remember" is set in the beginning of the Fourth Commandment,[1] partly because of the great benefit of remembering it, we being thereby helped in our preparation to keep it;[2] and, in keeping it, better to keep all the rest of the Commandments[3] and to continue a thankful remembrance of the two great benefits of creation and redemption, which contain a short abridgement of religion:[4] and partly because we are ready to forget it,[5] for that there is less light of nature for it, and yet it restraineth our natural liberty in things at other times lawful;[6] that it cometh but once in seven days, and many worldly businesses come between, and too often take off our minds from thinking of it, either to prepare for it, or to sanctify it;[7] and that Satan with his instruments much labor to blot out the glory, and even the memory of it, and to bring in all irreligion and impiety.[8]

7.232   **Q. 122. What is the sum of the six Commandments which contain our duty to man?**

A. The sum of the six Commandments which contain our duty to man is, to love our neighbor as ourselves,[1] and to do to others what we would have them to do to us.[2]

7.233   **Q. 123. Which is the Fifth Commandment?**

A. The Fifth Commandment is, "Honour thy father and thy mother: that thy days may be long upon the land which the Lord thy God giveth thee." [1]

7.234   **Q. 124. Who are meant by "father" and "mother," in the Fifth Commandment?**

A. By "father" and "mother" in the Fifth Commandment, are meant not only natural parents, but all superiors in age[1] and gifts;[2] and especially such as by God's ordinance are over us in place of authority, whether in family,[3] church,[4] or commonwealth.[5]

7.235   **Q. 125. Why are superiors styled "father" and "mother"?**

A. Superiors are styled "father" and "mother" both to teach them in all duties towards their inferiors, like natural parents, to express love and tenderness to them, according to their several relations,[1] and to work inferiors to a greater willingness and cheerfulness in performing their duties to their superiors, as to their parents.[2]

7.236   **Q. 126. What is the general scope of the Fifth Commandment?**

A. The general scope of the Fifth Commandment is, the performance of those duties which we mutually owe in our several relations, as inferiors, superiors, or equals.[1]

7.237   **Q. 127. What is the honor which inferiors owe to superiors?**

A. The honor which inferiors owe to their superiors is: all due reverence in heart,[1] word,[2] and behavior;[3] prayer and thanksgiving for them;[4] imitation of their virtues and graces;[5] willing obedience to their lawful commands and counsels,[6] due submission to their corrections;[7] fidelity to,[8] defense and maintenance of their persons and authority, according to their several ranks, and the nature of their places;[9] bearing with their infirmities, and covering them in love,[10] that so they may be an honor to them and to their government.[11]

Q. 128. What are the sins of inferiors against their superiors?   7.238
A. The sins of inferiors against their superiors are: all neglect of the duties required toward them;[1] envying at,[2] contempt of,[3] and rebellion[4] against their persons[5] and places,[6] in their lawful counsels,[7] commands, and corrections;[8] cursing, mocking,[9] and all such refractory and scandalous carriage, as proves a shame and dishonor to them and their government.[10]

Q. 129. What is required of superiors towards their inferiors?   7.239
A. It is required of superiors, according to that power they receive from God, and that relation wherein they stand, to love,[1] pray for,[2] and bless their inferiors;[3] to instruct,[4] counsel, and admonish them;[5] countenancing,[6] commending, and rewarding such as do well;[7] and discountenancing,[8] reproving, and chastising such as do ill;[9] protecting, and providing for them all things necessary for soul and body;[10] and, by grave, wise, holy, and exemplary carriage, to procure glory to God,[11] honor to themselves,[12] and so to preserve that authority which God hath put upon them.[13]

Q. 130. What are the sins of superiors?   7.240
A. The sins of superiors are, besides the neglect of the duties required of them[1] an inordinate seeking of themselves,[2] their own glory,[3] ease, profit or pleasure;[4] commanding things unlawful,[5] or not in the power of inferiors to perform;[6] counseling,[7] encouraging,[8] or favoring them in that which is evil;[9] dissuading, discouraging, or discountenancing them in that which is good;[10] correcting them unduly;[11] careless exposing or leaving them to wrong, temptation, and danger;[12] provoking them to wrath;[13] or any way dishonoring themselves, or lessening their authority, by an unjust, indiscreet, rigorous, or remiss behavior.[14]

Q. 131. What are the duties of equals?   7.241
A. The duties of equals are: to regard the dignity and worth of each other,[1] in giving honor to go one before another,[2] and to rejoice in each other's gifts and advancement as their own.[3]

Q. 132. What are the sins of equals?   7.242
A. The sins of equals are, besides the neglect of the duties required,[1] the undervaluing of the worth,[2] envying the gifts,[3] grieving at the advancement or prosperity one of another,[4] and usurping preeminence one over another.[5]

7.243   Q. 133. What is the reason annexed to the Fifth Commandment the more to enforce it?

A.   The reason annexed to the Fifth Commandment in these words, "that thy days may be long upon the land which the Lord thy God giveth thee," [1] is an express promise of long life and prosperity, as far as it shall serve for God's glory and their own good, to all such as keep this Commandment. [2]

7.244   Q. 134. Which is the Sixth Commandment?

A.   The Sixth Commandment is, "Thou shalt not kill." [1]

7.245   Q. 135. What are the duties required in the Sixth Commandment?

A.   The duties required in the Sixth Commandment are: all careful studies and lawful endeavors, to preserve the life of ourselves [1] and others, [2] by resisting all thoughts and purposes, [3] subduing all passions, [4] and avoiding all occasions, [5] temptations, [6] and practices, which tend to the unjust taking away the life of any; [7] by just defense thereof against violence; [8] patient bearing of the hand of God, [9] quietness of mind, [10] cheerfulness of spirit, [11] a sober use of meat, [12] drink, [13] physic, [14] sleep, [15] labor, [16] and recreation; [17] by charitable thoughts, [18] love, [19] compassion, [20] meekness, gentleness, kindness; [21] peaceable, [22] mild, and courteous speeches and behavior, [23] forbearance, readiness to be reconciled, patient bearing and forgiving of injuries, and requiting good for evil; [24] comforting and succoring the distressed, and protecting and defending the innocent. [25]

7.246   Q. 136. What are the sins forbidden in the Sixth Commandment?

A.   The sins forbidden in the Sixth Commandment are: all taking away the life of ourselves, [1] or of others, [2] except in case of public justice, [3] lawful war, [4] or necessary defense; [5] the neglecting or withdrawing the lawful or necessary means of preservation of life; [6] sinful anger, [7] hatred, [8] envy, [9] desire of revenge; [10] all excessive passions; [11] distracting cares; [12] immoderate use of meat, drink, [13] labor, [14] and recreation; [15] provoking words; [16] oppression, [17] quarreling, [18] striking, wounding, [19] and whatsoever else tends to the destruction of the life of any. [20]

7.247   Q. 137. Which is the Seventh Commandment?

A.   The Seventh Commandment is, "Thou shalt not commit adultery." [1]

7.248   Q. 138. What are the duties required in the Seventh Commandment?

A.   The duties required in the Seventh Commandment are: chastity in body, mind, affections, [1] words, [2] and behavior, [3] and the preservation of it in ourselves and others; [4] watchfulness over the eyes and all the senses; [5] temperance, [6] keeping of chaste company, [7] modesty in apparel, [8] marriage by those that have not the gift of continency,[9] conjugal love,[10] and cohabitation;[11] diligent labor in our callings;[12] shunning of all occasions of uncleanness, and resisting temptations thereunto.[13]

Q. 139. What are the sins forbidden in the Seventh Commandment?

A. The sins forbidden in the Seventh Commandment, besides the neglect of the duties required,[1] are: adultery, fornication,[2] rape, incest,[3] sodomy, and all unnatural lusts;[4] all unclean imaginations, thoughts, purposes, and affections;[5] all corrupt or filthy communications, or listening thereunto;[6] wanton looks,[7] impudent or light behavior, immodest apparel,[8] prohibiting of lawful,[9] and dispensing with unlawful marriages;[10] allowing, tolerating, keeping of stews, and resorting to them;[11] entangling vows of single life,[12] undue delay of marriage;[13] having more wives or husbands than one at the same time;[14] unjust divorce[15] or desertion;[16] idleness, gluttony, drunkenness,[17] unchaste company;[18] lascivious songs, books, pictures, dancings, stageplays,[19] and all other provocations to, or acts of, uncleanness either in ourselves or others.[20]

Q. 140. Which is the Eighth Commandment?

A. The Eighth Commandment is, "Thou shalt not steal."[1]

Q. 141. What are the duties required in the Eighth Commandment?

A. The duties required in the Eighth Commandment are: truth, faithfulness, and justice in contracts and commerce between man and man;[1] rendering to everyone his due;[2] restitution of goods unlawfully detained from the right owners thereof;[3] giving and lending freely, according to our abilities, and the necessities of others;[4] moderation of our judgments, wills, and affections, concerning worldly goods;[5] a provident care and study to get,[6] keep, use, and dispose of those things which are necessary and convenient for the sustentation of our nature, and suitable to our condition;[7] a lawful calling,[8] and a diligence in it;[9] frugality;[10] avoiding unnecessary lawsuits,[11] and suretyship, or other like engagements;[12] and an endeavor by all just and lawful means to procure, preserve, and further the wealth and outward estate of others, as well as our own.[13]

Q. 142. What are the sins forbidden in the Eighth Commandment?

A. The sins forbidden in the Eighth Commandment besides the neglect of duties required,[1] are: theft,[2] robbery,[3] man-stealing,[4] and receiving anything that is stolen;[5] fraudulent dealing,[6] false weights and measures,[7] removing landmarks,[8] injustice and unfaithfulness in contracts between man and man,[9] or in matters of trust;[10] oppression,[11] extortion, usury,[12] bribery,[13] vexatious lawsuits,[14] unjust enclosures and depopulations;[15] engrossing commodities to enhance the price,[16] unlawful callings,[17] and all other unjust or sinful ways of taking or withholding from our neighbor what belongs to him, or of enriching ourselves;[18] covetousness,[19] inordinate prizing and affecting worldly goods;[20] distrustful and distracting cares and studies in getting, keeping, and using them;[21] envying at the prosperity of others;[22] as likewise idleness,[23] prodigality, wasteful gaming, and all other ways whereby we do unduly prejudice our own outward estate;[24] and defrauding ourselves of the due use and comfort of that estate which God hath given us.[25]

7.253   **Q. 143. Which is the Ninth Commandment?**

A. The Ninth Commandment is, "Thou shalt not bear false witness against thy neighbour."[1]

7.254   **Q. 144. What are the duties required in the Ninth Commandment?**

A. The duties required in the Ninth Commandment are: the preserving and promoting of truth between man and man,[1] and the good name of our neighbor, as well as our own;[2] appearing and standing for the truth;[3] and from the heart, sincerely,[4] freely,[5] clearly,[6] and fully,[7] speaking the truth, and only the truth, in matters of judgment and justice,[8] and in all other things whatsoever;[9] a charitable esteem of our neighbors, [10] loving, desiring, and rejoicing in their good name;[11] sorrowing for,[12] and covering of their infirmities;[13] freely acknowledging of their gifts and graces,[14] defending their innocency;[15] a ready receiving of good report,[16] and unwillingness to admit of an evil report concerning them;[17] discouraging talebearers,[18] flatterers,[19] and slanderers;[20] love and care of our own good name, and defending it when need requireth;[21] keeping of lawful promises;[22] studying and practicing of whatsoever things are true, honest, lovely, and of good report.[23]

7.255   **Q. 145. What are the sins forbidden in the Ninth Commandment?**

A. The sins forbidden in the Ninth Commandment are: all prejudicing of the truth, and the good name of our neighbors as well as our own,[1] especially in public judicature;[2] giving false evidence,[3] suborning false witnesses,[4] wittingly appearing and pleading for an evil cause, outfacing and overbearing the truth;[5] passing unjust sentence,[6] calling evil good, and good evil; rewarding the wicked according to the work of the righteous, and the righteous according to the work of the wicked;[7] forgery,[8] concealing the truth, undue silence in a just cause,[9] and holding our peace when iniquity calleth for either a reproof from ourselves,[10] or complaint to others;[11] speaking the truth unseasonably,[12] or maliciously to a wrong end,[13] or perverting it to a wrong meaning,[14] or in doubtful and equivocal expression, to the prejudice of truth or justice;[15] speaking untruth,[16] lying,[17] slandering,[18] backbiting,[19] detracting,[20] talebearing,[21] whispering,[22] scoffing,[23] reviling;[24] rash,[25] harsh,[26] and partial censuring;[27] misconstruing intentions, words, and actions;[28]

flattering,[29] vainglorious boasting,[30] thinking or speaking too highly or too meanly of ourselves or others; denying the gifts and graces of God;[31] aggravating smaller faults;[32] hiding, excusing, or extenuating of sins, when called to a free confession;[33] unnecessarily discovering of infirmities;[34] raising false rumors;[35] receiving and countenancing evil reports,[36] and stopping our ears against just defense;[37] evil suspicion;[38] envying or grieving at the deserved credit of any;[39] endeavoring or desiring to impair it,[40] rejoicing in their disgrace and infamy;[41] scornful contempt,[42] fond admiration,[43] breach of lawful promises;[44] neglecting such things as are of good report;[45] and practicing or not avoiding ourselves, or not hindering what we can in others, such things as procure an ill name.[46]

Q. 146. Which is the Tenth Commandment?   7.256
A. The Tenth Commandment is, "Thou shalt not covet thy neighbour's house, thou shalt not covet thy neighbour's wife, nor his manservant, nor his maidservant, nor his ox, nor his ass, nor any thing that is thy neighbour's."[1]

Q. 147. What are the duties required in the Tenth Commandment?   7.257
A. The duties required in the Tenth Commandment are: such a full contentment with our own condition,[1] and such a charitable frame of the whole soul towards our neighbor, as that all our inward motions and affections touching him, tend unto and further all that good which is his.[2]

Q. 148. What are the sins forbidden in the Tenth Commandment?   7.258
A. The sins forbidden in the Tenth Commandment are: discontentment with our own estate;[1] envying,[2] and grieving at the good of our neighbor,[3] together with all inordinate motions and affections to anything that is his.[4]

Q. 149. Is any man able perfectly to keep the Commandments of God?   7.259
A. No man is able, either of himself,[1] or by any grace received in this life, perfectly to keep the Commandments of God;[2] but doth daily break them in thought,[3] word, and deed.[4]

Q. 150. Are all transgressions of the law of God equally heinous in themselves, and in the sight of God?   7.260
A. All transgressions of the law of God are not equally heinous; but some sins in themselves, and by reason of several aggravations, are more heinous in the sight of God than others.[1]

Q. 151. What are those aggravations that make some sins more heinous than others?   7.261

A. Sins receive their aggravations,

1. From the persons offending:[1] if they be of riper age, greater experience, or grace;[2] eminent for profession,[3] gifts,[4] place, office,[5] guides to others,[6] and whose example is likely to be followed by others.[7]

2. From the parties offended:[8] if immediately against God,[9] his attributes,[10] and worship;[11] against Christ, and his grace:[12] the Holy Spirit, his witness, and workings;[13] against superiors, men of eminency,[14] and such as we stand especially related and engaged unto;[15] against any of the saints,[16] particularly weak brethren, the souls of them or any other;[17] and the common good of all or many.[18]

3. From the nature and quality of the offense:[19] if it be against the express letter of the law,[20] break many commandments, contain in it many sins:[21] if not only conceived in the heart, but break forth in words and actions,[22] scandalize others,[23] and admit no reparation:[24] if against means,[25] mercies,[26] judgments,[27] light of nature,[28] conviction of conscience,[29] public or private admonition,[30] censures of the church,[31] civil punishments;[32] and our prayers, purposes, promises, vows, covenants, and engagements to God or men:[33] if done deliberately,[34] willfully,[34] presumptuously, impudently, boastingly,[35] maliciously,[36] frequently,[37] obstinately,[38] with light,[39] continuance,[40] or relapsing after repentance.[41]

4. From circumstances of time,[42] and place:[43] if on the Lord's Day,[44] or other times of divine worship;[45] or immediately before,[46] or after these,[47] or other helps to prevent or remedy such miscarriages;[48] if in public, or in the presence of others, who are thereby likely to be provoked or defiled.[49]

7.262   Q. 152. What doth every sin deserve at the hands of God?
A. Every sin, even the least,[1] being against the sovereignty,[2] goodness,[3] and holiness of God,[4] and against his righteous law,[5] deserveth his wrath and curse,[6] both in this life,[7] and that which is to come;[8] and cannot be expiated but by the blood of Christ.[9]

7.263   Q. 153. What doth God require of us, that we may escape his wrath and curse due to us by reason of the transgression of the law?
A. That we may escape the wrath and curse of God due to us by reason of the transgression of the law, he requireth of us repentance towards God, and faith towards our Lord Jesus Christ,[1] and the diligent use of the outward means whereby Christ communicates to us the benefits of his mediation.[2]

7.264   Q. 154. What are the outward means whereby Christ communicates to us the benefits of his mediation?
A. The outward and ordinary means, whereby Christ communicates to his church the benefits of his mediation, are all his

ordinances, especially the Word, sacraments, and prayer, all which are made effectual to the elect for their salvation.[1]

Q. 155. How is the Word made effectual to salvation? 7.265
A. The Spirit of God maketh the reading, but especially the preaching of the Word, an effectual means of enlightening, convincing, and humbling sinners,[1] of driving them out of themselves, and drawing them unto Christ,[2] of conforming them to his image,[3] and subduing them to his will;[4] of strengthening them against temptations and corruptions;[5] of building them up in grace,[6] and establishing their hearts in holiness and comfort through faith unto salvation.[7]

Q. 156. Is the Word of God to be read by all? 7.266
A. Although all are not permitted to read the Word publicly to the congregation, yet all sorts of people are bound to read it apart by themselves,[1] and with their families;[2] to which end, the Holy Scriptures are to be translated out of the original into the language of every people unto whom they come.[3]

Q. 157. How is the Word of God to be read? 7.267
A. The Holy Scriptures are to be read with an high and reverent esteem of them;[1] with a firm persuasion that they are the very Word of God,[2] and that he only can enable us to understand them;[3] with desire to know, believe, and obey, the will of God revealed in them;[4] with diligence,[5] and attention to the matter and scope of them;[6] with meditation,[7] application,[8] self-denial,[9] and prayer.[10]

Q. 158. By whom is the Word of God to be preached? 7.268
A. The Word of God is to be preached only by such as are sufficiently gifted,[1] and also duly approved and called to that office.[2]

Q. 159. How is the Word of God to be preached by those that are called thereunto? 7.269
A. They that are called to labor in the ministry of the Word are to preach sound doctrine,[1] diligently, in season, and out of season;[2] plainly,[3] not in the enticing word of man's wisdom, but in demonstration of the Spirit, and of power;[4] faithfully,[5] making known the whole counsel of God;[6] wisely,[7] applying themselves to the necessities and capacities of the hearers;[8] zealously,[9] with fervent love to God,[10] and the souls of his people;[11] sincerely,[12] aiming at his glory,[13] and their conversion,[14] edification,[15] and salvation.[16]

Q. 160. What is required of those that hear the Word preached? 7.270
A. It is required of those that hear the Word preached, that they attend upon it with diligence,[1] preparation,[2] and prayer;[3] examine what they hear by the Scriptures;[4] receive the truth with faith,[5] love,[6]

meekness,[7] and readiness of mind,[8] as the Word of God;[9] meditate,[10] and confer of it;[11] hide it in their hearts,[12] and bring forth the fruit of it in their lives.[13]

7.271   **Q. 161. How do the sacraments become effectual means of salvation?**

A.   The sacraments become effectual means of salvation, not by any power in themselves or any virtue derived from the piety or intention of him by whom they are administered; but only by the working of the Holy Ghost, and the blessing of Christ by whom they are instituted.[1]

7.272   **Q. 162. What is a sacrament?**

A.   A sacrament is an holy ordinance instituted by Christ in his Church,[1] to signify, seal and exhibit[2] unto those that are within the covenant of grace,[3] the benefits of his mediation;[4] to strengthen and increase their faith and all other graces;[5] to oblige them to obedience;[6] to testify and cherish their love and communion one with another,[7] and to distinguish them from those that are without.[8]

7.273   **Q. 163. What are the parts of a sacrament?**

A.   The parts of a sacrament are two: the one, an outward and sensible sign used according to Christ's own appointment; the other, an inward and spiritual grace thereby signified.[1]

7.274   **Q. 164. How many sacraments hath Christ instituted under the New Testament?**

A.   Under the New Testament Christ hath instituted in his church only two sacraments, baptism, and the Lord's Supper.[1]

7.275   **Q. 165. What is Baptism?**

A.   Baptism is a sacrament of the New Testament, wherein Christ hath ordained the washing with water in the name of the Father, and of the Son, and of the Holy Ghost,[1] to be a sign and seal of ingrafting into himself,[2] of remission of sins by his blood,[3] and regeneration by his Spirit;[4] of adoption,[5] and resurrection unto everlasting life:[6] and whereby the parties baptized are solemnly admitted into the visible church,[7] and enter into an open and professed engagement to be wholly and only the Lord's.[8]

7.276   **Q. 166. Unto whom is Baptism to be administered?**

A.   Baptism is not to be administered to any that are out of the visible church, and so strangers from the covenant of promise, till they profess their faith in Christ, and obedience to him;[1] but infants descending from parents, either both or but one of them, professing faith in Christ, and obedience to him, are, in that respect, within the covenant, and are to be baptized.[2]

Q. 167. How is our Baptism to be improved by us?   7.277

A. The needful but much neglected duty of improving our Baptism is to be performed by us all our life long, especially in the time of temptation,[1] and when we are presented at the administration of it to others, by serious and thankful consideration of the nature of it and of the ends for which Christ instituted it, the privileges and benefits conferred and sealed thereby, and our solemn vow made therein;[2] by being humbled for our sinful defilement, our falling short of, and walking contrary to, the grace of Baptism and our engagements;[3] by growing up to assurance of pardon of sin, and of all other blessings sealed to us in that sacrament;[4] by drawing strength from the death and resurrection of Christ, into whom we are baptized, for the mortifying of sin, and quickening of grace;[5] and by endeavoring to live by faith,[6] to have our conversation in holiness and righteousness,[7] as those that have therein given up their names to Christ, and to walk in brotherly love, as being baptized by the same Spirit into one body.[8]

Q. 168. What is the Lord's Supper?   7.278

A. The Lord's Supper is a sacrament of the New Testament wherein by giving and receiving bread and wine according to the appointment of Jesus Christ, his death is showed forth;[1] and they that worthily communicate, feed upon his body and blood to their spiritual nourishment and growth in grace;[2] have their union and communion with him confirmed; testify and renew their thankfulness and engagement to God,[3] and their mutual love and fellowship each with other, as members of the same mystical body.[4]

Q. 169. How hath Christ appointed bread and wine to be given and received in the sacrament of the Lord's Supper?   7.279

A. Christ hath appointed the ministers of his Word in the administration of this sacrament of the Lord's Supper, to set apart the bread and wine from common use by the word of institution, thanksgiving, and prayer; to take and break the bread, and to give both the bread and the wine to the communicants; who are by the same appointment to take and eat the bread, and to drink the wine; in thankful remembrance that the body of Christ was broken and given, and his blood shed for them.[1]

Q 170. How do they that worthily communicate in the Lord's Supper feed upon the body and blood of Christ therein?   7.280

A. As the body and the blood of Christ are not corporally or carnally present in, with, or under the bread and wine in the Lord's Supper;[1] and yet are spiritually present to the faith of the receiver, no less truly and really than the elements themselves are to their outward senses;[2] so they that worthily communicate in the sacrament of the Lord's Supper, do therein feed upon the body and blood of Christ, not after a corporal or carnal, but in a spiritual manner; yet truly and really,[3] while by faith they receive and apply unto themselves Christ crucified, and all the benefits of his death.[4]

7.281   **Q. 171. How are they that receive the sacrament of the Lord's Supper to prepare themselves before they come unto it?**

A. They that receive the sacrament of the Lord's Supper are, before they come, to prepare themselves thereunto; by examining themselves,[1] of their being in Christ,[2] of their sins and wants;[3] of the truth and measure of their knowledge,[4] faith,[5] repentance,[6] love to God and the brethren,[7] charity to all men,[8] forgiving those that have done them wrong;[9] of their desires after Christ,[10] and of their new obedience;[11] and by renewing the exercise of these graces,[12] by serious meditation,[13] and fervent prayer.[14]

7.282   **Q. 172. May one who doubteth of his being in Christ, or of his due preparation, come to the Lord's Supper?**

A. One who doubteth of his being in Christ, or of his due preparation to the sacrament of the Lord's Supper, may have true interest in Christ, though he be not yet assured thereof;[1] and in God's account hath it, if he be duly affected with the apprehension of the want of it,[2] and unfeignedly desirous to be found in Christ,[3] and to depart from iniquity;[4] in which case (because promises are made, and this sacrament is appointed, for the relief even of weak and doubting Christians)[5] he is to bewail his unbelief,[6] and labor to have his doubts resolved;[7] and so doing, he may and ought to come to the Lord's Supper, that he may be further strengthened.[8]

7.283   **Q. 173. May any who profess the faith, and desire to come to the Lord's Supper, be kept from it?**

A. Such as are found to be ignorant or scandalous, notwithstanding their profession of the faith, and desire to come to the Lord's Supper, may and ought to be kept from that sacrament by the power which Christ hath left in his Church,[1] until they receive instruction, and manifest their reformation.[2]

7.284   **Q. 174. What is required of them that receive the sacrament of the Lord's Supper in the time of the administration of it?**

A. It is required of them that receive the sacrament of the Lord's Supper that, during the time of the administration of it, with all holy reverence and attention, they wait upon God in that ordinance; diligently observe the sacramental elements and actions;[1] heedfully discern the Lord's body,[2] and affectionately meditate upon his death and sufferings,[3] and thereby stir up themselves to a vigorous exercise of their graces; in judging themselves,[4] and sorrowing for sin;[5] in earnest hungering and thirsting after Christ,[6] feeding on him by faith,[7] receiving of his fullness,[8] trusting in his merits,[9] rejoicing in his love,[10] giving thanks for his grace;[11] in renewing of their covenant with God,[12] and love to all the saints.[13]

7.285   **Q. 175. What is the duty of Christians after they have received the sacrament of the Lord's Supper?**

A. The duty of Christians after they have received the sacrament of the Lord's Supper is seriously to consider how they have behaved themselves therein, and with what success;[1] if they find quickening and comfort, to bless God for it,[2] beg the continuance of it, watch against relapse,[3] fulfill their vows,[4] and encourage themselves to a frequent attendance on that ordinance;[5] but if they find no present benefit, more exactly to review their preparation to, and carriage at, the sacrament;[6] in both which if they can approve themselves to God and their own consciences, they are to wait for the fruit of it in due time;[7] but if they see that they have failed in either, they are to be humbled,[8] and to attend upon it afterward with more care and diligence.[9]

Q. 176. Wherein do the sacraments of Baptism and the Lord's Supper agree?

7.286

A. The sacraments of Baptism and the Lord's Supper agree, in that the author of both is God;[1] the spiritual part of both is Christ and his benefits;[2] both are seals of the same covenant,[3] are to be dispensed by ministers of the gospel and by none other,[4] and to be continued in the Church of Christ until his second coming.[5]

Q. 177. Wherein do the sacraments of Baptism and the Lord's Supper differ?

7.287

A. The sacraments of Baptism and the Lord's Supper differ, in that Baptism is to be administered but once, with water, to be a sign and seal of our regeneration and ingrafting into Christ,[1] and that even to infants;[2] whereas the Lord's Supper is to be administered often, in the elements of bread and wine, to represent and exhibit Christ as spiritual nourishment to the soul,[3] and to confirm our continuance and growth in him,[4] and that only to such as are of years and ability to examine themselves.[5]

Q. 178. What is prayer?

7.288

A. Prayer is an offering up of our desires unto God,[1] in the name of Christ,[2] by the help of his Spirit,[3] with confession of our sins,[4] and thankful acknowledgment of his mercies.[5]

Q. 179. Are we to pray unto God only?

7.289

A. God only being able to search the heart,[1] hear the requests,[2] pardon the sins,[3] and fulfill the desires of all,[4] and only to be believed in,[5] and worshiped with religious worship;[6] prayer, which is a special part thereof,[7] is to be made by all to him alone, and to none other.[8]

Q. 180. What is it to pray in the name of Christ?

7.290

A. To pray in the name of Christ is, in obedience to his command, and in confidence on his promises, to ask mercy for his sake:[1] not by bare mentioning of his name;[2] but by drawing our encouragement to pray, and our boldness, strength, and hope of acceptance in prayer, from Christ and his mediation.[3]

7.291   Q. 181. Why are we to pray in the name of Christ?
A.   The sinfulness of man, and his distance from God by reason thereof, being so great, as that we can have no access into his presence without a mediator, and there being none in heaven or earth appointed to, or fit for, that glorious work but Christ alone, we are to pray in no other name but his only.[1]

7.292   Q. 182. How doth the Spirit help us to pray?
A.   We not knowing what to pray for as we ought, the Spirit helpeth our infirmities, by enabling us to understand both for whom, and what, and how prayer is to be made; and by working and quickening in our hearts (although not in all persons, nor at all times in the same measure) those apprehensions, affections, and graces, which are requisite for the right performance of that duty.[1]

7.293   Q. 183. For whom are we to pray?
A.   We are to pray for the whole church of Christ upon earth,[1] for magistrates,[2] and ministers,[3] for ourselves,[4] our brethren,[5] yea, our enemies,[6] and for all sorts of men living,[7] or that shall live hereafter;[8] but not for the dead.[9]

7.294   Q. 184. For what things are we to pray?
A.   We are to pray for all things tending to the glory of God,[1] the welfare of the church,[2] our own[3] or others' good;[4] but not for anything that is unlawful.[5]

7.295   Q. 185. How are we to pray?
A.   We are to pray with an awful apprehension of the majesty of God,[1] and deep sense of our own unworthiness,[2] necessities,[3] and sins;[4] with penitent,[5] thankful,[6] and enlarged hearts;[7] with understanding,[8] faith,[9] sincerity,[10] fervency,[11] love,[12] and perseverance,[13] waiting upon him[14] with humble submission to his will.[15]

7.296   Q. 186. What rule hath God given for our direction in the duty of prayer?
A.   The whole Word of God is of use to direct us in the duty of praying;[1] but the special rule of direction is that form of prayer which our Saviour Christ taught his disciples, commonly called, "the Lord's Prayer."[2]

7.297   Q. 187. How is the Lord's Prayer to be used?
A.   The Lord's Prayer is not only for direction, as a pattern according to which we are to make other prayers; but may be also used as a prayer so that it be done with understanding, faith, reverence, and other graces necessary to the right performance of the duty of prayer.[1]

7.298   Q. 188. Of how many parts doth the Lord's Prayer consist?
A.   The Lord's Prayer consists of three parts: a preface, petitions, and a conclusion.

Q. 189. What doth the preface of the Lord's Prayer teach us?   7.299

A. The preface of the Lord's Prayer (contained in these words, "Our Father which art in heaven")[1] teacheth us, when we pray, to draw near to God with confidence of his fatherly goodness, and our interest therein;[2] with reverence, and all other childlike dispositions,[3] heavenly affections,[4] and due apprehensions of his sovereign power, majesty, and gracious condescension:[5] as also to pray with and for others.[6]

Q. 190. What do we pray for in the first petition?   7.300

A. In the first petition (which is, "Hallowed be thy name"),[1] acknowledging the utter inability and indisposition that is in ourselves and all men to honor God aright,[2] we pray: that God would by his grace enable and incline us and others to know, to acknowledge, and highly esteem him,[3] his titles,[4] attributes,[5] ordinances, word,[6] works, and whatsoever he is pleased to make himself known by;[7] and to glorify him in thought, word,[8] and deed;[9] that he would prevent and remove atheism,[10] ignorance,[11] idolatry,[12] profaneness,[13] and whatsoever is dishonorable to him;[14] and by his overruling providence, direct and dispose of all things to his own glory.[15]

Q. 191. What do we pray for in the second petition?   7.301

A. In the second petition (which is, "Thy Kingdom come"),[1] acknowledging ourselves and all mankind to be by nature under the dominion of sin and Satan,[2] we pray: that the kingdom of sin and Satan may be destroyed,[3] the gospel propagated throughout the world,[4] the Jews called,[5] the fullness of the Gentiles brought in;[6] that the church may be furnished with all gospel-officers and ordinances,[7] purged from corruption,[8] countenanced and maintained by the civil magistrate; that the ordinances of Christ may be purely dispensed, and made effectual to the converting of those that are yet in their sins, and the confirming, comforting, and building up of those that are already converted;[9] that Christ would rule in our hearts here,[10] and hasten the time of his second coming, and our reigning with him forever;[11] and that he would be pleased so to exercise the Kingdom of his power in all the world, as may best conduce to these ends.[12]

Q. 192. What do we pray for in the third petition?   7.302

A. In the third petition (which is, "Thy will be done on earth as it is in heaven"),[1] acknowledging that by nature we and all men are not only utterly unable and unwilling to know and do the will of God,[2] but prone to rebel against his Word,[3] to repine and murmur against his providence,[4] and wholly inclined to do the will of the flesh, and of the devil:[5] we pray that God would by his Spirit take away from ourselves and others all blindness,[6] weakness,[7] indisposedness,[8] and perverseness of heart,[9] and by his grace make us able and willing to know, do, and submit to his will in all things,[10] with the like humility,[11] cheerfulness,[12] faithfulness,[13] diligence,[14] zeal,[15] sincerity,[16] and constancy,[17] as the angels do in heaven.[18]

7.303   **Q. 193. What do we pray for in the fourth petition?**

A. In the fourth petition (which is, "Give us this day our daily bread"),[1] acknowledging that in Adam, and by our own sin, we have forfeited our right to all the outward blessings of this life, and deserve to be wholly deprived of them by God, and to have them cursed to us in the use of them;[2] and that neither they of themselves are able to sustain us,[3] nor we to merit,[4] or by our own industry to procure them,[5] but prone to desire,[6] get,[7] and use them unlawfully:[8] we pray for ourselves and others, that both they and we, waiting upon the providence of God from day to day in the use of lawful means may, of his free gift, and as to his fatherly wisdom shall seem best, enjoy a competent portion of them,[9] and have the same continued and blessed unto us in our holy and comfortable use of them,[10] and contentment in them;[11] and be kept from all things that are contrary to our temporal support and comfort.[12]

7.304   **Q. 194. What do we pray for in the fifth petition?**

A. In the fifth petition (which is, "Forgive us our debts, as we forgive our debtors"),[1] acknowledging that we and all others are guilty both of original and actual sin, and thereby become debtors to the justice of God, and neither we nor any other creature can make the least satisfaction for that debt:[2] we pray for ourselves and others, that God of his free grace would, through the obedience and satisfaction of Christ apprehended and applied by faith, acquit us both from the guilt and punishment of sin,[3] accept us in his Beloved,[4] continue his favor and grace to us,[5] pardon our daily failings,[6] and fill us with peace and joy, in giving us daily more and more assurance of forgiveness;[7] which we are the rather emboldened to ask, and encouraged to expect, when we have this testimony in ourselves, that we from the heart forgive others their offenses.[8]

7.305   **Q. 195. What do we pray for in the sixth petition?**

A. In the sixth petition (which is, "And lead us not into temptation, but deliver us from evil"),[1] acknowledging that the most wise, righteous, and gracious God, for divers holy and just ends, may so order things that we may be assaulted, foiled, and for a time led captive by temptations;[2] that Satan,[3] the world,[4] and the flesh, are ready powerfully to draw us aside and ensnare us;[5] and that we, even after the pardon of our sins, by reason of our corruption,[6] weakness, and want of watchfulness,[7] are not only subject to be tempted, and forward to expose ourselves unto temptations,[8] but also of ouselves unable and unwilling to resist them, to recover out of them, and to improve them;[9] and worthy to be left under the power of them;[10] we pray: that God would so overrule the world and all in it,[11] subdue the flesh,[12] and restrain Satan,[13] order all things,[14] bestow and bless all means of grace,[15] and quicken us to watchfulness in the use of them, that we and all his people may by his providence be kept from being tempted to sin;[16] or, if tempted, that by his Spirit we may be powerfully supported and enabled to stand in the hour of temptation;[17]

or, when fallen, raised again and recovered out of it,[18] and have a sanctified use and improvement thereof;[19] that our sanctification and salvation may be perfected,[20] Satan trodden under our feet,[21] and we fully freed from sin, temptation, and all evil forever.[22]

Q. 196. What doth the conclusion of the Lord's Prayer teach us?   7.306

A. The conclusion of the Lord's Prayer (whch is, "For thine is the Kingdom, and the power, and the glory, for ever. Amen,"),[1] teacheth us to enforce our petitions with arguments,[2] which are to be taken, not from any worthiness in ourselves, or in any other creature, but from God,[3] and with our prayers to join praises,[4] ascribing to God alone eternal sovereignty, omnipotency, and glorious excellency;[5] in regard whereof, as he is able and willing to help us,[6] so we by faith are emboldened to plead with him that he would,[7] and quietly to rely upon him that he will, fullfill our requests.[8] And to testify our desires and assurance, we say, "Amen."[9]

Q. 1.

General Note.—At several points the Larger Catechism is more specific in its statements than in Scriptures. These statements are inferences from the Scriptures, or from statements based on the Scriptures, or from the experience and observation of the church. In such cases no texts are cited; but reference is made to this general note.

1. Rom. 11:36; I Cor. 10:31.
2. Ps. 73:24–26; John 17:22, 24.

Q. 2.

1. Rom. 1:19, 20; Ps. 19:1–4.
2. I Cor. 1:21; I Cor. 2:9, 10.

Q. 3.

1. Gal. 1:8, 9; Isa. 8:20; Luke 16:29, 31; II Tim. 3:15–17.

Q. 4.

1. See General Note.
2. John 16:13, 14; I Cor. 2:6–9.

Q. 5.

1. See General Note.

Q. 6.

1. John 4:24; Exod. 34:6, 7.
2. Matt. 28:19; II Cor. 13:14.
3. Eph. 1:11. See the context.
4. Acts 4:27, 28; Isa. 42:9.

Q. 7.

1. John 4:24.
2. I Kings 8:27; Isa. 40:20.
3. See General Note.
4. Acts 17:24, 25.
5. Ps. 90:2.
6. Mal. 3:6; James 1:17.
7. Rom. 11:33.
8. Jer. 23:24; Ps. 139.
9. Rev. 4:8.
10. Heb. 4:13; Ps. 147:5.
11. Rom. 16:27.
12. Isa. 6:3; Rev. 15:4.
13. Deut. 32:4.
14. Exod. 34:6.

Q. 8.

1. Deut. 6:4; I Cor. 8:4, 6; Jer. 10:10.

Q. 9.

1. Matt. 3:16, 17; Matt. 28:19; II Cor. 13:14.

Q. 10.

1. Heb. 1:5.
2. John 1:14.
3. Gal. 4:6; John 15:26.

Q. 11.

1. Jer. 23:6; I John 5:20; Ps. 45:6; Acts 5:3, 4.
2. John 1:1; Isa. 9:6; John 2:24, 25; I Cor. 2:10, 11; Heb. 9:14.
3. Col. 1:16; Gen. 1:2; Ps. 104:30; John 1:3.
4. Matt. 28:19; II Cor. 13:14.

Q. 12.

1. Eph. 1:4, 11; Acts 4:27, 28; Ps. 33:11.

Q. 13.

1. I Tim. 5:21.
2. Eph. 1:4–6; II Thess. 2:13, 14; I Peter 1:2.
3. Rom. 9:17, 18, 21, 22; Jude 4; Matt. 11:25, 26; II Tim. 2:20.

Q. 14.

1. Eph. 1:11; I Peter 1:1, 2.

Q. 15.

1. Heb. 11:3; Rev. 4:11; Gen. 1.

Q. 16.

1. Ps. 104:4; Col. 1:16.
2. Luke 20:36.
3. Gen. 1:31.
4. Matt. 24:36.
5. II Thess. 1:7.
6. Ps. 103:20, 21.
7. II Peter 2:4.

Q. 17.

1. Gen. 1:27.
2. Gen. 2:7.
3. Gen. 2:22.
4. Gen. 2:7; Matt. 10:28; Luke 23:43.
5. Gen. 1:27.
6. Col. 3:10; Gen. 2:19, 20.
7. Eph. 4:24.
8. Rom. 2:14, 15.
9. Rom. 1:28.
10. Gen. 2:16, 17; Gen. 3:6.

Q. 18.

1. Ps. 145:17.
2. Ps. 104:24; Isa. 28:29.
3. Heb. 1:3.
4. Ps. 103:19; Job Chapters 38–41.
5. Matt. 10:29, 30; Gen. 45:7; Ps. 135:6.
6. Rom. 11:36; Isa. 63:14.

Q. 19.

1. Jude 6; II Peter 2:4.
2. Job 1:12; Luke 10:17; Matt. 8:31.
3. I Tim. 5:21; Mark 8:38; Heb. 12:22.
4. Ps. 104:4; Heb. 1:14.

Q. 20.
1. Gen. 2:8; Gen. 2:15, 16.
2. Gen. 1:28.
3. Gen. 2:18.
4. Gen. 1:27, 28.
5. Gen. 2:3.
6. Compare Gen. 2:16, 17, with Rom. 5:12–14; 10:5; Luke 10:25–28, and with the covenants made with Noah and Abraham.
7. Gen. 2:17.

Q. 21.
1. Gen. 3:6–8, 13; II Cor. 11:3.

Q. 22.
1. Acts 17:16. See under figure 6 above.
2. Gen. 2:17. Compare with Rom: 5:12–20, and with I Cor. 15:21, 22.

Q. 23.
1. Rom. 5:12; Gal. 3:10.

Q. 24.
1. Rom. 3:23; I John 3:4; James 4:17.

Q. 25.
1. Rom. 5:12, 19; I Cor. 15:22.
2. Rom. 5:6; Eph. 2:1–3; Rom. 8:7, 8; Gen. 6:5; Rom. 3:10–20; Ps. 51:5; 58:3.
3. James 1:14, 15; Matt. 15:19.

Q. 26.
1. Ps. 51:5; John 3:6.

Q. 27.
1. Gen. 3:8, 24.
2. Eph. 2:2, 3.
3. II Tim. 2:26; Luke 11:21, 22; Heb. 2:14.
4. Rom. 6:23; Rom. 5:14.

Q. 28.
1. Eph. 4:18.
2. Rom. 1:28.
3. II Thess. 2:11.
4. Rom. 2:5.
5. Isa. 33:14; Gen. 4:13; Matt. 27:4; Heb. 10:27.
6. Rom. 1:26.
7. Gen. 3:17.
8. Deut. 28:15–68.
9. Rom. 6:21, 23.

Q. 29.
1. II Thess. 1:9; Mark 9:43, 44; Luke 16:24, 26; Matt. 25:41, 46; Rev. 14:11; John 3:36.

Q. 30.
1. I Thess. 5:9.
2. Titus 3:4–7; Titus 1:2; Gal. 3:21; Rom. 3:20–22.

Q. 31.
1. I Cor. 15:22, 45; Eph. 1:4; II Tim. 1:9; Isa. 53:10, 11; Heb. 2:10, 11, 14.

Q. 32.
1. I Tim. 2:5.
2. I John 5:11, 12.
3. John 3:16; John 1:12; John 3:36.
4. John 1:12, 13; John 3:5, 6, 8; Gal. 5:22, 28.
5. Ezek. 36:27.
6. James 2:18, 22.
7. II Cor. 5:14, 15.
8. Eph. 2:10, Titus 2:24; 3:8.

Q. 33.
1. II Cor. 3:6; Heb. 1:1, 2; 8:7, 8 ff.

Q. 34.
1. Rom. 15:8; Acts 3:20.
2. Acts 3:20, 24.
3. Heb. 10:1.
4. Rom. 4:11.
5. I Cor. 5:7; Exod. 12:14, 17, 24.
6. Heb. 11:13.
7. Gal. 3:7–9; Heb. 11.

Q. 35.
1. Matt. 28:19, 20.
2. Matt. 28:19.
3. I Cor. 11:23–26.
4. Heb. 8:6, 7.

Q. 36.
1. I Tim. 2:5.
2. John 1:1; John 10:30; Phil. 2:6; Gal. 4:4; Col. 2:9; Phil. 2:5–11.

Q. 37.
1. John 1:14; Matt. 26:38.
2. Luke 1:31, 35, 42; Gal. 4:4.
3. Heb. 4:15.

Q. 38.
1. See General Note.

Q. 39.
1. Rom. 5:19; Gal. 4:4, 5.
2. Heb. 2:14; Heb. 7:24, 25.
3. Heb. 4:15.
4. Gal. 4:5.
5. Heb. 4:14–16.

Q. 40.
1. See General Note.

Q. 41.
1. Matt. 1:21.

Q. 42.
1. John 3:34; Luke 4:18–21.
2. Luke 4:14; Heb. 9:14; Matt. 28:18–20.

3. Acts 3:22; Luke 4:18, 21.
4. Heb. 5:5, 6; Heb. 4:14, 15.
5. Rev. 19:16; Isa. 9:6, 7; Ps. 2:6.

Q. 43.
1. John 1:1, 4.
2. II Peter 1:21; II Cor. 2:9, 10.
3. Eph. 4:11–13; John 20:31.

Q. 44.
1. Heb. 9:14, 28.
2. Heb. 2:17.
3. Heb. 7:25.

Q. 45.
1. John 10:16, 27; Isa. 55:5.
2. I Cor. 12:28; Eph. 4:11, 12.
3. Matt. 28:19, 20.
4. Matt. 18:17, 18; I Cor. 5:4, 5; I Tim. 5:20; Titus 3:10.
5. Acts 5:31.
6. Rev. 22:12; Matt. 25:34–36; Rom. 2:7.
7. Rev. 3:19; Heb. 12:6, 7.
8. II Cor. 12:9, 10; Rom. 8:35–39.
9. I Cor. 15:25; Acts 12:17; Acts 18:9, 10.
10. Rom. 14:11; Col. 1:18; Matt. 28:19, 20.
11. Rom. 8:28.
12. II Thess. 1:8; Ps. 2:9.

Q. 46.
1. Phil. 2:6–8; II Cor. 8:9; Gal. 4:4.

Q. 47.
1. John 1:18. See Citations under Q. 46 above.

Q. 48.
1. Gal. 4:4.
2. Matt. 3:15; John 19:30; Rom. 5:19.
3. Heb. 12:2, 3; Isa. 53:2, 3; Ps. 22:6.
4. Matt. 4:1. See verses 2:12; Luke 4:1–14.
5. Heb. 2:17, 18; Heb. 4:15; Isa. 52:13, 14.

Q. 49.
1. Matt. 27:4.
2. Matt. 26:56.
3. Luke 18:32, 33; Isa. 53:3.
4. Matt. 27:26; John 19:34; Luke 22:63, 64.
5. Luke 22:44; Matt. 27:46; Rom. 8:32.
6. Rom. 4:25; I Cor. 15:3, 4; Isa. 53:10.
7. Phil. 2:8; Heb. 12:2; Gal. 3:13.

Q. 50.
1. I Cor. 15:3, 4.
2. Matt. 12:40; Luke 18:33.

Q. 51.
1. I Cor. 15:4.
2. Luke 24:51; Acts 1:9–11.
3. Eph. 1:20.
4. Acts 1:11; Acts 17:31.

Q. 52.
1. Acts 2:24; Ps. 16:10.
2. Luke 24:39.
3. Rev. 1:18.
4. John 10:18.
5. Rom. 1:4.
6. Rom. 4:25; I Cor. 15:17.
7. Heb. 2:14; Rev. 1:18.
8. Rom. 14:9.
9. I Cor. 15:21, 22.
10. Eph. 1:22, 23; Col. 1:18.
11. Rom. 4:25.
12. Eph. 2:5, 6; Col. 2:12.
13. I Cor. 15:25, 26; Acts 12:17; Acts 1 10.
14. I Cor. 15:20; I Thess. 4:13–18.

Q. 53.
1. Acts 1:2, 3.
2. Matt. 28:19, 20; Acts 1:8.
3. Heb. 6:20; Eph. 4:8; Acts 1:9.
4. Ps. 68:18.
5. Col. 3:1, 2.
6. John 14:2.
7. Acts 3:21.

Q. 54.
1. Phil. 2:9.
2. Acts 2:28. Compare Ps. 16:11.
3. John 17:5.
4. Eph. 1:22; I Peter 3:22.
5. Eph. 4:11, 12. See citations under Q.
6. Rom. 8:34. See citations under Q.

Q. 55.
1. Heb. 9:24.
2. Heb. 1:3.
3. John 17:9, 20, 24.
4. Rom. 8:33, 34.
5. Rom. 5:1, 2.
6. Heb. 4:16.
7. Eph. 1:6.
8. I Peter 2:5; Rev. 8:3, 4.

Q. 56.
1. Matt. 24:30; Luke 9:26; I Thess. 4 Acts 17:31; Matt. 25:31.

Q. 57.
1. Heb. 9:12; I Cor. 1:30; Rom. 8:32 Cor. 1:20.

Q. 58.
1. John 1:12, 13; John 3:5, 6; Titus 6.

Q. 59.
1. John 6:37, 39; John 10:15, 16; I 8:29, 30.
2. I Peter 1:2; II Thess. 2:13.

288

Q. 60.

1. Rom. 10:14; II Thess. 1:8, 9; Acts 4:12; Rom. 1:18–32.
2. I Cor. 1:21; Rom. 1:18–32; Rom. 3:9–19.
3. John 4:22; Phil. 3:4–10.
4. Acts 4:12.
5. John 6:39, 44; John 17:9.

Q. 61.

1. Rom. 9:6; Matt. 7:21; Matt. 13:41, 42.

Q. 62.

1. I Cor. 1:2; I Cor. 12:12, 13; Rom. 15:1–12.
2. Gen. 17:7. (See the context.) Compare Gal. 3:7, 9, 14; Rom. 4; Acts 2:39; I Cor. 7:14; Mark 10:13–16.

Q. 63.

1. I Cor. 12:28; Eph. 4:11, 12; Acts 13:1, 2; Isa. 49:14–16.
2. Matt. 16:18; Isa. 31:4, 5; Ps. 115:9–18.
3. Acts 2:42; Rom. 3:1, 2.
4. Ps. 147:19, 20; Rom. 9:4; Acts 16:31; Rev. 22:17.
5. John 6:37.

Q. 64.

1. John 11:52; John 10:16; Eph. 1:10, 22, 23.

Q. 65.

1. John 17:21; Eph. 2:5, 6; I John 1:3; John 17:24.

Q. 66.

1. Eph. 2:8. (See context.)
2. I Cor. 6:17; John 10:28; Eph. 5:23, 30; John 15:1–5.
3. I Cor. 1:9; I Peter 5:10.

Q. 67.

1. Eph. 1:18–20; II Tim. 1:9.
2. Titus 3:4, 5; Rom. 9–11; Eph. 2:4–10.
3. II Cor. 5:20; John 6:44; II Thess. 2:13, 14.
4. Acts 26:18.
5. Ezek. 11:19; Ezek. 36:26, 27.
6. John 6:45; Phil. 2:13; Deut. 30:6; Eph. 2:5.

Q. 68.

1. Acts 13:48; John 6:39, 44; John 17:9.
2. Matt. 22:14.
3. Matt. 13:20, 21; Heb. 6:4–6.
4. Ps. 81:11, 12; John 12:38–40; Acts 28:25–27; John 6:64, 65; Prov. 1:24–32; Ps. 95:9–11.

Q. 69.

1. Rom. 8:30.
2. Eph. 1:5.
3. I Cor. 1:30.

Q. 70.

1. II Cor. 5:19, 21; Rom. 3:22, 24, 25; Rom. 4:5.
2. Eph. 1:6, 7; Rom. 3:28.
3. Rom. 3:24, 25; Rom. 5:17–19; Rom. 4:6–8.
4. Rom. 5:1; Acts 10:43; Gal. 2:16; Phil. 3:9; Rom. 3:25, 26.

Q. 71.

1. See citations under Question 70.

Q. 72.

1. Heb. 10:39.
2. Rom. 10:14, 17; II Thess. 2:13.
3. John 16:8, 9; Acts 16:30; Acts 2:37; Eph. 2:1; Acts 4:12; Rom. 7:9.
4. Rom. 10:8–10.
5. Acts 10:43; Gal. 2:15, 16; Acts 16:31.
6. Phil. 3:9; Acts 15:11.

Q. 73.

1. Gal. 3:11; Rom. 3:28.
2. Titus 3:5–7; Rom. 4:5–8.
3. Phil. 3:9.

Q. 74.

1. I John 3:1.
2. Eph. 1:5; Gal. 4:4, 5.
3. John 1:12.
4. Rev. 3:12; II Cor. 6:18.
5. Gal. 4:6.
6. Ps. 103:13; Prov. 14:26; Matt. 6:32.
7. Rom. 8:17; Heb. 6:12.

Q. 75.

1. Eph. 1:4; I Cor. 6:11; II Thess. 2:13.
2. Rom. 6:4–6; Eph. 4:23, 24; Phil. 3:10.
3. Acts 11:18; I John 3:9.
4. Jude 20; Eph. 3:16–18; Col. 1:10, 11. Rom. 6:4, 6, 14.

Q. 76.

1. II Tim. 2:25; Luke 24:47.
2. Acts 11:18, 20, 21; Zech. 12:10; Acts 2:37.
3. Ezek. 18:30, 32; Luke 15:17, 18; Hos. 2:6, 7.
4. Ezek. 36:31; Ezek. 16:61, 63; Isa. 30:22.
5. Luke 22:61, 62; Zech. 12:10.
6. II Cor. 7:11; Acts 2:37.
7. Acts 26:18; Ezek. 14:6; I Kings 8:47, 48; I Sam. 7:3.
8. Ps. 119:59, 128.

Q. 77.
1. I Cor. 6:11; I Cor. 1:30; Rom. 8:30.
2. Rom. 4:6, 8; Phil. 3:8, 9; II Cor. 5:21.
3. Ezek. 36: 27.
4. Rom. 3:24, 25.
5. Rom. 6:6, 14.
6. Rom. 8:1, 33, 34.
7. I Cor. 3:1, 2; Mark 4:8, 28.
8. I John 1:8, 10.
9. II Cor. 7:1; Phil. 3:12–14; Eph. 4.11–15.

Q. 78.
1. Rom. 7:18, 23.
2. Gal. 5:17; Heb. 12:1.
3. Exod. 28:38; Rom. 7:18, 23.

Q. 79.
1. Jer. 31:3; John 13:1.
2. I Cor. 1:8; Heb. 6:17; Heb. 13:20, 21; Isa. 54:10.
3. I Cor. 12:27. Compare with Rom. 8:35–39.
4. Heb. 7:25; Luke 22:32.
5. I John 3:9; I John 2:27.
6. Jer. 32:40; John 10:28; I Peter 1:5; Phil. 1:6.

Q. 80.
1. I John 2:3; I Cor. 2:12; I John 4:13, 16; I John 3:14, 18, 19, 21, 24; Rom. 8:16; I John 5:13.

Q. 81.
1. Isa. 50:10; Ps. 88.
2. Ps. 31:22; Ps. 77:1–12; Ps. 30:6, 7; Ps. 51:8, 12.
3. Job 13:15; Ps. 73:13–15, 23; I John 3:9; Isa 54:7–11.

Q. 82.
1. II Cor. 3:18.
2. Luke 23:43.
3. I John 3:2; I Thess. 4:17; Rev. 22:3–5.

Q. 83.
1. Eph. 2:4–6.
2. Rom. 5:5; II Cor. 1:22.
3. Rom. 5:1, 2; Rom. 14:17.
4. Gen. 4:13; Matt. 27:3–5; Heb. 10:27; Mark 9:44; Rom. 2:9.

Q. 84.
1. Rom. 6:23.
2. Heb. 9:27.
3. Rom. 5:12.

Q. 85.
1. Cor. 15:26, 55–57; Heb. 2:15.
2. Isa. 57:1, 2; II Kings 22:20.
3. Luke 16:25; II Cor. 5:1–8.
4. Luke 23:43; Phil. 1:23.

Q. 86.
1. Luke 16:23; Luke 23:43; Phil. 1:23; II Cor. 5:6–8.
2. Rom. 8:23; Ps. 16:9.
3. I Thess. 4:14.
4. Rom. 8:23.
5. Luke 16:23, 24; Acts 1:25; Jude 6.

Q. 87.
1. Acts 24:15.
2. I Cor. 15:51–53; I Thess. 4:15–17; John 5:28, 29.
3. I Cor. 15:21–23, 42–44 [It is evidently the scope of the apostle's argument in this passage, to prove, that as all the natural seed of Adam, their covenant–head, were subjected to death by his offence; so all the spiritual seed of Christ, their new covenant–head, shall be raised from death, to an immortal life of glory and blessedness, by virtue of his resurrection. It is therefore a perversion of the Scripture, to adduce this text as a proof of universal redemption.] Phil 3:21.
4. John 5:28, 29; Dan. 12:2; Matt. 25:33.

Q. 88.
1. II Peter 2:4; Rev. 20:11–13.
2. Matt. 24:36, 42, 44; Luke 21:35, 36.

Q. 89.
1. Matt. 25:33.
2. Rom. 2:15, 16. (See the context.)
3. Matt. 25:41, 42.
4. Matt. 25:46; II Thess. 1:8, 9; Luke 16:26; Mark 9:43, 44; Mark 14:21.

Q. 90.
1. I Thess. 4:17.
2, Matt. 25:33; Matt. 10:32.
3. I Cor. 6:2, 3.
4. Matt. 25:34, 46.
5. Eph. 5:27; Rev. 7:17.
6. Ps. 16:11, I Cor. 2:9.
7. Heb. 12:22, 23.
8. I John 3:2; I Cor. 13:12; I Thess. 4:17, 18; Rev. 22:3–5.

Q. 91.
1. Deut. 29:29; Micah 6:8; I Sam. 15:22.

Q. 92
1. Rom. 10:5; Rom. 2:14, 15; Gen. 2:17.

Q. 93.
1. James 2:10; Deut. 5:1, 31, 33; Luke 10:26, 27; I Thess. 5:23.
2. Rom. 10:5; Gal. 3:10.

Q. 94.

1. Rom. 8:3; Gal. 2:16.
2. I Tim. 1:8; Gal. 3:19, 24.

Q. 95.

1. Rom. 7:12.
2. Micah 6:8, Luke 10:26, 28, 37.
3. Ps. 19:11, 12; Rom. 3:20; Rom. 7:7.
4. Rom. 3:9, 23; Rom. 7:9, 13.
5. Gal. 3:21, 22.

Q. 96.

1. Rom. 7:9; I Tim. 1:9, 10.
2. Gal. 3:24.
3. Rom. 1:20. (Compare Rom. 2:15.)
4. Gal. 3:10.

Q. 97.

1. Rom. 7:4, 6; Rom. 6:14; Rom. 3:20; Rom. 8:1, 34; Gal. 3:13, 14; Rom. 8:3, 4; II Cor. 5:21.
2. Col. 1:12–14; Rom. 7:22; Titus 2:11–14.

Q. 98.

1. Matt. 19:17–19.
2. Deut. 10:4; Exod. 34:1–4.

Q. 99.

Rule 1.
1. Ps. 19:7; James 2:10; Matt. 5:22, 28, 37, 44.
Rule 2.
1. Rom. 7:14; Deut. 6:5; Matt. 22:37–39; Matt. 12:36, 37. See citations under Rule 1 above.
Rule 3.
1. Col. 3:5; I Tim. 6:10; Exod. 20:3–5; Amos 8:5.
Rule 4.
1. Isa. 58:13; Matt. 15:4–6; Deut. 6:12. Compare with Matt. 4:9, 10.
2. Eph. 4:18.
3. Exod. 20:12. Compare with Prov. 30:17.
4. Jer. 18:7, 8; Exod. 20:7. Compare with Ps. 15:1, 4, 5; Ps. 24:4, 5.
Rule 5
1. Rom. 3:8; Heb. 11:25.
2. Deut. 4:9.
3. Matt. 12:7; Mark 14:7.
Rule 6.
1. I Thess. 5:22; Gal. 5:26; Heb. 10:24; Col. 3:21.
Rule 7.
1. Exod. 20:10; Deut. 6:6, 7; Josh. 24:15.
Rule 8.
1. Heb. 10:24.
2. I Tim. 5:22; Eph. 5:11.

Q. 101.

1. Exod. 20:2.

Q. 102.

1. Luke 10:27.

Q. 103.

1. Exod. 20:3.

Q. 104.

1. The exposition of the Ten Commandments contained in the answers to Questions 104 to 148 are deduced from the Commandments themselves, and from the "Rules" set forth in Question 99. Texts under the specifications are given in order to show that the specifications are in accord with the general teaching of the Scriptures.
2. I Chron. 28:9; Deut. 26:17; Isa. 43:10; Jer. 14:22.
3. Ps. 95:6, 7; Matt. 4:10; Ps. 29:2.
4. Mal. 3:16.
5. Ps. 63:6.
6. Eccl. 12:1.
7. Ps. 18:1, 2.
8. Mal. 1:6.
9. Isa. 45:23; Ps. 96.
10. Josh. 24:22.
11. Deut. 6:5.
12. Ps. 73:25.
13. Isa. 8:13.
14. Exod. 14:31; Rom. 10:11; Acts 10:43.
15. Isa. 26:4; Ps. 40:4.
16. Ps. 130:7.
17. Ps. 37:4.
18. Ps. 32:11.
19. Rom. 12:11; Rev. 3:19; Num. 25:11.
20. Phil. 4:6.
21. Jer. 7:23; James 4:7; Rom. 12:1.
22. I John 3:22.
23. Neh. 13:8; Ps. 73:21; Ps. 119:136; Jer. 31:18, 19.
24. Micah 6:8.

Q. 105.

1. Ps. 14:1.
2. Jer. 2:27, 28. Compare I Thess. 1:9.
3. Ps. 81:11.
4. Isa. 43:22, 23.
5. Jer. 4:22; Hos. 4:1, 6.
6. Jer. 2:32; Ps. 50:22.
7. Acts 17:23, 29.
8. Ps. 50:21.
9. Deut. 29:29.
10. Titus 1:16; Heb. 12:16.
11. Rom. 1:30.
12. II Tim. 3:2.

13. Phil. 2:21.
14. I John 2:15; I Sam. 2:29; Col. 3:2, 5.
15. I John 4:1.
16. Heb. 3:12.
17. Gal. 5:20; Titus 3:10.
18. Acts 26:9.
19. Ps. 78:22.
20. Ezek. 37:11.
21. Jer. 5:3.
22. Rom. 2:5.
23. Jer. 13:15.
24. Ps. 19:13.
25. Zeph. 1:12.
26. Matt. 4:7.
27. Rom. 3:8.
28. Jer. 17:5.
29. II Tim. 3:4.
30. Gal. 4:17; Rom. 10:2; John 16:2; Luke 9:54, 55.
31. Rev. 3:16.
32. Rev. 3:1.
33. Ezek. 14:5; Isa. 1:4, 5.
34. Hos. 4:12; Rev. 19:10; Col. 2:18; Rom. 1:25.
35. Lev. 20:6; I Sam. 28:7–11. Compare I Chron. 10:13, 14.
36. Acts 5:3.
37. Matt. 23:9.
38. Deut. 32:15; Prov. 13:13; II Sam. 12:9.
39. Acts 7:51; Eph. 4:30.
40. Ps. 73:2, 3. See verses 13–15, 22.
41. Dan. 5:23.
42. Deut. 8:17; Dan. 4:30.
43. Hab. 1:16.

Q. 106.

1. Ps. 44:20, 21; Ezek. 8:15–18.
2. I Chron. 28:9.

Q. 107.

1. Exod. 20:4–6.

Q. 108.

1. Deut. 32:46; Matt. 28:20; I Tim. 6:13, 14; Acts 2:42.
2. Phil. 4:6; Eph. 5:20.
3. Deut. 17:18, 19; Acts 15:21; II Tim. 4:2; James 1:21; Acts 10:33.
4. Matt. 28:19; I Cor. 11:23–30.
5. Matt. 16:19; Matt. 18:17; I Cor. 5; I Cor. 12:28; John 20:23.
6. Eph. 4:11, 12; I Tim. 5:17, 18; I Cor. 9:1–15.
7. Joel 2:12; I Cor. 7:5.
8. Deut. 6:13.
9. Ps. 76:11; Isa. 19:21; Ps. 116:14, 18.
10. Acts 17:16, 17; Ps. 16:4.
11. Deut. 7:5; Isa. 30:22.

Q. 109.

1. Num. 15:39.
2. Deut. 13:6, 8.
3. Hos. 5:11; Micah 6:16.
4. I Kings 11:33; I Kings 12:33.
5. Deut. 12:30, 32.
6. Deut. 4:15, 16; Acts 17:29; Rom. 1:21–25.
7. Gal. 4:8; Dan. 3:18.
8. Exod. 32:5.
9. Exod. 32:8.
10. I Kings 18:26, 28; Isa. 65:11.
11. Acts 19:19.
12. Mal. 1:7, 8, 14.
13. Deut. 4:2.
14. Ps. 106:39.
15. Matt. 15:9.
16. I Peter 1:18.
17. Jer. 44:17.
18. Isa. 65:3–5; Gal. 1:13, 14.
19. I Sam. 13:12; I Sam. 15:21.
20. Acts 8:18.
21. Rom. 2:22; Mal. 3:8.
22. Exod. 4:24–26.
23. Matt. 22:25; Mal. 1:7, 12, 13.
24. Matt. 23:13.
25. Acts 13:45; I Thess. 2:15, 16.

Q. 110.

1. Exod. 20:5, 6.
2. Exod. 34:13, 14.
3. I Cor. 10:20–22; Deut. 32:16–19; J 7:18–20; Ezek. 16:26, 27.
4. Hos. 2:2–4.
5. Deut. 5:29.

Q. 111.

1. Exod. 20:7.

Q. 112.

1. Matt. 6:9; Deut. 28:58; Ps. 68:4; 29:2; Rev. 15:3, 4.
2. Mal. 1:14.
3. Ps. 138:2.
4. I Cor. 11:28, 29. See context.
5. I Tim. 2:8.
6. Jer. 4:2.
7. Ps. 76:11.
8. Acts 1:24, 26.
9. Ps. 107:21, 22.
10. Mal. 3:16.
11. Ps. 8.
12. Ps. 105:2, 5; Col. 3:17.
13. Ps. 102:18.
14. I Peter 3:15; Micah 4:5.
15. Phil. 1:27.
16. I Cor. 10:31.
17. Jer. 32:39.
18. I Peter 2:12.

113.

1. Mal. 2:2.
2. Acts 17:23.
3. Prov. 30:9.
4. Mal. 1:6, 7, 12; Mal. 3:14.
5. Jer. 7:4. See context. Col. 2:20 22.
6. Exod. 5:2; Ps. 139:20.
7. Ps. 50:16, 17.
8. Isa. 5:12.
9. II Kings 19:22; Lev. 24:11.
10. Zech. 5:4.
11. Rom. 12:14; I Sam. 17:43; II Sam. 16:5.
12. Jer. 5:7; Jer. 23:10.
13. Deut. 23:18; Acts 23:12.
14. Esth. 3:7; Esth. 9:24.
15. Ps. 24:4; Ezek. 17:19. See context.
16. Mark 6:26; I Sam. 25:22, 32–34.
17. Rom. 9:14, 19, 20.
18. Deut. 29:29.
19. Rom. 3:5, 7. See context.
20. Ps. 73:12, 13.
21. Matt. 5:21–48.
22. Ezek. 13:22.
23. II Peter 3:16; Matt. 22:29. See context, verses 23–32.
24. Eph. 5:4.
25. I Tim. 6:4, 5, 20; II Tim. 2:14; Titus 3:9.
26. Deut. 18:10, 11. See context. Acts 19:13.
27. II Tim. 4:3, 4; Jude 4; Rom 13:13, 14; I Kings 21:9, 10.
28. Acts 13:45.
29. II Peter 3:3; Ps. 1:1.
30. I Peter 4:4.
31. Acts 13:50. See verses 45, 46; Acts 4:18; Acts 19:9; I Thess. 2:16, Heb. 10:29.
32. II Tim. 3:5; Matt. 23:14; Matt. 6:1–3, 5, 16.
33. Mark 8:38.
34. Ps. 73:14, 15.
35. Eph. 5:15, 17; I Cor. 6:5, 6.
36. Isa. 5:4; II Peter 1:8, 9.
37. Rom. 2:23, 24.
38. Gal. 3:1, 3; Heb. 6:6.

114

1. Exod. 20:7.
2. Lev. 19:12.
3. Deut. 28:58, Zech. 5:2–4; Ezek. 36:21–23.
4. I Sam. 2:12, 17, 22.

115.

1. Exod. 20:8–11.

116.

1. Isa. 56:2, 4, 6, 7.
2. Gen. 2:3; Luke 23:56.
3. I Cor. 16:2; Acts 20:7; John 20:19–27.

Q. 117.

1. Exod. 20:8, 10.
2. Jer. 17:21, 22; Exod. 16:25–29; Neh. 13:15–22.
3. Matt. 12:1–14.
4. Lev. 23:3; Isa. 58:13; Luke 4:16; Acts 20:7.
5. Exod. 20:8; Luke 23:54, 56; Neh. 13:19.

Q. 118.

1. These statements are necessary inferences from the relations which exist between governors and the governed.

Q. 119.

1. Ezek. 22:26.
2. Ezek. 33:31, 32; Mal. 1:13; Amos 8.5.
3. Ezek. 23:38.
4. Jer. 17:27. See context. Isa. 58:13, 14.

Q. 120.

1. Exod. 20:9.
2. Exod. 20:10.
3. Exod. 20:11.

Q. 121.

1. Exod. 20:8.
2. Exod. 16:23; Luke 23:54. Compare Mark 15:42; Neh. 13:19.
3. Ezek. 20:12, 20.
4. Gen. 2:2, 3; Ps. 118:22, 24; Heb. 4.9.
5. Num. 15:37, 38, 40. See context.
6. Exod. 34:21.
7. See citation under figure 5 above.
8. Lam. 1:7; Neh. 13:15–23; Jer. 17:21–23.

Q. 122.

1. Matt. 22:39.
2. Matt. 7:12.

Q. 123

1. Exod. 20:12.

Q. 124.

1. I Tim. 5:1, 2.
2. Gen. 4:20, 21; Gen. 45:8.
3. II Kings 5:13.
4. Gal. 4:19; II Kings 2:12; II Kings 13:14.
5. Isa. 49:23.

Q. 125.

1. Eph. 6:4; I Thess. 2:7, 8, 11; Num. 11:11, 12, 16.
2. I Cor. 4:14–16.

Q. 126.

1. Eph. 5:21; I Peter 2:17; Rom. 12:10.

Q. 127.

1. Mal. 1:6; Lev. 19:3.
2. Prov. 31:28; I Peter 3:6.
3. Lev. 19:32; I Kings 2:19.
4. I Tim. 2:1, 2.
5. Heb. 13:7; Phil. 3:17.
6. Eph. 6:1, 5–7; I Peter 2:13, 14; Rom. 13:1–6; Heb. 13:17; Prov. 4:3, 4; Prov. 23:22.
7. Heb. 12:9; I Peter 2:18–20.
8. Titus 2:9, 10.
9. Matt. 22:21; Rom. 13:6, 7; I Tim. 5:17, 18; Gal. 6:6; Gen. 45:11; Gen. 47:12.
10. Gen. 9:23; I Peter 2:18; Prov. 23:22.
11. Ps. 127:3, 5; Prov. 31:23.

Q. 128.

1. Matt. 15:5, 6.
2. Ps. 106:16.
3. I Sam. 8:7; Isa. 3:5.
4. II Sam. 15:1–12.
5. Exod. 21:15.
6. I Sam. 10:27.
7. I Sam. 2:25.
8. Deut. 21:18, 20, 21.
9. Prov. 30:11, 17.
10. Prov. 19:26.

Q. 129.

1. Col. 3:19; Titus 2:4.
2. I Sam. 12:23; Job. 1:5.
3. I Kings 8:55, 56; Gen. 49:28.
4. Deut. 6:6, 7.
5. Eph. 6:4.
6. I Peter 3:7.
7. Rom. 13:3; I Peter 2:14.
8. Rom. 13:4.
9. Prov. 29:15; Rom 13:4.
10. I Tim. 5:8; Isa. 1:10, 17; Eph. 6:4.
11. I Tim. 4:12; Titus 2:2–14.
12. I Kings 3:28.
13. Titus 2:15.

Q. 130.

1. Ezek. 34:2, 4.
2. Phil. 2:21.
3. John 5:44, John 7:18.
4. Isa. 56:10, 11; Deut. 17:17.
5. Acts 4:18; Dan. 3:4–6.
6. Exod. 5:10–19; Matt. 23:2, 4.
7. Matt. 14:8. Compare with Mark 6:24.
8. Jer. 5:30, 32; II Sam. 13:28.
9. Jer. 6:13, 14; Ezek. 13:9, 10.
10. John 7:46–49; John 9:28.
11. I Peter 2:19, 20; Heb. 12:10; Deut. 25:3.
12. Lev. 19:29; Isa. 58:7; Gen. 38:11, 26.
13. Eph. 6:4.
14. Gen. 9:21; I Kings 12:13, 14; I Kings 1:6; I Sam. 3:13.

Q 131.

1. I Peter 2:17.
2. Rom. 12:10; Phil. 2:3.
3. Rom. 12:15, 16; Phil. 2:4.

Q. 132.

1. Rom. 13:8.
2. Prov. 14:21; Isa. 65:5; II Tim. 3.3.
3. Acts 7:9; Gal. 5:26.
4. I John 3:12; Matt. 20:15; Num. 12:2; Luke 15:28, 29.
5. Matt. 20:25–27; III John 9; Luke 2:24–26.

Q. 133.

1. Exod. 20:12.
2. Eph. 6:2, 3; Deut. 5:16; I Kings 8.2.

Q. 134.

1. Exod. 20:13.

Q. 135.

1. Eph. 5:29; Matt. 10:23.
2. Ps. 82:4; Deut. 22:8.
3. Matt. 5:22; Jer. 26:15, 16.
4. Eph. 4:26.
5. Prov. 22:24, 25; I Sam. 25:32, 33; Deu 22:8.
6. Prov. 1:10, 11, 15; Matt. 4:6, 7.
7. I Kings 21:9, 10, 19; Gen. 37:21, 22; Sam. 24:12 and 26:9–11.
8. Prov. 24:11, 12; I Sam. 14:45.
9. Luke 21:19; James 5:8; Heb. 12:5.
10. Ps. 37:8, 11; I Peter 3:3, 4.
11. Prov. 17:22; I Thess. 5:16.
12. Prov. 23:20; Prov. 25:16.
13. Prov. 23:29, 30; I Tim. 5:23.
14. Matt. 9:12; Isa. 38:21.
15. Ps. 127:2.
16. II Thess. 3:10, 12.
17. Mark 6:31; I Tim. 4:8.
18. I Cor. 13:4, 5; I Sam. 19:4, 5.
19. Rom. 13:10; Prov. 10:12.
20. Zech. 7:9; Luke 10:33, 34.
21. Col. 3:12.
22. Rom. 12:18.
23. I Peter 3:8, 9; I Cor. 4:12, 13.
24. Col. 3:13; James 3:17; I Peter 2:2(Rom. 12:20, 21; Matt. 5:24.
25. I Thess. 5:14; Matt. 25:35, 36; Prov 31:8, 9; Isa. 58:7.

Q. 136.

1. Acts 16:28; Prov. 1:18.
2. Gen. 9:6.
3. Exod. 21:14; Num. 35:31, 33.
4. Deut. 20:1; Heb. 11:32–34; Jer. 48:10.

5. Exod. 22:2.
6. Matt. 25:42, 43; James 2:15, 16.
7. Matt. 5:22.
8. I John 3:15; Prov. 10:12; Lev. 19:17.
9. Prov. 14:30.
10. Rom. 12:19.
11. James 4:1; Eph. 4:31.
12. Matt. 6:34.
13. Luke 21:34.
14. Exod. 20:9, 10.
15. I Peter 4:3, 4.
16. Prov. 15:1; Prov. 12:18.
17. Isa. 3:15; Exod. 1:14.
18. Gal. 5:15.
19. Num. 35:16.
20. Prov. 28:17; Exod. 21:18–36.

. 137.

1. Exod. 20:14.

. 138.

1. I Thess. 4:4, 5.
2. Eph. 4:29; Col. 4:6.
3. I Peter 3:2.
4. I Cor. 7:2; Titus 2:4, 5.
5. Matt. 5:28.
6. Prov. 23:31, 33; Jer. 5:7.
7. Prov. 2:16, 20; I Cor. 5:9.
8. I Tim. 2:9.
9. I Cor. 7:9.
10. Prov. 5:18, 19.
11. I Peter 3:7; I Cor. 7:5.
12. I Tim. 5:13, 14; Prov. 31:27.
13. Prov. 5:8.

139.

1. Prov. 5:7; Prov. 4:23, 27.
2. Heb. 13:4; Eph. 5:5; Gal. 5:19.
3. II Sam. 13:14; Mark 6:18; I Cor. 5:1, 13.
4. Rom. 1:26, 27; Lev. 20:15, 16.
5. Matt. 15:19; Col. 3:5; Matt. 5:28.
6. Eph. 5:3, 4; Prov. 7:5, 21; Prov. 19:27.
7. Isa. 3:16; II Peter 2:14.
8. Prov. 7:10, 13.
9. I Tim. 4:3.
10. Lev. 18:1–21.
11. II Kings 23:7; Lev. 19:29; Jer. 5:7.
12. Matt. 19:10–12.
13. I Tim. 5:14, 15; Gen. 38:26.
14. Matt. 19:5; I Cor. 7:2.
15. Matt. 5:32; Mal. 2:16.
16. See citations under Question 138. I Cor. 7:12, 13.
17. Ezek. 16:49; Jer. 5:7.
18. Eph. 5:11; Prov. 5:8.
19. Rom. 13:13; I Peter 4:3; Mark 6:22.
20. Rom. 13:14; II Peter 2:17, 18.

Q. 140.

1. Exod. 20:15.

Q. 141.

1. Ps. 15:2, 4; Micah 6:8; Zech. 8:16.
2. Rom. 13:7.
3. Lev. 6:4, 5; Luke 19:8.
4. Deut. 15:7, 8, 10; Gal. 6:10; Luke 6:30, 38.
5. I Tim. 6:8, 9.
6. I Tim. 5:8.
7. Prov. 27:23, 24; I Tim. 6:17, 18.
8. Eph. 4:28; Rom. 12:5–8.
9. Prov. 10:4; Rom 12:11.
10. Prov. 12:27; Prov. 21:20; John 6:12.
11. I Cor. 6:7.
12. Prov. 11:15; Prov. 6:1–5.
13. Lev. 25:35; Phil. 2:4; Deut. 22:1–4; Exod. 23:4, 5.

Q 142.

1. Prov. 23:21; I John 3:17; James 2:15, 16.
2. Eph. 4:28.
3. Ps. 62:10.
4. I Tim. 1:10; Exod. 21:16.
5. Prov. 29:24; Ps. 50:18.
6. I Thess. 4:6.
7. Prov. 11:1; Prov. 20:10.
8. Deut. 19:14; Prov. 23:10.
9. Amos 8:5; Ps. 37:21.
10. Luke 16:11.
11. Ezek. 22:29; Lev. 25:17.
12. Matt. 23:25; Ezek. 22:12.
13. Isa. 33:15.
14. Prov. 3:30; I Cor. 6:7.
15. Isa. 5:8; Micah 2:2.
16. Prov. 11:26.
17. Acts 19:19. See context.
18. James 5:4; Prov. 21:6.
19. Luke 12:15; Prov. 1:19.
20. I John 2:15, 16; Prov. 23:5; Ps. 62:10.
21. Matt. 6:25, 34.
22. Ps. 73:3; James 5:9.
23. II Thess. 3:11; Prov. 18:9.
24. Prov. 21:17; Prov. 23:20, 21; Prov. 28:19.
25. Deut. 12:7; Deut. 16:14.

Q. 143.

1. Exod. 20:16.

Q. 144.

1. Eph. 4:25.
2. III John 12.
3. Prov. 31:9.
4. Ps. 15:2.
5. Jer. 9:3.
6. Jer. 42:4; Acts 20:20.
7. Acts 20:27.

8. Lev. 19:15; Prov. 14:15.
9. Isa. 63:8; Col. 3:9; II Cor. 1:17.
10. Heb. 6:9; I Cor. 13:4, 5.
11. III John 4; Rom. 1:8.
12. II Cor. 12:21; Ps. 119:158.
13. Prov. 17:9; I Peter 4:8.
14. I Cor. 1:4, 5; II Tim. 1:4, 5.
15. Ps. 82:3.
16. I Cor. 13:4, 6, 7.
17. Ps. 15:3.
18. Prov. 25:23.
19. Prov. 26:24, 25.
20. Ps. 101:5.
21. II Cor. 11:18, 23; Prov. 22:1; John 8:49.
22. Ps. 15:4.
23. Phil. 4:8.

Q. 145.

1. Luke 3:14.
2. Lev. 19:15; Hab. 1:4.
3. Prov. 19:5; Prov. 6:16, 19.
4. Acts 6:13.
5. Jer. 9:3; Ps. 12:3, 4; Ps. 52:1–4.
6. Prov. 17:15.
7. Isa. 5:23.
8. I Kings 21:8.
9. Lev. 5:1; Acts 5:3.
10. Lev. 19:17; Isa. 58:1.
11. Isa. 59:4.
12. Prov. 29:11.
13. I Sam. 22:9, 10; Ps. 52:1.
14. Ps. 56:5; Matt. 26:60, 61. Compare John 2:19.
15. Gen. 3:5; Gen 26:7, 9.
16. Isa. 59:13.
17. Col. 3:9; Lev. 19:11.
18. Ps. 50:20.
19. Ps. 15:3; Rom. 1:30.
20. James 4:11; Titus 3:2.
21. Lev. 19:16.
22. Rom. 1:29; Prov. 16:28.
23. Isa. 28:22; Gen. 21:9; Gal. 4:29.
24. I Cor. 6:10.
25. Matt. 7:1.
26. James 2:13.
27. John 7:24; Rom 2:1.
28. Rom. 3:8; Ps. 69:10.
29. Ps. 12:2, 3.
30. II Tim. 3:2.
31. Luke 18:11; Gal. 5:26; Exod. 4:10, 14; Acts 12:22.
32. Isa. 29:20, 21; Matt. 7:3.
33. Gen. 3:12, 13; Prov. 28:13; Gen. 4:9.
34. Prov. 25:9; Gen. 9:22.
35. Exod. 23:1.
36. Jer. 20:10; Prov. 29:12.
37. Acts 7:57.

38. I Cor. 13:4, 5; I Tim. 6:4.
39. Matt. 21:15; Num. 11:29.
40. Dan. 6:3, 4; Ezra 4:12, 13.
41. Jer. 48:27.
42. Matt. 27:28, 29; Ps. 35:15, 16.
43. I Cor. 3:21; Jude 16; Acts 12:22.
44. Rom. 1:31; II Tim. 3:3.
45. II Sam. 12:14; I Sam. 2:24.
46. Phil. 3:18, 19; II Peter 2:2; II S
   12:13, 14.

Q. 146.
1. Exod. 20:17.

Q. 147.
1. Heb. 13:5; I Tim. 6:6.
2. Rom. 12:15; Phil. 2:4; I Tim. 1:5.

Q. 148.
1. I Cor. 10:10.
2. Gal. 5:26; James 3:14, 16.
3. Ps. 112:9, 10; Neh. 2:10.
4. Rom. 7:7; Deut. 5:21; Col. 3:5; R
   13:9.

Q. 149.
1. James 3:2; John 15:5.
2. I Kings 8:46; Ps. 17:15; I John 1:8–
3. Gen. 8:21; James 1:14; Gen. 6:5.
   citations under figure 2 above.
4. Ps. 19:12; James 3:2, 8.

Q. 150.
1. Heb. 2:2, 3; Ezra 9:14; Ps. 78:17,
   56.

Q. 151.
1. Jer. 2:8.
2. I Kings 11:9.
3. II Sam. 12:14; I Cor. 5:1.
4. James 4:17; Luke 12:47.
5. John 3:10; Jer. 5:4, 5; II Sam.
   12:7–9; Ezek. 8:11, 12.
6. Rom. 2:21, 23, 24.
7. Gal. 2:14; II Peter 2:2.
8. I John 5:10; Matt. 21:38, 39.
9. I Sam. 2:25; Acts 5:4.
10. Rom. 2:4.
11. Mal. 1:14; I Cor. 10:21, 22.
12. John 3:18, 36; Heb. 12:25
13. Heb. 6:4–6; Heb. 10:29; Matt. 12
    32; Eph. 4:30.
14. Num. 12:8; Jude 8.
15. Prov. 30:17; Ps. 41:9; Ps. 55:12–1
16. Zech. 2:8.
17. I Cor. 8:11, 12; Rom. 14:13, 15,
18. I Thess. 2:15, 16; Matt. 23:34–38
19. Isa. 3:9.
20. Ezek. 20:12, 13.
21. Col. 3:5; I Tim. 6:10.

22. Micah 2:1, 2.
23. Rom. 2:23, 24; Matt. 18:7.
24. Prov. 6:32–35; Matt. 16:26.
25. Matt. 11:21–24; John 15:22.
26. Deut. 32:6; Isa. 1:2, 3; Ezra 9:13, 14.
27. Jer. 5:3; Amos 4:8–11.
28. Rom. 1:20, 21.
29. Rom. 1:32; Dan. 5:22.
30. Prov. 29:1.
31. Matt. 18:17; Titus 3:10.
32. Rom. 13:1–5.
33. Ps. 78:34, 36, 37; Jer. 42:5, 6, 20–22; Prov. 20:25; Lev. 26:25; Jer. 31:32; Prov. 2:17; Ezek. 17:18.
34. Ps. 36:4; Jer. 6:16.
34. Num. 15:30; Jer. 6:15; Ps. 52:1.
36. Ezek. 35:5, 6; III John 10.
37. Num. 14:22.
38. Zech. 7:11, 12.
39. Prov. 2:14.
40. Jer. 9:3, 5; Isa. 57:17.
41. II Peter 2:20, 21; Heb. 6:4, 6.
42. Isa. 22:12–14; II Kings 5:26.
43. Jer. 7:10, 11.
44. Ezek. 23:38.
45. Isa. 58:3, 4.
46. I Cor. 11:20, 21; Jer. 7:9, 10.
47. Prov. 7:14, 15.
48. Neh. 9:13–16; II Chron. 36:15, 16.
49. Isa. 3:9; I Sam. 2:22–24.

152.
1. James 2:10, 11.
2. Mal. 1:14.
3. Deut. 32:6.
4. Hab. 1:13; I Peter 1:15, 16; Lev. 11:45.
5. I John 3:4; Rom. 7:12.
6. Gal. 3:10; Eph. 5:6.
7. Deut. 28:15; Prov. 13:21.
8. Matt. 25:41; Rom. 6:21, 23.
9. Heb. 9:22; I John 1:7; I Peter 1:18, 19.

153.
1. Acts 20:21; Mark 1:15; John 3:18.
2. See texts cited under Q. 154.

154.
1. Matt. 28:19, 20; Acts 2:42, 46; I Tim. 4:16; I Cor. 1:21; Eph. 5:19, 20; Eph. 6:17, 18.

155.
1. Jer. 23:28, 29; Heb. 4:12; Acts 17:11, 12; Acts 26:18.
2. Acts 2:37, 41; Acts 8:27–38.
3. II Cor. 3:18; Col. 1:27.
4. II Cor. 10:4, 5; Rom. 6:17.
5. Ps. 19:11; Col. 1:28; Eph. 6:16, 17; Matt. 4:7, 10.

6. Eph. 4:11, 12; Acts 20:32; II Tim. 3:15, 16; I Cor. 3:9–11.
7. Rom. 16:25; I Thess. 3:2, 13; Rom. 10:14–17.

Q. 156.
1. Deut. 17:18, 19; Isa. 34:16; John 5:39; Rev. 1:3.
2. Deut. 6:6, 7; Ps. 78:5, 6.
3. I Cor. 14:18, 19. See context.

Q. 157.
1. Ps. 119:97; Neh. 8:5; Isa. 66:2.
2. I Thess. 2:13; II Peter 1:16–21.
3. Ps. 119:18; Luke 24:44–48.
4. James 1:21, 22; I Peter 2:2; Mark 4:20.
5. Acts 17:11; Deut. 11:13.
6. Acts 8:30, 34; Matt. 13:23.
7. Ps. 1:2; Ps. 119:97.
8. Acts 2:38, 39; II Sam. 12:7; II Chron. 34:21.
9. Gal. 1:15, 16; Prov. 3:5.
10. Ps. 119:18; Luke 24:45.

Q. 58.
1. I Tim. 3:2, 6; II Tim. 2:2; Mal. 2:7.
2. Rom. 10:15; I Tim. 4:14.

Q. 159.
1. Titus 2:1, 8.
2. Acts 18:25; II Tim. 4:2.
3. I Cor. 14:9.
4. I Cor. 2:4.
5. Jer. 23:28; I Cor. 4:1, 2; Matt. 24:45–47.
6. Acts 20:27.
7. Col. 1:28; II Tim. 2:15.
8. I Cor. 3:2; Heb. 5:12–14; I Thess. 2:7; Luke 12:42.
9. Acts 18:25; II Tim. 4:5.
10. II Cor. 5:13, 14; Phil. 1:15–17.
11. II Cor. 12:15; I Thess. 3:12.
12. II Cor. 4:2; II Cor. 2:17.
13. John 7:18; I Thess. 2:4–6.
14. I Cor. 9:19–22.
15. II Cor. 12:19; Eph. 4:12.
16. I Tim. 4:16; II Tim. 2:10; Acts 26:16–18.

Q. 160.
1. Ps. 84:1, 2, 4; Ps. 27:4; Prov. 8:34.
2. Luke 8:18; I Peter 2:1, 2; James 1:21.
3. Ps. 119:18; Eph. 6:18, 19.
4. Acts 17:11.
5. Heb. 4:2.
6. II Thess. 2:10.
7. James 1:21; Ps. 25:9.
8. Acts 17:11; Acts 2:41.
9. I Thess. 2:13.
10. Heb. 2:1.
11. Deut. 6:6, 7.

12. Ps. 119:11; Prov. 2:1–5.
13. Luke 8:15; James 1:25.

Q. 161.
1. I Peter 3:21; Acts 8:13, 23; I Cor. 3:7; I Cor. 6:11.

Q. 162.
1. Matt. 28:19; Matt. 26:26, 27.
2. Rom. 4:11; I Cor. 11:24, 25.
3. Rom. 9:8; Gal. 3:27, 29; Gal. 5:6; Gal. 6:15.
4. Acts 2:38; I Cor. 10:16; Acts 22:16.
5. I Cor. 11:24–26.
6. Rom. 6:4; I Cor. 10:21.
7. I Cor. 12:13; I Cor. 10:17; Eph. 4:3–5.
8. I Cor. 10:21.

Q. 163.
1. See Confession of Faith, Chapter XXIX, Section 2, and passages there cited.

Q 164.
1. Matt. 28:19; Matt. 26:26, 27; I Cor. 11:23–26.

Q. 165.
1. Matt. 28:19.
2. Gal. 3:27; Rom. 6:3.
3. Acts 22:16; Mark 1:4; Rev. 1:5.
4. John 3:5; Titus 3:5.
5. Gal. 3:26, 27.
6. I Cor. 15:29.
7. Acts 2:41.
8. Rom. 6:4.

Q 166.
1. Acts 2:41.
2. Acts 2:38, 39; I Cor. 7:14; Luke 18:16; Rom. 11:16; Gen. 17:7–9, compare with Col. 2:11, 12; Gal. 3:17, 18, 29.

Q. 167.
1. Ps. 22:10, 11.
2. Rom. 6:3–5.
3. Rom. 6:2, 3; I Cor. 1:11–13.
4. I Peter 3:21; Rom. 4:11, 12.
5. Rom. 6:2–4.
6. Gal. 3:26, 27.
7. Rom. 6:22.
8. I Cor. 12:13, 25, 26. See context.

Q. 168.
1. I Cor. 11:26.
2. Matt. 26:26, 27; I Cor. 11:23–27.
3. I Cor. 10:16, 21.
4. I Cor. 10:17.

Q. 169.
1. See General Note.

Q. 170.
1. The specifications enumerated in answers to Questions 170–175 are deduced from the nature of the Lord's Supper as set forth in the New Testament. The texts are given to show that these specifications are in accord with the general tenor of the Scriptures. Acts 3:21.
2. Gal. 3:1; Heb. 11:1.
3. John 6:51, 53. See context.
4. I Cor. 10:16.

Q. 171.
1. I Cor. 11:28.
2. II Cor. 13:5.
3. I Cor. 5:7. Compare Exod. 12:15.
4. I Cor. 11:29.
5. II Cor. 13:5. See citation under figure above.
6. I Cor. 11:31.
7. I Cor. 10:17.
8. I Cor. 5:8; I Cor. 11:18, 20.
9. Matt. 5:23, 24.
10. John 7:37; Luke 1:53; Isa. 55:1.
11. I Cor. 5:8.
12. Heb. 10:21, 22, 24; Ps. 26:6.
13. I Cor. 11:24.
14. Matt. 26:26; II Chron. 30:18, 19.

Q 172.
1. Isa. 50:10.
2. Isa. 54:7, 8, 10; Matt. 5:3, 4; Ps. 31:22.
3. Ps. 42:11.
4. II Tim. 2:19; Rom. 7:24, 25.
5. Matt. 26:28; Matt. 11:28; Isa. 4:11, 29, 31.
6. Mark 9:24.
7. Acts 16:30; Acts 9:6.
8. I Cor. 11:28; Matt. 11:28.

Q. 173.
1. I Cor. 11:29; I Cor. 5:11; Matt. 7:6.
2. I Cor. 5:4, 5; II Cor. 2:5–8.

Q 174
1. Gal. 3:1.
2. I Cor. 11:29.
3. Luke 22:19.
4. I Cor. 11:31.
5. Zech. 12:10.
6. Ps. 63:1, 2.
7. Gal. 2:20; John 6:35.
8. John 1:16; Col. 1:19.
9. Phil. 3:9.
10. I Peter 1:8; I Chron. 30:21.
11. Ps. 22:26.
12. Jer. 50:5; Ps. 50:5.
13. I Cor. 10:17; Acts 2:42.

Q. 175.
1. I Cor. 11:17, 30, 31.
2. II Cor. 2:14; Acts 2:42, 46, 47.
3. I Cor. 10:12; Rom. 11:20.
4. Ps. 50:14.
5. I Cor. 11:25, 26; Ps. 27:4; Acts 2:42.
6. Ps. 77:6; Ps. 139:23, 24.
7. Ps. 123:1, 2; Isa. 8:17.
8. Hos. 14:2; Hos. 6:1, 2.
9. II Cor. 7:11; I Chron. 15:12–14.

Q. 176.
1. Matt. 28:19; I Cor. 11:23.
2. Rom. 6:3, 4; I Cor. 10:16.
3. Col. 2:11, 12. Compare with Rom. 4:11; Matt. 26:27, 28.
4. See General Note.
5. Matt. 28:20; I Cor. 11:26.

Q. 177.
1. Matt. 3:11; Gal. 3:27; Titus 3:5.
2. Acts 2:38, 39; I Cor. 7:14. See citations under Q. 166, figure 2.
3. I Cor. 11:26; Col. 2:19.
4. I Cor. 10:16; John 6:51–53.
5. I Cor. 11:28.

Q. 178.
1. Ps. 62:8.
2. John 16:23, 24.
3. Rom. 8:26.
4. Dan. 9:4; Ps. 32:5, 6.
5. Phil. 4:6.

Q. 179.
1. I Kings 8:39; Acts 1:24; Rom. 8.27.
2. Ps. 65:2.
3. Micah 7:18.
4. Ps. 145:16, 19.
5. II Sam. 22:32; John 14:1.
6. Matt. 4:10.
7. I Cor. 1:2.
8. Luke 4:8; Isa. 42:8; Jer. 3:23.

Q 180.
1. John 14:13, 14; Dan. 9:17.
2. Luke 6:46; Matt. 7:21.
3. Heb. 4:14–16; I John 5:13–15.

Q 181
1. John 14:6; Eph. 3:12; I Tim. 2:5; John 6:27; Col. 3:17; Heb. 7:25–27; 13:15.

Q. 182.
1. Rom. 8:26; Ps. 80:18; Ps. 10:17; Zech. 12:10.

Q 183.
1. Eph. 6:18; Ps. 28:9.
2. I Tim. 2:1, 2.
3. II Thess. 3:1; Col 4:3.
4. Gen. 32:11.

5. James 5:16; II Thess. 1:11.
6. Matt. 5:44.
7. I Tim. 2:1, 2. See under figure 2. above.
8. John 17:20; II Sam. 7:29.
9. This statement is based on the absence of any command to pray for the dead, and of any example in the Scriptures of such prayer.

Q. 184.
1. Matt. 6:9.
2. Ps. 51:18; Ps. 122:6.
3. Matt. 7:11.
4. Ps. 125:4; I Thess. 5:23; II Thess. 3:16.
5. I John 5:14; James 4:3.

Q. 185.
1. Ps. 33:8; Ps. 95:6.
2. Gen. 18:27; Ps. 144:3.
3. Ps. 86:1; Luke 15:17–19.
4. Ps. 130:3; Luke 18:13.
5. Ps. 51:17; Zech. 12:10–14.
6. Phil. 4:6; I Thess. 5:18.
7. Ps. 81:10; Eph. 3:20, 21.
8. I Cor. 14:15.
9. Heb. 10:22; James 1:6.
10. Heb. 10:22; Ps. 145:18; Ps. 17:1; John 4:24.
11. James 5:16.
12. I Tim. 2:8; Matt. 5:23, 24.
13. Eph. 6:18.
14. Micah 7:7.
15. Matt. 26:39.

Q. 186.
1. II Tim. 3:16, 17; I John 5:14.
2. Matt. 6:9–13; Luke 11:2–4.

Q. 187.
1. Matt. 6:9; Luke 11:2.

Q. 189.
1. Matt. 6:9.
2. Luke 11:13; Rom. 8:15.
3. Ps. 95:6, 7; Isa. 64:9.
4. Ps. 123:1; Lam. 3:41.
5. Ps. 104:1; Isa. 63:15; Ps. 113:4–6.
6. Acts 12:5; Zech. 8:21.

Q. 190
1. Matt. 6:9.
2. II Cor. 3:5; Ps. 51:15.
3. Ps. 67:2, 3; Ps. 72:19; Eph. 3:20, 21.
4. Ps. 83:18.
5. Ps. 145:6–8; Ps. 86:10–15.
6. II Thess. 3:1; Ps. 107:32; II Cor. 2:14.
7. Ps. 8 and 145, throughout.
8. Ps. 19:14.

9. Phil. 1:11.
10. Ps. 79:10; Ps. 67:1–4.
11. Eph. 1:17, 18.
12. Ps. 97:7.
13. Ps. 74:18, 22.
14. Jer. 14:21; II Kings 19:16.
15. Isa. 64:1, 2; II Chron. 20:6, 10–12.

Q. 191.
1. Matt. 6:10.
2. Eph. 2:2, 3.
3. Ps. 68:1; Rev. 12:9.
4. II Thess. 3:1.
5. Rom. 10:1; Ps. 67:2.
6. Rom. 11:25; Ps. 67:1–7.
7. Matt. 9:38.
8. Eph. 5:26, 27; Mal. 1:11.
9. II Cor. 4:2; Acts 26:18; II Thess. 2:16, 17.
10. Eph. 3:14, 17.
11. Rev. 22:20.
12. Isa. 64:1, 2; II Chron. 20:6, 10–12.

Q. 192.
1. Matt. 6:10.
2. I Cor. 2:14; Rom. 8:5, 8.
3. Rom. 8:7.
4. Matt. 20:11, 12; Ps. 73:3.
5. Titus 3:3; Eph. 2:2, 3. See Q. 191 under figure 2.
6. Eph. 1:17, 18.
7. Eph. 3:16.
8. Matt. 26:40, 41; Rom. 7:24, 25.
9. Ezek. 11:19; Jer. 31:18.
10. Ps. 119:35; Acts 21:14; I Sam. 3:18.
11. Ps. 123:2; Ps. 131:2; Micah 6:8.
12. Ps. 100:2.
13. Isa. 38:3; Eph. 6:6.
14. Ps. 119:4.
15. Rom. 12:11.
16. II Cor. 1:12.
17. Ps. 119:112; Rom. 2:7.
18. Ps. 103:20–22; Dan. 7:10.

Q. 193.
1. Matt. 6:11.
2. Gen. 3:17; Lam. 3:22; Deut. 28:15–68.
3. Deut. 8:3.
4. Gen. 32:10.
5. Deut. 8:18; Prov. 10:22.
6. Luke 12:15; Jer. 6:13.
7. Hos. 12:7.
8. James 4:3.
9. Gen. 28:20, 21; James 4:13, 15; Ps. 90:17; Ps. 144:12–15.

10. I Tim. 4:4, 5; Prov. 10:22.
11. I Tim. 6:6, 8.
12. Prov. 30:8, 9.

Q. 194.
1. Matt. 6:12.
2. Matt. 18:24; Rom. 5:19; Rom. 3:9, 19. See context. Ps. 130:3; Micah 6:6, 7.
3. Rom. 5:19; Rom. 3:24, 25; Acts 13:39.
4. Eph. 1:6.
5. II Peter 1:2.
6. Hos. 14:2; Ps. 143:2; Ps. 130:3.
7. Rom. 15:13; Rom. 5:1, 2; Ps. 51:7–12.
8. Luke 11:4; Matt. 18:35; Matt. 6.14, 15.

Q. 195.
1. Matt. 6:13.
2. II Chron. 32:31; Job 2:6.
3. I Peter 5:8; Job 2:2.
4. Luke 21:34; Mark 4:19.
5. James 1:14.
6. Gal. 5:17; Rom. 7:18.
7. Matt. 26:41.
8. I Tim. 6:9; Prov. 7:22.
9. Rom. 7:18, 19.
10. Ps. 81:11, 12.
11. John 17:15; Rom. 8:28.
12. Ps. 51:10; Ps. 119:133.
13. Heb. 2:18; I Cor. 10:13; II Cor. 12:8.
14. Rom. 8:28.
15. Heb. 13:20, 21; Eph. 4:11, 12.
16. Matt. 26:41; Ps. 19:13.
17. I Cor. 10:13; Eph. 3:14–16.
18. Ps. 51:12.
19. I Peter 5:10; I Peter 1:6, 7.
20. I Thess. 3:13.
21. Rom. 16:20.
22. I Thess. 5:23.

Q. 196.
1. Matt. 6:13.
2. Job. 23:3, 4; Jer. 14:20, 21.
3. Dan. 9:4, 7–9, 16, 19.
4. Phil. 4:6.
5. I Chron. 29:10–13.
6. Eph. 3:20, 21; Luke 11:13; Ps. 84:11.
7. Eph. 3:12; Heb. 10:19–22.
8. I John 5:14; Rom. 8:32.
9. I Cor. 14:16; Rev. 22:20, 21.

THE THEOLOGICAL
DECLARATION OF BARMEN

Introduction to the Theological Declaration of Barmen

In May of 1934, one hundred thirty-nine delegates representing eighteen Lutheran, Reformed, and United churches from throughout Germany met in the town of Barmen-Wurppertal to reiterate their common faith in the gospel of Jesus Christ. In so doing, they were contesting the imposition of Adolf Hitler's National Socialist agenda on the churches in Germany. To appreciate the significance of the Barmen Declaration, one must remember that to oppose the Nazis in 1934 was considered by many Germans to be at the very least unpatriotic and, at the worst, an act of treason. Thus, the Confessing Church's stand at Barmen, which by today's lights seems so prescient, so courageous, and so daring, was at the time by no means self-evident.

National Socialism's long ascent to power had been sealed on January 30, 1933, when Adolf Hitler was elected Reich Chancellor of Germany. Although early on, Hitler's Nazi party had feigned compatibility with Christianity, it became increasingly apparent that the movement was far more pagan than Christian in its basic orientation. As the power of the Nazis grew, so too did that of their ardent supporters in the churches, the so-called German Christians. While officially organized on June 6, 1932, the German Christians drew strength from earlier movements that, among other things, championed the need for racial purity, asserted the racial superiority of the German people or "folk" (*Volk*), and prosecuted a fierce opposition to Marxists, Jews, and others. These convictions drew support not only from the rank and file but also from many of the leading intellectuals in the German academy such as the theologians Friedrich Gogarten and Paul Althaus, the church historians Emanuel Hirsch and Reinhold Seeberg, and the philosopher Martin Heidegger.

Once Hitler's grip on power was assured, the Nazis began intervening coercively in church affairs. Among the most notorious laws that the Nazis enacted during these years was the so-called Aryan paragraph, which called for the exclusion from the church of all Christians with Jewish ancestry. This had the egregious effect of making race a direct criterion for church membership.

In response to all this, an opposition movement called for a free and confessing church. On October 20, 1932, Martin Niemöller organized the Pastors' Emergency League, a resistance effort that attracted thousands of church leaders. Niemöller was later to be held for seven years as Hitler's personal prisoner, first in solitary confinement in Sachsenhausen and later in Dachau. Not long after Niemöller's initiative, a group of pastors led by the Lutheran Hans Asmussen promulgated the Altona declaration, in part as a response to the events of July 17, 1932, known as Bloody Sunday, when, just months prior to Hitler's victory, the Nazis had moved into the streets of Altona in the name of law and order to ruthlessly quash opposition to National Socialism. The Altona declaration held that when secular authorities violate their mandate to seek the good of civil society, then Christians, in turn, must make a decision whether to cast their obedience to human authorities or to God. Other gestures of protest prior to Barmen included the Düsseldorf Theses issued by Reformed theologians (among them Karl Barth) in May of 1933; the Bethel Confession of August 1933 with an important paragraph drafted by Dietrich Bonhoeffer against the Aryan paragraph; and a Confession of Faith from the Synod of Bielfeld on June 29, 1933, just one day following the seizure of the headquarters of the German Evangelical Church by Nazi troopers.

It was in these explosive circumstances that the Confessing Church called for a free national synod of the German churches to be held at Barmen. With a synod of the Reformed churches already having been held in Barmen in January, the Confessing Church on May 2, 1934, appointed a theological committee to prepare for the national synod. It consisted of Hans Asmussen and Thomas Breit, for the Lutheran side, and Karl Barth for the Reformed. This committee met on May 15–16 in Frankfurt am Main two weeks before the Barmen synod was to open. It was in the afternoon of May 15 in Frankfurt that Barth, building on his previous work in the resistance movement and "fortified by strong coffee and one or two Brazilian cigars," drafted the lion's share of the declaration.

Although Barth was the declaration's chief author, he never spoke publicly at the synod when it convened on the evening of May 29. Instead he worked behind the scenes as part of a theological commission that included—in addition to himself and Hans Asmussen—Joachim Beckmann, Georg Merz, Wilhelm Niesel, Harmannus Obendiek, Eduard Putz, and Hermann Sasse. In the end, Sasse, a theologian from the faculty at Erlangen, would leave the synod in protest, offering what now seems the overly narrow objection that only a Lutheran synod was competent to speak with binding authority on Lutherans. To appease this concern, the declaration was approved on May 31 but with Hans Asmussen's opening lecture affixed as a fitting Lutheran interpretation of the text.

The Barmen Declaration, as adopted in the Presbyterian *Book of Confessions,* contains two parts. The first part, "An Appeal to the Evangelical Congregations and Christians in Germany," states the purpose of the declaration as uniting the church in obedience to the Word of God by the power of the Holy Spirit. The second part, "Theological Declaration Concerning the Present Situation of the German Evangelical Church," insists that the unity of the church stood imperiled by the alien principles being advanced by the so-called German Christians. The *Book of Confessions* does not include various legal and miscellaneous resolutions also enacted by the synod.

The nucleus of the declaration comes down to the six theses enumerated in Part II. Each lays forth one or more quotations of Scripture, underscoring that the church's confessions are always an explication and application of Scripture in a particular context. In addition, each of Barmen's six affirmations is accompanied by a corresponding denial using the phraseology "We reject the false doctrine. . . ." The "yes" of the gospel, in other words, always entails a necessary "no." That is, there are certain beliefs that stand outside the pale of Christian faith and conviction.

Everything in Barmen hangs on the first thesis, which states the one presupposition by which the Christian church must live or die. That presupposition, deceptive in its simplicity, is that Jesus Christ is the one source of the church's proclamation. In his very being and act, Jesus Christ is the Way, the Truth, and the Life, and hence the one Word to whom alone the church must listen, the one Word to whom alone the church owes obedience.

The first thesis is a classic restatement of some essential Reformation tenets. First, it renders explicit what has remained implicit in the church's confession from the outset, namely, that Jesus Christ himself is God's Word. This underscores the Reformation insistence on "Christ alone" (*solus Christus*). It is not merely a Christ principle or some abstract message about God's goodness that sent missionaries into the world and martyrs to their deaths; rather, it was and is the very personhood of Jesus Christ—true divinity and true humanity, the Word made flesh—that gives birth to the church's faith.

In so reiterating and intensifying the historic Reformation principle of "Christ alone" (*solus Christus*), Barmen also reaffirmed a second Reformation conviction, which is the competence of "scripture alone" (*sola scriptura*) to bear the essential and unparalleled witness to who Jesus Christ is. In this way, the church's confession of "Christ alone" and "scripture alone" sound forth two mutually implicating convictions. In order to know who Jesus Christ is, the church is tied to the texts of scripture; but at the same time the church is dependent upon the self-witness of the living, resurrected Christ in order to hear the biblical witness for what it is.

Third, it is by hearing this Word—and by trusting and obeying it—that the church may be saved. Here Barmen also underscores, at least by implication, two other red-letter Reformation principles: grace alone (*sola gratia*) and faith alone (*sola fide*). It is only through God's grace in Jesus Christ, which must be received by faith, that a true gospel obedience is born.

The confession of Jesus Christ as Lord in the first thesis led, in its turn, to the rejection of the false doctrine that there are "still other events and powers, figures and truths" that qualify as God's revelation other than the one Word, Jesus Christ. Barmen does not deny that Christians can, do, and indeed must listen to the many words spoken in their surrounding culture. What Barmen does deny, however, is that any of these other words can in themselves become the source of gospel proclamation.

Barmen's second thesis extends the crucial Reformation conviction about salvation into the realm of ethics. Jesus Christ is God's salvific "assurance of forgiveness" and, as such, God's "mighty claim upon our whole life." This means, in the first place, that Jesus Christ, who has been "made our wisdom, our righteousness and sanctification and redemption"

(1 Cor. 1:30), confronts us as both gospel and law. As gospel, he reconciles us; as law, he redeems us. It means, in the second place, that the powerful claim of God's law is comprehensive, leaving no sphere of life out of bounds. It thereby effectuates a superb freedom and a joyful deliverance from all forms of godlessness.

This interplay between law and gospel in the second thesis was understood differently by Lutheran and Reformed Christians at the synod. Lutherans have always emphasized the law more as an accusation that convicts one of sin, while the Reformed have stressed the law as a transformation that leads one to renewal. The text of Barmen does not resolve this debate, but it does clarify that the law of God is not to be confused with any of the imperatives that may arise from nature, biology, or politics. Instead, the true law of God must have the gospel of Jesus Christ as both its presupposition and its goal. Thus, the corresponding denunciation calls into question the false doctrine "as though there were areas of our life in which we would not belong to Jesus Christ."

Having articulated the centrality of Jesus Christ in theses one and two, theses three and four speak to the nature of the church and its ministry. According to the third thesis, the church is the community of sisters and brothers in which, by the Spirit's power, Jesus Christ acts as the living Lord in Word and sacrament. Barmen bases this view on Eph. 4:15–16, which speaks of the community as a body knit together and growing into maturity in Christ, who is the church's head. As such, the community is charged with bearing testimony to a sinful world. It is thus a false doctrine that asks the church to hand over either the form of its message or its polity to the prevailing ideological convictions of the day.

The mention of "Word and Sacrament" was a Lutheran addition, born of the traditional Reformation insistence that a true church exists where the Word is rightly preached and the sacraments rightly administered. This Lutheran addition prompted the Reformed theologians, in turn, to insist on a counterbalancing reference to the Holy Spirit. This was in keeping with the Reformed penchant for not considering the sacrament as an end in itself and with Barth's own tendency to subordinate the role of the sacraments to the dynamic work of the Spirit.

According to the fourth thesis, the ministry of the church belongs to the whole community, and therefore church officers "do not establish a dominion of some over the others." Instead, officers must be instructed by the great Matthean injunction that "whoever would be great among you must be your servant" (Matt. 20:25–26). Accordingly, it is a false doctrine to subject the church to a "special leader" (literally, a *"Führer")* who lords it over others.

The fifth thesis addresses the appropriate roles of church and state. Beginning with the bare directive from 1 Peter 2:17, "Fear God. Honor the emperor," Barmen acknowledges that in the sinfulness of a not-yet-redeemed world, the state's task is to maintain justice and peace, and to do this even if by means of force. It is not that the use of force defines the essential function of the state, but the state may from time to time be called on to use force to promote the cause of justice and peace. Thesis five expresses the church's desire to remain loyal to the state, but it also insists that the state's function is to remain true to a dynamic divine "ordering" and not to maintain a fixed and immutable "order" that is beyond question. In fulfilling this role, admittedly, the state's labor grants a benefit to the church. Yet it is still the church's office to call the state's attention to the larger and more encompassing matter of God's reign (Reich). The state is indeed to be "honored," as First Peter puts it, but God alone is to be "feared."

Two negations flow from this fifth thesis. First, Barmen rejects as false doctrine any ideology calling for the state to overstep its limits by exercising a totalitarian claim upon the whole of life. In so doing, the state would defy the God who upholds all things and whom alone the church must trust and obey. Second, it is false doctrine to reduce the church to an organ of the state. For this constitutes both a violation of the church's freedom and a transgression of its singular vocation to call the whole world to obedience to the reign of God.

The means of carrying out this unique vocation, according to the sixth thesis, is the proclamation of the free grace of God in sermon and sacrament. The free grace of God is both a consolation to a church under affliction ("Lo, I am with you always, to the close of the age," Matt. 28:20) and the guarantor of the church's freedom ("The word of God is not fettered," 2 Tim. 2:9). It is thus an arrogant and false doctrine to attempt to subject God's Word and God's work to "any arbitrarily chosen desires, purposes, and plans."

Certain aspects of the Barmen Declaration have proved controversial. Some, for example, have wondered about Barmen's utter rejection of so-called natural theology. Natural theology is a theology derived from a construal of nature rather than God's revelation in Jesus Christ. By no means can Barmen's repudiation of natural theology be understood as a rejection of created nature, as some have charged. The point is, rather, that nothing in the natural world possesses its own *intrinsic* capacity to comprehend or make reference to God. God can be known only through an act of God. But this does not preclude God using what Barth himself sometimes called "secular parables of truth," or true words of God uttered by non-Christian voices, to shed light on the truth of God's grace in Jesus Christ.

In addition, some felt that Barmen should have been more forthright in naming and condemning specific Nazi atrocities. Dietrich Bonhoeffer, although not a member of the Barmen Synod, felt the need for a much stronger statement about the Nazi persecution of the Jews. Barth himself considered it "a failing" that the Jewish question was not a "decisive feature" of Barmen, though he believed that "in 1934 no text in which I had done that would have been acceptable even to the Confessing Church. . . . But that does not excuse me for not having at least gone through the motions of fighting."[1] After the war Martin Niemöller and others in the Confessing Church movement believed they could have done more to resist Nazi evils, and so in October of 1945 they signed an admission called the Stuttgart Confession of Guilt embracing their collective responsibility for the sins of the war years. Whether one believes a more explicit stand against Nazi atrocities was needed during the years leading up to the war, it is still to the Confessing Church's credit that many, including Barth, paid the price of expulsion from teaching posts or from pastorates, and that some, not least Bonhoeffer, even lost their lives for espousing the theological convictions of Barmen.

Perhaps more than any other theological statement in our time, Barmen raises the issue of how the church is to discern when the gospel itself is at stake. By calling on the church to trust and obey Jesus Christ alone and not to follow Adolf Hitler, Barmen was implicitly declaring a condition of *status confessionis,* a dire situation in which enough is enough—in which a confession of faith has become unavoidable. Some years later, Barth extended the concept of status confessionis to embrace the nuclear threat, arguing in a 1958 declaration that the church's confession requires the unequivocal repudiation of weapons of mass destruction. More recently, a similar rationale was used by the World Alliance of Reformed Churches to declare apartheid in South Africa a matter of heresy and thus of status confessionis.

In short, Barmen's legacy has been to remind Christian believers that no human being or institution can usurp the place of the living God. Hence, whenever the integrity of either its doctrinal theology or its ethical and political witness is at stake, the church must take a stand. In the freedom of the gospel, the church must confess its faith in Jesus Christ, and do so against all odds and no matter what the cost.

QUESTIONS FOR STUDY

1. What does it mean for Jesus Christ to be the sole source of Christian proclamation—the one Word whom we must trust and obey in life and in death?

2. How does Jesus Christ's "assurance of forgiveness" place a "mighty claim upon our whole life"?

3. What is Barmen's view of the nature of the church, of church leadership, and of the church's mission?

4. How do you understand the relationship between church and world in the light of Barmen?

---

[1] Letter to Eberhard Bethge (1968), cited in Eberhard Busch, *Karl Barth: His Life from Letters and Autobiographical Texts,* trans. John Bowden (Philadelphia: Fortress Press, 1976), 247–48.

THE THEOLOGICAL DECLARATION OF BARMEN[1]

I. An Appeal to the Evangelical Congregations and Christians in Germany

The Confessional Synod of the German Evangelical Church met in Barmen, May 29-31, 1934. Here representatives from all the German Confessional Churches met with one accord in a confession of the one Lord of the one, holy, apostolic Church. In fidelity to their Confession of Faith, members of Lutheran, Reformed, and United Churches sought a common message for the need and temptation of the Church in our day. With gratitude to God they are convinced that they have been given a common word to utter. It was not their intention to found a new Church or to form a union. For nothing was farther from their minds than the abolition of the confessional status of our Churches. Their intention was, rather, to withstand in faith and unanimity the destruction of the Confession of Faith, and thus of the Evangelical Church in Germany. In opposition to attempts to establish the unity of the German Evangelical Church by means of false doctrine, by the use of force and insincere practices, the Confessional Synod insists that the unity of the Evangelical Churches in Germany can come only from the Word of God in faith through the Holy Spirit. Thus alone is the Church renewed.   **8.01**

Therefore the Confessional Synod calls upon the congregations to range themselves behind it in prayer, and steadfastly to gather around those pastors and teachers who are loyal to the Confessions.   **8.02**

Be not deceived by loose talk, as if we meant to oppose the unity of the German nation! Do not listen to the seducers who pervert our intentions, as if we wanted to break up the unity of the German Evangelical Church or to forsake the Confessions of the Fathers!   **8.03**

Try the spirits whether they are of God! Prove also the words of the Confessional Synod of the German Evangelical Church to see whether   **8.04**

---

[1] Reprinted from *The Church's Confessions Under Hitler* by Arthur C. Cochrane. Phila.: Westminster Press, 1962, pp. 237-242. Used by permission.

they agree with Holy Scripture and with the Confessions of the Fathers. If you find that we are speaking contrary to Scripture, then do not listen to us! But if you find that we are taking our stand upon Scripture, then let no fear or temptation keep you from treading with us the path of faith and obedience to the Word of God, in order that God's people be of one mind upon earth and that we in faith experience what he himself has said: "I will never leave you, nor forsake you." Therefore, "Fear not, little flock, for it is your Father's good pleasure to give you the kingdom."

II. Theological Declaration Concerning the Present Situation of the German Evangelical Church

8.05 According to the opening words of its constitution of July 11, 1933, the German Evangelical Church is a federation of Confessional Churches that grew out of the Reformation and that enjoy equal rights. The theological basis for the unification of these Churches is laid down in Article 1 and Article 2(1) of the constitution of the German Evangelical Church that was recognized by the Reich Government on July 14, 1933:

> Article 1. The inviolable foundation of the German Evangelical Church is the gospel of Jesus Christ as it is attested for us in Holy Scripture and brought to light again in the Confessions of the Reformation. The full powers that the Church needs for its mission are hereby determined and limited.
> Article 2(1). The German Evangelical Church is divided into member Churches (*Landeskirchen*).

8.06 We, the representatives of Lutheran, Reformed, and United Churches, of free synods, Church assemblies, and parish organizations united in the Confessional Synod of the German Evangelical Church, declare that we stand together on the ground of the German Evangelical Church as a federation of German Confessional Churches. We are bound together by the confession of the one Lord of the one, holy, catholic, and apostolic Church.

8.07 We publicly declare before all evangelical Churches in Germany that what they hold in common in this Confession is grievously imperiled, and with it the unity of the German Evangelical Church. It is threatened by the teaching methods and actions of the ruling Church party of the "German Christians" and of the Church administration carried on by them. These have become more and more apparent during the first year of the existence of the German Evangelical Church. This threat consists in the fact that the theological basis, in which the German Evangelical Church is united, has been continually and systematically thwarted and rendered ineffective by alien principles, on the part of the leaders and spokesmen of the "German Christians" as well as on the part of the Church administration. When these principles are held to be valid, then, according to all the Confessions in force among us, the Church ceases to be the Church and the German Evangelical Church, as a federation of Confessional Churches, becomes intrinsically impossible.

As members of Lutheran, Reformed, and United Churches, we may and must speak with one voice in this matter today. Precisely because we want to be and to remain faithful to our various Confessions, we may not keep silent, since we believe that we have been given a common message to utter in a time of common need and temptation. We commend to God what this may mean for the interrelations of the Confessional Churches. **8.08**

In view of the errors of the "German Christians" of the present Reich Church government which are devastating the Church and are also thereby breaking up the unity of the German Evangelical Church, we confess the following evangelical truths: **8.09**

1. "I am the way, and the truth, and the life; no one comes to the Father, but by me." (John 14:6). "Truly, truly, I say to you, he who does not enter the sheepfold by the door but climbs in by another way, that man is a thief and a robber. . . . I am the door; if anyone enters by me, he will be saved." (John 10:1, 9.) **8.10**

Jesus Christ, as he is attested for us in Holy Scripture, is the one Word of God which we have to hear and which we have to trust and obey in life and in death. **8.11**

We reject the false doctrine, as though the Church could and would have to acknowledge as a source of its proclamation, apart from and besides this one Word of God, still other events and powers, figures and truths, as God's revelation. **8.12**

2. "Christ Jesus, whom God made our wisdom, our righteousness and sanctification and redemption." (I Cor. 1:30.) **8.13**

As Jesus Christ is God's assurance of the forgiveness of all our sins, so in the same way and with the same seriousness is he also God's mighty claim upon our whole life. Through him befalls us a joyful deliverance from the godless fetters of this world for a free, grateful service to his creatures. **8.14**

We reject the false doctrine, as though there were areas of our life in which we would not belong to Jesus Christ, but to other lords—areas in which we would not need justification and sanctification through him. **8.15**

3. "Rather, speaking the truth in love, we are to grow up in every way into him who is the head, into Christ, from whom the whole body [is] joined and knit together." (Eph. 4:15–16.) **8.16**

The Christian Church is the congregation of the brethren in which Jesus Christ acts presently as the Lord in Word and Sacrament through the Holy Spirit. As the Church of pardoned sinners, it has to testify in the midst of a sinful world, with its faith as with its obedience, with its message as with its order, that it is solely his property, and that it lives and wants to live solely from his comfort and from his direction in the expectation of his appearance. **8.17**

We reject the false doctrine, as though the Church were permitted to abandon the form of its message and order to its own pleasure or to changes in prevailing ideological and political convictions. **8.18**

8.19   4. "You know that the rulers of the Gentiles lord it over them, and their great men exercise authority over them. It shall not be so among you; but whoever would be great among you must be your servant." (Matt. 20:25–26.)

8.20   The various offices in the Church do not establish a dominion of some over the others; on the contrary, they are for the exercise of the ministry entrusted to and enjoined upon the whole congregation.

8.21   We reject the false doctrine, as though the Church, apart from this ministry, could and were permitted to give to itself, or allow to be given to it, special leaders vested with ruling powers.

8.22   5. "Fear God. Honor the emperor." (I Peter 2:17.)

Scripture tells us that, in the as yet unredeemed world in which the Church also exists, the State has by divine appointment the task of providing for justice and peace. [It fulfills this task] by means of the threat and exercise of force, according to the measure of human judgment and human ability. The Church acknowledges the benefit of this divine appointment in gratitude and reverence before him. It calls to mind the Kingdom of God, God's commandment and righteousness, and thereby the responsibility both of rulers and of the ruled. It trusts and obeys the power of the Word by which God upholds all things.

8.23   We reject the false doctrine, as though the State, over and beyond its special commission, should and could become the single and totalitarian order of human life, thus fulfilling the Church's vocation as well.

8.24   We reject the false doctrine, as though the Church, over and beyond its special commission, should and could appropriate the characteristics, the tasks, and the dignity of the State, thus itself becoming an organ of the State.

8.25   6. "Lo, I am with you always, to the close of the age." (Matt. 28:20.) "The word of God is not fettered." (II Tim. 2:9.)

8.26   The Church's commission, upon which its freedom is founded, consists in delivering the message of the free grace of God to all people in Christ's stead, and therefore in the ministry of his own Word and work through sermon and Sacrament.

8.27   We reject the false doctrine, as though the Church in human arrogance could place the Word and work of the Lord in the service of any arbitrarily chosen desires, purposes, and plans.

8.28   The Confessional Synod of the German Evangelical Church declares that it sees in the acknowledgment of these truths and in the rejection of these errors the indispensable theological basis of the German Evangelical Church as a federation of Confessional Churches. It invites all who are able to accept its declaration to be mindful of these theological principles in their decisions in Church politics. It entreats all whom it concerns to return to the unity of faith, love, and hope.

THE CONFESSION OF 1967

Introduction to the Confession of 1967

For most of their history, American Presbyterians have looked to the Westminster Confession of Faith (and the Larger and Shorter Catechisms) to define themselves theologically. The writing of the Confession of 1967 (often called C67) broke with this past and challenged the church to think anew about the authority and role of confessions.

In adopting C67, the church did not eliminate the Westminster Standards but placed them within a *Book of Confessions* that included key creeds and confessions from the early centuries of the church, the Reformation, and the twentieth century. (The Larger Catechism, however, did not become part of the *Book of Confessions* until the reunion of the Northern and Southern churches in 1983.) Further, C67 clarified that "confessions and declarations are subordinate standards in the church, subject to the authority of Jesus Christ, the Word of God, as the Scriptures bear witness to him" (9.03).

The Confession of 1967 recovered key insights of the Protestant Reformation, drawing on the thought of Karl Barth, the great Swiss theologian of the twentieth century, who forcefully articulated their meaning for today. Faith was to be understood primarily as trust in Christ, to whom Scripture witnesses, not as mastery of a theological system. At the same time, C67 rightfully insisted that confessional standards aid and guide the church today in understanding the gospel (9.04). They are neither irrelevant nor dispensable.

The committee that prepared C67 also proposed new ordination questions. Up to this time, candidates for ordained office had promised to "sincerely receive and adopt the confession of faith of this church [that is, Westminster] as containing the system of doctrine taught in the holy Scriptures." The new vows, reflecting C67, asked persons to exercise their office in "obedience to Jesus Christ, under the authority of Scripture, and continually guided by our Confessions."

IMPULSES FOR CONFESSIONAL CHANGE

The decision to augment Westminster was a century in the making. By the end of the nineteenth century, Presbyterians were openly debating Westminster's adequacy. In Westminster, Scripture seemed to be viewed as a collection of divinely revealed, timeless truths. Changing understandings of truth and authority in the wider intellectual world challenged this position. Biblical scholars—and increasingly pastors and lay people—were learning to read Scripture as a historical document that reflected the particular circumstances, and ways of thinking, of ancient cultures.

Other impulses for change came from the great missionary movement of the late nineteenth and early twentieth centuries. Whereas Westminster declared that God had "appointed the elect unto glory . . . [and]

the rest of mankind . . . to dishonour and wrath for their sin" (6.019–.020), the church now emphasized that God's love was available to all. In response to such concerns, the Northern church finally amended Westminster in 1903, though it largely reaffirmed the confession's basic theology.

In the 1950s, the question of the adequacy of Westminster came to a head again. With the union of the United Presbyterian Church of North America and the Presbyterian Church in the U.S.A. in 1958 to become the United Presbyterian Church in the U.S.A., the General Assembly appointed a Special Committee on a Brief Contemporary Statement of Faith, headed by Professor Edward Dowey of Princeton Theological Seminary.

The committee argued that Westminster should not be abandoned, but that more than a revision was needed. In 1965, it offered the church a draft of a new confession, solicited response, and made revisions. A year later, a Special Committee of Fifteen proposed minor changes, and the General Assembly sent the revised confession to the presbyteries for their consideration. The confession found widespread interest among pastors and in congregations. The committee received more than 140,000 requests for study materials, and major national publications such as the *New York Times* and *Time* magazine reported on the church's debate. In the end, more than 90 percent of the presbyteries voted their approval.

STRUCTURE AND KEY THEMES

The fact that the confession carries no title other than the year of its adoption was not the result of careless editing or lack of creativity. C67 was understood to be a confession for its time, not necessarily for all time. (Even the term "C67" is reminiscent of the acronyms that began to flourish in the 1960s.) As C67 notes, the church is called to confess its faith in every age, not only in word but also in deed. Confessions will differ not only in content but also in form, as "the need of the time requires" (9.02).

While C67 builds on the traditional theological teachings of the Christian faith, it does not attempt to speak to them all. Rather, it focuses on the theme of reconciliation, both because reconciliation is always at the heart of the gospel, and because "our generation stands in peculiar need of reconciliation in Christ" (9.06).

The choice of the word "reconciliation" is noteworthy (and again suggests the influence of Barth, who had devoted the fourth and final part of his *Church Dogmatics* to "the doctrine of reconciliation"). Key to the Reformation was the insight that God is a God of grace alone, who promises to forgive us our sin. C67 suggests that the term "reconciliation" may best state for people in the second half of the twentieth century the full meaning of God's forgiveness. Forgiveness is not just a matter of words; rather, it opens us to a new way of life. Forgiveness is not just a legal transaction between God and individuals; rather, it restores community between them, as well as among individuals and groups that have been alienated from one another.

These basic understandings are summarized in the preamble to C67, which cites Paul's words in the Second Letter to the Corinthians (5:19) that "in Jesus Christ God was reconciling the world to himself." Through the Holy Spirit, God continues this work of reconciliation in the church, and the church in response "calls men to be reconciled to God and to one another" (9.07).

The structure of C67 also reflects these understandings of the meaning and work of reconciliation. In keeping with the emphases of the Reformation and that particular strand of it known as the Reformed tradition (descended from the reformer John Calvin), C67 begins with God and God's work of reconciliation (Part I), rather than with an explication of human needs and insights. The church's ministry of reconciliation (Part II) is not a good work that springs from ourselves, but is a joyful response to God's gracious activity in Jesus Christ.

Just as the church lives out of what God has already done in Christ and what God continues to do in Christ through the Holy Spirit, it also lives in anticipation of God's final triumph. Thus, C67 moves from God (Part I) to church and world (Part II) to the hope of God's coming kingdom (Part III). It moves from what we believe (theology) to what we are called to do (ethics) to a vision of the new order that is already dawning and that God promises to bring to fulfillment (eschatology).

The structure of each part is also significant theologically. Drawing on the trinitarian benediction that concludes Second Corinthians (13:14), Part I is divided into three sections: "The Grace of Our Lord Jesus Christ," "The Love of God," and "The Communion of the Holy Spirit." While this ordering of the persons of the Trinity differs from that of the early confessions (Father, Son, and Holy Spirit), it reminds us that we come to know God most clearly and completely through God's revelation in Jesus Christ. Only as we understand God's will to redeem us in Jesus Christ can we also understand God's purposes as the Lord and Creator who has "made all things to serve the purpose of his love" (9.15) and who "creates and renews the church as the community in which men are reconciled to God and to one another" (9.20). This ordering—Christ, God, Holy Spirit (note that the Brief Statement of Faith uses a similar order)—parallels that of the entire confession: God's grace again stands at the beginning; God's desire to be in relationship with us and to offer us blessing is the appropriate starting point for all reflection on Christian faith and life.

The threefold division of Part I is significant in another respect as well. It lifts up the work of the Holy Spirit. The confessions of the early church focus on the person and work of Jesus Christ. The confessions of the

317

Reformation expand on the work of God the Creator, and the life of the church. C67, by contrast, gives significant attention to all three persons of the Trinity and makes clear that life in community is the gift and work of the Holy Spirit.

The structure of Part II lifts up key points about the character of this community. Reformed confessions had traditionally identified key "marks" of the true church: the pure preaching of the gospel, the right administration of the sacraments, and (sometimes) church discipline. C67, by contrast, first speaks (Part II, Section A) of the mission of the church. Only then does it discuss preaching, prayer, and sacraments (Part II, Section B). What makes the church "the church" is above all its message to the world.

This way of ordering the confession suggests that the church's worship is not exhausted in human words to God. Rather, worship undergirds the church's witness to the world. Worship provides "means of fulfilling [the church's] service of God among men" (9.48). Worship feeds into the life of ethical responsibility (see also 9.36–.37).

THE CHURCH: THEN AND NOW

This understanding of the church reflects particular features of the time. C67 was addressed to a church that had sufficient social standing and self-confidence to believe that it could influence society and its leaders. In an era of public protest (including marches, sit-ins, and acts of civil disobedience), C67 called on the church to risk its forms and structures in order to witness to God's work of reconciliation in society (9.40). It spoke concretely to the need for reconciliation between races ("the abolition of all racial discrimination" [9.44]), between nations ("even at risk to national security" [9.45]), between economic classes ("enslaving poverty in a world of abundance is an intolerable violation of God's good creation" [9.46]), and in sexual relations ("to lead men and women into the full meaning of life together" [9.47]).

Since 1967, the social influence of the mainline churches has come to seem less impressive. From one direction, declining numbers and budgets have focused these churches on questions of institutional survival. From another, profound shifts in American society have challenged values long associated with the Christian tradition. Presbyterians find themselves thinking anew about the church's relationship to culture and the dangers of accommodating the gospel to foreign values.

We are also aware of just how much C67 reflects the limits—and cultural values—of its time. A contemporary reader is apt to be struck in particular by C67's failure to grapple with the changing status of women in society. The composition of the committee itself was all male, and the confession unrelentingly uses masculine pronouns such as "man" and "men" to refer to humans in general.

Even so, C67 may have a helpful word for the church in our time. The church is perennially tempted to withdraw from the world. In a time of disorienting cultural change, this temptation may become overwhelming. C67 reminds us that we dare not focus on the church's inner life, whether spiritual or organizational, to the detriment of the church's mission to the world.

SCRIPTURE

In finding orientation for its life in times of change and cultural confusion, the church throughout the ages has turned to Scripture. Against the Roman claims for the authority of the church, Westminster (like the Second Helvetic Confession) opens with declarations about the authority of Scripture. In response to the Nazi threat, the Barmen Declaration cites Scripture prior to each of its propositions.

The understanding of Scripture in C67 is no less significant. The discussion of Scripture comes not at the beginning of the confession, but in the context of "The Communion of the Holy Spirit." Here, again, C67 recovers Reformation insights. First, we can read Scripture rightly only as the Spirit guides and illumines us. Through the Spirit, our bond to Christ, Scripture becomes the "unique and authoritative witness" to Jesus Christ (9.27). Second, Scripture is the church's book. The Spirit that binds us to Christ also binds us to one another as members of the body of Christ. God speaks in Scripture above all to a community that has been called into new life and is ready "to receive [Scripture's] truth and direction" (9.30).

Influenced by Barth's theology, C67 distinguishes the Word of God, God's revelation in Jesus Christ, from the word of God (that is, the words of Scripture). As C67 notes, the Scriptures, "given under guidance of the Holy Spirit, are nevertheless the words of men, conditioned by . . . the places and times at which they were written" (9.29). C67 calls on the church to pay attention to scholarship that examines the historical and literary context of Scripture.

Since 1967, issues of biblical authority and interpretation have continued to receive attention. We have greater awareness of the significance of social location (race, ethnicity, class, gender, and other social factors) in shaping a person's (or community's) reading of Scripture. The growing pluralism of North American society has also made us more aware of other religions and their claim to have authoritative Scriptures.

C67 also speaks to questions of biblical authority and interpretation in its actual use of Scripture. C67 relies less on propositional statements from Scripture than on key biblical images that redirect our imagination. These images challenge us to look beyond the constraints and unspoken assumptions of our time and place to the new thing that God has already done—and continues to do—in Jesus Christ and the church. Jesus' life, ministry, death, and resurrection send us in the "direction" of new life

319

(9.24). They set a "pattern" for the church's mission (9.32). C67 suggests that the authority of Scripture finally rests not on abstract declarations, but on Scripture's continuing capacity to invite the church into life in Christ.

CONCLUDING REFLECTIONS

Issues of reconciliation remain more urgent than ever. Recent decades have seen ethnic warfare in Bosnia and Rwanda, race riots in south-central Los Angeles, and bitter conflict in the church over such matters as human sexuality. C67 challenges the church to examine itself continually, reform its structures where necessary, and speak God's good news in Jesus Christ in light of a careful reading of the larger social context.

In an age where the theological foundations of the church sometimes seem shaky, C67 demonstrates how even one theological theme, reconciliation, can speak powerfully to specific social needs and ills. At its best, C67 invites us to look for God's active presence in the world, and to respond to God's coming kingdom through concrete acts of love and justice.

QUESTIONS FOR STUDY

1. How does the church benefit from having a *Book of Confessions,* rather than just one confession of faith? What are the potential problems?

2. As you think about the needs and opportunities of the church today, which of the marks of the church would you lift up: mission, preaching, sacraments, church discipline, or something else?

3. Which parts of C67 now seem outdated? Which seem to speak with more urgency than ever? If the church were to revise it for the present, what would it need to add or delete?

THE CONFESSION OF 1967

PREFACE

The church confesses its faith when it bears a present witness to God's grace in Jesus Christ. **9.01**

In every age, the church has expressed its witness in words and deeds as the need of the time required. The earliest examples of confession are found within the Scriptures. Confessional statements have taken such varied forms as hymns, liturgical formulas, doctrinal definitions, catechisms, theological systems in summary, and declarations of purpose against threatening evil. **9.02**

Confessions and declarations are subordinate standards in the church, subject to the authority of Jesus Christ, the Word of God, as the Scriptures bear witness to him. No one type of confession is exclusively valid, no one statement is irreformable. Obedience to Jesus Christ alone identifies the one universal church and supplies the continuity of its tradition. This obedience is the ground of the church's duty and freedom to reform itself in life and doctrine as new occasions, in God's providence, may demand. **9.03**

The United Presbyterian Church in the United States of America acknowledges itself aided in understanding the gospel by the testimony of the church from earlier ages and from many lands. More especially it is guided by the Nicene and Apostles' Creeds from the time of the early church; the Scots Confession, the Heidelberg Catechism, and the Second Helvetic Confession from the era of the Reformation; the Westminster Confession and Shorter Catechism from the seventeenth century; and the Theological Declaration of Barmen from the twentieth century. **9.04**

The purpose of the Confession of 1967 is to call the church to that unity in confession and mission which is required of disciples today. This Confession is not a "system of doctrine," nor does it include all the traditional topics of theology. For example, the Trinity and the Person of Christ are not redefined, but are recognized and reaffirmed as forming the basis and determining the structure of the Christian faith. **9.05**

321

9.06   God's reconciling work in Jesus Christ and the mission of reconciliation to which he has called his church are the heart of the gospel in any age. Our generation stands in peculiar need of reconciliation in Christ. Accordingly, this Confession of 1967 is built upon that theme.

THE CONFESSION

9.07   In Jesus Christ, God was reconciling the world to himself. Jesus Christ is God with man. He is the eternal Son of the Father, who became man and lived among us to fulfill the work of reconciliation. He is present in the church by the power of the Holy Spirit to continue and complete his mission. This work of God, the Father, Son, and Holy Spirit, is the foundation of all confessional statements about God, man, and the world. Therefore, the church calls men to be reconciled to God and to one another.

PART I

GOD'S WORK OF RECONCILIATION

Section A. The Grace of Our Lord Jesus Christ

1. JESUS CHRIST

9.08   In Jesus of Nazareth, true humanity was realized once for all. Jesus, a Palestinian Jew, lived among his own people and shared their needs, temptations, joys, and sorrows. He expressed the love of God in word and deed and became a brother to all kinds of sinful men. But his complete obedience led him into conflict with his people. His life and teaching judged their goodness, religious aspirations, and national hopes. Many rejected him and demanded his death. In giving himself freely for them, he took upon himself the judgment under which all men stand convicted. God raised him from the dead, vindicating him as Messiah and Lord. The victim of sin became victor, and won the victory over sin and death for all men.

9.09   God's reconciling act in Jesus Christ is a mystery which the Scriptures describe in various ways. It is called the sacrifice of a lamb, a shepherd's life given for his sheep, atonement by a priest; again it is ransom of a slave, payment of debt, vicarious satisfaction of a legal penalty, and victory over the powers of evil. These are expressions of a truth which remains beyond the reach of all theory in the depths of God's love for man. They reveal the gravity, cost, and sure achievement of God's reconciling work.

9.10   The risen Christ is the Savior for all men. Those joined to him by faith are set right with God and commissioned to serve as his reconciling community. Christ is head of this community, the church, which began with the apostles and continues through all generations.

9.11   The same Jesus Christ is the judge of all men. His judgment discloses the ultimate seriousness of life and gives promise of God's final victory over the power of sin and death. To receive life from the risen Lord is to have life eternal; to refuse life from him is to choose the death which is separation from God. All who put their trust in Christ face divine judgment without fear, for the judge is their redeemer.

2. THE SIN OF MAN

The reconciling act of God in Jesus Christ exposes the evil in men as sin in the sight of God. In sin, men claim mastery of their own lives, turn against God and their fellow men, and become exploiters and despoilers of the world. They lose their humanity in futile striving and are left in rebellion, despair, and isolation. **9.12**

Wise and virtuous men through the ages have sought the highest good in devotion to freedom, justice, peace, truth, and beauty. Yet all human virtue, when seen in the light of God's love in Jesus Christ, is found to be infected by self-interest and hostility. All men, good and bad alike, are in the wrong before God and helpless without his forgiveness. Thus all men fall under God's judgment. No one is more subject to that judgment than the man who assumes that he is guiltless before God or morally superior to others. **9.13**

God's love never changes. Against all who oppose him, God expresses his love in wrath. In the same love, God took on himself judgment and shameful death in Jesus Christ, to bring men to repentance and new life. **9.14**

Section B. The Love of God

God's sovereign love is a mystery beyond the reach of man's mind. Human thought ascribes to God superlatives of power, wisdom, and goodness. But God reveals his love in Jesus Christ by showing power in the form of a servant, wisdom in the folly of the cross, and goodness in receiving sinful men. The power of God's love in Christ to transform the world discloses that the Redeemer is the Lord and Creator who made all things to serve the purpose of his love. **9.15**

God has created the world of space and time to be the sphere of his dealings with men. In its beauty and vastness, sublimity and awfulness, order and disorder, the world reflects to the eye of faith the majesty and mystery of its Creator. **9.16**

God has created man in a personal relation with himself that man may respond to the love of the Creator. He has created male and female and given them a life which proceeds from birth to death in a succession of generations and in a wide complex of social relations. He has endowed man with capacities to make the world serve his needs and to enjoy its good things. Life is a gift to be received with gratitude and a task to be pursued with courage. Man is free to seek his life within the purpose of God: to develop and protect the resources of nature for the common welfare, to work for justice and peace in society, and in other ways to use his creative powers for the fulfillment of human life. **9.17**

9.18   God expressed his love for all mankind through Israel, whom he chose to be his covenant people to serve him in love and faithfulness. When Israel was unfaithful, he disciplined the nation with his judgments and maintained his cause through prophets, priests, teachers, and true believers. These witnesses called all Israelites to a destiny in which they would serve God faithfully and become a light to the nations. The same witnesses proclaimed the coming of a new age, and a true servant of God in whom God's purpose for Israel and for mankind would be realized.

9.19   Out of Israel, God in due time raised up Jesus. His faith and obedience were the response of the perfect child of God. He was the fulfillment of God's promise to Israel, the beginning of the new creation, and the pioneer of the new humanity. He gave history its meaning and direction and called the church to be his servant for the reconciliation of the world.

Section C. The Communion of the Holy Spirit

9.20   God the Holy Spirit fulfills the work of reconciliation in man. The Holy Spirit creates and renews the church as the community in which men are reconciled to God and to one another. He enables them to receive forgiveness as they forgive one another and to enjoy the peace of God as they make peace among themselves. In spite of their sin, he gives them power to become representatives of Jesus Christ and his gospel of reconciliation to all men.

1.   THE NEW LIFE

9.21   The reconciling work of Jesus was the supreme crisis in the life of mankind. His cross and resurrection become personal crisis and present hope for men when the gospel is proclaimed and believed. In this experience, the Spirit brings God's forgiveness to men, moves them to respond in faith, repentance, and obedience, and initiates the new life in Christ.

9.22   The new life takes shape in a community in which men know that God loves and accepts them in spite of what they are. They therefore accept themselves and love others, knowing that no man has any ground on which to stand, except God's grace.

9.23   The new life does not release a man from conflict with unbelief, pride, lust, fear. He still has to struggle with disheartening difficulties and problems. Nevertheless, as he matures in love and faithfulness in his life with Christ, he lives in freedom and good cheer, bearing witness on good days and evil days, confident that the new life is pleasing to God and helpful to others.

9.24   The new life finds its direction in the life of Jesus, his deeds and words, his struggles against temptation, his compassion, his anger, and his willingness to suffer death. The teaching of apostles and prophets guides men in living this life, and the Christian community nurtures and equips them for their ministries.

The members of the church are emissaries of peace and seek the **9.25** good of man in cooperation with powers and authorities in politics, culture, and economics. But they have to fight against pretensions and injustices when these same powers endanger human welfare. Their strength is in their confidence that God's purpose rather than man's schemes will finally prevail.

Life in Christ is life eternal. The resurrection of Jesus is God's sign **9.26** that he will consummate his work of creation and reconciliation beyond death and bring to fulfillment the new life begun in Christ.

2. THE BIBLE

The one sufficient revelation of God is Jesus Christ, the Word of **9.27** God incarnate, to whom the Holy Spirit bears unique and authoritative witness through the Holy Scriptures, which are received and obeyed as the word of God written. The Scriptures are not a witness among others, but the witness without parallel. The church has received the books of the Old and New Testaments as prophetic and apostolic testimony in which it hears the word of God and by which its faith and obedience are nourished and regulated.

The New Testament is the recorded testimony of apostles to the **9.28** coming of the Messiah, Jesus of Nazareth, and the sending of the Holy Spirit to the Church. The Old Testament bears witness to God's faithfulness in his covenant with Israel and points the way to the fulfillment of his purpose in Christ. The Old Testament is indispensable to understanding the New, and is not itself fully understood without the New.

The Bible is to be interpreted in the light of its witness to God's **9.29** work of reconciliation in Christ. The Scriptures, given under the guidance of the Holy Spirit, are nevertheless the words of men, conditioned by the language, thought forms, and literary fashions of the places and times at which they were written. They reflect views of life, history, and the cosmos which were then current. The church, therefore, has an obligation to approach the Scriptures with literary and historical understanding. As God has spoken his word in diverse cultural situations, the church is confident that he will continue to speak through the Scriptures in a changing world and in every form of human culture.

God's word is spoken to his church today where the Scriptures are **9.30** faithfully preached and attentively read in dependence on the illumination of the Holy Spirit and with readiness to receive their truth and direction.

PART II

THE MINISTRY OF RECONCILIATION

Section A. The Mission of the Church

1. DIRECTION

To be reconciled to God is to be sent into the world as his re- **9.31** conciling community. This community, the church universal, is entrusted with God's message of reconciliation and shares his labor of healing the enmities which separate men from God and from each other. Christ has called the church to this mission and given it the gift of the Holy Spirit. The church maintains continuity with the apostles and with Israel by faithful obedience to his call.

9.32   The life, death, resurrection, and promised coming of Jesus Christ has set the pattern for the church's mission. His life as man involves the church in the common life of men. His service to men commits the church to work for every form of human well-being. His suffering makes the church sensitive to all the sufferings of mankind so that it sees the face of Christ in the faces of men in every kind of need. His crucifixion discloses to the church God's judgment on man's inhumanity to man and the awful consequences of its own complicity in injustice. In the power of the risen Christ and the hope of his coming, the church sees the promise of God's renewal of man's life in society and of God's victory over all wrong.

9.33   The church follows this pattern in the form of its life and in the method of its action. So to live and serve is to confess Christ as Lord.

2. FORMS AND ORDER

9.34   The institutions of the people of God change and vary as their mission requires in different times and places. The unity of the church is compatible with a wide variety of forms, but it is hidden and distorted when variant forms are allowed to harden into sectarian divisions, exclusive denominations, and rival factions.

9.35   Wherever the church exists, its members are both gathered in corporate life and dispersed in society for the sake of mission in the world.

9.36   The church gathers to praise God, to hear his word for mankind, to baptize and to join in the Lord's Supper, to pray for and present the world to him in worship, to enjoy fellowship, to receive instruction, strength, and comfort, to order and organize its own corporate life, to be tested, renewed, and reformed, and to speak and act in the world's affairs as may be appropriate to the needs of the time.

9.37   The church disperses to serve God wherever its members are, at work or play, in private or in the life of society. Their prayer and Bible study are part of the church's worship and theological reflection. Their witness is the church's evangelism. Their daily action in the world is the church in mission to the world. The quality of their relation with other persons is the measure of the church's fidelity.

9.38   Each member is the church in the world, endowed by the Spirit with some gift of ministry and is responsible for the integrity of his witness in his own particular situation. He is entitled to the guidance and support of the Christian community and is subject to its advice and correction. He in turn, in his own competence, helps to guide the church.

9.39   In recognition of special gifts of the Spirit and for the ordering of its life as a community, the church calls, trains, and authorizes certain members for leadership and oversight. The persons qualified for these duties in accordance with the polity of the church are set apart by ordination or other appropriate act and thus made responsible for their special ministries.

The church thus orders its life as an institution with a constitution, **9.40** government, officers, finances, and administrative rules. These are instruments of mission, not ends in themselves. Different orders have served the gospel, and none can claim exclusive validity. A presbyterian polity recognizes the responsibility of all members for ministry and maintains the organic relation of all congregations in the church. It seeks to protect the church from exploitation by ecclesiastical or secular power and ambition. Every church order must be open to such reformation as may be required to make it a more effective instrument of the mission of reconciliation.

3. REVELATION AND RELIGION

The church in its mission encounters the religions of men and in that **9.41** encounter becomes conscious of its own human character as a religion. God's revelation to Israel, expressed within Semitic culture, gave rise to the religion of the Hebrew people. God's revelation in Jesus Christ called forth the response of Jews and Greeks and came to expression within Judaism and Hellenism as the Christian religion. The Christian religion, as distinct from God's revelation of himself, has been shaped throughout its history by the cultural forms of its environment.

The Christian finds parallels between other religions and his own **9.42** and must approach all religions with openness and respect. Repeatedly God has used the insight of non-Christians to challenge the church to renewal. But the reconciling word of the gospel is God's judgment upon all forms of religion, including the Christian. The gift of God in Christ is for all men. The church, therefore, is commissioned to carry the gospel to all men whatever their religion may be and even when they profess none.

4. RECONCILIATION IN SOCIETY

In each time and place, there are particular problems and crises **9.43** through which God calls the church to act. The church, guided by the Spirit, humbled by its own complicity and instructed by all attainable knowledge, seeks to discern the will of God and learn how to obey in these concrete situations. The following are particularly urgent at the present time.

a. God has created the peoples of the earth to be one universal **9.44** family. In his reconciling love, he overcomes the barriers between brothers and breaks down every form of discrimination based on racial or ethnic difference, real or imaginary. The church is called to bring all men to receive and uphold one another as persons in all relationships of life: in employment, housing, education, leisure, marriage, family, church, and the exercise of political rights. Therefore, the church labors for the abolition of all racial discrimination and ministers to those injured by it. Congregations, individuals, or groups of Christians who exclude, dominate, or patronize their fellowmen, however subtly, resist the Spirit of God and bring contempt on the faith which they profess.

9.45   b.   God's reconciliation in Jesus Christ is the ground of the peace, justice, and freedom among nations which all powers of government are called to serve and defend. The church, in its own life, is called to practice the forgiveness of enemies and to commend to the nations as practical politics the search for cooperation and peace. This search requires that the nations pursue fresh and responsible relations across every line of conflict, even at risk to national security, to reduce areas of strife and to broaden international understanding. Reconciliation among nations becomes peculiarly urgent as countries develop nuclear, chemical, and biological weapons, diverting their manpower and resources from constructive uses and risking the annihilation of mankind. Although nations may serve God's purposes in history, the church which identifies the sovereignty of any one nation or any one way of life with the cause of God denies the Lordship of Christ and betrays its calling.

9.46   c.   The reconciliation of man through Jesus Christ makes it plain that enslaving poverty in a world of abundance is an intolerable violation of God's good creation. Because Jesus identified himself with the needy and exploited, the cause of the world's poor is the cause of his disciples. The church cannot condone poverty, whether it is the product of unjust social structures, exploitation of the defenseless, lack of national resources, absence of technological understanding, or rapid expansion of populations. The church calls every man to use his abilities, his possessions, and the fruits of technology as gifts entrusted to him by God for the maintenance of his family and the advancement of the common welfare. It encourages those forces in human society that raise men's hopes for better conditions and provide them with opportunity for a decent living. A church that is indifferent to poverty, or evades responsibility in economic affairs, or is open to one social class only, or expects gratitude for its beneficence makes a mockery of reconciliation and offers no acceptable worship to God.

9.47   d.   The relationship between man and woman exemplifies in a basic way God's ordering of the interpersonal life for which he created mankind. Anarchy in sexual relationships is a symptom of man's alienation from God, his neighbor, and himself. Man's perennial confusion about the meaning of sex has been aggravated in our day by the availability of new means for birth control and the treatment of infection, by the pressures of urbanization, by the exploitation of sexual symbols in mass communication, and by world overpopulation. The church, as the household of God, is called to lead men out of this alienation into the responsible freedom of the new life in Christ. Reconciled to God, each person has joy in and respect for his own humanity and that of other persons; a man and woman are enabled to marry, to commit themselves to a mutually shared life, and to respond to each other in sensitive and lifelong concern; parents receive the grace to care for children in love and to nurture their individuality. The church comes under the judgment of God and invites rejection by man when it fails to lead men and women into the full meaning of life together, or withholds the compassion of Christ from those caught in the moral confusion of our time.

Section B.   The Equipment of the Church

Jesus Christ has given the church preaching and teaching, praise and prayer, and Baptism and the Lord's Supper as means of fulfilling its service of God among men. These gifts remain, but the church is obliged to change the forms of its service in ways appropriate to different generations and cultures.

9.48

1.   PREACHING AND TEACHING

God instructs his church and equips it for mission through preaching and teaching. By these, when they are carried on in fidelity to the Scriptures and dependence upon the Holy Spirit, the people hear the word of God and accept and follow Christ. The message is addressed to men in particular situations. Therefore, effective preaching, teaching, and personal witness require disciplined study of both the Bible and the contemporary world. All acts of public worship should be conducive to men's hearing of the gospel in a particular time and place and responding with fitting obedience.

9.49

2.   PRAISE AND PRAYER

The church responds to the message of reconciliation in praise and prayer. In that response, it commits itself afresh to its mission, experiences a deepening of faith and obedience, and bears open testimony to the gospel. Adoration of God is acknowledgement of the Creator by the creation. Confession of sin is admission of all men's guilt before God and of their need for his forgiveness. Thanksgiving is rejoicing in God's goodness to all men and in giving for the needs of others. Petitions and intercessions are addressed to God for the continuation of his goodness, the healing of men's ills, and their deliverance from every form of oppression. The arts, especially music and architecture, contribute to the praise and prayer of a Christian congregation when they help men to look beyond themselves to God and to the world which is the object of his love.

9.50

3.   BAPTISM

By humble submission to John's baptism, Christ joined himself to men in their need and entered upon his ministry of reconciliation in the power of the Spirit. Christian baptism marks the receiving of the same Spirit by all his people. Baptism with water represents not only cleansing from sin, but a dying with Christ and a joyful rising with him to new life. It commits all Christians to die each day to sin and to live for righteousness. In baptism, the church celebrates the renewal of

9.51

the covenant with which God has bound his people to himself. By baptism, individuals are publicly received into the church to share in its life and ministry, and the church becomes responsible for their training and support in Christian discipleship. When those baptized are infants, the congregation, as well as the parents, has a special obligation to nurture them in the Christian life, leading them to make, by a public profession, a personal response to the love of God shown forth in their baptism.

4. THE LORD'S SUPPER

9.52   The Lord's Supper is a celebration of the reconciliation of men with God and with one another, in which they joyfully eat and drink together at the table of their Savior. Jesus Christ gave his church this remembrance of his dying for sinful men so that by participation in it they have communion with him and with all who shall be gathered to him. Partaking in him as they eat the bread and drink the wine in accordance with Christ's appointment, they receive from the risen and living Lord the benefits of his death and resurrection. They rejoice in the foretaste of the kingdom which he will bring to consummation at his promised coming, and go out from the Lord's Table with courage and hope for the service to which he has called them.

PART III

THE FULFILLMENT OF RECONCILIATION

9.53   God's redeeming work in Jesus Christ embraces the whole of man's life: social and cultural, economic and political, scientific and technological, individual and corporate. It includes man's natural environment as exploited and despoiled by sin. It is the will of God that his purpose for human life shall be fulfilled under the rule of Christ and all evil be banished from his creation.

9.54   Biblical visions and images of the rule of Christ, such as a heavenly city, a father's house, a new heaven and earth, a marriage feast, and an unending day culminate in the image of the kingdom. The kingdom represents the triumph of God over all that resists his will and disrupts his creation. Already God's reign is present as a ferment in the world, stirring hope in men and preparing the world to receive its ultimate judgment and redemption.

9.55   With an urgency born of this hope, the church applies itself to present tasks and strives for a better world. It does not identify limited progress with the kingdom of God on earth, nor does it despair in the face of disappointment and defeat. In steadfast hope, the church looks beyond all partial achievement to the final triumph of God.

9.56   "Now to him who by the power at work within us is able to do far more abundantly than all we ask or think, to him be glory in the church and in Christ Jesus to all generations, forever and ever. Amen."

A BRIEF STATEMENT OF FAITH—
PRESBYTERIAN CHURCH (U.S.A.)

Introduction to a Brief Statement of Faith —
Presbyterian Church (U.S.A.)

It was a glorious day in Atlanta. The date was June 9, 1983. On the morning of that day the General Assemblies of the Presbyterian Church in the United States and the United Presbyterian Church in the United States of America convened in separate meeting rooms in the Atlanta convention center. Each had the same agenda item before it: to vote on whether these two denominations, separated from each other since 1859, should become one.

The process of forging a reunion had been long and arduous. Thoughtfully and prayerfully, with great sensitivity to diverse perspectives and to many anxieties, a joint committee or union had shepherded a Plan for Reunion through the official and unofficial labyrinths of the two denominations. Its fourteen years of labor were culminating in the votes about to be taken.

The members of the special committee were not to be disappointed. The votes to adopt and enact a Plan for Reunion were resoundingly positive. In each case the affirmative vote was followed by cheers and shouts of gladness. Tears of gratitude and joy mingled with embraces by friends and strangers. Separated brothers and sisters became once again an ecclesiastical family in Jesus Christ.

Following a prayer of thanksgiving, bagpipes began their sacred squawks. The now one General Assembly, joined by friends and ecclesiastical staff, poured out of separate doors in the convention center, forming one great, rejoicing parade. Usually sober and dour Presbyterians were transformed into a people overwhelmed by an unrestrained joyfulness. Following the pipers through the streets of Atlanta they marched, ending at the city hall where Atlanta's Mayor Andrew Young and ecclesiastical leaders extended greeting and congratulations. It was a glorious day in Atlanta, one filled with a sense of the rush of God's Holy Spirit.

The 1983 reunion was a momentous event. But reuniting was a process that stretched out into the future. There were tasks to be done, to which the new church now turned its attention.

One such task was that of seeking a statement of belief that could be endorsed and used by the new church, the Presbyterian Church (U.S.A.). The Plan for Reunion specified that the reunited church's confessional ground would be the confessional documents of the two previous denominations. But true to its Reformed heritage, there was also the call to say what the new reunited church believed. Such a statement was deemed desirable for both the integrity and the identity of the new denomination. Provision was therefore made for establishing a Special Committee to draft a brief statement of Reformed faith for possible inclusion in the *Book of Confessions*. J. Randolph Taylor, Moderator of the 1983 reuniting assembly, appointed that committee in the spring of

1984. Its membership was diverse and representative of the richness of the church.

For five years the special committee studied, prayed, and discussed the shape and content of such a statement. It consulted widely with ecumenical partners, theological faculties, and the church at large. In 1989 it sent a proposal to the 201st General Assembly for its action. That assembly voted to approve the draft as worthy of further consideration and, in keeping with constitutional procedures, voted to establish a second special committee to review the statement of belief and submit a revised draft to the next General Assembly, with appropriate recommendations.

The 202nd General Assembly (1990) overwhelmingly endorsed the proposed confession, sending it to the presbyteries where it was approved by far more than the required two-thirds majority. Finally the 203rd General Assembly (1991) voted to approve and enact A Brief Statement of Faith—Presbyterian Church (U.S.A.), adding it to The Book of Confessions.

The question immediately arises as to the functions of this particular confession in the life of the church. One is its role as a teaching resource. A Brief Statement of Faith rehearses enduring Reformed beliefs, while assuming latitude in how such beliefs will be interpreted. Indeed its style is one that names such beliefs while inviting and encouraging its readers to explore more fully their rich meanings.

A Brief Statement is also a document to be used in worship. Though too long in its entirety to be regularly incorporated into the liturgy, sections of the statement may be appropriated from time to time. For example, the lines on the Holy Spirit, in part or in whole, are often used on Pentecost Sunday.

Further, in conjunction with the historic confessions A Brief Statement has the function of pointing to beliefs that form the core of the church's faith, essential tenets as the ordination questions call them. They are to serve as guides to the exercise of leadership by the church's officers (Book of Order, G-14.040).

One continuing question in the writing of confessions concerns their organization and structure. Often the Apostles' Creed is used as a pattern to be followed, moving from God the Creator to God the Redeemer to God the Holy Spirit. A Brief Statement, however, follows the order of the apostolic benediction: "The grace of our Lord Jesus Christ, the love of God, and the communion of the Holy Spirit be with all of you" (2 Cor. 13:14). It consists of an introduction (lines 1–6); an initial section on the second person of the Trinity, our Lord Jesus Christ (lines 7–26); a middle section on the first person of the Trinity, God the Creator (lines 27–51); a concluding section on the Holy Spirit (lines 52–76); and a doxological affirmation (lines 77–80). The central structure of A Brief Statement is trinitarian. A Brief Statement follows the lead of its immediate predecessor in the Book of Confessions, the Confession of

1967, as well as other creedal documents in beginning with Jesus Christ, through whom we know God the Creator and Spirit.

A Brief Statement is a summary of beliefs confessed through the ages and an application of such convictions to the life of the church today. The Preface to a Brief Statement—received but not adopted as a part of the constitution of the denomination—orients the reader to the intention of all confessions. It reads: "No confession of faith looks merely to the past; every confession seeks to cast the light of a priceless heritage on the needs of the present moment, and so to shape the future." In keeping with that understanding A Brief Statement both draws from the church's heritage and addresses the present.

We can review only a few of the historic doctrines in A Brief Statement. Unlike the Confession of 1967, which adopted the theological principle of reconciliation as its dominant theme, A Brief Statement invokes several foundational Reformed convictions. Perhaps the most central one is the sovereignty of God. From the initial sentence—"In life and in death we belong to God"—to the concluding paragraph, God's rule over life and death is affirmed, reflecting Rom. 8:31–39, as well as other biblical passages. (See the Appendix to A Brief Statement for other references both to Scripture and to other confessions.) And A Brief Statement at its very beginning ties itself to confessional teaching about God's sovereignty. It echoes the Heidelberg Catechism's first question and answer: "What is your only comfort, in life and in death?" The response is: "That I belong—body and soul, in life and in death—not to myself but to my faithful Savior, Jesus Christ." And the affirmation of God's sovereignty is woven into the full text of A Brief Statement. The reign of God over all worldly powers and principalities is heralded in line 9 as the heart of Jesus' ministry. And the concluding line save one concludes the confession as it began, "We rejoice that nothing in life or in death can separate us from the love of God in Christ Jesus our Lord."

The sovereignty of God is the throbbing heartbeat of faith confessed in A Brief Statement. It underlies the entire document. But what is as important as God's rule is the nature of that rule. A Brief Statement insists that the content of that ruling is most clearly manifest in Jesus Christ. God's ruling is affirmed to be one of love, the love demonstrated in Jesus' life and death for others, and the vindication of that love as authentic by the resurrection's overruling of death as the ultimate power. "God raised this Jesus from the dead, . . . delivering us from death to life eternal" (lines 23–26). In the love of Christ we experience and see the love of God crucially and concretely breaking into the world, a sign of the ultimate victory to which the church looks with confidence, praying, "Come, Lord Jesus" (line 76).

Another theme in A Brief Statement drawn from both Scripture and earlier confessions is human sinfulness. A Brief Statement does not allow one to go around rather than through the confrontation with one's own self-chosen alienation from God and neighbors. Unlike other confessions that often treat human sinfulness as abstract propositions to be acknowledged, A Brief Statement addresses sin's reality as attitudes and behaviors in which those of us confessing are immediately implicated. Sin is not something that refers us to the past chronologically. It is about what we do; it is about what we don't do; it is about our relation to God and neighbors here and now. Sin as alienation from God and neighbor wears two costumes. It appears in the guise of rebellion against God and of sloth, ignoring or denying our gifts that are to be used for God's purposes of reconciliation and redemption. "But we rebel against God; we hide from our Creator" (line 33). Lines 34–38 outline some of the manifestations of our sinfulness. They lead to the fearsome conclusion: "We deserve God's condemnation." But our sinfulness is overruled. For God's love is one that forgives and restores us to the integrity of our lives as they were intended to be. God replies to our sin with justice and mercy (line 40).

Another mark of continuity between A Brief Statement and earlier confessions is the attention given to the full range of categories grouped under the doctrine of the Holy Spirit. A Brief Statement recognizes that the Spirit will blow where it will and cannot be limited to imposed boundaries. But the disciplines of discerning what the Spirit is doing and how Christians are to respond are essential for the church's and individual Christians' faithfulness. That is why A Brief Statement is more than an ethereal confession. It roots the discerning of God's Spirit in the concrete gifts God gives to the church: Scripture, preaching, sacraments, church order, and the ministries of the Church (lines 58–64). Also the Christian life is directed and strengthened by the Spirit, who gives courage for a comprehensive witness to God's love and justice (lines 66–74).

A Brief Statement carries forward the "priceless heritage" of the faith. It also sounds new dimensions of the faith or differently accented aspects of what we believe in this time and place. For example, A Brief Statement includes both proportionally and actually more attention to the life and ministry of Jesus than other confessions. While confessing that Jesus is fully human, fully God, it is Jesus as the human face of God that is given more attention than is typical. In doing so A Brief Statement helps to fill the void that exists in, for instance, the Apostles' Creed, between Jesus as "born of the Virgin Mary" and as "crucified under Pontius Pilate." The life of Jesus in proclaiming the reign of God with both words and deeds is recognized as integral to what we believe. And to what we do.

At the highest level of generality, the recounting of significant elements of Jesus' life is a claim about what it means to follow him now. The familiar theme of "the imitation of Christ," part of the heritage of the past, is reaffirmed and reinvigorated by spelling out significant ingredients in what it means to be "fully human." Thus, in providing food for the homeless we follow Jesus, who ate with the outcast. In seeking to assure that all children live up to their potential, we emulate one who "blessed the children." In sharing the good news of God's love, we call "all to repent and believe the gospel."

A Brief Statement gives more specific, though still general, direction for life in Christ in the here and now. One way it does so is by citing what we have not done, how we have sinned. The front side of what we confess we have failed to do is a positive task or tasks in which we are to be engaged. It takes little imagination to turn the negatives of what we have done wrong into the positives of what we are to do, individually and corporately. So to confess that we have exploited neighbor and nature (line 37), misusing God's creation, turns us to seeking ways by which we may care for our human family and the environment that we inhabit. Similarly, to "threaten death to the planet entrusted to our care" calls on Christians and the others to exercise a stewardship that works for an environment that will contribute to the health of this and future generations. It is also a call to do all in our power to assure that no nuclear exchange will ever occur, even if that means a disavowal of the production and employment of all such weaponry.

Another contemporary issue A Brief Statement addresses both directly and indirectly is that of gender inclusiveness with reference to what is said and done. Both in what is said and in what is not said, the language of A Brief Statement fosters such inclusiveness. With reference to language about human beings, the document is free of gender-exclusive terms. In its language about God a way of using such inclusive language is demonstrated. Lines 47–51 give parallel similes, both drawn from Scripture: "God makes us heirs with Christ of the covenant. Like a mother who will not forsake her nursing child, like a father who runs to welcome the prodigal home, God is faithful still." Together these lines point to masculine and feminine characteristics of God, who is neither male nor female. This method of complementarity suggests one way of addressing the issue of gender-inclusive language about God. It also legitimates an ongoing discussion and consideration of how the church shall speak faithfully and persuasively of God.

The attention to gender-inclusive language is not "just" a language issue. It is a question of justice, of how all people are to be treated as those created "equally in God's image, male and female" (lines 30–31). One way is for the church to open its offices of ministry equally to men and women. The Presbyterian Church (U.S.A.) did so long ago by amending its Book of Order. But the confessional position was not changed. Both the Second Helvetic Confession and the Scots Confession explicitly bar women from ordination. Ironically the Scots Confession rejects the Roman Catholic clergy as illegitimate because women are approved for the administration of a sacrament. In Chapter XXII, "The Right Administration of the Sacraments," two things are identified as necessary for the right administration of the sacraments. One is that they should be "ministered in the elements and manner which God has appointed. Otherwise they cease to be the sacraments of Christ Jesus. This is why we abandon the teaching of the Roman Church and withdraw from its sacraments; firstly, because their ministers are not true ministers of Christ

Jesus (indeed they even allow women, whom the Holy Ghost will not permit to preach in the congregation to baptize). . . ."

A Brief Statement remedies the confessional exclusion of women by the presence of one line, number 64. There the Holy Spirit is confessed as calling "women and men to all ministries of the Church."

A Brief Statement is a theological and a pastoral document. It affirms the traditions of Reformed doctrines while addressing certain pressing issues. Not all doctrines and not all human issues are addressed, nor could they be. But A Brief Statement is a starting point for exploring who we Presbyterians are, what we believe, and what we are to do in obedience to Jesus Christ. For finally the validity of A Brief Statement will be measured by its truthfulness to the biblical proclamation and teaching, and by whether it receives the approbation of the people of God by being incorporated into the practices of the church, its teaching, its worship, and its witness. It will become authentic as it assists the church in its thinking and its acting, and as it casts a light into the future into which God calls. As that occurs it will have contributed to the reuniting process, assisting the church to make a good confession. Finally A Brief Statement will be measured by whether it contributes to the reuniting of all members of Christ's body. For the reuniting of the two Presbyterian communions was and is, theologically, only a partial recovery, but a strong promise of the one church that God intends and will give.

QUESTIONS FOR STUDY

1. One of the goals of a confession is to make more accessible the official beliefs of the church. Does A Brief Statement accomplish that purpose, and if so how, and if not how could it be improved? How do you see the congregation of which you are a part using A Brief Statement?

2. Besides the theological themes explicitly discussed in the text above, what other doctrines do you discern in the statement itself? What issues or questions are not addressed in A Brief Statement and why are they important?

3. How would you give more explicitness to the Christian life than is given in the broad categories of A Brief Statement?

4. How does A Brief Statement compare and contrast with other documents in the Book of Confessions?

PREFACE[1]
TO
A BRIEF STATEMENT OF FAITH
PRESBYTERIAN CHURCH (U.S.A.)

In 1983 the two largest Presbyterian churches in the United States reunited. *The Plan for Reunion* called for the preparation of a brief statement of the Reformed faith for possible inclusion in the *Book of Confessions*. This statement is therefore not intended to stand alone, apart from the other confessions of our church. It does not pretend to be a complete list of all our beliefs, nor does it explain any of them in detail. It is designed to be confessed by the whole congregation in the setting of public worship, and it may also serve pastors and teachers as an aid to Christian instruction. It celebrates our rediscovery that for all our undoubted diversity, we are bound together by a common faith and a common task.

The faith we confess unites us with the one, universal church. The most important beliefs of Presbyterians are those we share with other Christians, and especially with other evangelical Christians who look to the Protestant Reformation as a renewal of the gospel of Jesus Christ. Diversity remains. But we are thankful that in our time the many churches are learning to accept, and even to affirm, diversity without divisiveness, since the whole counsel of God is more than the wisdom of any individual or any one tradition. The Spirit of Truth gives new light to the churches when they are willing to become pupils together of the Word of God. This statement therefore intends to confess the catholic faith.

We are convinced that to the Reformed churches a distinctive vision of the catholic faith has been entrusted for the good of the whole church. Accordingly, "A Brief Statement of Faith" includes the major themes of the Reformed tradition (such as those mentioned in the *Book of Order*, Form of Government, Chapter 2),[2] without claiming them as our private possession, just as we ourselves hope to learn and to share the wisdom and insight given to traditions other than our own. And as a confession that seeks to be both catholic and Reformed, the statement (following the apostle's blessing in 2 Cor. 13:14) is a trinitarian confession in which the grace of Jesus Christ has first place as the foundation of our knowledge of God's sovereign love and our life together in the Holy Spirit.

No confession of faith looks merely to the past; every confession seeks to cast the light of a priceless heritage on the needs of the present moment, and so to shape the future. Reformed confessions, in particular, when necessary even reform the tradition itself in the light of the Word of God. From the first, the Reformed churches have insisted that the renewal of the church must become visible in the

---

[1] The preface and the appendix do not have confessional authority.

[2] The appendix provides cross-references that will enable the reader to place the affirmations of "A Brief Statement of Faith" in the context of the Reformed tradition.

transformation of human lives and societies. Hence "A Brief Statement of Faith" lifts up concerns that call most urgently for the church's attention in our time. The church is not a refuge from the world; an elect people is chosen for the blessing of the nations. A sound confession, therefore, proves itself as it nurtures commitment to the church's mission, and as the confessing church itself becomes the body by which Christ continues the blessing of his earthly ministry.

THE STATEMENT

1 In life and in death we belong to God.
2   Through the grace of our Lord Jesus Christ,
3   the love of God,
4   and the communion of the Holy Spirit,
5   we trust in the one triune God, the Holy One of Israel,
6   whom alone we worship and serve.

7 We trust in Jesus Christ,
8   fully human, fully God.
9 Jesus proclaimed the reign of God:
10   preaching good news to the poor
11   and release to the captives,
12   teaching by word and deed
13   and blessing the children,
14   healing the sick
15   and binding up the brokenhearted,
16   eating with outcasts,
17   forgiving sinners,
18   and calling all to repent and believe the gospel.
19 Unjustly condemned for blasphemy and sedition,
20 Jesus was crucified,
21   suffering the depths of human pain
22   and giving his life for the sins of the world.
23 God raised this Jesus from the dead,
24   vindicating his sinless life,
25   breaking the power of sin and evil,
26   delivering us from death to life eternal.

27 We trust in God,
28   whom Jesus called Abba, Father.
29 In sovereign love God created the world good
30   and makes everyone equally in God's image,
31   male and female, of every race and people,
32   to live as one community.
33 But we rebel against God; we hide from our Creator.
34   Ignoring God's commandments,
35   we violate the image of God in others and ourselves,
36   accept lies as truth,
37   exploit neighbor and nature,
38   and threaten death to the planet entrusted to our care.
39   We deserve God's condemnation.
40   Yet God acts with justice and mercy to redeem creation.

41	In everlasting love,
42	the God of Abraham and Sarah chose a covenant people
43	to bless all families of the earth.
44	Hearing their cry,
45	God delivered the children of Israel
46	from the house of bondage.
47	Loving us still,
48	God makes us heirs with Christ of the covenant.
49	Like a mother who will not forsake her nursing child,
50	like a father who runs to welcome the prodigal home,
51	God is faithful still.

10.4

52	We trust in God the Holy Spirit,
53	everywhere the giver and renewer of life.
54	The Spirit justifies us by grace through faith,
55	sets us free to accept ourselves and to love God and neighbor,
56	and binds us together with all believers
57	in the one body of Christ, the Church.
58	The same Spirit
59	who inspired the prophets and apostles
60	rules our faith and life in Christ through Scripture,
61	engages us through the Word proclaimed,
62	claims us in the waters of baptism,
63	feeds us with the bread of life and the cup of salvation,
64	and calls women and men to all ministries of the Church.
65	In a broken and fearful world
66	the Spirit gives us courage
67	to pray without ceasing,
68	to witness among all peoples to Christ as Lord and Savior,
69	to unmask idolatries in Church and culture,
70	to hear the voices of peoples long silenced,
71	and to work with others for justice, freedom, and peace.
72	In gratitude to God, empowered by the Spirit,
73	we strive to serve Christ in our daily tasks
74	and to live holy and joyful lives,
75	even as we watch for God's new heaven and new earth,
76	praying, "Come, Lord Jesus!"

10.5

77	With believers in every time and place,
78	we rejoice that nothing in life or in death
79	can separate us from the love of God in Christ Jesus our Lord.

10.6

80	Glory be to the Father, and to the Son, and to the Holy Spirit. Amen.*

*Instead of saying this line, congregations may wish to sing a version of the Gloria.

APPENDIX
to
A Brief Statement of Faith—
Presbyterian Church (U.S.A.)

Cross-Reference

The writers of "A Brief Statement of Faith" have endeavored to establish this confession on the broad base of Scripture as a whole and the consensus of Reformed theology, not upon isolated or particular texts either in Scripture or theology.

These cross-references identify sources that have significantly shaped the specific part of the faith being confessed at the lines indicated. They show the congruence of "A Brief Statement of Faith" with the teachings of the Scriptures and of earlier confessional documents. They point to only a selected few of the passages and contexts that congregations could study in comparing the ways the faith has been re-confessed in diverse historical situations.

The verse references and abbreviations for books of the Bible are based on the *Revised Standard Version*. Biblical passages are listed in the order of their occurrence in the English Bible, except that the parallel passages from the Synoptic Gospels (Matthew, Mark, and Luke) have been grouped together. Portions of the verses cited in italics are quoted or closely paraphrased in "A Brief Statement of Faith."

Documents in the *Book of Confessions* are abbreviated as follows: NC, Nicene Creed; AC, Apostles' Creed; SC, Scots Confession; HC, Heidelberg Catechism; SHC, Second Helvetic Confession; WCF, Westminster Confession of Faith [numbered according to the edition used by the former United Presbyterian Church U.S.A.]; WSC, Westminster Shorter Catechism; WLC, Westminster Larger Catechism; BD, Theological Declaration of Barmen; C67, Confession of 1967.

Citations are listed in the order of their occurrence in the *Book of Confessions*.

Lines 1–6

1	Scripture	Deut 7:6–11; Ps 100; 139:1–12; Is 43:1–9; Jer 31; Rom 8:31–39; 14:7–9; 2 Cor 5:1–5.
	Confessions	SC, 1; HC, q 1; WLC, q 1; BD, II, 1, 2.

2–6	Scripture	Ex 20:3–6; Deut 6:4–9; 11:16; 2 Kings 19:14–22; Ps 56:3–4; 62:1–8; 71:22–24; 103; Is 10:20; 12:5–6; 17:7–8; 43:14–15; 54:5; Jer 17:5–8; 25:5–6; Dan 3:28; Mt 28:16–20; Jn 3:16; 14:8–17; Acts 2:41–42; 27:21–26; 1 Cor 8:1–6; *2 Cor 13:14;* Eph 2:8–10; 1 Pet 1:2–9.
	Confessions	NC; SC, I, IV; HC, q 25; SHC, III, V; WCF, II, VII, 5; WSC, q 6; WLC, qq 6–11; C67, "The Confession," IA–C.

Lines 7–26

7–8	Scripture	Ps 86:1–2; Is 12:2; Mt 1:18–25; 11:27; Mk 8:27–30; 14:61–62; Lk 2:1–52; Jn 1:1–18; 5:1–18; 7:25–31; 10:30–39; Gal 4:1–7; Phil 2:5–11; Col 1:15–20; 2:8–10; Heb 1; 2:14–18; 4:14–15; 5:7–10; 13:8; 1 Jn 1:1–2.
	Confessions	NC, 2nd art.; SC, VI; HC, qq 31, 35, 47; SHC, XI; WCF, VIII, 2; WSC, q 21; WLC, qq 36–42; C67, IA1.

9–18	Scripture	Ps 34:6–18; 146:5–9; 147:1–6; Is 42:1–7; *61:1*–3; Ezek 34:15–16; Zeph 3:19; Mt 4:23–25; 9:10–13; 13:1–58; 15:21–28; 18:21–35; 23:1–4; Mk *1:14–15;* 5:1–20; 6:30–44; 9:33–37; 10:13–16; Lk *4:16*–22 *(18)*; 5:17–32; 6:17–36; 7:1–27, 33–50; 8:1–3; 10:38–42; 15:1–32; Jn 4:1–42; 8:1–11; 10:1–18; 11:1–44; 16:33; Acts 10:34–43.
	Confessions	SC, XIV, XVI; HC, qq 1, 31, 74, 107; SHC, XIII–XV; WCF, VIII, XII, XXV; WSC, qq 21–30, 36; WLC, qq 43–50, 135; BD, I; C67, IA1, IIA4c, III.

19–22	Scripture	
	Lines 19–20	Mt 26:57–68; Mk 14:53–65; Lk 22:63–71; Mt 27:32–37; Mk 15:21–26; Lk 23:32–35; Jn 10:22–39; 19:1–22; 1 Cor 1:20–25.
	Lines 21–22	Ps 22; 88:1–9; Is 52:13–53:12; Mt 27:27–31, 39–50; Mk 15:16–20, 29–37; Lk 23:11, 39–46; Mk 8:31–35; 10:45; Lk 22:39–46; Jn 1:29–34; 3:16–18; 10:7–18; 19:28–37; Rom 5; 2 Cor 5:17–21; 1 Tim 2:5–6; Heb 2; 5:7–10; 9:11–22; 1 Pet 2:21–24; 3:18; 1 Jn 2:1–2; 4:9–10; Rev 5.

	Confessions	SC, VIII, IX; HC, qq 29–44; SHC, XI; WCF, VIII; WSC, qq 28–31; WLC, qq 44, 49.

23–26	Scripture	
	Lines 23–24	Ps 24:4–5; 26:1; 37:5–6; Is 50:4–9; Matt 27:3–4; 28:1–17; Mk 16:1–8; Lk 24:1–47; Jn 20–21; Acts 2:22–36 *(32)*; 17:16–34; Rom 1:1–7; 1 Cor 15:3–57; 1 Tim 3:14–16.
	Lines 25–26	Ps 49:13–15; Is 25:6–8; Dan 12:2–3; Jn 3:16–18; 5:19–24; 11:17–27; Rom 4:24–25; 5:1–21; 6:1–23; 8:1–11; 1 Cor 15:20–28; Eph 2:1–7; Col 1:9–14; 2:8–15; 1 Thess 4:13–18; 2 Tim 1:10; Heb 13:20–21; Rev 21:3–4.
	Confessions	SC, X; HC, qq 45–52; SHC, XI; WCF, VIII, 4–8; WLC, qq 52–56; BD, II, 2–4; C67, IA1.

Lines 27–51

27–28	Scripture	2 Kings 18:5–6; Ps 28:6–7; 71:5–6; Prov 3:5–8; Mt 6:25–34; *Mk 14:32–36*; Lk 11:2–4; Rom 8:12–17; Gal 4:1–7.
	Confessions	NC, 1st art.; AC, 1st art.; HC, qq 26–28; WCF, XII; WLC, q 100.

29–32	Scripture	
	Line 29	Gen 1:1–25; Ps 33:1–9; 104; Is 40:21–28; Jn 1:1–5; Col 1:15–20; 1 Tim 4:4.
	Lines 30–32	Gen 1:26–2:25; 5:1–32 (esp. 1–5, 32); 10:32–11:1; Lev 19:9–18; Ps 22:25–31; 67; 133; Is 56:3–8; 66:18–21; Mic 4:1–4; Lk 10:29–37; Acts 17:22–28; Eph 1:9–10; Rev 7:9–12; 22:1–2.
	Confessions	HC, q 6; SHC, VII; WCF, IV, 1–2; WSC, qq 9, 10; WLC, qq 12–17; C67, IIA4a.

33–38	Scripture	
	Line 33	Gen 3:1–24; 4:1–6; Ex 3:6; 4:1–17; Judg 11:29–40; 1 Sam 10:20–24; Ps 2:1–3; 14:1–4; Is 1:1–6; Jer 5:20–25; 23:24; Jon 1:1–4; Mt 5:14–16; Mk 4:21–23; Lk 8:16–18; Mt 19:16–22; 25:14–30 (esp. 18, 24–25); Lk 8:43–48; 10:38–42 (Martha); Rom 1:16–3:26; Heb 4:13; Rev 2–3; 6:12–17.
	Line 34	Gen 1:28; 2:15–16; Ex 20:1–17; 21:1–23:19; Lev 19:1–37; Deut 6:4–9; 10:19; Neh 7:73b–8:18; Ps 119:169–176; Amos 5:24; Mic 6:8; Mt 5:17–6:21; 7:12; 22:34–40; Jn 13:34; 14:15; 15:12–17; Rom 13:8–10; 1 Cor 8; 1 Jn 2:3–11.

	Line 35	Gen 1:27; 4:8; 6:11–12; 16; 21:9–21; Judg 19; 2 Sam 11; 13:1–20; 18:5–15; Ps 14:1–4; Is 1:12–23; 59:1–8; Ezek 7:10–11; 45:9; Zeph 3:1–4; Mt 23:13–28; 25:31–46; Lk 16:19–31; Rom 1:28–32; Eph 4:17–22; Col 3:5–11; 2 Tim 3:1–9; Tit 1:15–16.
	Line 36	Gen 2:16–17; 3:1–4; Job 13:1–12; Ps 4:2; Is 5:20–21; 28:14–15; 59:3b, 12–15a; Jer 5:1–3; 14:13–14; Jn 8:42–45.
	Lines 37–38	Gen 2:15; Ps 8; Is 5:7–8; 24:4–6; 33:7–9; Jer 2:7–8; 9:4–6; Hos 4:1–3; Amos 2:6–8; Acts 16:16–24.
	Confessions	SC, II; HC, qq 3–11, 106, 107; SHC, VIII, IX; WCF, VI; WSC, q 77; WLC, qq 22–28, 105, 131, 132, 136, 145, 149; C67, IA2.
39	Scripture	Gen 6:5–7; Deut 28:15–68; 30:15–20; 2 Sam 12:1–12; Is 1:24–25; 5:9–10, 24–25; 28:16–22; 59:9–11, 15b–19; Jer 2:9; 9:7–11; 14:15–16; Amos 2:13–16; Jn 3:16–21; Rom 5:18–21; 8:1–4.
	Confessions	SC, III, XV; HC, qq 10–12; SHC, XII, XIII; WCF, VI, 6; WSC, qq 82–85; WLC, q 27; C67, IA2.
40	Scripture	2 Chron 7:11–14; Ps 34:22; 51; 78:36–39; 103:1–14; 130; 145:8–9; Is 2:2–4; 6:5–7; 11:1–9; 30:18; 51:4–6; Jer 31:20; Lam 3:22–33; Ezek 36:8–15; Hos 11:1–9; 14:4–8; Mt 1:18–21; Lk 1:67–79; 15:1–7; Jn 3:16–17; Rom 5:15–17; 8:18–25; Eph 2:4–7; 1 Pet 1:13–21.
	Confessions	SC, I, IV; HC, qq 26–28; SHC, VI, X; WCF, V; WSC, q 31; WLC, q 30.
41–51	Scripture	
	Lines 41–43	Gen 12:1–7; 15; 17:1–21; 18:1–15; 21:1–7; 28:10–17; Deut 7:6–7; Neh 9:6–8; Ps 65:1–4; Is 41:8–10; 44:1–8; 51:1–2; Jer 31:3, 31–34; Mt 9:9–13; 26:26–28; Rom 4:13–25; 11; 1 Cor 1:26–29; Gal 3:6–9; Eph 1:3–10; 1 Thess 1; Heb 11:8–12; Jas 2:5; 1 Pet 2:9–10.
	Lines 44–46	Ex 2:23–3:10; 6:2–8; 15:1–21; 18:5–12; 20:1–2; 22:21–24; Deut 7:8; Judg 6:7–16; 10:10–16; 2 Chron 32:9–23; Ezra 9:6–9; Neh 9:9–15; Ps 18:1–19; 34; 77; 105:23–45; 107; 136; Is 40:3–5, 9–11; 43:14–21; 51:9–16; Dan 3; 6; Mic 6:4; Mt 6:13; 15:21–28; Mk 5:1–20; 2 Cor 1:8–11; Rev 1:4–11; 15:2–4.
	Lines 47–48	Ps 33:20–22; 36:7–9; Is 54:4–10; 63:7–9; Mic 7:18–20; Mt 26:26–29; *Rom 8:15–17*, 38–39; 1 Cor 11:23–26; Gal 3:15–29; 4:6–7, 21–31; Eph 1:3–6; 2:11–22; Heb 13:20–21: 1 Pet 1:1–9; 1 Jn 3:1–2.

Lines 49–51	Gen 33:1–11; Deut 7:9; 32:10–12; Neh 9:16–23; Ps 27:7–10; 36:5–12; 91; 117; Is 42:14–16; 46:3–4; 49:7; *49:14–15*; 66:13; Jer 31:15–20; Lam 3:22–23; Hos 11:3–4; Lk 13:34–35; 15:11–32 (esp. 20); *1 Cor 1:9*; 1 Thess 5:23–24; 2 Thess 2:16–17.
Confessions	SC, IV, V; HC, qq 12–15, 18, 19, 34, 49, 51, 52, 54, 128; SHC, XIII; XVII–XIX; WCF, VI, 4, VII, VIII, 8, XVII, XVIII, XXXV, "Declaratory Statement" of 1903; WSC, q 36; WLC, qq 31–34, 74; BD, II, 2; C67, IB.

Lines 52–76

52–53	Scripture	Gen 1:1–2; Ps 23; 139:1–12; Ezek 37:1–14; Lk 1:26–35; Jn 3:1–15; Acts 2:1–21; 10; Rom 8:1–11; 2 Cor 3.
	Confessions	NC, 3rd art.; AC, 3rd art; SC, XII; HC, q 53; WCF, XX, XXXIV; WLC, qq 58, 89, 182.

54–57	Scripture	
	Line 54	Gen 15:1–6; Hab 2:4; Rom 1:16–17; *3:21–28 (24–25)*; 4:1–5; 5:1–2; Gal 3:1–14; Eph 2:8–9; Tit 3:3–7.
	Lines 55–57	Lev 19:18; Deut 6:4–5; Mk 12:28–34; Lk 10:25–37; Jn 3:1–15; Rom 8:26–27; 12; 13:8–10; 1 Cor 12:1–31 (esp. 13, 27); 13; 2 Cor 3:17–4:2; Gal 5; 6:1–10; Eph 2:11–22; 4:1–6; Phil 4:1–7; Col 1:24; 3:12–17; 1 Pet 4:8–11; 1 Jn 4:19–5:5.
	Confessions	SC, XVI–XX; HC, qq 1, 21, 54, 55, 86, 87; SHC, XV–XVII; WCF, XI, XX, XXV, XXVI, XXXIV, XXXV; WSC, qq 29–36; WLC, qq 63–66, 70–73; BD, II, 1–3; C67, IC1.

58–61	Scripture	
	Lines 58–59	Num 11:24–30; Deut 18:15–22; 2 Chron 20:13–19; 24:20–22; Ezek 3:22–27; 8:1–4; 11:5–12; 13:3; Mic 3:5–8; Mk 12:35–37; Jn 20:19–23; Acts 1:1–9; 2:1–4; 9:17–19a; 1 Pet 1:10–11; 2 Pet 1:20–21.
	Lines 60–61	2 Kings 22:8–13; 23:1–3; Ps 119:1–16; Zech 7:11–12; Mt 5:17; Mk 13:9–11; Lk 24:13–27, 44; Jn 5:30–47; 16:13; Acts 2:14–36; 4:13–20; 8:4–8; 9:17–22; 10:34–44; 13:4–5; 17:1–4; Rom 15:17–21; Eph 2:19–3:6; 2 Tim 1:11–14; 3:14–17; Heb 1:1–4; 3:7–11; 1 Pet 1:12; 2 Pet 1:16–19; 3:1–2; Rev 3:22.
	Confessions	SC, XIX, XX; HC, qq 19–21; SHC, I, II; WCF, I, XXXIV, 2; WSC, qq 2, 3; WLC, qq 2–6, 108; BD, I, II, 1; C67, IC2, IIB1.

62–64	Scripture	
	Line 62	Mk 1:1–12; 6:30–52; Jn 1:19–34; 3:5; 7:37–39; Acts 2:38–42; 8:26–39; 9:10–19; 10:44–11:18; Rom 6:1–4; 1 Cor 12:12–13; Gal 3:27–28; Eph 1:13–14; Col 2:8–15; Tit 3:3–7; 1 Jn 5:6–8.
	Line 63	*Ps 116:*12–14 *(13)*; Mt 26:17–29; Mk 14:22–25; Lk 22:14–20; 24:13–35; *Jn 6:*22–59 *(35, 48);* Acts 2:41–42; 1 Cor 10:16–17; 11:17–34; Heb 9:11–28.
	Line 64	Gen 1:26–27; Ex 15:1–21; Judg 4:4–10; 2 Kings 22:8–20; Joel 2:28–32; Lk 1:46–55; 2:25–38; 8:1–3; 10:38–42; Jn 4:7–42; 20; Acts 1:12–2:47; 13:1–4; 16:1–15; 18:24–28; Rom 16:1–16; 1 Cor 12:4–7; 2 Cor 4–5; Gal 3:27–29; Eph 4:7–16; Phil 4:1–3; 1 Pet 2:9–10.
	Confessions	SC, XVIII, XXI–XXIII; HC, qq 65–85; SHC, XVIII–XXVIII; WCF, XXVI–XXXI; WSC, qq 88–98; WLC, qq 157, 158, 164–177; BD, II, 1, 3–6; C67, IIA1–2, IIB.
65–71	Scripture	
	Lines 65–66	Gen 15:1; Ps 23:1–4; 27:1–6; 46:1–3; Is 41:8–10; Hag 2:4–5; Acts 4:13–31; Phil 1:19–20; 2 Cor 1:18–22.
	Line 67	Gen 18:16–33; 2 Sam 7:18–29; Dan 6; Mt 6:5–15; Mk 14:32–42; Lk 18:1–8; Jn 17; Rom 12:12; Eph 6:18–20; Col 1:3–14; 4:2; *1 Thess 5:*16–18 *(17);* Jas 5:13–18; Jude 20–21.
	Line 68	Is 60:1–3; Mt 28:19–20; Lk 24:45–47; Acts 1:8; 9:27–29; 23:11; Rom 1:1–6; 1 Thess 2:1–8; 2 Tim 1:8–14; 4:1–2.
	Line 69	Ex 20:2–6; 1 Kings 18:21–39; Ps 115:1–11; Is 31:1–3; 44:6–20; Jer 7:1–20; Zech 4:6; Mt 6:24; Lk 18:18–23; Acts 19:21–41; 1 Cor 8:1–6; Phil 3:18–19; Col 3:5; 1 Jn 5:20–21.
	Line 70	Gen 41:1–45; Ruth 1–4; 1 Kings 12:1–20; Jer 36; Zeph 3:1–2; Mt 15:21–28; Mk 5:15–20; 9:38–41; 16:9–11; Lk 7:36–50; 10:30–35; Jn 4:27–30, 39; 20:11–18; Acts 24; 1 Cor 14:33b–35; 1 Tim 2:11–12.
	Line 71	Lev 25:25–55; Deut 15:1–11; Ps 34:14; 72:1–4, 12–14; Is 58; Amos 5:11–24; Mic 6:6–8; Mt 5:9; 25:31–46; Rom 14:17–19; Gal 5:13–26; Heb 12:14; 13:1–3, 20–21; Jas 1:22–2:26.
	Confessions	SC, XIII, XIV, XXIV; HC, qq 86–129; SHC, IV, XVII, XXIII, XXX; WCF, IX, XII, XIX–XXIII, XXV, XXXIV, 3, XXXV; WSC, qq 35, 36, 98–107; WLC, qq 75, 76, 91–148; BD, II; C67, IB, IIA1, 3, 4, IIB2.

2–76   Scripture

Lines 72–74   Lev 19:1–4; Neh 7:73b–8:12; Ps 68:32–35; 96; 100; Mt 13:44; Lk 9:23; 24:44–53; Jn 15:10–11; Acts 1:8; 13:52; Rom 7:4–6; 12:1–3, 9–21; 15:13; 1 Cor 3:16–17; 13; 2 Cor 1:12; Eph 1:3–2:21; 1 Thess 1:4–8; 5:16–18; 1 Pet 1:13–16.

Lines 75–76   Is 65:17; 66:22–23; Mt 24:42–44; 25:1–13; Mk 13:32–37; Lk 14:15–24; 1 Cor 15:51–58; 16:21–24; 2 Pet 3; *Rev 21:1–22:5; 22:20.*

Confessions   HC, qq 31, 32, 86 and all of Part III; SHC, XIV, XVI, XXIX; WCF, VII, 5, XIII–XVI, XIX, XXI–XXIV, XXXIV; WSC, qq 39–82; WLC, qq 56, 175; BD, II, 2; C67, IB, IC1, IIA, III.

Lines 77–80

7–80   Scripture   Ps 27:1–10; 91; 118:1–6; 139:1–18; Is 25:6–9; Jn 3:16; *Rom 8:31–39;* Eph 2:1–10; 2 Tim 2:8–13; Jas 1:12; 1 Pet 1:3–9; 1 Jn 4:7–21.

Confessions   NC, 3rd art.; AC, 3rd art.; SC, XVI, XVII; HC, qq 1, 50–58; SHC, XXVI; WCF, XVII, XVIII; WLC, qq 67, 196; BD, II, 2; C67, IB, IC, IC1, III.

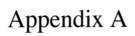

Appendix A

THE CONFESSIONAL NATURE OF THE CHURCH

The 209th General Assembly of the Presbyterian Church (U.S.A.) (1997) mandated that the following document, which was commended for study by the 198th General Assembly (1986), be included in future editions of the *Book of Confessions*.

I. THE NATURE AND PURPOSE OF CONFESSIONS

Many people are confused by talk of "confessing," "confessions," and "confessional" churches. Both inside and outside the church confession is ordinarily associated with admission of wrongdoing and guilt: Criminals "confess" that they have committed a crime; famous people write "true confessions" about their scandalous lives; persons visit a "confessional" to tell of their sin. In Christian tradition, however, confession has an earlier, positive sense. To confess means openly to affirm, declare, acknowledge, or take a stand for what one believes to be true. The truth that is confessed may include the admission of sin and guilt but is more than that. When Christians make a confession, they say, "This is what we most assuredly believe, regardless of what others may believe and regardless of the opposition, rejection, or persecution that may come to us for taking this stand."

A distinction must be made between confession as an act of Christian faith and a confession as a document of Christian faith.

On the one hand, all Christians are by definition people who confess their faith—people who make their own the earliest Christian confession: "Jesus Christ Is Lord." The Christian church, called and held together by Jesus Christ himself, lives only through the continual renewal of this fundamental confession of faith that all Christians and Christian bodies make together.

On the other hand, a confession of faith is an officially adopted statement that spells out a church's understanding of the meaning and implications of the one basic confession of the lordship of Christ. Such statements have not always been called confessions. They have also been called creeds, symbols, formulas, definitions, declarations of faith, statements of belief, articles of faith, and other similar names. All these are different ways of talking about the same thing, although "creed" has ordinarily been used for short affirmations of faith, while other names have been used for longer ones.

While the first and primary meaning of confession as an act of faith must always be kept in mind, this document will concentrate on the second meaning, confession as an officially adopted church document.

Presbyterian and Reformed churches are not the only churches with confessional standards. The Roman Catholic, Eastern Orthodox, Lutheran, and to a lesser extent the Anglican, Episcopal, and Methodist churches are also confessional bodies. Even so-called free churches that acknowledge only the Bible as their creed have often made semiauthoritative confessions of faith. Most Christian churches officially or informally share the faith of the Apostles' and Nicene Creeds. Therefore what is said in this section about the role of creeds and confessions is applicable not only to Presbyterian and Reformed churches but also to the Christian church as a whole. Most of the examples cited come from the Reformed tradition but similar examples could also be drawn from other traditions.

A. *The Three Directions of Confessions of Faith*

A confession of faith may be defined more precisely as a public declaration before God and the world of what a church believes.

A confession is a public declaration of what a church believes. Individual Christians may and should confess their own personal faith, but a confession of faith is more than a personal affirmation of faith. It is an officially adopted statement of what a community of Christians believe. This communal character of confessions of faith is made explicitly clear in confessions such as the Scots and Second Helvetic Confessions and the Barmen Declaration, which speak of what "we" believe. But it is also implicit in such confessions as the Apostles' Creed and the Heidelberg Catechism, which speak of what "I" believe, and in other confessions such as the Westminster Confession of Faith and the Confession of 1967, which speak more objectively. Whatever their form, confessions of faith express what a body of Christians believe in common.

These affirmations of the church's faith always have three reference points: God, the church itself, and the world. Confessions of faith are first of all the church's solemn and thankful response to God's self-revelation, expressed with a sense of responsibility to be faithful and obedient to God. Second, in a confession of faith members of a Christian community seek to make clear to themselves who they are, what they believe, and what they resolve to do. Finally, Christians confess their common faith not only to praise and serve God and not only to establish their self-identity but to speak to the world a unified word that declares who they are and what they stand for and against. Confessions thus have a social and political as well as theological and ecclesiological significance.

B. *The Time for Confession*

Throughout the history of the Christian movement churches have written confessions of faith because they feel that they must do so, not just because they think it would be a good idea. Confessions of faith may result from a sense of urgent need to correct some distortion of the truth and claim of the gospel that threatens the integrity of the church's faith and life from within the church. They may result from some political or cultural movement outside the church that openly attacks or subtly seeks to compromise its commitment to the gospel. Sometimes the urgency to confess comes from the church's conviction that it has a great new insight into the promises and demands of the gospel that is desperately needed by both church and world. Frequently, all three occasions — internal danger, external threat, and great opportunity — are behind the great confessions of the church at the same time. In any case, the church writes confessions of faith when it faces a situation of life or a situation of death so urgent that it cannot remain silent but must speak, even at the cost of its own security, popularity, and success. Or to put it negatively, when all the church has to say is the restatement of what everyone already knows and believes, or when it has no word to speak other than safe generalities that ignore or cover over the concrete, specific issues of a crisis situation — then it is not the time for confession even though what is confessed might be true in itself.

C. *The Content of Confessions of Faith*

At the heart of all confessions is the earliest confession of the New Testament church, "Jesus Is Lord." (Strictly speaking, therefore, Christians confess not what but in whom they believe.) But the church discovered very early that in order to protect this simple confession from misunderstanding and misuse, it had to talk about the relation between Jesus and the God of Israel, and between Jesus and the Holy Spirit. The earliest christological confession became a trinitarian confession. That led to further reflection on biblical witness to the reality and work of God the Father, Son, and Holy Spirit in the past, present, and future history of the world in general, in the particular history of the people of God, and in the life of every individual Christian. Moreover, the church could not talk about the "lordship" of Jesus without also talking about the claim the triune God has on the lives of people in their personal and social relationships in the church and in the world. The confession "Jesus Is Lord" necessarily led to the development of a full theology and ethic.

The length and focus of the church's confessions have varied according to which elements of this developing and expanding faith it has believed should be emphasized to meet the needs and challenges of particular situations.

Sometimes the situation has called not for a summary of everything Christians believe but for a short pointed confession dealing with one or more specific issues. The Nicene and Chalcedon Creeds, for instance, were the church's response to fundamental heresies in the ancient church concerning the identity of Jesus Christ. The Barmen Declaration was the response of some Reformed and Lutheran churches in Germany to what they believed was the one most critical issue in their situation in 1933, the relation between loyalty to Jesus Christ and loyalty to the state. The Confession of 1967 reformulated important themes of Christian doctrine in confessional literature and showed their social ethical implications.

Other confessions such as the Apostles' Creed are short summaries of elements of the whole of Christian faith.

The Lutheran and Reformed confessions of the sixteenth and seventeenth centuries tended to be longer and more comprehensive summaries of faith. In reforming the church they dealt with the most critical theological and political issues that divided Roman Catholics and Protestants—and Lutheran, Reformed, and Anabaptist Protestants—in the Reformation and post-Reformation period.

In every time and place the church is called to make the implications of its fundamental confession of the lordship of Jesus Christ unmistakably clear and relevant. But in order to do that it has had in every new situation to decide afresh what to say and what to leave unsaid, how much and how little to say, what to emphasize and what for the time being to pass over, which internal and external dangers are critical and which are less critical.

D. *The Functions of Confessions*

The shape of confessions has been determined not only by the historical situation in which they were written but also by the uses for which they have been intended.

1. *Worship.* Like the Apostles' and Nicene Creeds, some creeds and confessions have been used as acts of worship in the church's liturgy. This use is a reminder of the fact that the church's confessions are first of all acts of praise, thanksgiving, and commitment in the presence of God.

2. *Defense of Orthodoxy.* Most confessions have been intended as polemical defense of true Christian faith and life against perversion from within as well as attacks from outside the church. They are the church's means of preserving the authenticity and purity of its faith.

3. *Instruction.* The confessions have been used for the education of leaders and members of the church in the right interpretation of Scripture and church tradition and to guard against the danger of individuals or groups selecting from the Bible or church tradition only that which confirms their personal opinions and desires. Confessions written in question-and-answer form (like the Heidelberg and Westminster Catechisms) were written to prepare children and adult converts for baptism and participation in the fellowship of believers.

4. *Rallying Point in Times of Danger and Persecution.* Confessions have often prepared and strengthened Christians to stand together in faithfulness to the gospel when they have been tempted to surrender to powerful forces of political, racial, social, or economic injustice.

5. *Church Order and Discipline.* Some churches, like the Presbyterian Church (U.S.A.), have sought to preserve the purity and unity of the church by requiring its ministers and church officers to accept the teachings of its confessions in order to be ordained. The government of these churches is also determined by their confessions of faith.

Some confessions were originally intended to serve more than one of these purposes. Others have in fact served multiple purposes, although their writers may not have foreseen how they would be used.

E. *The Historical Limitations of Confessions*

Confessions address the issues, problems, dangers, and opportunities of a given historical situation. But confessions are related to their historical situation also in another way. Even when their writers have believed they were formulating Christian truth valid for all time and places, their work has been not only directed to but limited by their particular time and place. Throughout the history of the church — and also in our time — confessions have been deliberately or unconsciously expressed in the language and thought forms that were commonly accepted when they were written. God's self-revelation in Jesus Christ has sometimes been clarified but also distorted by the language and presuppositions of this or that ancient or current philosophy. The great classical confessions were written before the discoveries of modern science and reflect an outdated understanding of the structure of the world and its natural processes (just as our "modern" confessions will one day seem outdated and "primitive" to a later world). The theology and ethics of confessions of every age are shaped by what seem to be the normative or preferable sexual, familial, social economic, cultural, and political patterns of a particular period of history. Even those confessions that have sought to be grounded exclusively in biblical revelation have often confused the revelation itself with various historically conditioned thought forms and cultural patterns in which it was received and preserved by people who lived in the ancient Near East. Modern scholarship has shown how extensively earlier confessions of faith saw in Scripture only the confirmation of what they thought they already knew about God, the world, and human life in it (just as future scholarship will reveal how we have done the same thing in our time).

The confessions of the church, in other words, have indeed interpreted, defended, and preserved biblical-Christian truth. They have united the Christian community in its one task of bearing witness to the one Christian confession that Jesus is Lord. But at the same time, despite all good intentions, they have also distorted the truth revealed in Jesus Christ, been unable to grasp parts of the biblical witness to God's presence and work in Christ, and divided the church into churches with conflicting views of what Christian faith and life are all about. Is there any way to distinguish between the truth to which confessions of faith seek to bear witness and their inadequate witness to the truth? Christians in the Presbyterian-Reformed tradition believe they know at least how to go about this task. Their solution will be discussed in the proper place in the following section.

II. CONFESSIONS OF FAITH IN THE REFORMED TRADITION

Everything we have said about confessions in general applies also to Reformed confessions. But now we turn to some of the most important characteristics of the Reformed understanding of the nature and purpose of confessions that distinguish it from other confessional traditions and theological movements.

A. *The Ecumenical Character of Reformed Churches*

From the very beginning and throughout their history the Reformed churches have sought to represent the church catholic. Their confessions do not speak only of what Reformed churches or Presbyterians believe but seek to confess what Christians believe. They have not claimed to be the only true church, with a monopoly on Christian faith and life, but have always been open to learn from other churches and traditions and eager to participate in conversations with them that could lead to mutual correction and reconciliation.

We must not exaggerate this ecumenical openness, of course. Individuals, groups, and whole denominations who claim to be Reformed have sometimes assumed or openly declared that only this or that particular Reformed church is the true church, that all other churches (including other Reformed denominations) are false or at least fatally corrupted, and that conversation with them can only compromise the true understanding of Christian faith and life which is completely, infallibly, and unchangeably contained in this or that particular Reformed confession. But such an attitude is itself un-Reformed and contrary to the very confessional documents used to support it.

Characteristic of the ecumenicity of the genuine Reformed tradition and its confessions is this statement in the confession of the Synod of Bern in 1528:

> But where something is brought before us by our pastors or by others, which brings us closer to Christ, and in accordance with God's word is more conducive to mutual friendship and Christian love than the interpretation now presented, we will gladly accept it and will not limit the course of the Holy Spirit, which does not go backwards towards the flesh but always forward towards the image of Jesus Christ our Lord.

B. *Faith and Practice*

It is typical of confessions in the Reformed tradition that they emphasize not only what Christians believe but also how Christians live, not only orthodox Christian faith but also thankful and obedient Christian "practice," not only justification by grace through faith but also sanctification by grace evidenced in "good works." All Christian traditions acknowledge the fact that faith without works is dead. But in Reformed confessions the active Christian life is given special and unique emphasis.

1. *The Claim of God on All of Life.* Reformed confessional tradition follows Calvin in emphasizing the authority of God over every area of human life: over personal and familial relationships, over the organization and government of the Christian community, and over social, economic, and political "secular" communities as well. Reformed confessions therefore contain both personal and social ethics, a gospel of salvation and a social gospel. (See, for instance, the comprehensive and detailed exposition of the Ten Commandments in the Westminster Larger Catechism.)

Reformed confessions of different periods differ in their understanding of precisely what God requires. Sometimes they have been too certain that the will of God was identical with the historically and socially conditioned presuppositions of Reformed Christians in a particular time and place. Sometimes they have confused the rule of God in the world with the rule of the church. But however they differ and whatever mistakes they may have made, a consistent theme in Reformed confessions of all periods and places is the responsibility of individual Christians and the Christian church to seek to order all of human life according to the sovereign will of the God who is known in Jesus Christ through Scripture. No room is left for the belief of Christians in some other traditions that there are some areas of individual and social life that are not claimed by God and in which they are excused or prohibited from serving God.

2. *Grace and Law.* Reformed confessional tradition follows Calvin in believing that because the meaning and purpose of God's sovereign will is made known in Jesus Christ, and because sin separates humanity from God and each other, God's rule over and in the world must be understood as gracious rule exercised for our good. God gives us commands and requirements in order to guide and help us to the achievement of wholeness and happiness in our individual lives and justice, freedom, and peace in human society. The Heidelberg Catechism therefore expresses the theology of all Reformed confessions when it put its exposition of the law of God under the heading "Thankfulness." The demands of God are understood in Reformed tradition as the good gift of God to be received with gratitude, exercised for the welfare of all human beings, and obeyed in confidence that God's grace gives us the ability to do what God's law requires. Law, in other words, is a part of the gospel of saving grace, not something opposed to it or some alternative to it.

This theology of grace and law is one of the most important things that distinguishes the Reformed tradition from other traditions and theologies. (a) It distinguishes Reformed Christians from other Christians who understand obedience to God's commandments as a means of earning or cooperating with the saving grace of God rather than as a thankful response to saving grace already freely given and powerfully at work. (b) It distinguishes Reformed Christians from other Christians who believe that the law of God serves primarily the negative purpose of exposing sin, leading to repentance, and leading to the gospel of God's saving grace rather than the positive purposes of guidance offered by the gospel. (c) It distinguishes Reformed Christians from the belief of some other Christians that Christian freedom is freedom from rather than freedom for obedience to the commands of God. (d) It distinguishes Reformed Christians from other Christians for whom obedience to the law is an end in itself rather than a means of loving and serving God and other people. (e) Finally, it distinguishes Reformed Christians from those who use the law of God to justify oppressive "order" in society for the benefit of a few rather than to achieve a free and just society for all.

One can of course find in the present as well as in the past individuals, groups, and whole denominations of Christians who call themselves Reformed yet understand and use the law of God in all of the un-Reformed ways we have mentioned. But insofar as they do so, they have misunderstood and misused the very theology of grace and law based on God's gracious sovereignty that is one of the most distinctive elements of their own Reformed confessions.

C. *The Authority of Confessions in the Reformed Tradition*

The Reformed tradition is unique in its understanding of the authority of its confessions. The most revealing clue to this unique understanding is the great number of confessions it has produced. Other Protestant confessional traditions have been content with only a few confessional statements written by a few people within narrow geographical or historical limits. All the Lutheran confessions, for instance, were written by a few Germans in Germany between 1529 and 1580. Authoritative Roman Catholic teaching comes from church councils or from the Pope. But from the beginning of the Reformation wherever the Reformed church spread, Reformed Christians made new confessions of their faith, first city by city then country by country. The confessions of Bern, Basel, Zurich, Geneva, and other Swiss cities were followed by one or more confessions written for Germany, Switzerland, Belgium, Holland, Hungary, and Scotland. The great period of confession writing came to an end for two centuries after the seventeenth century (because under the influence of Protestant orthodoxy the Reformed churches lost sight of the reason for multiple confessions and because the liberal theology that dominated the eighteenth and nineteenth centuries was suspicious of confessional restraint). But the twentieth century has seen a revival of Reformed confessional writing. Reformed churches have participated in the preparation of well over thirty new confessions that have been completed or are in process.

This multiplicity of confessions, written by many people in many places over such a great span of time, obviously means that the Reformed tradition has never been content to recognize any one confession or collection of confessions as an absolute, infallible statement of the faith of Reformed Christians for all time. In the Reformed tradition confessional statements do have authority as statements of the faith of Reformed Christians at particular times and places, and there is a remarkable consistency in their fundamental content. Some have had convincing power for a long time. Nevertheless, for Reformed Christians all confessional statements have only a provisional, temporary, relative authority.

Reformed confessions themselves provide three interrelated reasons for this unique attitude toward confessional authority:

1. Confessions have a *provisional authority* (and are therefore subject to revision and correction) because all confessions are the work of limited, fallible, sinful human beings and churches. In our time we have perhaps become more aware than most of those who wrote and adopted Reformed confessions in the past that even when confessions intend to serve only the revealed truth and will of God, they are also influenced by the sexual, racial, and economic biases and by the scientific and cultural limitations of a particular situation. But from the very beginning and throughout its history Reformed Christians and their confessions have acknowledged with the Westminster Confession of 1646: "All

synods or councils since the apostles' times, whether general or particular, may err, and many have erred; therefore they are not to be made the rule of faith or practice, but to be used as a help in both" (6.175).

2. Confessions have a *temporary authority* (and are therefore subject to revision and correction) because faith in the living God present and at work in the risen Christ through the Holy Spirit means always to be open to hear a new and fresh word from the Lord. As the multiplicity of Reformed confessions indicates, Reformed Christians have never been content to learn only how Christians before them discerned and responded to the word and work of God; they have continually asked in every new time, place, and situation, "What is the living Lord of Scripture saying and doing here and now, and what do we have to say and do to be faithful and obedient in our time?" The Barmen Declaration speaks for the best intentions of the whole Reformed tradition when it says, "Jesus Christ, as he is attested for us in Holy Scripture, is the one Word of God which we have to hear and which we have to trust and obey in life and in death" (8.11).

3. Confessions have a *relative* authority (and are therefore subject to revision and correction) because they are subordinate to the higher authority of Scripture, which is the norm for discerning the will and work of God in every time and place. A frequently repeated theme in Reformed confessions is their subjection of their own theological and ethical thought—including their interpretation of Scripture itself—to this higher authority, or to the authority of the Holy Spirit who speaks through it:

> We protest that if any man will note in this confession of ours any article or sentence repugnant to God's holy word, that it would please him of his gentleness and for Christian charity's sake to admonish us of the same in writing; and we upon our honor and fidelity, by God's grace do promise unto him satisfaction from the mouth of God, that is, from his holy scriptures, or else reformation of that which he shall prove to be amiss. (Preface to the Scots Confession)

> The Supreme Judge, by which all controversies of religion are to be determined, and all decrees of councils, opinions of ancient writers, doctrines of men, and private spirits, are to be examined, and in whose sentence we are to rest, can be no other but the Holy Spirit speaking in the Scripture. (Westminster Confession, 6.010)

> Confessions and declarations are subordinate standards in the church, subject to the authority of Jesus Christ, the Word of God, as the Scriptures bear witness to him. No one type of confession is exclusively valid, no one statement is irreformable. Obedience to Jesus Christ alone identifies the one universal church and supplies the continuity of its tradition. (Preface to the Confession of 1967, 9.03)

Reformed Christians are put in a difficult position with their self-limiting, self-relativizing confessions. On the one hand they are bound: So long as they are faithful members of a Reformed church they are not free to interpret Christian faith and life (or even Scripture itself) however seems best to them personally, but are committed to submit themselves to the authority and guidance of the confessional standards of their church. On the other hand they are free: The very confessions to which they are bound allow—require—them to remember the human limitations and fallibility of their church's confessional standards, to be open to hear a new and perhaps different word from the living Lord the standards confess, and to examine critically the church's teachings in the light of further study of Scripture. It is not surprising, then, that Reformed Christians and whole Reformed denominations have sometimes been unable to maintain this balance between authority and freedom. Some have contradicted the very Reformed tradition they confess by claiming for this or that confession the absolute, infallible, unchangeable truth and authority that the Roman Catholic Church has traditionally claimed for its official teaching. Others, while calling themselves Reformed, have acted as if they were members of a nonconfessional "free" church, insisting on their freedom to interpret Scripture for themselves without regard for the guidance and restraint of their church's confessional consensus. Those who choose confessional authority over personal freedom make impossible the continual reformation of the church called for by Reformed confessions themselves. They run the risk of idolatrously giving to the church the ultimate authority that belongs alone to the living God we come to know in Jesus Christ through the Bible. On the other hand, those who choose personal freedom over the confessional consensus of the church destroy the church's unity, cut themselves off from the guidance of the church as they interpret Scripture, and run the risk of serving not biblical truth but the personal biases they read into Scripture.

Difficult as it is to find the way between church authority without personal freedom and personal freedom without church authority, a distinctive mark of the Reformed tradition is the belief that it is only by seeking this difficult way that the church can be a united community of Christians who are both "reformed and always being reformed."

III. THE PRESBYTERIAN *BOOK OF CONFESSIONS*

This section will deal with some questions concerning the particular confessional documents included in the *Constitution of the Presbyterian Church (U.S.A.)*.

A. *Why a* Book of Confessions

For most of their history Presbyterians in the United States were guided by essentially a single confessional standard: the Westminster Confession of Faith with the Larger and Shorter Catechisms that translated it into question and answer form for educational purposes. It is not surprising then that many Presbyterians have been disturbed by the idea of a book of confessions: Is it not contrary to Reformed tradition? Does not the adoption of a plurality of confessions water down or compromise the confessional nature of the Presbyterian Church? Will not Presbyterians be confused by so many documents, especially since they do not always say the same thing? Will they not tend to pay little attention to any of them because they are overwhelmed by so much confessional material? Two answers can be given to these questions, the first historical and the second theological.

In the first place there is a historical answer. Although the idea of a collection of confessions is relatively new for North American Presbyterians, it is not at all new in the history of the Reformed tradition. In 1581 (still in the period of the Reformation itself) the Reformed churches of Europe issued a *Harmonia Confessionum Fidei (A Harmony of Confessions of Faith)* which set out in parallel form the main doctrines of the confessions of eight Reformed and three Lutheran churches. This harmony listed the agreement between the various confessions but pointed out the disagreements as well. Moreover, in the eighteenth century, the Church of Scotland officially authorized eight different confessional documents besides the Westminster Confession as teaching instruments of the church. Both the Heidelberg Catechism and the Second Helvetic Confession have long been standards for most Reformed bodies around the world. Reformed churches in America have been the exception rather than the rule with their single standard. Most Reformed churches have believed that a plurality of confessions enriches rather than compromises Reformed faith and practice.

Second, there is a theological reason for a book of confessions. We have just discussed the reasons why Reformed Christians cannot recognize any one confession as a final, infallible encapsulation of true Christian faith and life for all Christians, everywhere, now and forever. A book of confessions that includes some classical Reformed confessions and leaves room for new confessions makes unmistakably clear one of the most distinctive marks of the Reformed tradition.

B. *Why This* Book of Confessions

The most immediate explanation for the content of the *Book of Confessions* is that it is the result of the combination of doctrinal standards that came with Presbyterian reunion in 1983. This amounted to adding the Larger Catechism from the three Westminster documents that were standards in the former Presbyterian Church in the United States to the *Book of Confessions* already adopted by the former United Presbyterian Church in the United States of America.

But the question remains, Why this selection from the great number of authentic Reformed confessions that could have been chosen? The answer is that the *Book of Confessions* contains a cross-section of ecumenical and Reformed confessions with wide geographical and historical representation.

The Nicene and Apostles' Creeds from the ancient church come as close as any other confessional statements to expressing the faith of all Christians, of all traditions, throughout church history. Their inclusion points to the ecumenical character of our church.

The Scots Confession (1560) was written mostly by John Knox, student of Calvin and father of English-speaking Reformed Christianity.

The German Heidelberg Catechism (1563) and the Swiss Second Helvetic Confession (1566) are, as we have noted, probably the two most widely accepted confessional statements among Reformed Christians throughout the world.

The originally British Westminster Confession and Catechisms (1647) have been the primary standard for the Presbyterian branch of the Reformed family not only in our country but wherever Presbyterian Churches have sent missionaries.

The Barmen Declaration (1934), written by Lutheran and Reformed Christians working together (and thus another ecumenical document), confesses the lordship of Christ especially in relation to political issues that are critical for all Christians in the modern world.

The Confession of 1967, the only specifically American confession in the book, addresses critical issues of Christian faithfulness in our time and place.

The *Book of Confessions* as a whole enriches our understanding of what it means to be Reformed Christians, helps us escape the provincialism to which we have been prone, and expresses our intention to join the worldwide family of Reformed churches that is far bigger and more inclusive than our particular denomination.

C. *The Relation of the Confessions in the Book to Each Other*

There is both unity and diversity in the theological and ethical teachings of the various confessions in the book.

1. *Unity*. Comparison of the individual confessions in the book with each other reveals an easily recognizable fundamental agreement among them:

a. All the confessions in the book share the same convictions about Jesus Christ as the one truly human and truly divine Mediator, Lord, and Savior.

b. All explicitly or implicitly confess the doctrine of the Trinity.

c. All the specifically Reformed confessions acknowledge the unique authority of Scripture and agree on principles for the right interpretation of Scripture.

d. All the Reformed confessions assume or articulate the conviction that the Holy Spirit is the source of all right interpretation of Scripture and true Christian faith and life.

e. All the Reformed confessions have the same theology concerning the true preaching of the Word and right administration of the sacraments.

f. All the Reformed confessions emphasize God's sovereign claim on both personal and corporate life, and thankful human obedience to it. (All the catechisms contain expositions of the Ten Commandments and the Lord's Prayer.)

g. With the exception of the Nicene and Apostles' Creeds, comparison of any of these confessions with the confessional literature of other Christian traditions clearly reveals the same distinctively Reformed understanding of Christian faith and life.

2. *Differences*. There are of course differences in style, purpose, and sometimes content among confessions written by different people directed to the problems and issues of different situations and shaped by the patterns of thought of different periods of history.

The most obvious differences are differences in form. The Apostles' Creed is a very brief summary of Christian faith in general. The Scots, Second Helvetic, and Westminster Confessions are extended theological discussions that cover all or most of the main elements of Reformed faith in particular. The Nicene Creed, Barmen Declaration, and Confession of 1967 concentrate on a few major critical issues without intending to be comprehensive. The Heidelberg and the two Westminster Catechisms are written in question and answer form for the sake of the Christian education of children and adults. The Westminster documents and the Confession of 1967 differ from all the other confessions in the book in confessing our faith mostly in objective language rather than in terms of what "I" or "we" believe. So long as there is no expectation for any confession to serve purposes for which it was not written, these differences are not confusing or disturbing but can only help the church as it uses different confessions in the book to meet different needs.

But there are also differences, even apparent contradictions, in theological and ethical content that are more difficult to deal with. Without attempting to be exhaustive, the following point to some of the more important of them:

a. The sixteenth- and seventeenth-century confessions, most notably the Scots, contain an anti-Roman Catholic polemic that would be unfair and inappropriate in contemporary confessions.

b. The classical confessions show little interest in the mission of the church in the world, seeming to imply that the church's task is exhausted in worship, preaching, and sacraments. Barmen and the Confession of 1967 reflect the awareness of the church in our time that the church does not exist for itself but for the sake of mission.

c. The doctrine of "double predestination" in Chapter III of the Westminster Confession is not taught in the doctrine of election in Chapter VIII of the Scots Confession, or in Chapter X of the Second Helvetic Confession. The Heidelberg Catechism has no explicit doctrine of predestination at all.

d. With the exception of Chapter II of the Second Helvetic Confession, the classical confessions were not concerned with the historical interpretation of Scripture, whereas the contemporary Confession of 1967 of necessity deals with this issue.

e. Chapter XXII of the Scots Confession and Chapter XX of the Second Helvetic Confession reflect the sixteenth-century view that women should not be allowed to preach or administer the sacraments. Contemporary confessions do not express this view, and the present Form of Government precludes it.

f. Chapter XVIII of the Scots Confession, 8.11 of the Declaration of Barmen, and 9.27 of the Confession of 1967 have a Christocentric understanding of the authority of Scripture, holding that Scripture is to be understood as witness to Jesus Christ. This Christocentric emphasis is missing in Chapters I and II of the Second Helvetic Confession and in Chapter I of the Westminster Confession.

g. Speaking or praying in "tongues" is forbidden in Chapter XXII of the Second Helvetic Confession and in Chapter XXIII (XXI) of the Westminster Confession, but not in the other confessions of the book.

h. Some issues that in the confessions of the sixteenth and seventeenth centuries were important enough to be issues of fundamental Christian faithfulness seem relatively unimportant in our time, for instance, the observance of canonical hours or the choice of food in fasting (Second Helvetic Confession) or the taking of oaths and vows (Westminster Confession).

3. *Dealing with the Differences.* Presbyterians who expect one right answer to every theological and ethical question are especially confused and deeply disturbed by these differences. ("What then does our church believe?") But the differences also puzzle others who understand that there is room for variety within the fundamental unity of the church. It is therefore important that agreement be reached on some guidelines for dealing with divergences among the confessions. Following are some suggestions based on the theology of the confessions themselves:

a. Differences should not be exaggerated but should be understood and evaluated in light of the christological and trinitarian faith shared in common by all the confessions.

b. Differences should be judged central or peripheral, critical or relatively unimportant, in light of the confessions' common christological and trinitarian faith, and in consideration of the most pressing problems and needs that confront the church in our time.

c. Where there are conflicts, decision in favor of one or another alternative — or in favor of a totally new alternative — should be sought by subjection of all confessional statements to possible correction in light of fresh reading of Scripture.

d. In light of the confessions' acknowledgment of their own fallibility, differences between them should be understood and evaluated with consideration of the scientific limitations, cultural influences, and theological language and style of the particular time in which they were written.

e. Both Scripture and the confessions teach us to have confidence in the Holy Spirit's continuing guidance of the church through the centuries as the Spirit enables the church to hear the Word of God through Scripture in every new time and situation. Therefore when there are differences between the confessions, initial priority should be given to contemporary confessions. This is only initial preference because further reflection may reveal that at some points the church in earlier times was more able and willing to be guided by the Spirit than the contemporary church.

f. The confessions are the church's confessions. Therefore when a governing body of the church has ruled in favor of one over another alternative in the confessions, the consensus of the whole church should take precedence over the opinions of individual church members or groups of church members. Because individual members or groups who disagree with the consensus of the church sometimes may have a better understanding of Scripture and be more open to the guidance of the Spirit than the church as a whole, the church should listen to them respectfully, with openness to be reformed by them. But until such time as the church as a whole is convinced that it should change its position, its interpretation of the confessions should be considered authoritative.

g. So long as the church as a whole has not taken a stand on differences among the confessions, its ministers and officers should have the freedom to choose the confessional interpretation that they believe best reflects the witness of Scripture.

h. When there is no real consensus in the church, differences among the confessions should ordinarily be allowed to stand until such time as a genuine consensus is possible and necessary. Even if a bare majority were able to defeat a very large minority in voting for one option in preference to another, it would ordinarily be premature and dishonest for the church to claim, "This is what we Presbyterians believe."

D. *The* Book of Confessions *and Ordination*

The church does not require acceptance of the church's confessions for church membership. All who acknowledge Jesus Christ as Lord and Savior are welcome to join and participate in fellowship. But to ensure that those who lead the church do so in faithfulness to its doctrine and form of government, the church does require ordained ministers, elders, and deacons to declare their adherence to the confessions of the church. In order to understand what they commit themselves to when they do this, it is important to note the sequence of questions asked at ordination and the precise wording of the third question. The first five questions are:

a. Do you trust in Jesus Christ your Savior, acknowledge him Lord of all and Head of the church, and through him believe in one God, Father, Son, and Holy Spirit?

b. Do you accept the Scriptures of the Old and New Testaments to be, by the Holy Spirit, the unique and authoritative witness to Jesus Christ in the church universal, and God's Word to you?

c. Do you sincerely receive and adopt the essential tenets of the Reformed faith as expressed in the confessions of our church as authentic and reliable expositions of what Scripture leads us to believe and do, and will you be instructed and led by those confessions as you lead the people of God?

d. Will you fulfill your office in obedience to Jesus Christ, under the authority of Scripture, and be continually guided by our confessions?

e. Will you be governed by our church's polity, and will you abide by its discipline? Will you be a friend among your colleagues in ministry, working with them, subject to the ordering of God's Word and Spirit?

These questions are very carefully worded to preserve in the church the same understanding of the authority of confessions characteristic of the Reformed tradition in general. That is, they seek to protect both freedom and variety in the church and the authority and unity of the church. The following two sections must therefore be held closely together.

1. *Freedom and Variety in the Church.* The same freedom and variety that is characteristic of the Reformed tradition in general is expressed in the questions asked of candidates for ordination in the Presbyterian Church (U.S.A.):

a. Ordained persons are asked to acknowledge the *Book of Confessions* as "authentic and reliable expositions of what Scripture leads us to believe and do." These words limit the authority of the book by making its authority subordinate to the high authority of Scripture, which in turn (according to the first two questions) derives its authority from its witness to the triune God revealed in Jesus Christ who alone has the right to claim absolute and unqualified loyalty and obedience.

b. Ordained persons are required to be "instructed and led" and "continually guided" by the church's confessions. These words demand study of the confessions. They also provide freedom from a demand for unqualified assent to everything the confessions ask us to think, say, and do and freedom from a legalistic interpretation of the confessions.

c. Since 1983 ordained persons are asked to receive and adopt the "essential tenets" of the Reformed faith as expressed in the confessions. Although some other wording may better express the intent, the phrase "essential tenets" is intended to protect freedom with the limits of general commitment to the confessions. That this is indeed the purpose of the phrase is made clear by the fact that both the former United Presbyterian Church in the U.S.A. and Presbyterian Church in the U.S. repeatedly answered in the negative overtures requesting that the church make a precise list of a few fundamental doctrines (once called "essential and necessary articles of faith") that must be accepted by ordained officers. Moreover, while Chapter II of the Form of Government lists a number of general theological affirmations to summarize the broad general character of Presbyterian faith and life, it too prescribes no specific understanding of any of these affirmations to test the acceptability of people for ordained office in the church.

The ordination question that asks for commitment to the "essential tenets" of the confessions brings freedom in the church at several levels. Ordained persons are free to be "instructed," "led," and "continually guided" by the confessions without being forced to subscribe to any precisely worded articles of faith drawn up either by the General Assembly or by a presbytery. (Presbyteries, too, are bound to the constitutional language that excludes demand for adherence to any specifically worded interpretations of a few selected doctrines. In a presbytery the decision for ordination is always determined by the concrete encounter between the presbytery and the candidate.) Presbyteries (in the case of ministers) and church sessions (in the case of elders and deacons) are free to decide for themselves what acceptable loyalty to the confessions means in their particular situation without being bound to any "check list" prescribed by higher governing bodies of the church.

2. *The Authority and Unity of the Church.* The ordination questions make room for freedom in the church but not for unlimited freedom. They also protect the authority and unity of the church:

a. To be an ordained Presbyterian is not only to acknowledge the superior authority of God in Christ as proclaimed by Scripture but also to recognize the church's confessions as "authentic and reliable expositions of what Scripture leads us to believe and do."

"While confessional standards are subordinate to the Scriptures, they are, nonetheless, standards. They are not lightly drawn up or subscribed to, nor may they be ignored or dismissed. The church is prepared to counsel with or even to discipline one ordained who seriously rejects the faith expressed in the confessions" (*Book of Order*, G-2.0200).

b. To be an ordained Presbyterian is to promise to be "instructed," "led," and "continually guided" by the confessions of the church—not just by one's own personal theological and ethical preferences or even by one's own personal understanding of God or Jesus Christ or Scripture. The church should not "bind the conscience" of those who disagree with its confessions and interpretation of their meaning. When an individual or group of individuals disagree with the consensus of the church, the church must first examine itself to see whether it needs to reform its confessional stance. Nevertheless, in the Presbyterian Church the consensus of the church concerning the meaning of faith and life takes precedence over the opinions and preferences of individuals and groups in the church, and may lead to the refusal of ordination to those who disagree with the church.

c. To be an ordained Presbyterian is to acknowledge the authority of each individual confession in the *Book of Confessions* and the book as a whole, not just the authority of selected sections from the confessions or the authority of one or another preferred confession in the book. While reception and adoption of the *Book of Confessions* means freedom from the imposition of a list of specific doctrinal formulations, it does not mean freedom to select from the book whatever an individual or group in the church chooses. An appropriate governing body as a whole may decide that some statements in the confessions are central and others peripheral, some no longer authoritative and others still authoritative for the church in our place and time. It may decide that there is or is not room for difference in the church regarding the authority of this or that statement. But in the Presbyterian Church the decision about what is "essential and necessary" belongs not to individuals or groups in the church but to the appropriate governing body of the church as it makes decisions in particular cases.

It is important to emphasize that it is not only individual ordained persons but also General Assemblies, presbyteries, and synods that are to be instructed, led, and continually guided by the church's confessions.

3. *Guidelines.* In light of the foregoing discussion of the freedom and variety and authority and unity of the church, the following guidelines may be seen as conclusions drawn from these discussions and as guidance for individuals and groups concerned with the ordination of pastors, elders, and deacons:

a. General Assemblies, synods, presbyteries, and sessions, as well as individual church officers, should be led, instructed, and continually guided by the whole *Book of Confessions*.

b. The confessions of the *Book of Confessions* are standards, in response to the historical context of the time, which are subordinate to Scripture; they are subject to criticism in light of the word of God in Jesus Christ as witnessed in the Scriptures of the Old and New Testaments and may be revised by the Church following duly prescribed procedures. (*The Confessional Nature of the Church,* 29.207.)

c. The confessions are serious statements and are "not to be taken lightly." While neither the General Assembly nor any presbytery or session should demand adherence to any specific list of beliefs or doctrinal formulations as if the content of the faith could be reduced to a few selected and precisely worded statements of doctrine, General Assemblies, synods, presbyteries, and sessions have the responsibility of determining on a case by case basis whether candidates for ordination adhere to the standards of doctrine as set out in the confessions.

d. When individuals or groups in the church call into question some aspect of the confessions or of the church's interpretation of them, those who hear that objection should consider the possibility that the dispute may point to a deficiency in present confessional standards, remembering that, indeed, synods or councils may err and that the church is always to be reformed (*semper reformanda*). However, after due consideration, the court of jurisdiction must decide whether such objection is to be allowed to stand or is to be ruled as being out of conformity with the confessional standards of the church.

e. Thus, when individuals or groups in the church persist in disagreeing with the confessions or the church's interpretation of them, the appropriate church body has the responsibility of determining whether the disagreement is sufficient to prevent the approval of a candidate for ordination to the office of pastor, elder, or deacon.

f. So long as presbyteries do not contradict specific interpretations of the confessions made by the General Assembly, and so long as sessions do not contradict those made by the assembly or by their presbytery, presbyteries and sessions have the right and responsibility to interpret for themselves whether candidates for ordination and ordained persons, for whom they are responsible, hold to the "essentials" of the faith as articulated by the confessions of the church (the constitutional right of appeal being understood).

E. *Other Important Uses of the* Book of Confessions *in the Church*

If our church is to be a truly confessional church in the Reformed tradition, every aspect of its life must be informed and shaped by the understanding of Christian faith and life expressed in the *Book of Confessions*. Without attempting to be exhaustive in discussing them, we suggest the following areas in which the book should have the normative function the church acknowledges it to have:

1. *The Church's Ministry in General.* Prerequisite to faithful and responsible use of the book in every particular aspect of the church's life is its being carefully taught in the seminaries, seriously and properly used in the ordination process, and continually studied and utilized by the leaders and governing bodies of the church at all levels.

2. *Worship.* Remembering that one of the main functions of confession in the New Testament and in the ancient church was liturgical, we should seek ways to use the language of the confessions in the church's worship so that people in our congregations may make them their own confessions of faith before God and the world. Even when explicit language of the confessions would be inappropriate, their theological and ethical teachings should determine decisions about the order, forms, content, and purpose of worship.

3. *Preaching.* The task of preaching is to proclaim the God we meet in Jesus Christ through the biblical witness, not to proclaim the theology of the confessions. Nevertheless, preachers may, and should also be "instructed," "led," and

"continually guided" by the confessions as they choose and interpret their biblical texts and prepare their sermons.

4. *Christian Education.* After the Bible itself, the *Book of Confessions* should be a primary resource and standard of the church's responsibility to enable children, youth, new and longtime Presbyterians to understand what it means to be a Christian in the Reformed tradition, claim that tradition for themselves, and be guided by it in every area of their daily lives. If this is to happen: (a) Unordained as well as ordained teachers in the church should understand, be able to interpret, and be themselves committed to the Reformed faith as contained in the confessions of our church. (b) Ministers must be teachers and especially the teachers of teachers. (c) The best education theories and methods must be chosen and used in a way consistent with the Reformed tradition so that true learning and claiming of the tradition can take place and authoritarian indoctrination or brainwashing avoided. (d) The *Book of Confessions* itself should be part of the church's educational curriculum—especially in officer and teacher education, in confirmation instruction, and in adult church school classes. (e) All curriculum material need not be informed by the Reformed tradition, but all curriculum material should be continually evaluated and taught in light of that tradition as expressed in the *Book of Confessions.*

5. *Pastoral Care.* Faithful and effective pastoral care in our time requires ministers gratefully and diligently to use the wisdom, tools, and skills of such "secular" disciplines as psychology and sociology, and (increasingly) to be able to deal with issues raised by modern medical science and technology. If pastors are to be faithful to their ordination vows and if they are to offer people in need the distinctive resources of Christian and Reformed faith, they must continually evaluate the presuppositions, claims, methods, and goals of these disciplines in light of the theological and ethical teaching of the church's confessions. Pastors should also find guidance in the theology and language of the confessions for what they should say and do in ministering to people both in crisis situations and in situations of everyday life.

6. *Evangelism.* The theology of the confessions should shape the motives, content, methods, and goals of the church's evangelistic programs. Special care must be taken lest concern for "results" or "success" lead to evangelistic preaching and techniques that compromise either the fundamental commitment of our confessions to the gospel of salvation by God's grace alone or their emphasis on costly Christian discipleship in every area of life.

7. *Mission.* The church must continually evaluate its mission programs, strategies, and goals to be sure that they are determined by the theology and ethics of its confessions and not by this or that liberal, conservative, or revolutionary ideology or by the cultural or racial preferences of the leaders and members of the church.

8. *Administration.* Governing bodies of the church and church leaders properly seek the most efficient styles of leadership, management, decision making, and priority and goal setting. But all administrative and operational processes and goals should be measured by the confessional standards of the church and choices determined by the "essential tents of the Reformed faith" expressed in them.

Our church will have become a truly confessional church when we no longer have to remind ourselves to test what we think and say and do by reference to the *Book of Confessions,* but when we do so automatically, and when it becomes so much a part of us that we are always unconsciously guided by our commitment to the Reformed tradition it expresses and serves.

Appendix B

THE ASSESSMENT OF PROPOSED AMENDMENTS TO THE *BOOK OF CONFESSIONS*

The 209th General Assembly of the Presbyterian Church (U.S.A.) (1997) mandated that the following document be commended to the church for study and guidance and be included in future editions of the *Book of Confessions.*

I. PREAMBLE

The *Constitution of the Presbyterian Church (U.S.A.)* consists of the *Book of Confessions* and the *Book of Order.* The *Book of Confessions* includes the following: "The Nicene Creed, The Apostles' Creed, The Scots Confession, The Heidelberg Catechism, The Second Helvetic Confession, The Westminster Confession of Faith, The [Westminster] Shorter Catechism, The [Westminster] Larger Catechism, The Theological Declaration of Barmen, The Confession of 1967, and A Brief Statement of Faith—Presbyterian Church (U.S.A.)."[1]

The Presbyterian Church (U.S.A.) does not recognize any one confession or collection of confessions as an absolute, infallible statement of the faith for Christians of all times and places. In the Reformed tradition, the authority of all confessional statements is "subject to the authority of Jesus Christ, the Word of God, as the Scriptures bear witness to him,"[2] and therefore provisional, temporary, and relative. Thus, any confession or collection of confessions is subject to revision and correction. Nevertheless, as a constitutional matter, change in the *Book of Confessions* is a momentous decision, affecting the church's understanding of its faith and life.

When the Presbyterian Church (U.S.A.) considers amending the *Book of Confessions* by the inclusion or deletion of a confessional document, it has enduring resources for assessing the wisdom of the proposal. In its *Book of Order* and the General Assembly study, *The Confessional Nature of the Church,* Presbyterians have articulated an understanding of the place of confessions in the church's life. This understanding embodies considerations that guide the church in its determination of the scope and shape of the *Book of Confessions.*

Chapter II of the *Book of Order,* "The Church and Its Confessions," clarifies the significance of confessions for the faith and life of the church. Any proposed change in the *Book of Confessions*—whether by inclusion of an additional confessional document, by deletion of a current confessional document, or by clarification of a current confessional document—should be considered in light of these constitutional understandings, grounded in the church's theological tradition and expressed in the *Book of Order.*

Possible changes in the *Book of Confessions* cannot be governed by a formula or a brief checklist of criteria. As the church weighs any proposal for altering its confessional standards, it must consider carefully a broad range of issues. The following considerations are drawn from the church's articulated position in the *Book of Order* and *The Confessional Nature of the Church.* They do not exhaust the issues related to the place and function of confessions in the church. They do provide a necessary framework for actions affecting the scope and shape of the *Book of Confessions.*

II. CONFESSIONAL STANDARDS

The *Book of Order* is clear that "confessional statements are subordinate standards in the church, subject to the authority of Jesus Christ, the Word of God, as the Scriptures bear witness to him."[3] This order of authority—Christ, Scriptures, Confessions—is nicely expressed in the fourth ordination question:

> d. Will you fulfill your office in obedience to Jesus Christ, under the authority of Scripture, and be continually guided by our confessions?[4]

While all creeds and confessions, including those in the *Book of Confessions,* are subordinate standards, they are *standards* for the church and its ordered ministries. "[The confessions] are not lightly drawn up or subscribed to," states the *Book of Order,* "nor may they be ignored or dismissed."[5] Thus, the church requires that ministers of the Word and Sacrament, elders, and deacons give affirmative answer to an ordination question that specifies the source and the function of confessional authority:

> Do you sincerely receive and adopt the essential tenets of the Reformed faith as expressed in the confessions of our church as authentic and reliable expositions of what Scripture [teaches] us to believe and do, and will you be instructed . . . by those confessions as you lead the people of God?[6]

Because the church's confessions are central to its identity and integral to its ordered ministries, changes in the *Book of Confessions* require an exacting amendment process. Nevertheless, the church is clear that obedience to Jesus Christ opens it to the reform of its standards of doctrine. Change in the *Book of Confessions* is an ever-present possibility that must always be approached with discernment of the truth of the gospel and the leading of the Holy Spirit.

III. THE CHURCH AND ITS CONFESSIONS

The church's commitment to its confessions is an expression of its determination to shape its life in faithful response to the grace of the Lord Jesus Christ, the love of God, and the koinonia of the Holy Spirit. The church's confessions are far more than ecclesial artifacts or intellectual abstractions, for

> The Presbyterian Church (U.S.A.) states its faith and bears witness to God's grace in Jesus Christ in the creeds and confessions in the *Book of Confessions.* In these confessional statements the church declares to its members and to the world
>
> who and what it is,
> what it believes,
> what it resolves to do.[7]

Thus, any proposed change to the *Book of Confessions* should enhance the church's understanding and declaration of who and what it is, what it believes, and what it resolves to do. There are numerous reasons to know, respect, and use creeds and confessions that may not be sufficient to warrant their inclusion in the *Book of Confessions.* The central functions of identifying and proclaiming the church's faithful identity, beliefs, and actions are necessary elements in determining the content of the *Book of Confessions.*

THE ASSESSMENT OF PROPOSED AMENDMENTS

A. *The Church Declares to Its Members and to the World Who and What It Is*

1. *The Faith of the Church Catholic*

> In its confessions, the Presbyterian Church (U.S.A.) gives witness to the faith of the church catholic. The confessions express the faith of the one, holy, catholic, and apostolic church . . .[8]

Thus, any confession within the *Book of Confessions* should articulate the breadth and depth of what Christians believe, not only the distinctive features of what Reformed churches or Presbyterians believe. The Presbyterian Church (U.S.A.) affirms that there is one church and that "the unity of the church is a gift of its Lord. . . ."[9] Thus the confessional standards of the Presbyterian Church (U.S.A.) should acknowledge gratefully the gift of unity as they seek faithfully the visible oneness of the church catholic.

2. *The Affirmations of the Protestant Reformation*

"In its confessions, the Presbyterian Church (U.S.A.) identifies with the affirmations of the Protestant Reformation."[10] The Presbyterian Church (U.S.A.) understands itself to be part of the tradition emerging from the sixteenth-century Reformation in Europe. Thus, any confession within the *Book of Confessions* should be compatible with the "Protestant watchwords"—Christ alone, grace alone, faith alone, Scripture alone—that remain guides to Christian faith and life.

3. *The Faith of the Reformed Tradition*

"In its confessions, the Presbyterian Church (U.S.A.) expresses the faith of the Reformed tradition."[11] The Presbyterian Church (U.S.A.) understands itself to be one ecclesial expression of the Reformed tradition. Thus, any confession within the *Book of Confessions* should be compatible with central elements of Reformed faith and life. As one church within the Reformed family of churches, the Presbyterian Church (U.S.A.) should ensure that its confessions enrich understanding of what it means to be Reformed Christians. Historical and geographic representation help the church overcome a tendency toward provincialism and reflect the church's intention to be a member of the worldwide family of Reformed churches.

B. *The Church Declares to Its Members and to the World What It Believes*

1. *Affirmations*

Ecclesial confessions "identify the church as a community of people known by its convictions. . . ."[12] As an expression of what a body of Christians believe in common, any confession within the *Book of Confessions* should help members of the community define and give witness to what they believe.

2. *Renunciations*

Ecclesial confessions of faith speak a unified word that declares what the church opposes as well as what it affirms. Confessions within the *Book of Confessions* should help members of the community resist the seductions of ideologies, institutions, and images that are inimical to the gospel, and should embolden the church to announce its opposition to all that denies the good news.[13]

3. *Scripture, Tradition, Doctrine, Proclamation*

As expressions of the "yes" and the "no" of the gospel, the confessions within the *Book of Confessions* should

—guide the church in its study and interpretation of the Scriptures;

—summarize the essence of Christian tradition;

—direct the church in maintaining sound doctrine;

—equip the church for its work of proclamation.[14]

4. *Unity*

The *Book of Confessions* evidences a fundamental theological unity. While confessional unity does not mean uniformity, confessions within the *Book of Confessions* should display consistent convictions concerning central affirmations of Christian faith.

C. *The Church Declares to Its Members and to the World What It Resolves to Do*

1. *Mission*

Confessions of faith are not timeless abstractions, but expressions of the actual life of communities of faith. They identify the church as a community of people known by its actions as well as by its convictions.[15] Thus, confessions within the *Book of Confessions* should shape the church's faithfulness and courage in its mission:

> The Church is called to undertake this mission even at the risk of losing its life, trusting in God alone as the author and giver of life, sharing the gospel, and doing those deeds in the world that point beyond themselves to the new reality in Christ.[16]

2. *Actions*

The *Book of Confessions* is meant to be used in the church. Thus, the church should ask how a proposed confessional statement might function in the life of the church. Among the possibilities are the following:

—In the church's ministry and mission: the church's confessions should be used to shape faithful witness and service in the world.

—In worship: the church's confessions are acts of praise, thanksgiving, and commitment in the presence of God: confessions should help to shape the liturgy in addition to their use as elements within the liturgy.

—In teaching: the church's confessions should be used for the education of leaders and members of the church in the right interpretation of Scripture, tradition, theology, and ethics.

—In preaching: preachers should be instructed, led, and guided by the confessions of the church as they proclaim the gospel.

—In church order and discipline: the confessions of the church should be used to preserve the peace, unity, and purity of the church by serving as standards for ordered ministry and governance.

—In defense of the gospel: the confessions of the church may be elements in resisting perversions of the faith from within and temptations or attacks from without.[17]

IV. THE CONFESSIONAL COLLECTION

The *Book of Confessions* includes creeds, catechisms, and confessions from the early church, the Reformation and post-Reformation eras, and the twentieth century. Each document was a genuine expression of Christian faith in its own time and place. Each has been received by the Presbyterian Church (U.S.A.) as a significant expression of Christian faith for our time and place.

Confessional statements emerge from a variety of circumstances in the church's life. Among the realities that lead to the formulation and reception of creeds, catechisms, and confessions are the following:

1. A sense of urgent need to clarify the faith over and against some distortion of the gospel that threatens the integrity of the church's faith and life.

2. A political or cultural movement outside the church that openly attacks or subtly seeks to compromise the church's commitment to the gospel.

3. The church's conviction that it has a new insight into the promise and demand of the gospel that is needed by both church and world.

When the church considers a proposal to add a confessional document to the *Book of Confessions,* all considerations are sharply focused by the issue of the church's reception of the proposed confession.

1. When a *new confession* is proposed for inclusion in the *Book of Confessions,* the church must understand the occasion for its formulation. However, the *intention* of the new document should be tested by a period of reception in the church. A confessional statement should prove itself foundational to the church's faith and life before it is proposed for inclusion in the church's confessional standards.

2. When the proposed confession is a *historic document,* the church should understand the original circumstances of formulation and reception. Additionally, the contemporary need for the confession and the possibilities for reception should be demonstrated. Then, the value of the historical confession should be tested by a period of reception in the church. A confessional statement should prove itself foundational to the church's faith and life before it is proposed for inclusion in the church's confessional standards.

Thus, the creeds and confessions of this church reflect a particular stance within the history of God's people. They are the result of prayer, thought, and experience within a living tradition. They serve to strengthen personal commitment and the life and witness of the community of believers.[18]

ENDNOTES

1. *Book of Order*, G-1.0501.
2. *Book of Order*, G-2.0200.
3. *Book of Order*, G-2.0200.
4. *Book of Order*, G-14.0207d, passim.
5. *Book of Order*, G-2.0200.
6. *Book of Order*, G-14.0207c, passim.
7. *Book of Order*, G-2.0100a.
8. *Book of Order*, G-2.0300.
9. *Book of Order*, G-4.0201.
10. *Book of Order*, G-2.0400.
11. *Book of Order*, G-2.0500.
12. *Book of Order*, G-2.0100b.
13. *The Confessional Nature of the Church,* 29.120.
14. Taken from the *Book of Order*, G-2.0100b.
15. *Book of Order*, G-2.0100b.
16. *Book of Order*, G-3.0400.
17. *The Confessional Nature of the Church,* 29.129-.135; 29.211-.219.
18. *Book of Order*, G-2.0500b.